Complete
Student **A**ssistance **P**rogram
Handbook

Student Assistance Program

Techniques and Materials for Alcohol/Drug Prevention and Intervention in Grades 7-12

Barbara Sprague Newsam
Illustrated by Jim Burke

THE CENTER FOR APPLIED
RESEARCH IN EDUCATION
West Nyack, New York 10995

Library of Congress Cataloging-in-Publication Data

Newsam, Barbara Sprague, 1963–
     Complete student assistance program handbook : techniques and
materials for alcohol/drug prevention and intervention in grades
7–12 / Barbara Sprague Newsam : illustrated by Jim Burke.
          p.   cm.
     ISBN 0-87628-878-6
     1. Student assistance programs—United States—Handbooks, manuals,
etc.   2. Students—United States—Substance use.   3. Alcoholism—
United States—Prevention.   I. Title.
LB3430.5.N48   1992   92-22749
373.14′6—dc20   CIP

Printed in the United States of America

10   9   8   7   6   5   4   3

ISBN 0-87628-878-6

**THE CENTER FOR APPLIED RESEARCH
IN EDUCATION**
West Nyack, NY 10994
A Simon & Schuster Company

On the World Wide Web at http://www.phdirect.com

Prentice-Hall International (UK) Limited, *London*
Prentice-Hall of Australia Pty. Limited, *Sydney*
Prentice-Hall Canada Inc., *Toronto*
Prentice-Hall Hispanoamericana, S.A., *Mexico*
Prentice-Hall of India Private Limited, *New Delhi*
Prentice-Hall of Japan, Inc., *Tokyo*
Simon & Schuster Asia Pte. Ltd., *Singapore*
Editora Prentice-Hall do Brasil, Ltda., *Rio de Janeiro*

Acknowledgments

I am grateful to a number of very special people for their encouragement and friendship throughout the writing of this book. First and foremost, my thanks to David, who just keeps getting better and is even learning to cook.

Personal thanks go to

- My mother, Linda Sprague, who for years has encouraged me to write and who has provided me with all the tools and opportunity to do it
- My old and new soulmate friends—Suzi, Eve, Lauren, Luanne, Dana, and Sandy—who have simultaneously encouraged me and allowed me my "hermitude"
- George Sprague, whose example of kindness and self-discipline inspired me all summer
- Alexandra and Bryan Sprague and Ryan, Johnny, and Allie Moran, who have prompted me to try to make a dent in the problems of the future
- Sandra Hutchison, my editor, without whose reassurance I would never have started, let alone completed, this project
- Jim Burke, my illustrator, for his enthusiasm, willingness, and great talent.

In addition, I'd like to thank these wonderful people that I have met through my work: Bill Burns, who has believed in me and has helped the student assistance program (SAP) sail since its inception; Tina Craig and Mary-Jo Bourque, without whom the ship would have sunk long ago; the SAP Core Team and George, Cleo, Bonnie, and Sofia for making Central High School a nice place for me to be; SAP interns and consultants Steve, Jenny, Cathy, Jon, and Deane, for giving so fully of themselves; Joanne Smogor, for believing I could do it; New Hampshire Office of Alcohol and Drug Abuse Prevention OADAP, and especially Linda King, whose support has been unfaltering.

Most importantly, I'd like to thank the hundreds of teenagers who have given me a privileged window into their lives and have made my work and this book possible.

Barbara Sprague Newsam

To David

About the Author

BARBARA SPRAGUE NEWSAM currently directs the Student Assistance Program at Central High School, which serves a heterogeneous population of 1700 students in the city of Manchester, New Hampshire. She has a Masters in Education from Harvard Graduate School of Education and a Bachelors degree from the University of New Hampshire. She is a member of the National Association of Alcohol and Drug Abuse Counselors.

In addition to her duties at Central High School, she presents workshops to adolescents, parents and community groups and provides training to school district personnel on issues surrounding alcohol and other drug use. She has served on numerous community task forces, including the city's Task Force on Adolescent Alcohol and Other Drug Abuse, the United Way Adolescent Substance Abuse Network, and the Manchester school district's Wellness Initiative. She has also taught English at the high school level.

About This Resource

The *Complete Student Assistance Program Handbook* provides counselors, administrators, and student assistance personnel with everything necessary to set up, refine, or overhaul any secondary school effort to help students with personal problems, especially those related to alcohol or other drug use.

The motivation behind any student assistance program (SAP) is fundamentally educational: Students who are alcohol or drug dependent or live in families affected by addiction often cannot work to their full academic potential. While the cause of their problems may not be readily apparent, these students are at high risk for disruptive behavior, truancy, academic failure, and dropping out—as well as for teen pregnancy, AIDS, depression, and suicide. Also helped by SAPs are students who suffer from a variety of problems not related to alcohol or other drug abuse.

The *Complete Student Assistance Program Handbook* places in your hands a wealth of practical techniques and materials for helping these students and others so they can focus their energy on the normal social and academic challenges of adolescence.

Part I, "Setting It Up and Making It Work," is a comprehensive guide to setting up and running a student assistance program in any school, at any level of funding. It includes sample faculty information handouts, model letters and forms, and other materials that can be easily reproduced or adapted for use in your school.

- Chapter 1, "How Student Assistance Programs Work," explains the rationale behind SAPs, including how they help high-risk students and improve the overall climate of schools.

- Chapter 2, "Designing a Structure That Works," describes the basic ingredients of any SAP and offers five different structures you can adapt for your situation, along with practical advice on gaining and keeping funding.

- Chapter 3, "Insuring Confidentiality," helps you safely navigate the sometimes treacherous waters of federal and state laws applying to alcohol and other drug information, school records, and parental consent, with sample forms, letters, and more.

- Chapter 4, "Starting a School-Based Student Assistance Program," helps you "sell" a program and handle the nuts and bolts of setting it up, including ways to form a Core Team, set up a chemical use policy, and build support from both administration and faculty.

- Chapter 5, "Promoting Your Student Assistance Program," helps you publicize your program to faculty, students, parents, and the community, with numerous samples of newsletters, handouts, and more.

- Chapter 6, "Training Faculty and Staff," gives you detailed advice on training the school board, administrators, your Core Team, and the faculty in general.

- Chapter 7, "Reaching High-Risk Students," describes the major indications for referral of students and helps you build a referral system that can overcome institutional denial and student and faculty mistrust.

- Chapter 8, "Assessment and Referral," details effective techniques for individual assessment, provides a number of intake and assessment forms, and suggests a range of options for referral.

- Chapter 9, "General Guidelines for SAP Groups," helps you start a number of time- and cost-efficient groups, including survival tips for handling the complex logistics involved. It also offers a troubleshooting guide to group problems ranging from students under the influence to "dead group syndrome."

- Chapter 10, "Additional Programming," suggests a myriad of additional programming the SAP can either implement or encourage in the drive to prevent alcohol and other drug abuse, including ways to work with many existing student and parent groups.

- Chapter 11, "Field Survival Guide for SAP Personnel," offers seasoned advice on coping with the special stresses of SAP work, including specific ways to keep the lines of communication open to faculty and staff while maintaining confidentiality, avoiding territorial disputes, staying organized, and preventing burnout.

Part II, "Three Group Curricula for Use in School-Based Programs," offers complete, session-by-session guidelines and ready-to-use materials for three vital groups, along with specific tips for screening students and facilitators.

- Chapter 12, "Friends' Group," addresses the particular needs of students coping with addiction in their homes, with guidelines and materials for ten one-period sessions.

- Chapter 13, "Challenge Group," offers an intensive curriculum that challenges students to examine their own drinking and drugging in six double-period sessions. Complete materials are provided for students who may be in the group as a result of low grades, disciplinary problems, chemical use violations, or personal choice.

- Chapter 14, "Recovery Group," offers ten sample sessions and suggestions for ongoing group support of students in recovery, with the double aim of helping them stay sober and helping them address developmental issues they may have missed while they were chemically involved.

The *Complete Student Assistance Program Handbook* is about new solutions to old problems. Student assistance programming is a proactive response to the continuing alcohol and other drug problems we face in our schools—*and it works*. You will find that it helps not only individual students, but the overall school climate and staff morale as well.

SAP work is hard work, and the rewards are sometimes difficult to discern through the tragic realities SAP personnel face every day. This handbook was written to help you with every aspect of your job, including the most challenging ones. I urge you to take what fits your particular program, add your individual creative touches, and watch your school take a giant step toward wellness.

Barbara Sprague Newsam

Contents

Part II: Three Group Curricula for Use in School-Based Programs 245

Chapter 12: Friends' Group 247

PART I

Setting It Up and Making It Work

1

How Student Assistance Programs Work: An Overview

CHAPTER 1

How Student Assistance Programs Work: An Overview

A senior boy is referred to the student assistance program by a concerned teacher because he is always late to science class. He arrives at the SAP office very defiant and angry, but the SAP counselor reassures him that he is not in any trouble. The SAP counselor briefly goes over the confidentiality regulations governing SAPs and then begins an intake interview. Two appointments later, the student reports that he's been doing "speedballs" (shots of vodka followed by lines of cocaine) every day before science class since the beginning of the semester. He wants to stop using alcohol and other drugs because his life is changing in ways he cannot understand, but he doesn't know how. Because he feels that he cannot stay clean and sober for even a day if he is unassisted, he reluctantly agrees to go to chemical dependency treatment. With the student's permission, the student assistance program at his school contacts his mother and helps her make all the necessary arrangements for treatment. When the student returns to school, he attends the student assistance program recovery group and Alcoholics Anonymous meetings in the evenings. In June, he is sporting a cap and gown and five months of hard-won sobriety.

A freshman girl who has spent three days in internal suspension because of attendance problems is referred to a suspension alternative program by the assistant principal. Because of her participation in the alternative program, she recognizes that some of her problems originate with her mother's drug use. Though she is reluctant and shy at first, she joins a student assistance program friends' group (for children affected by the drinking or drug use of a close friend or relative), where she is encouraged to share the challenges that face her with other students who have similar experiences. Her attendance improves significantly, and she plans on staying in school. Several of her friends follow her into the friends' group.

A timid junior boy is referred to the student assistance program office by a concerned teacher, who reports that the student seems withdrawn in class. He is painfully shy and cannot make eye contact. The initial interview with the SAP counselor reveals that the boy doesn't have any friends at school and feels lonely and unwanted. He is considering getting a job and going to night school. Because his isolation puts him at a high risk for becoming involved with *alcohol and other drugs, the student assistance program counselor asks him to consider joining a discussion group where he could meet other students in a small, safe setting. After several group meetings, the student looks forward to the meetings every week and begins to come out of his shell a bit. He is thinking about staying in school instead of going to night school.*

A sophomore girl comes to the student assistance program office complaining of "problems at home" and after three appointments reports that her stepfather is sexually abusing her. The counselor calls Child Protective Services. The case is then investigated. There follows a combined effort on the part of the school and the protective agency. Through the protective agency, the girl is referred to a therapist who specializes in sexual abuse cases. Through the student assistance program, she sees the in-school counselor three or four times and then joins a small in-school support group of other young people who have been sexually abused. With the guidance of the student assistance program counselor, this group of young people reflect on their experiences, support one another, and help each other avoid the pitfall of medicating their pain with alcohol and other drugs.

WHY SCHOOLS NEED STUDENT ASSISTANCE PROGRAMS

Student assistance programs (SAPs) are a response to the many and varied personal problems that students bring with them to school, including alcohol and other drug-related problems. The sheer weight of some of this "baggage" makes it impossible for some students to concentrate on the emotional and developmental tasks they face as children and adolescents. Both academically and socially, these students are at a decided disadvantage. Any student assistance program effort demonstrates that a school system recognizes, first, that such problems do plague students and, second, that a responsible system of adults must respond and help.

Student assistance programs aim to identify troubled students and connect them with the helping services available to them in school or in the community. The confidential service that SAPs provide is based on an educational premise: Students who receive help and support to deal with pressing personal concerns will be able to focus their remaining energy more efficiently on their schoolwork and important tasks of developing academically, socially, and emotionally.

Chief among the challenges children and adolescents face today are those related to alcohol and other drugs. Many more problems than we once recognized are indeed related to alcohol and other drug use. Whether you teach in a large urban high school or a rural elementary school, your students' lives are touched by alcohol and other drug use. Basic to the nature of student assistance programs is the notion that if you had to choose just one issue which accounts for the largest number of student problems, what would it be? The answer always comes back alcohol and other drugs. Once you target that issue, by association you get access to school failure, pregnancy, violence, neglect, sexual abuse, school adjustment problems, depression, and suicidality. Once schools begin to address this range of very real problems children face, students have a better chance of developing into healthy adults.

PREVENTION, INTERVENTION, TREATMENT, AND AFTERCARE

When alcohol and other drug concerns are targeted, there are four basic areas where helping efforts can be concentrated, referred to as the "continuum of care": prevention, intervention, treatment, and aftercare, in that order. This model is used in the public health field to conceptualize comprehensive responses to disease. It is, of course, no coincidence that it is used in this handbook in this context, as alcohol and other drug addiction is recognized as a primary, progressive, and chronic disease. The disease of alcoholism is estimated to affect one in eight Americans.

School-based student assistance programs generally concentrate their efforts in the prevention and intervention areas while touching both treatment and aftercare in specific ways. Once you understand the continuum of care, you can see how any SAP effort can make significant inroads in all four areas.

Prevention: Student assistance programs offer prevention first by providing an in-house educational resource for alcohol and other drug information for students to use. Troubled students may use this service to discuss or evaluate their own use or nonuse of substances. SAP personnel can be called on to share their expertise in varied forums, from school assemblies, guest lectures in academic classes, to teacher and staff trainings. A successful SAP can legitimize the nonuse of chemicals by students and may foster climatic change. Involving children of alcoholics and addicts in support groups and educating them about their own risk of developing alcohol and other drug problems can prevent these students from becoming harmfully involved with chemicals themselves. Schools also provide prevention through traditional extracurricular activities such as sports and drama and music, which can provide healthy outlets.

Intervention: The main task of a student assistance program is to identify and intervene with students who are experiencing difficulties in school because of personal problems. A referral system is used to identify troubled students by targeting behavior which is of concern. The purpose of identifying troubling behavior early is to curtail further or future involvement with alcohol and other drugs while providing access to helping services. Intervention really begins when teachers and other staff are trained to recognize at-risk students and refer them for assessment. Some students will be identified as being troubled who have no alcohol or other drug-related concerns. Some SAPs also coordinate or run ancillary programs which are used to screen for students who may be at high risk.

Groups which are run to help students assess their own relationship to alcohol and other drugs are intervention efforts. The challenge group, discussed in chapter 13, is such an intervention program.

Treatment and Support: Strictly speaking, SAPs do not offer treatment for alcohol and other drug *dependency*. However, one role of student assistance programs is to provide bridges to such treatment, either outpatient counseling or chemical dependency treatment. Most SAPs also offer individual counseling and assessment services.

SAPs offer in-school support groups for students who want to stay clean and

THE STUDENT ASSISTANCE PROGRAM'S CONTINUUM OF CARE

PREVENTION	INTERVENTION	TREATMENT/SUPPORT	AFTERCARE
In-school resource	Behaviorally based referral system	Support group participation	Monitoring of student progress
Legitimize nonuse message	Identifying troubled students and their families	Access to treatment, both inpatient and outpatient	Constant support
Education for high-risk populations	Ancillary programs to screen for at-risk populations	Individual counseling	Continuing contact with families of students in recovery
School climate change	Teacher training to identify at-risk students	Coordinated school response (SAP, guidance, administration)	Peer monitoring of progress
Teacher training			

sober, or for students who are affected by a loved one's alcoholism or other drug addiction, though these groups do not provide intensive therapy and therefore should not be considered treatment. Some SAP efforts offer educational and support group programs for any or all of many populations considered at risk for developing alcohol and other drug-related problems.

Aftercare: Aftercare refers to the process of monitoring a person's actions for signs of relapse and reintervening if a return to negative patterns seems imminent. SAPs can be instrumental in monitoring students who have returned from chemical dependency treatment facilities by watching students' disciplinary records, attendance, and appropriate class participation closely. You can construe SAP recovery groups as aftercare efforts or, in the broader sense, as prevention efforts—because they are relapse prevention strategies while simultaneously providing legitimacy to students who choose not to use.

UNDERSTANDING THE "BROAD-BRUSH" PHILOSOPHY

Student assistance programs can be structured in any number of ways, depending on your particular resources and commitment. (See chapter 2 for a full explanation of the different structures.) However, a very good argument can be made for basing your program on the "broad-brush" philosophy because it tends to attract both those students who readily admit that they are troubled and know the source of the problem, and those whose trouble boils under the surface, unknown perhaps even to them.

The broad-brush philosophy posits that students who are displaying troubling behavior should be referred to the student assistance program, regardless of whether that trouble indicates any involvement or association with alcohol and other drug-related concerns. What has been found is that *a large percentage of troubled students do have alcohol and other drug-related concerns but may not identify them as a source of trouble.* A student who lives with an alcoholic, for instance, may know of his mother's problem, but he may not connect that problem to his own truancy or school failure problems. Those who cannot make the connection may be at higher risk for developing problems themselves.

In a broad-brush program, teachers are encouraged to make referrals based on student behavior that is troubling, without making any diagnosis of what the behavior indicates. So a student who is experiencing academic failure may be referred to the SAP by the teacher. The question of whether that student is experiencing academic failure because of his or her own or a parent's alcohol or other drug use or because he or she is overextended at an after-school job is answered by the SAP personnel after seeing the student. A key advantage of the broad-brush approach is that it allows students to seek help from the SAP without fearing that they will be labeled as alcohol and other drug users. In effect, this allows the SAP to reach many more of the students who are at risk than a program that specifically targets alcohol and other drug use.

Students who do not have alcohol and other drug concerns can still be helped in the context of a student assistance program by referral to an outside agency, an in-school support group, or other helping services in the school, including traditional guidance departments. And in fact this sort of involvement with the SAP is a prevention effort, because students get help which may prevent them from becoming harmfully involved with alcohol and other drugs later on. However, although SAPs want to extend open arms to the entire student population, the population you are trying to touch most significantly is children who are already involved with alcohol and other drugs and those who are statistically at extremely high risk for becoming involved.

TARGETING HIGH-RISK STUDENTS

SAPs aim to isolate and intervene with very high-risk students. The trick is that not every student who is high risk *appears* high risk. The policies and procedures of most SAPs reflect this reality and utilize specific behavioral indications to identify high-risk behavior. Among the most obvious high-risk populations are the following:

Alcohol and Other Drug Users: Clearly, one population that needs educators' immediate attention is students who are currently using alcohol and other drugs. Students who are themselves harmfully involved with alcohol and other drugs are clearly at risk of harming themselves or others, or for not realizing their full potential as human beings, students, athletes, artists, musicians, parents, and so on.

The more obviously affected students tend to experience a negative spiral of grades, attendance, and interest in school. Without help, many will drop out of school. Their relationships with their families are often strained or worse, and their involvement with alcohol and other drugs can expose them to earlier sexual activity, violence, and trouble with the law. In terms of school climate, it is unconscionable for us to leave these students who are suffering from the disease of addiction without access to helping resources and proper treatment. Unfortunately, there are a great number of students suffering from chemical dependency who don't look the part and so may go unnoticed. Your SAP policies and procedures must reflect this reality.

SAPs hope to intervene with this population by identifying troubling behaviors and getting at-risk students into the SAP system. Once in, they can be involved in challenge groups (to take a look at their own drinking and drugging) or recovery groups. Access to in-patient treatment is also provided through an SAP.

Children Affected by Addiction[1] Children who live with or are related to an alcoholic or other drug addict (including prescription drug addicts) are at significantly higher risk for experiencing all sorts of problems. It is estimated that there are currently 28.6 million children of alcoholics in the United States; 6.6 million are under the age of 18 and most are enrolled in our schools. Research about children of alcoholics is more readily available, but experience has shown that children who live with other drug addiction experience similar problems. Children of illegal drug addicts may experience even more problems because of the social stigma attached to illegal drug use and the constant anxiety that their parents will be caught by the police. Research about children of alcoholics[2] shows that

- Children of alcoholics are more likely to develop alcoholism and other drug addiction than other children.
- Children of alcoholics are more likely to be truant, drop out of school, repeat grades, or be referred to the school counselor or school psychologist.
- Children of alcoholics score lower on tests measuring verbal ability.
- Existing research suggests that alcoholism is more strongly related to child abuse than are other disorders, such as parental depression.
- Children of alcoholics exhibit symptoms of depression and anxiety more than children of nonalcoholics.

---

[1]Throughout this book, children who live with or are related to an alcoholic or addict will be referred to as children of addiction, or COAs; in this book, the acronym refers both to children of alcoholics and those who live with other drug addiction.

[2]National Clearinghouse for Alcohol and Drug Information, NCADI, P.O. Box 2345, Rockville, MD, 20852, Office of Substance Abuse Prevention, May, 1991.

Ongoing research indicates that grandchildren of alcoholics may also experience some of these difficulties.

Other At-Risk Populations: There are a number of other variables which can predict if a student is at high risk for becoming involved with alcohol and other drugs. Children who experience multiple traumas, such as physical, emotional, or sexual abuse, school failure, chronic pain, pregnancy, mental illness, violence, or poverty, are statistically at risk for becoming involved with alcohol and other drugs. For students who are not already involved with alcohol and other drugs, student assistance programming is a prevention effort.

It is also an unfortunate fact that *any* student can be at risk for developing alcohol and other drug problems, even if there is no indication or predisposition to the disease of addiction. Without developing an addiction to the chemical, any adolescent can be hurt while under the influence or while someone else is under the influence.

EMPHASIZING THE EDUCATIONAL PERSPECTIVE

Years ago, employee assistance programs (on which student assistance programs are based) were developed to help employees deal with personal problems affecting their ability to work. Employers provided this much needed service while keeping their eye on the bottom line, because they found it was cost-effective to help employees help themselves.

In education, there is a different bottom line. We want our students to be able to learn in our classrooms so they can become the adults they choose to be. They will all pursue different career and family paths, but we want them to do those things without the ball and chain of alcohol or other drug addiction. Further, we want them to enjoy their childhood and teenage years as much as possible given their circumstances.

Student assistance programs work backward, starting at the research. For instance, because children of alcoholics display depression, more physical complaints than other students, poorer schoolwork, and so on, the idea is to target students who are depressed, who are in the nurse's office more than usual, and who are not reaching their potential academically. If you target these populations, you will find a significant percentage who are affected by addiction. Student assistance programs target these students because they are at incredibly high risk for repeating the patterns they have grown up with.

How a Student Assistance Program Can Improve School Climate

Student assistance programs can be the beginning of climatic change in your school and community. This is a positive change, as student and faculty alike begin to recognize that seeking help for personal problems is perfectly acceptable and indeed encouraged in your school setting. Student assistance programs embrace the magnitude of the alcohol and other drug-related problems facing educators and students today. Although they target at-risk populations specifically, the effect of having a student assistance program in operation can be felt throughout the school community. Students come to understand that there is an identified and confidential place to bring personal concerns. A student assistance program also encourages faculty to pay attention to what is happening with students and to refer them for help.

As you begin implementing an SAP, you may become discouraged because of the magnitude and pervasiveness of the problems you face. It helps to remember that SAPs, although they can't do the job alone, can be the catalyst for a more caring atmosphere in schools, where educators acknowledge the new and sometimes frightening reality of life for children and adolescents Only by addressing the serious personal problems that affect our students' ability to perform well in school can we make significant changes for this generation of young people and the generations to come. Student assistance programs address what have seemed like insurmountable problems for students and empower educators to do something about them.

The handout "Student Assistance Programs," which follows, can be used to acquaint faculty with a new SAP program.

FACULTY INFORMATION HANDOUT
STUDENT ASSISTANCE PROGRAMS

You may have heard a lot about a student assistance program being proposed or started in your school or district. Here are some of the fundamentals to help you understand the mission of the program:

What is a Student Assistance Program?

A student assistance program (SAP) aims to identify troubled students so they can receive the helping services they need. The SAP tries to help students who are dealing with a variety of personal problems, including those related to alcohol and other drugs. The SAP is not a disciplinary program, and teachers who refer students to the program are not getting students into trouble.

How Do Students Access the Program?

Students can get to the SAP in three ways: (1) They can be referred by a teacher or a friend *out of concern* about specific behavior which indicates that the student may be dealing with personal problems. (2) They can come to the SAP on their own, seeking a confidential place to discuss personal issues. (3) They can be caught in violation of the school's alcohol and other drug policy and be asked to participate, on the premise that students who are using at school may have well-developed problems with alcohol or other drugs.

What Should I Be Looking for to Make a Referral to the SAP?

Use your years of teaching experience to identify troubling behavioral patterns: students who are always late to class, who sleep in class, who speak freely about the problems that face them, who present problems to you that you feel need further attention, who have a lot of absences, or who are inappropriate in class or in their interaction with other students.

How Can I Refer a Student When I Am Concerned?

The student assistance program uses a simple form which you can use to refer students. There may be specific behaviors listed which are clues that a student is experiencing difficulty in his or her personal life. Ask your student assistance program coordinator or team member for more information.

What if a Student Is Upset Because I Make a Referral?

You make referrals based on observations of troubling behavior, not on accusations. If there is specific behavior which concerns you, you are not accusing the student of anything. The SAP counselor will make this clear to the student.

2

Designing a Structure That Works

CHAPTER 2

Designing a Structure That Works

Every student assistance program will be structured differently, depending on the vision, resources, and constraints of your particular system. If you are reading this, you are already considering instituting an SAP in your school system; perhaps you have already decided to do it. You may already be part of an SAP team or committee. Your school's programming should reflect the subtle differences in administrative style, personalities, physical plant, and so forth that distinguish your school or school system. However, there are some basic structures which have worked well in school settings, and they are included in this chapter as a starting point for your own design. If you already have a successful SAP structure, you may still want to read this chapter for a sense of other designs that can work.

BASIC INGREDIENTS OF A SUCCESSFUL SAP

All formalized student assistance programs include some basic elements, but the proportions will vary. As you know, a sports team must have elements of defense and offense, technique, coaching, practice, and play to be successful, but proportions of these elements are decided by whoever is in charge of the team. If the coaching staff emphasizes defense, the team may be known for its great defense. Another team might have great technique or a strong offense. Your program may emphasize certain elements over others, but you must have *all* the following elements to constitute a student assistance program:

- An SAP staff
- A core team
- A referral procedure
- Administrative support
- Student participation
- A chemical use policy for the school or district.

The SAP Staff

Someone must oversee the SAP effort. In some models, this will be a person or persons hired full time for just this purpose. This is the ideal situation, because this professional will bring experience dealing with alcohol and other drug concerns, confidentiality, educational systems, and adolescents. This person may also have extensive knowledge about student assistance programs and can guide the start-up operation. The coordinator/counselor usually has the most direct contact with students. In large schools, there may be more than one SAP person hired to fulfill these responsibilities. In districts comprised of small schools, this counselor might be hired by the school district and "float" from one school to another, in which case there must be a faculty member who acts as a liaison to the coordinator/counselor.

In some models, the person who oversees the SAP will be a professional who already works in the school in some other capacity. Usually a teacher or guidance counselor will be relieved of some other duties to perform this function.

In other cases, the school hires an agency that sends an SAP professional to the school on a regular basis. The only difference here is that the person hired is an employee of the agency, not of the school.

Even if the student assistance program is run as an in-school team effort, without a hired SAP coordinator or counselor, someone must be the recognized contact person. So, even when the core team performs the duties of the coordinator/counselor, someone must be in charge of the core team to delegate and organize its efforts.

A Core Team: The core team is a group of teachers, staff, and administrators from the school who are interested and invested in the success of the student assistance program. This group can be large or small, depending on the job it aims to do. Most successful core teams are comprised of people who express a desire to work in this capacity. Depending on the model chosen, this team can perform one or all of the following functions:

- Serve as ambassadors, transmitting information about the program and how it works to other members of the faculty. This team promotes the program through teaching other faculty members to utilize the referral system and by referring students to a coordinator/counselor and/or team.

- Gain training in the area of adolescent chemical dependency, parental addiction, and surrounding issues. Such training may be the catalyst for whole-school change as other faculty learn from those core team members trained.

- Serve as an information-gathering team, finding information about particular students so either the core team, the coordinator/counselor, or an outside agency can intervene more effectively.

- After receiving specific training, provide direct services to students, either performing formal interventions, cofacilitating groups, or conducting assessments.

- Provide the public relations element of student assistance programming by keeping the school community up to date about what is going on in the program, informing the community at large about the program's operation, and keeping the public aware of program efficacy. Core team members may serve on community task forces and advisory boards to promote recognition of the program.

A great deal of the core team's function will be determined by whether there is a hired, faculty-based or floating coordinator/counselor. The core team's composition will also vary. Some core teams include the entire guidance staff, for instance, while others have only representative participation from several departments.

A Referral Procedure: There must be a formalized way and a specific set of criteria which qualify students for referral and/or participation in the program. Faculty should be aware of these parameters. For instance, if you choose to have a program which identifies only those students whose parents are involved with alcohol and other drugs, you will need a way to identify such students. Some of the core team's role will be determined by the referral procedure. Some referral procedures require that students who meet some sweeping criteria (like failing three classes) be assessed by the SAP as a matter of course. Other structures allow for students to access the program on their own, only when they feel the need.

Administrative Support: The only way a student assistance program can operate effectively is to have the support of building-level and top administrators. This may vary from expressions of support to actual participation on the core team, depending on the model and the personalities of the administrators in your school.

Student Participation: There is no student assistance program without student participation. Your program design will determine how students access the program—whether they are referred by concerned teachers, peers, or parents, whether they refer themselves, or whether they can do both. Will student participation be voluntary, or will there be situations in which participation is mandatory? A great deal of your program's success depends on how students perceive your program, so you will want to consider that in your design.

A Chemical Use Policy: A student assistance program operates at top efficiency in a school system where there is a clear chemical use policy. If your policy is old, outdated, or erratically enforced, part of the start-up (or revitalization) of the student assistance program should include a long, hard look at the chemical use policy. Participation in the student assistance program should be part of the automatic consequence of violating the chemical use policy. Depending on the model, this policy may generate a few or a lot of referrals.

Now that you know the six fundamental elements of a student assistance program, your next task is to combine them in whatever proportion is needed and feasible in your setting. Five preformed combinations are briefly described in the remainder of this chapter, and more detailed explanations of all the elements are included in chapters 4 to 8.

FIVE BASIC STRUCTURES

The structure determines how much an SAP can accomplish. An SAP without a director or counselor is obviously going to work at the slowest pace, because members of the core team have teaching, counseling, or administrative duties and have to "borrow" time for the logistical tasks of an SAP start-up. (However, these efforts are not in vain, and if this is the only possible arrangement, don't wait!)

Starting on a Shoestring: A Core Team with no SAP Counselor:

The purpose of student assistance programs is to notice students who are in trouble, find out what's going on, and get them the appropriate help. Some of the premise is that a lot of students who display behavioral difficulties—declining grades, changing moods, and so on—are in fact in some way touched by their own or someone else's use of alcohol or other drugs. In schools across the nation, concerned school personnel have been getting together to see what can be done about the problem, and some of them have formed various task forces, coalitions, and community boards. Such a motivated group of individuals can quickly change gears, call themselves a core team of a student assistance program, and make significant headway.

Without a hired coordinator/counselor, the core team must take on the responsibility of identifying troubled students and must also provide a great deal of direct services to assess students and make referrals to outside agencies. Any function that would normally be accomplished by a trained SAP professional must be carried out by the team, and therefore you will have to secure some basic training for your core team. The number of students your SAP can serve may also be smaller than if you have a coordinator/counselor on staff. But don't be discouraged! As the saying goes, "better to light a single candle than to sit and curse the dark."

When forming a core team without a coordinator/counselor, some school personnel will have to obtain or refresh some basic training in counseling techniques so they can intervene one-on-one with students. You will want to secure alcohol and other drug training for these individuals as a condition of their participation on the core team. Some SAP consultants will come into schools and help you set up a core team, providing training for the members in alcohol and other drug-related issues. If your system does have some financial resources but is not yet ready to hire someone full time, this arrangement can work well. The consultant can bring expertise and clarity to the often confusing and emotionally charged issues surrounding alcohol and other drug use and can help members understand their roles more clearly. (You can read more about core team training in chapter 6.)

Guidance counselors who are core team members can provide some of the counseling and assessment. Core teams are typically comprised of between eight and ten individuals who can give significant time to this important work. Without a hired coordinator/counselor, there are choices to be made about how you want to structure your program.

Structure 1: Using Your Core Team as a Referral Agency:

When there is no hired, full-time counselor, one model views the core team as a referral agency itself. The team's purpose in this model is to accept referrals from concerned teachers, parents, staff, and peers (or any subset of those) and to follow them up by meeting with the student and referring him or her to an outside agency or existing in-school service. In some cases, the SAP's only function is to screen for alcohol and other drug-related issues; in others, the team is equipped to deal with any or all personal problems. This will depend on the training and composition of your team. In this model, identifying troubled students and offering them a referral is the main thrust.

Someone must still head up the operation of the core team in school, usually a counselor or teacher who is relieved of some other duties to make time for this important work.

In this structure, if a teacher or other staff member has a concern about a specific student, he or she brings this student's case to the attention of the core team, either by contacting the faculty-appointed coordinator or by presenting the case to the team at a scheduled meeting. (Some SAPs have core team meetings at a set time every week so teachers can present cases.) The concerned staff member may refer the student using a behavioral checklist or by expressing his or her concerns verbally to a core team member.

The faculty-appointed coordinator may use other options:

- Bring the student's case to the attention of the team to gather additional information, and the team may make a referral to the guidance staff or an outside agency. If another person on the team has an established relationship with the student and is sufficiently trained, that person might conduct the original assessment.

- Gather additional information about the student and, before the student is contacted, contact the parents to make them aware that the student's case has been brought before the core team. This works best in junior and senior high school populations, where alcohol and other drug users are targeted. In this case, parents can become part of a formal intervention if one is to take place.

As you will notice, the functions the core team emphasizes in this structure are identification and referral (noticing and identifying the trouble and securing appropriate help), and the assessment generally takes a short time but involves the entire team. This is because there are fewer resources within the school to get to the root of the student's trouble. The most important tool the SAP needs in this structure is an updated and reliable list of resources for the area, including agencies, self-help groups, private therapists, hotlines, mediators, Child Protective Services offices, and hospitals. What you cannot provide in school, you must have access to out of school. Core team members must have good powers of observation and some basic training in what identifies students as being at high risk for alcohol and other drug involvement.

In terms of the confidentiality regulations, the only confidential information is that gathered from the student that identifies him or her as an alcohol or other drug user. (Confidentiality is discussed at length in chapter 3.) If you've never met with the student, you don't yet have the information that he or she is an alcohol or other drug abuser. You can gather a lot of information that does not come from the student's self-disclosure previous to your meeting with him or her. For example, absenteeism, declining grades, inappropriate behavior in class, and other directly observable behaviors are not covered by the laws surrounding confidentiality.

Although the practice of discussing students' cases with a team previous to meeting with students is certainly within the law, students may perceive that a hostile team of teachers is discussing their personal lives, so be careful of this approach if you use it. Core team members must have sophisticated understanding of the confidentiality regulations for this approach to work well.

In some cases, after gathering information from team members, it will be clear that a student has a well-developed and dangerous relationship with alcohol and/or other drugs and referral to chemical dependency treatment is in order. In some models, the core team is trained in intervention techniques, and members close to the student perform formal interventions, hopefully motivating students into inpatient chemical dependency treatment, sometimes with the consultant help of hired alcohol and other drug counselors. This approach works especially well when the parents have brought their concerns to the school and are involved in the process. This is using the core team for very specific, limited, direct services.

Structure 2: Using Your Core Team to Provide Direct Service:

In this structure, the team itself performs the duties of a coordinator/counselor. This may include gathering information about students, taking teacher, parent, and peer referrals, acting as a referral agency, and seeing students individually and in groups to deal with ongoing personal issues, especially those pertaining to alcohol and other drug use.

In this structure, core team members provide both identification of troubled students, assessment, and direct services for students. Team members may cofacilitate student assistance program groups or may alternately staff an office or "drop-in center" throughout the day. Because most team members may not have extensive training, they must be aware of their limitations and must have clear guidelines for when a student should be referred to an outside agency or alcohol and other drug professional. When core team members are not professionally trained, it may be best to have them work in pairs and to discuss their meetings soon after with trained counselors on staff. The scope of a team-based program can only be as wide as the team's ability to process referrals in a timely fashion.

In some cases, professionals from the community will volunteer an hour or so each week to cofacilitate a special topic group with an SAP core team member. For instance, a professional counselor with specialized training in children of alcoholics might agree to help run an eight-week educational group to help the SAP effort get underway and to help familiarize a cofacilitator core team member with the pertinent issues. Other SAP efforts may be to hire an outside professional on a consultant or hourly basis to facilitate or cofacilitate an in-school group.

In this structure, when students are referred to the core team for follow-up, the team may take other optional courses of action:

- Discuss the case, adding any information team members might individually have about a particular student's situation.
- Decide to have one of the trained team members see a referred student to assess the situation. This may be a core team member who has a previous

history with the student and may be able to gain the student's trust more readily. Depending on the team member's level of training, the student's situation will either be assessed by the team member, or the team member will recommend that a more formal assessment of chemical dependency or depression, for instance, be conducted by an outside professional, and may try to gain a release of information from the student to notify the parents. (If there is evident imminent suicidality, homicidality, abuse, or neglect, parents and the proper authorities are notified regardless of consent.)

- Decide, after gathering additional information, that the student's situation is very serious and plan for a formal intervention.

- After the initial meeting with the student, encourage him or her to join one of the in-school groups offered by the student assistance program and cofacilitated by trained core team members.

Structure 3: Using an Outside Contract:

Some schools utilize the core team to generate referrals and then provide direct service through an agency which is hired to assess and service troubled students. The agency sends counselor(s) to the school who are not on the faculty of the school but work in it on a consultant basis. It is best when the agency sends particular counselors to the school on a regular basis so students can become familiar with them. This can be a workable situation for all involved, particularly in smaller systems that cannot afford to hire a person full time. The agency then takes on the role of the coordinator/counselor, providing assessments, individual counseling, and groups for children of addiction, recovering students, or special populations (sexual abuse survivors, children from chaotic homes, etc.). It is essential that the agency send counselors who are familiar with the workings of schools and who have a sophisticated understanding of alcohol and other drug-related issues and the surrounding confidentiality issues. Because the counselor may not be at the school full time, the number of students served by the SAP may be small.

The significant drawback to this model is that since the person is agency-hired, there may not be the same level of trust between the school community and the person. It is always better to have someone at the school full time, because students' problems are a full-time job. However, this drawback is balanced by the access to a specifically trained professional.

When students are referred to the SAP in this structure, the following optional courses of action may be taken:

- Students may be referred directly to the counselor, and the core team acts in an advisory capacity to the counselor or agency.

- A core team member conducts an interview with the student to see whether a referral to the contracted counselor is appropriate. If it isn't, the student might be referred to his or her guidance counselor (who may be a core team member) or to some other school-based or agency-based program for further follow-up.

If the student is referred to the counselor, the counselor then assesses the student's trouble and helps him or her decide what is the best route. This may include outpatient counseling, continued counseling with the SAP counselor, participation in an in-school group, referral back to the guidance staff, or referral to inpatient treatment.

MAXIMIZING RESULTS: COUNSELOR-BASED PROGRAMS

Structures 4 and 5 are in-school, counselor-based student assistance programs. An SAP director hired by an enthusiastic school district, working with a cooperative principal and core team, will make great progress quickly. Because time is of the essence, this is the best way to go. In both structures that follow, the assumption is that a person(s) will be hired onto the staff of the school or district either full time or part time to head up the student assistance program. This person(s) may provide all the necessary preliminary work, such as training faculty to use a referral system and training them to identify at-risk populations. In addition, the SAP staff usually offers in-school individual counseling, in-school groups, and perhaps in-school assessment. The scope of the program with a counselor can be as wide as the counselor or staff has time and energy. It is an ideal situation to have a full-time person on board, as students and teachers alike begin to trust this person and treat him or her like another member of the faculty. The only difference between the two structures that follow is the role of the core team.

Structure 4: Counselor/Staff Base with Core Team as Advisory Board

In some systems, there is a hired student assistance program counselor/coordinator who operates autonomously, seeing all students who are referred and making all referrals without any help or input from anyone else at the school. This person may also facilitate or cofacilitate most or all of the in-school groups. These people work hard and are generally underappreciated, mostly because other people do not know what they do.

For this reason, it is unwise to operate completely without input from other faculty and staff. A core team can be formed to act as an advisory board to the SAP counselor/coordinator. By definition, an advisory core team learns about the work the SAP does and can advocate for the coordinator/counselor. Especially when programs are new, it is helpful to have a group of friendly faces who can make inroads with other faculty and concentrate on the public relations end of the program. Advisory core teams also have important information about the inner workings of the school and can provide invaluable information about what will work and what won't work, historical information, and inside information on who will be easy to work with and who may present obstacles to the SAP. Even SAPs that have operated without core teams for some time may find that their road becomes less bumpy and territorial disputes less harrowing once a core team is formed.

At the start-up phase of an SAP, an advisory core team guides the policy and practices of the SAP and helps the coordinator/counselor or staff get the operation underway. As a continuing effort, the core team troubleshoots political problems within the system and disseminates information to other faculty members. Because they are familiar with referral procedures, members generally refer a large number of students to the program. An advisory core team may help to secure funding for personnel, or help to obtain the proper facilities. Even an advisory core team should get some basic training in alcohol and other drug-related issues so they can be better equipped to identify and refer troubled students. After such basic training, an advisory core team may also be instrumental in drafting or redrafting the chemical use policy for the school or district. (Often, refining or creating such a policy is the first task core teams complete.)

Some SAP structures extend the core team advisory board to include community members. This larger board meets less often but performs essentially the same function, serving as the public relations bridge to the community at large. Often, an extended advisory board includes representation from community agencies, parent groups, business, and so on. This larger advisory board is never made aware of the problems of specific students, but serves to educate the community and to act as a political force should the program's funding be threatened.

In this structure, students are referred directly to the SAP staff, who may do the following:

- See the student individually to assess his or her trouble and then make a referral to an outside agency (including the possibility of inpatient chemical dependency treatment).
- See the student individually and refer him or her to existing in-school services.
- See the student individually and/or refer him or her to SAP services, suggesting a specific number of individual sessions with the SAP counselor/coordinator or encouraging the student to join a group offered by the SAP. (As in all other models, if suicidality, homicidality, abuse, or neglect are apparent, the proper authorities and parents will be contacted.)

Structure 5: Counselor/Staff Base with Core Team Participation

In this structure, the core team performs all the duties of an advisory board, and some or all members are involved in providing direct services to students. This is perhaps the best-case scenario in student assistance programming. This structure combines the best elements of all the other structures: first, a hired SAP counselor/coordinator with specialized expertise in alcohol and other drug-related issues, experience with adolescents, and knowledge of SAP operation and, second, a core team that is trained and whose membership participates actively in providing direct services to students.

In this structure, the SAP coordinator can train or coordinate the initial training of the core team in alcohol and other drug-related issues. This is an important phase in this model of SAP. The core team then acts in cooperation with the counselor, providing him or her with student referrals. Core team members who are specifically trained (or who are willing to become trained) can serve as group cofacilitators or can provide preliminary screenings for students with whom they are acquainted. Core team members can also cofacilitate groups and can use the counselor/coordinator for technical assistance and clinical supervision or referral of difficult cases. Depending on the structure of your school, some core team members may be released from other duties to cofacilitate groups or to perform assessments or interviews with students. Core teams in this structure may also set up and staff an informal drop-in center where students can bring concerns. Those that are of a serious nature can then be referred to the SAP counselor. This structure, combining a hired SAP staff and active participation by veteran faculty members, is the most desirable because it combines the talents and energies of a number of different people while providing some technical expertise in the area of alcohol and other drugs and their related issues.

In this structure, students may be

- Referred to a core team member who does an initial assessment to determine whether the student can benefit from SAP services
- Referred to the SAP staff for assessment and referral to outside agencies, or existing in-school services
- Referred from the initial assessment to extended SAP services, such as group or one-on-one sessions with SAP staff or core team members. Core team members may cofacilitate groups or staff an office or drop-in center.

GAINING AND KEEPING FUNDING FOR YOUR SAP

Funding often determines your structure. In start-up SAPs, core teams often form as some sort of task force to try to address the personal problems they see their students facing—these teachers and administrators are fed up with alcohol and other drug concerns and have put their heads together to do something about it. When they do their research, they find that many schools are instituting student assistance programs to combat these problems. It is these same teams and task forces that may eventually lobby to hire a coordinator/counselor or an outside contract because they feel they need additional people-power and specialized expertise about alcohol and other drug use in student populations. Some SAPs are started using federal Drug-Free Schools and Communities allocations, which most publicly assisted schools have received since the mid-1980s. Sometimes community task forces can be instrumental in securing funding—by conducting a needs survey, for instance, which indicates that student assistance programs are necessary in the district. If you are in a large school district and you are curious about funding, make phone calls to find out who is in charge of federal projects and Drug-Free Schools funding.

However, there's an old saying about people entering therapy for personal problems: It only works if you pay for it. Much the same can be said for student assistance programming and its relationship to the community it serves. If a community pays for SAPs, it is much more likely to be invested in them and to understand their wide target population and their broad-brush educational mission. While we can be grateful that some SAPs are getting underway with start-up grants through the federal government or private funding, we must be vigilant that cities, towns, states, and school departments begin to take financial responsibility for their SAPs and don't let federally funded SAP efforts fall by the wayside or stop abruptly when the terms of the grants are up. Federal grants are not required for math departments or guidance personnel, and there's no reason why outside funds should have to be elicited for what is an "inside" problem in most American schools.

The best possible scenario is to have SAP personnel on the faculty of schools, paid like any other full-time teacher or counselor. This means that the commitment for SAP programming comes directly from the district, town, or city it serves. This is one of the first steps a community can take toward recognizing its own problems and dealing with them. If the community is only willing to have these services if someone else pays for them, then the commitment is shaky.

If you have been hired to head up an SAP effort and don't know how your SAP is funded, find out. If you are on an SAP team, operating on barefaced spirit and dedication, congratulations—but take steps to insure that your efforts can continue if your spirit is daunted or if you lose some key personnel. A dedicated SAP team can drum up support from the school board by presenting what you have accomplished already without funds, and what you could do given an SAP counselor(s) and other resources. This is a difficult prospect in these belt-tightening days, but it is feasible.

Although it is necessary to aim for the best possible program, the budgets and logistics of smaller school systems may make it impossible to hire full-time SAP people right away. Some very good things can happen on a shoestring, however, so do not be discouraged. Of course, a great many more good things can happen on even a moderate budget. In larger systems, if SAP personnel cannot be hired right away, it is still best to include the eventual hiring of a full-time SAP person in the plan for the near future.

Some Final Words about Structuring Your SAP

This has been just a quick overview of the different SAP structures and funding options that can work in a school setting. Details about setting up the programs, training faculty, and marketing the programs are covered in subsequent chapters. Most SAP structures are evolving, depending on the people who staff them and the individual characteristics of the school system. For instance, in my first years in SAP work, my core team acted in an advisory capacity only. Then as years went by and team members became more familiar with the issues surrounding alcohol and other drugs, some wanted to try their hand at cofacilitating groups. Others began taking over some of the responsibilities associated with other alcohol and drug initiatives (awareness campaigns, assemblies, etc.). Decide on a structure as a starting point and then, as your core team gets trained and invested in the success of the program, watch the evolution. You will surely arrive at a structure that will help students in your particular setting.

3

Insuring Confidentiality

CHAPTER 3

Insuring Confidentiality

Confidentiality is the cornerstone of student assistance programming and what sets an SAP slightly apart from the rest of the school. This is why we devote a whole chapter to these complex but fundamental issues. The more carefully you work out the confidentiality issues surrounding student assistance programming, the more successful your program will ultimately be. Therefore, your core team, administration, and SAP people need to hash out ahead of time how the tangle of SAP confidentiality constraints will be managed consistently in your school or district. The confidentiality regulations can seem arbitrary—like hurdles you have to jump before you can get students the help they need—but there are compelling reasons for SAPs to adhere to strictest principles of confidentiality. It is not an option to disregard the confidentiality regulations. Your program must work within or around them.

Unfortunately, school systems may have to disprove the reputation that school confidentiality has traditionally been "fast and loose." Students know that in some schools, teachers, counselors, and staff talk freely about students' problems and family histories in the teachers' cafeteria or in the teachers' rooms. Student assistance programs have to battle that reputation while guiding school systems to an updated understanding of confidentiality as it relates to SAPs.

Those people with work experience in chemical dependency treatment, social work, and private practice will probably be more comfortable with SAP confidentiality than people from the school setting, because they are more familiar with this level of confidentiality. Once your school administration and faculty have received some training and understand the meaning and intent of the confidentiality regulations, it will be much easier to maneuver within the confines of them. Once students understand that SAP services are in fact confidential, and your SAP has an established record of trustworthiness, more students will access the system for help.

DEALING WITH RESISTANCE

Your student assistance program may come up against some resistance to the confidentiality standards, first because most people believe that they *are* adhering to strict confidentiality when in fact they are not. Second, most people would like access to the same information that the SAP people have, simply due to their natural human curiosity. There are two important reasons why SAPs should focus on confidentiality early on: It has a direct effect on the ultimate success of your program, and it is the law.

Confidentiality is extremely complex, especially with adolescents. Someone once said that "to not decide is to decide," and in this case the axiom holds true. If a school system disregards the regulations because they don't mesh with the opinions of those in charge, it has essentially decided to break the law. Even if you do not agree with their basic premises, they are laws and you must either break the law, abide by the law, or study the regulations and design programming that works within both the law and the collective conscience of your system.

It is important that you have a clear understanding of the federal confidentiality regulations and those for your state, because you will be asked to explain them over and over again, and you should be prepared. The more succinctly you can present them, the more confidence you'll instill in others about conforming to them.

UNDERSTANDING THE LAW

This discussion of the regulations[1] is meant to provide a framework for understanding, but it is not legal counsel. Your core team training should include a workshop on the confidentiality regulations and surrounding issues, and you should keep in touch with your school lawyer or district lawyer. There is still much controversy surrounding these issues, so carefully check the state and local laws governing student assistance programs in your area.

At present, federal regulations (42 C.F.R., part 2) provide that any person can seek assistance for alcohol or other drug-related problems without anyone else's knowledge or consent. Each state decides at what age a person can apply for such services; many states stipulate that any person over the age of twelve can seek these services without anyone's consent. In some states, there is no age minimum. You *must* know at what age students can access services without parental consent in your state. Call your single state agency (Appendix B: "State Government Agencies for Drug and Alcohol Information") to find out.

Federal regulation 42 C.F.R., part 2 was originally intended for drug and/or alcohol treatment facilities, and its translation into the domain of the school has been tricky at best, especially when student assistance programs hope to make treatment available but do not necessarily intend to provide treatment themselves. However, currently these regulations seem to cover federally assisted, school-based SAPs. (This includes all programs in public schools and some in private schools.) You cannot get around this by calling your SAP something other than treatment. If you serve a population that uses alcohol or other drugs, and you tout your program as an identified referral source for alcohol and other drug-related issues in schools, then you are providing treatment according to the federal law and fall under these regulations. Broad-brush programs are covered, too, because the description emphasizes that if your program specializes in whole *or in part* in providing referral services, treatment, counseling, and/or assessment for students with alcohol and drug problems, then you must comply with the federal regulations.

---

[1] Federal Confidentiality Regulations (42 U.S.C. § 290dd–3 and § 290 ee–3; 42 C.F.R., part 2).

Who Has Access to Information?

The way you structure your program will determine who can have access to what information. Information can always be shared if you have consent from the student (and in states that require it, from the parent). Information can also be shared within the program (for instance, within a core team) if the shared information is needed to provide treatment, referral services, etc., to the student. This approach seems to work well when there is no SAP counselor and core team members need to brainstorm ways of securing treatment for students. Core teams cannot get together to discuss students' cases just for the heck of it, or to satisfy core team members' curiosity about student cases.

Similarly, the law allows disclosure of participation to an entity having direct administrative control over the SAP, but again, only when needed to provide services for the student. If your principal oversees the SAP operation, disclosure would be permitted, for example, to gain permission to take a student out of a class to attend a counseling session. Disclosure would not be permitted to levy disciplinary consequences on a student. If the principal does not have direct administrative control over the SAP, some schools solve this dilemma by having the administrative office in question sign a QSOA (Qualified Service Organization Agreement), which allows the administrator to provide services (like handling attendance records) to the SAP without gaining individual student consent.[2]

When there is an SAP counselor who performs intakes and assessments, sharing information with the whole team after seeing the student seems unnecessary and risky, unless it is needed to procure additional treatment for the student. Team members who receive this information are bound by the same confidentiality regulations, and the more people who have the information, the greater the likelihood that some of it will leak.

In broad-brush programs, a number of people (teachers, counselors, and administrators) may know that students are involved in the program, because participation neither explicitly nor implicitly identifies students as alcohol and other drug abusers. The information that identifies them as alcohol and other drug abusers, however, remains confidential, even if faculty members know that students are participating in the program. The law also allows for disclosures to medical personnel in medical emergencies, or in coping with a substantial threat to the life or well-being of the minor or someone else. However, even in these extreme cases, the information that identifies the student as an alcohol or other drug abuser is confidential.

NARROW-FOCUS PROGRAMS AND CONFIDENTIALITY

The only information that is protected under the federal regulations is that which identifies a student as an alcohol or drug abuser. This stipulation has interesting ramifications for the way in which you design your program, because if your SAP

---

[2]This QSOA would prohibit any further disclosure by the principal without written consent. A QSOA can only be used when providing services to the student, not for other purposes.

attempts to intervene with only alcohol or other drug abusers, a student's mere participation in the program must be kept completely confidential. If your SAP is structured this way, simple questions like, "Was Sam with you in period 4?" become difficult because the admission of his participation in your program labels him an alcohol or other drug abuser, which is against the law.

Another problem with narrow-focus programs is that your program may suffer if only students with drug problems attend. Students who utilize your services may feel stigmatized if it becomes the "drug program." This is clearly another argument for using the broad-brush targeting technique. Students need to know that just walking in your door won't cause the label "alcohol or other drug abuser" to be slapped on their back.

However, there are going to be situations in which a narrow-focus program is the only feasible alternative. In this case, great care must be taken to insure that no information that identifies a student as an alcohol or other drug abuser leaks from the program staff. That staff may be a hired SAP counselor or may be a school-based team. A member of the team, trained in the issues of confidentiality, should be responsible for intercepting attendance troubles that could identify the student as a participant in the program.

Luckily, however, information that you obtain about a student prior to meeting with him or her is not protected. Confidentiality starts when the student applies for or receives services. In other words, a team could gather information about a student which could indicate that the student was experiencing problems (i.e., declining grades, attendance, negative attitude in school, etc.). *Before* meeting with the student, the parents could be contacted and informed that the SAP team had identified behavior that could indicate problems. This type of set-up is most common in team-based, intervention-oriented programs that aim to identify alcohol and other drug abusers and immediately motivate them into treatment. Because your state may require written release of information from the student to contact his or her parents after the student meets with you, these programs attempt to motivate the student into treatment on the *first* attempt, with the help of the parents.

ALCOHOL AND OTHER DRUG EDUCATION AND CONFIDENTIALITY

On the other end of the spectrum, if a program is merely educational in nature (for instance, part of a comprehensive health curriculum, or part of a K–12 comprehensive alcohol and other drug curriculum), then no one's participation would be considered confidential. A lot of schools currently have a unit in their health curriculum which deals directly with alcohol and other drug issues. Any parent, friend, etc., could call up and ask what the students were doing in health class, and it would break no one's confidentiality to volunteer that information. Also, if a student were to volunteer information in class which made it clear that the student or a family member was abusing alcohol and other drugs, the teacher is under no legal obligation to keep that information confidential. This helps SAPs gain referrals, because in many classrooms students confide in teachers after class or through written assignments. However, it is still good practice for teachers to tell students what they want to do with the information, though they are under no legal obligation to do so. For instance, a teacher might say, "Jane, I read your journal last night and it seems to me like you have a lot to deal with. We have a person here at school who knows a lot about what your situation must be like, and I'd really like to refer you. What do you think?" A great number of referrals are generated this way and through health class units on alcohol and other drugs.

Most people in the SAP business would like to see alcohol and other drug education continue to be part of the regular school curriculum in all grades. Bear in mind that SAPs and health education are two very separate entities. Education is prevention. SAPs provide education *and* intervention.

MANAGING CONFIDENTIALITY IN BROAD-BRUSH PROGRAMS

Most student assistance programs are broad brush in nature and occupy that murky, gray area where a variety of problems are handled, though a large percentage of them are in fact related to alcohol or other drugs. For example, students who have been sexually abused are often (though not always) from homes in which there are alcohol and other drug-related problems. School failure can sometimes be attributable to an adolescent's alcohol or other drug use, and children affected by parental addiction show a myriad of maladaptive behaviors directly attributable to the parent's involvement with chemicals. So, in an SAP's practice, there will be students who are bona-fide alcohol and other drug abusers, but there will also be others who are not.

If your program is broad brush in nature, you will be receiving a lot of information about the students you serve, but the only information that is legally confidential (by federal regulation) is the information that identifies a student as being an alcohol or other drug user. So how does this translate into practice? What do you tell the students who participate in your SAP? That you'll keep confidential only the information that identifies them as alcohol or other drug abusers? Clearly, that is not the answer. Ethically, all information that is not life threatening needs to be treated with the same level of respect.

SAP confidentiality is meant to foster a sense of trust—the feeling in a young adult that he or she can share information that won't be shared with anyone else unless his or her life or someone else's is in danger, or there is evidence of abuse or neglect. Confidentiality is not that same thing as secrecy, but we must be aware that many people still judge students harshly who are chemically dependent or whose family situations are less than perfect. While we do not want to create a feeling of mystery and distance, we *do* want to insure a safe place for students to explore the issues that will define them as adults. Students deserve respect and privacy, but they also need adult monitoring to keep them safe. Student assistance programs hope to provide that safety while encouraging students to bring others into their confidence, if it will make it easier for the student to get further help.

In broad-brush programs, confirming attendance at groups is much easier because mere participation in the program implies nothing about whether a student is an alcohol or other drug abuser. A student might access the program for help with family problems or difficulty dealing with a peer group. Communication with other staff members in the school is eased considerably because as long as you have groups which do not have alcohol or other drug-related issues as well as those that do, you can confirm a student's participation in a group. You still cannot identify which group a student attends or the nature of the issues discussed there, but it makes the SAP personnel's role easier.

CONFIDENTIALITY AND PARENTS

Legally, you must keep all information that identifies a student as being an alcohol or other drug abuser completely confidential. In states where students under the age of eighteen can seek services, that means that no one but the person who conducts the assessment of the situation has access to that information, including parents. To let anyone else know the results of the assessment, the interviewer would need the written consent of the student. These are some of the most difficult questions that SAPs have to grapple with—finding the balance between respect for the law, the school community, the student, and the student's parents. This may seem to be an impossible situation. One way of handling it is to use a release of information.

Using Releases of Information

Some school systems insist that all students sign a release of information routinely (see sample release of information, next page) before even talking with the SAP person. This insures that SAP personnel can get back to parents with any essential information. Using a release of information may seem cumbersome at first, but it does help students understand that their privacy is being taken very seriously. That goes a long way in building trust. The following release of information form can be altered as long as it contains the following information:

- Name of the student
- Name of the person and the student assistance program disclosing the information
- Name of the agency to which the information is being disclosed
- A brief and clear explanation of the statutes that protect this information
- Content and extent of the information to be disclosed
- A clear expiration date of the consent
- Student's signature indicating his or her understanding of the release of information (and in some states, a parent's signature as well)
- A statement regarding the student's ability to revoke the consent at any time, except after disclosure has been made (Students cannot retroactively deny consent once you have acted on their initial consent.)
- Expiration of the consent for release of confidential information
- A reminder to the recipient of this information that the information cannot be redisclosed without additional permission

CONSENT FOR RELEASE OF CONFIDENTIAL INFORMATION

I, _____ of _____
              (student's name)   (student's address)

authorize the student assistance program to disclose to:

☐ the person that referred me _____

☐ appropriate school personnel (guidance, teachers, etc.)

☐ my parents _____

☐ school administration (if this is a mandatory referral, this is required)

☐ other _____

The student assistance program is authorized to disclose to the above persons the following information:

☐ that I kept my first appointment

☐ that I kept my first appointment and that I will continue to be involved with the Student Assistance Program, either individually or in group support

☐ that I completed whatever was required of me (for mandatory referral)

☐ recommendations for treatment or placement services

☐ other (please specify) _____

_____

I understand that my records are protected under Federal Regulations and State statutes and cannot be disclosed without my written consent unless otherwise provided for in the regulations. I also understand that I may revoke this consent at any time except to the extent that action has been taken and reliance contingent on it. In any event, this consent expires automatically as described below:

☐ This consent will expire 180 days from the date of execution

☐ This consent will expire on _____

I acknowledge with my signature here that the information to be released was fully explained to me and this consent is given of my own free will.

_____ _____
(signature of student)   (date)

Note to recipients of information: Federal regulations and state statutes require that information released to you covered by this consent must be held in strict confidence and may not be released to others without the written consent of the above-named student.

This information may only be used to support the student in his or her best interest.

If you require a release of information to be signed by the student before conducting the initial interview, then when the assessment through the SAP indicates that the student is chemically dependent or harmfully involved, a release has already been signed and the parents can be contacted. While this approach may work, it is essentially school oriented rather than student oriented, and it may discourage some students from coming to the program or from speaking truthfully. Although it may enhance the comfort level of the school administration, you will get a lot of students coming in to talk about "this friend I know...," forced to conceal information to talk about themselves.

Other districts manage the problem of parental knowledge by waiting for the assessment to be completed and, if treatment is indicated, telling the student that the easiest way to pursue further help is to have the SAP contact his or her parents. Most agencies or hospitals to which an SAP would refer require payment, and most students need their parents' help in that regard. The SAP person would be responsible for gaining the release of information from the student at this point.

One other option is to conduct the assessment in the SAP office with a "pending release of information" understanding, and a written contract between the SAP counselor and the student, that if the assessment indicates harmful involvement or beyond, parents will be contacted. This is a very workable deal because it includes caution on the part of the SAP, respect for the fact that most parents want to know that their child may be in trouble, and respect for the student as well. The only danger here is that some students may answer assessment questions dishonestly, hoping to "seal the deal" in their favor. Of course, in states that require parental consent for treatment, you would need to gain permission even before you made the original contact with the student.

Although it goes against some people's grain, in states that allow it, the law says that students can get this help without their parents' knowledge or consent. In the strictest interpretation of the law, a chemically dependent student could hypothetically have an assessment through the SAP and decide to treat himself or herself by going to Alcoholics Anonymous (AA) or Narcotics Anonymous (NA) meetings in the area and participating in an in-school SAP group without the parents ever knowing about the student's involvement with alcohol or other drugs. I believe that for a small portion of the adolescent population, this is a necessary course of action and it is best that their rights are protected in this regard. However, we must also recognize that for some other students, no real healing can begin until their families are aware of their situations, and some SAP policies should reflect that philosophy. A school-based SAP must think long and hard about how cases like this will be managed.

Handling Suicidality and Homicidality, Abuse and Neglect

The appropriate people must be contacted in the event that a student poses a substantial threat to his or her own life or someone else's or is being abused or neglected. It is a good rule of thumb to err on the side of caution when these issues are concerned. It is unlikely that parents will sue you because you let them know that their son or daughter was suicidal. Also, the law allows disclosure if a student indicates that he or she is being abused or neglected. These boundaries must be made clear to students before they entrust you with their thoughts. If a student knows the rules and discloses this information anyway, despite vocal protest when you make the call, it is clear that he or she wanted help. If a student discloses without knowing the rules, however, then you may shatter not only his or her trust of you, but trust of people in the helping professions for years to come. This is a high price to pay.

You may want to post your "rules" and ask students to sign a statement underscoring their understanding of them. For instance, I have recited this little speech literally thousands of times:

> Whatever you tell me is completely confidential. What you tell me, I won't tell your teachers, your guidance counselor, the administration of the school, the police, or your parents without your express written consent. There are some exceptions to this rule that you need to understand: If I think you are a threat to your own life or someone else's, I'll need to tell your parents. If you are being abused or neglected, I'll tell someone who can help.

Making the Call to Parents

Whatever you do, do not contact a student's parent without the student knowing about it. Students then regard the SAP as a spy ring, doing the dirty work and spying for the parents. It may take years for your SAP to shake this reputation. But do not confuse that warning with a call to inaction. If you have sufficiently outlined your rules from the start, any breaking of a student's confidentiality will be an expected, if protested, event. Once students really understand the operating procedure of the SAP, they may even use this procedure to get the message to their parents that they need to be taken seriously by telling you that they are feeling suicidal. If you can, have the student in the office with you when you make a call to the parents, an outside agency, or to your department of Child and Family Services (in abuse cases). This way, you show the student respect by keeping him or her informed of everything that is said.

Even when there is no evidence of suicidality, homicidality, abuse, or neglect, it is sometimes clear that a parent should be contacted. This is where the power of persuasion really helps. After you have reached the limit of individual sessions and a student really should have further assistance from an outside professional, it will become necessary to get a written release of information from the student to contact the parent.

If a student absolutely refuses to let you contact his or her parents, document the refusal thoroughly in your notes, and if you feel anxious about it, eliminate all identifying details and bounce the case off your clinical supervisor or off another SAP director in your area. Document your calls to other professionals, and if their advice warrants it (because of suicidality, homicidality, abuse, or neglect), call the student back to your office and contact the parents. There are some situations when you are simply going to have to trust your gut. If a student seems to be a danger to himself or herself or you have a funny feeling about it, act on it.

CONFIDENTIALITY AND CONTACTING OUTSIDE AGENCIES

When contacting an outside agency for a referral, make sure you have a written release of information from the student and familiarity with the agency. If you can, get to know someone there by name, and if possible meet with him or her for lunch and get a working familiarity with the agency and this person. You'll get faster responses if you have a personal relationship with someone there. In states that require parental permission for treatment, parental permission is also required for release of information. If you needed permission to treat a student initially, you need parental permission to call an outside therapist to refer the student for additional counseling.

You don't need a release of information if you are reporting suicidality or homicidality, abuse or neglect, but you might want to get one anyway, as it helps to maintain some level of trust between the SAP person and the student. Some agencies can see students without parental consent and do so, but most will require at least parents' knowledge. Obviously, when you are reporting parental abuse or neglect, you would contact the Division of Child and Youth Services of the Child Protective Services in your area.

If a matter is serious enough to be referred to an outside agency, it is wise in most cases to contact parents as well with a written release of information from the student. Consider this example: In some states, a crime like rape must be reported to the Division of Child Protective Services. If the student goes to the hospital, the hospital is required to contact the police. Everyone is required to contact someone, but no one is explicitly required to contact the parents. Here is a case, however, in which the parents definitely should be contacted. In a number of cases like this, the parents will find out what is going on eventually anyway because the police will come by for questioning, or the bill from the hospital will arrive at the student's home. The SAP's job may be to convince the student to sign the release of information right at the outset so the parents can be involved early on.

A word of caution from experience: It is perfectly normal adolescent behavior for a student to leave your office after signing a release of information, reporting that he or she feels OK about your calling the parents or an outside agency, and then to have the student hold court in the hallway about what a mean and nasty so-and-so the SAP director is. Out of a sense of loyalty to both friends and family, developmentally and socially, the student must believe the call is your fault. Don't take it personally. Students need you to "take the fall" for them when parents or agencies are contacted. Particularly in cases where abuse is reported, you need to reassure students that they didn't report the parent—you did. A student who arrives at school with a black eye and confirms that her stepfather punched her did not report her stepfather to the authorities. The adults at the school acted like adults and took care of the child. A student should never be made to feel that a report was his or her fault.

CONFIDENTIALITY AND SAP GROUPS

Because groups are part of the SAP's regular operation, in states where people under the age of eighteen can access services, students are entitled to this service without anyone's knowledge or consent. In the school setting, this poses certain challenges. Again, if your program caters only to those students who are abusing chemicals, and that fact is common knowledge, then a student's mere participation in the program is protected by law. This is why it is preferable for SAPs to offer a number of different groups focusing on different subject areas: Students who are in the alcohol and other drug groups are protected because some of the groups are not for students who are abusing alcohol or other drugs.

Teachers and Group Participation

If the only SAP group is for identified alcohol and other drug abusers, you will need to take great care in handling attendance records. An administrator trained in confidentiality issues will have to intercept "cut" slips from teachers when students miss their classes to attend groups that could identify them as alcohol and other drug abusers. This can cause further problems down the road if, for instance, your school has an attendance policy and the teacher records that a student has gone over his or her limits of absences, but the administrator keeping the confidential attendance records knows that the student has not, indeed, gone over the limit. You would have to include some sort of procedure for that administrator to override the teacher's attendance records. It is far better to start a divorce and separation support group or a grief and loss group through the SAP, expanding the parameters of the program so attendance is not a confidentiality issue.

In a broad-brush program, teachers are certainly entitled to know that a student is attending a group, and which classes he or she might miss, if any, but teachers are not entitled to know which group a student is attending. Most teachers truly care about their students and would like to know which group a student is attending so they can help in some way, but students will quickly catch on that information is leaking from SAP personnel back to teachers. It is difficult to resist a teacher who is trying to reassure himself that a student's group participation is important and comments to the SAP person, "John is in group because his father's a real heavy hitter, right?," but SAP people have to resist this unconscious baiting. John might be in group because his father is a heavy hitter, or because his mother is chronically ill, or because he is in recovery from addiction himself. That is John's business. Developing a conversational style that deflects probing questions like this without appearing aloof is one of the greatest challenges of people involved directly with student assistance programs. (See chapter 11 for tips on how to handle this.)

In a broad-brush program, there is likely to be a "pass" system to account for students' absences from classes. In this case, teachers will be aware that students are missing classes to attend group. Homeroom teachers will probably also be aware of students who are involved in the program because of group reminders that may be delivered through the homeroom. Encourage teachers to be discreet about group participation but to insist on confirmation from the SAP that students did indeed make it to group and didn't drift off to the cafeteria or library. In a broad-brush program, teachers needn't be secretive, just respectful. For instance, some homeroom teachers simply leave group passes in a certain place in their classroom, and students who are involved with the SAP pick up their passes there on days when their groups meet. Students who are not in the program don't know to look there.

Guidance and Administration and Group Participation

Guidance counselors and administrators need know about a student's participation in group only if it has some direct bearing on their interaction with the student. There is no reason why the administration should have a list of students involved in the program, unless it is required for attendance purposes. Such a list is potentially dangerous, even in a broad-brush program, because people will automatically try to figure out which group is which and which students belong to which group. Potentially, this list could identify every student's most personal concerns. I prefer to handle the attendance between the SAP and the teachers to minimize the number of people involved in the process. I keep attendance records for groups and issue passes to students who participate. If teachers have questions about a particular student's participation, I can check my attendance records for them.

Parents and Group Participation

Parents should understand that groups are offered through the SAP at your school or in your district. Some schools introduce the SAP through a letter at the beginning of each year which is sent to all parents. (You will find a sample of one of these in chapter 4.) This is a balanced approach, because then everyone is informed from the start, and parents who are concerned can vent their frustrations at the time the letter goes out. The letter should describe all the services of the SAP, including groups, and instruct parents that if they have concerns, they should contact the school. At the high school level, very few parents will take you up on this offer, as most parents hope that there are places for students to bring personal concerns. A thorough discussion of the confidentiality regulations with concerned parents usually soothes them; however, in states where parental consent is required for treatment, an order from parents not to see a student would have to be honored.

In some states, notification is required, but consent is not. When a conflict with parents arises in states where parental permission for services is not required, your core team, administrators, and legal counsel should confer, taking into consideration the ultimate success of the program, the parent, and the particular student. When federal confidentiality regulations cover your program, it appears that you have the option of providing such services against the parent's will. Obviously, it can get messy if you do so, so have your administration and program personnel in agreement and steeled for the potential conflict. Fortunately, most of these conflicts subside over time.

Using a Parental Permission Form

At the junior high school level, the issues may be less confusing because *most* of the students will require parental consent to participate, regardless of the state laws. And in states where parental consent is required, *all* students under eighteen would have to obtain parental permission. In these cases, most student assistance programs draft parental permission forms that speak fairly generally about group participation. In addition to gaining written permission, some SAP counselors also make phone calls to explain the groups and to make initial contact with the parents. Student assistance program counselors can still give their students quite a bit of privacy by alerting parents beforehand that "to build trust in the group, I won't be able to get back to you with very much specific information. If I think your son or daughter is in trouble, I will contact you, but we're trying to foster an atmosphere in which students feel free to share." Most parents will respond well to that sort of information. A sample letter and permission form is provided on the following page.

SPECIAL TOPIC GROUPS AND CONFIDENTIALITY

Some schools offer support groups through the SAP on very sensitive subjects and require parental permission for attendance. These are usually not alcohol or other drug related, but they deal with subjects such as sexual abuse or grief or are formed because of a crisis at school or in the community (a suicide, natural disaster, war, etc.). In the case of sexual abuse, one SAP director I know uses parental permission as a way to insure that the incidents have been reported to the proper authorities and that parents are willing for their children to participate. (Treatment for sexual abuse is not treatment for alcohol and other drug issues and may require parental permission.) In this case, a student cannot attend the support group without the parental permission signed because the permission form requires that the incident has been reported. Student assistance program counselors, like any other school personnel, are required by law to report sexual abuse to the proper authorities and are similarly protected by the "in-good-faith" statutes.

FEDERAL CONFIDENTIALITY REGULATIONS AND FERPA

Federal regulations surrounding SAPs seem to conflict directly with FERPA (Family Educational Rights and Privacy Act)[3] laws, which allow parents access to all students' school records. Luckily, there are not too many requests for information under this law, though care should be taken to minimize the damage to student confidentiality in the event that you receive such a request. There are no easy answers to these very difficult questions, because one law sometimes requires that you disclose information to parents when they request it, and another law explicitly prohibits you from doing so.

FERPA applies only to written educational records, and it seems that it would cover written records from a school-based SAP. FERPA does not cover personal notes kept in the sole possession of the maker, however. Once records are shown to anyone else in the program, they become program records and are subject to FERPA. One way to minimize the damage here is to make sure that your program files do not contain information that identifies a student as an alcohol or other drug abuser, but this is difficult, too. In response to these potential conflicts, some programs choose to ask students to sign a release of information specifically outlining that information can only be shared in the event that a parent makes a request under FERPA, underscoring that this is an extremely rare event. Other programs will simply wait until such an occasion arises and then try to gain the student's consent to release the information, or get further legal counsel about what to do. Court orders can sometimes be secured so SAPs don't have to release information under FERPA if the information can be secured elsewhere or if the

---

[3]Family Educational Rights and Privacy Act (FERPA) (20 U.S.C. § 1232g, 34 C.F.R., Part 99).

SAMPLE LETTER TO PARENTS (WHEN PERMISSION IS REQUIRED)

Formal Letterhead
Central Junior High School
Anytown, USA

Dear Parent:

The student assistance program at Central Junior High is offering a program of group participation for interested students called the "friends' group." All participation in these groups is completely voluntary.

These groups of 8–15 students will meet once a week on a rotating period basis. Your child has expressed an interest in joining, and we would like your permission to include him/her.

The groups are designed to help students

- feel better about themselves
- learn to express their feelings
- build self-esteem
- learn about making decisions and setting limits
- learn about alcohol and other drug use and the consequences of such use.

The group will be run by a member of our student assistance program team. If you have

any questions, please contact _____

at the following number: _____.

_____   _____
Principal   Student Assistance Program

- -

I give permission for my son/daughter _____
                                              (name of student)

to participate in a "friends' group" through the student assistance program at Central Junior High School.

                    _____   _____
                    Parent/Guardian   Date

release of information will adversely affect the counselor/patient relationship or the general operation of the student assistance program.

Your school or district will need to wrestle with these conflicts and come up with a comfortable solution. One word of advice: Do not waste time fretting about the confidentiality regulations, and don't let them discourage you from getting a program off the ground. Many schools have fully functioning student assistance programs and have managed to gain some facility with the regulations and work within or around them. The regulations seem complicated and intimidating, but it simply requires some advance planning and the understanding that these are difficult issues.

KEEPING SAP RECORDS, PERSONAL NOTES, OR FILES

Documentation is an important part of SAP effectiveness, but care must be taken to respect confidentiality. Information that identifies a student as an alcohol or other drug abuser should never make its way into a student's permanent school record. This is clearly a violation of the federal confidentiality regulations, and this identification is why the statutes protecting this information were adopted. Someone must keep notes about the progress of an individual participating in the SAP, but none of that information has any place in a permanent school record.

SAP directors may keep personal notes which are not shared with anyone else. To respect confidentiality, a great deal of memory jogging may be done in the form of personal notes, with SAP counselors and directors keeping notebooks in their sole possession. Verbal communications are not covered by FERPA, so it would seem that information can be shared with additional SAP staff, but notes cannot. Once you share notes, they are in fact school records, and in some states, school records can be examined under FERPA laws without a student's consent. Another option is just to create very few records. Keeping SAP personal notes completely separate from a school record helps, though it doesn't eliminate the possibility that records will be requested. The mere request doesn't, however, insure that the records requested will be relinquished.

FINDING ADDITIONAL RESOURCES

If you are unsure of the regulations or how they will translate into practice in your particular setting, ask for help. Your state agency for alcohol and other drug issues can be of great help. Call them and ask for someone to present a workshop to your core team or administration about the regulations. Contact your state attorney general's office and ask them the same thing. You are likely to get some conflicting information, but the dust will settle eventually and you will make sense of everything with the help of your administration and core team. Another great resource for SAPs is the Legal Action Center—a group that concentrates on legal issues surrounding alcohol and other drug treatment. Contact them at

Legal Action Center
153 Waverly Place
New York, NY 10014
(212) 243-1313

Also, utilize other SAP directors in your immediate area for information. Spend an afternoon on the phone finding out how they are managing the regulations.

INSIST ON A CONFIDENTIAL TELEPHONE LINE

Because of the sensitive nature of issues dealt with in the SAP, it is clear that the program needs a direct, confidential telephone line. In most schools, the main office is a busy place, full of students, secretaries, teachers, and administrators coming and going. It may compromise the confidentiality of students if they or their parents are calling or if you are trying to give or get information about a treatment option for a particular student and their calls have to be directed through a school-wide switchboard. Even the question "May I ask who's calling?" can prompt some referring parents or concerned individuals to hang up the phone. In some schools, student helpers answer the phones and post messages for teachers, and this practice is totally inappropriate for a student assistance program.

If the SAP has a full-time secretary who is trained in the issues of confidentiality, calls can be directed through him or her. If there is no secretary, the SAP should be equipped with an answering machine with adjustable volume so the program can monitor calls and so parents, students, teachers, and administrators alike can leave confidential messages.

GETTING BACK TO REFERRAL SOURCES

When a teacher, student, parent, or staff member makes a referral to the SAP, it is usually something they have thought long and hard about. They have considered all the angles and have decided that it is the best thing to do, which means they are invested in the outcome. They also usually like the students they refer, and they believe, or at least hope, that SAP participation will help. This is where the confidentiality constraints seem to tie our hands, because in some cases getting back to the referral source with an assessment without a written release from the student is clearly a violation of confidentiality. But to leave teachers hanging, after they have given of themselves by referring a student, is a dangerous public relations policy for your SAP.

Casual communications with teachers need to be carefully thought out. (See more about this in chapter 11.) Teachers desperately want to know what is going on with the students they refer to the program. But SAP personnel cannot choose which students' confidence to compromise. If the SAP counselor makes a habit of soothing the teachers of those students whose problems aren't alcohol or other drug related, it won't take a faculty of rocket scientists to figure out that silence from the SAP person means the student is harmfully involved with chemicals. A faculty information handout such as the one provided on the following page can head off a number of problems.

Many SAPs have settled on using a thank-you letter, which thanks the teacher for his or her concern and willingness to transfer that concern into action by referring. Some SAP policies have included a clause that referral sources will be notified if a student at least shows up for the appointment and will be told whether or not the student will continue to use the services of the SAP. If it is a

FACULTY INFORMATION HANDOUT
UNDERSTANDING CONFIDENTIALITY AND SAPs

Student assistance programs are covered under some pretty strict federal confidentiality regulations (42 C.F.R. part 2), and it is important that you understand them so you don't misunderstand the SAP personnel and the program. These regulations can make communication with staff difficult, but please understand that the SAP wants to give you as much information as possible.

What's the Big Secret? The federal confidentiality regulations require that SAPs don't give out any information that could identify a student as being an alcohol or other drug user. If our SAP only works with alcohol and other drug users, that means that we can't even tell you which student is coming to the program, because to do so would break legal confidentiality.

What Can You Tell Me? If our SAP works with a variety of student problems, we can tell you who is coming to the program and when they were at the office or in a support group. We are happy to confirm passes and let you know when a student's group will be meeting next.

What Can I Ask the SAP? If we deal with a variety of student problems, you can ask us when a student came to see us. You can ask if he or she is planning to use the services of the SAP in the future. You can ask if the student is in a group. However, we can't tell you which group a student is in, nor can we tell you the nature of his or her difficulty. Even if the student is not an alcohol or drug user, we cannot give you that information because it would implicate others who are. For instance, if we reassured you that Susie did not use alcohol and other drugs, but that we couldn't comment on Sam, we would break Sam's confidentiality.

How Can I Find out More? The only way we can let you know the specifics of a student's case is if he or she signs a release of information so we can speak directly to you. If you are interested in finding out how a student is doing, the easiest way is to ask him or her when you have a private moment.

Can I Give You Information? You are always encouraged to make or update referrals to the SAP. While we can't give you any information about a student's particular case, we can reassure you that the student is involved in support through the SAP. If you have information which you think would help the SAP help the student, please don't hesitate to contact us. We rely mostly on the observations of teachers and staff to reach our student participants, and we appreciate all the help you give us. If we can answer any of your questions, feel free to stop by the SAP office.

broad-brush program, this doesn't in any way identify the student as being an alcohol and other drug abuser and can be done without consent. In a narrowly defined program, you would need the student's (and in some states, the parent's) consent. A sample thank-you form is provided for your use.

When using thank-you notes, it is good practice to complete them in the presence of the student to whom they refer, except in cases when students don't show up. It is important to let the teachers know when students aren't showing up so they are not looking for signs of improvement in students who are dodging the school's efforts to help. If students are informed of the referral source, they are usually happy to let the SAP get back to the teacher with simple information like, "John showed up for his first appointment and has decided to continue using SAP services." When students are referred anonymously, it is best to tell the referral source that you won't be able to get back to him or her with information concerning the student. Otherwise, the SAP counselor is in the very delicate position of trying to convince the student that the referral is anonymous while at the same time trying to gain permission to get back to the source with information.

CONFIDENTIALITY AND YOUR PERSONAL LIFE

SAPs are setting a new standard for confidentiality in schools, a standard which must be taken very seriously if the regulations are to work in the way they were intended. As a professional, you must maintain the very highest standards of confidentiality to set an example and to assure students that you practice what you preach. My mother once counseled me, "Never dress for the job you have; dress for the job you want." A similar analogy can be drawn when talking about confidentiality: Don't only adhere to the regulations you have—set a standard slightly above what is required of you. This translates into your personal life as well and means that you must watch yourself at all times, not just when you are at school. For some of us who are accustomed to being able to discuss our work lives openly, this is new, awkward, and sometimes difficult. Here are some reminders:

- Avoid discussing the specifics of cases with your spouse or partner. Even though you may feel that he or she can't tell anyone, or won't be in any position to break your confidence, you can't be too careful. For example, my husband works in a youth music project in our area, and when I first went to see a performance, I recognized several of his kids as "my" kids too. My husband also once hired someone to do a job for us, and I soon discovered that this person was the parent of a student involved in the SAP.

- Avoid discussing cases with anyone in a restaurant or other public place. You don't know who is within earshot. In a small community, you will often run across students who are involved with the SAP and their parents in very public places. If you live in the same community where you work, it is likely that parents, siblings, and your students themselves will at some time wait on your table, provide legal assistance, book your vacation, bag your groceries, and see you in your hospital gown if you happen to land in the hospital. All it takes is one misplaced comment that gets passed on

TEACHER REFERRAL ACKNOWLEDGMENT FORM

Date _____

Dear _____:
     (name of teacher)

Thank you for your recent referral of _____ to the
                                      (use student's initials)
student assistance program.

I'd like to get back to you with some simple information.

- ☐ The student has not shown up for any appointments. The SAP will continue to try to make contact.
- ☐ The student did attend an individual SAP session and has decided not to pursue any further assistance.
- ☐ The student attended individual session(s) and has decided to seek further help either through in-school services or an outside referral.
- ☐ The student would like to speak to you privately about your referral.

Thank you for translating your concern into positive action!

Sincerely,

_____
SAP director or team member

down the line, and your credibility is shot. I happen to live in a neighborhood which is served by my school, with students living on both sides of me. When the windows are open, I have to be very careful what I say, even in my own kitchen.

• Avoid becoming exhausted. Though you may be wondering why this seemingly general advice is included here, it is because when you get too tired, or too overwhelmed, it is so much easier to say, "Forget it! Who cares who knows about this anyway!" and to lose your own commitment to confidentiality. Share appropriate nonidentifying information with fellow professionals in settings such as peer supervision or clinical supervision. If there isn't anything formal set up in your area, call another SAP professional in your area with whom you feel comfortable and arrange a meeting. Change identifying information to talk about your particular concerns, and lend an ear to your listener's concerns as well. This sort of arrangement can be a good investment in your sanity.

Handling Students Outside of the SAP

If you see a student who is involved in the student assistance program in the grocery store and ask how he's doing, whoever is with him is going to ask him who you are and how he knows you. Even in a broad-brush program, this may put the student on the spot. Worse yet, in the school setting, students know who you are already and may mercilessly tease their friends when you speak to them. You can't go up to a member of your "Children Affected by Addiction" group at her basketball game and congratulate her in front of all her teammates, potentially breaking her trust. Perhaps this particular student wouldn't mind, or perhaps this particular student's parents are in the audience and she would mind a great deal. After you have taken such great care to protect this student's confidentiality through the school administration and with teachers, you can blow the whole thing by acknowledging that you know a student in the wrong place at the wrong time. On the other hand, you don't want to snub students as a matter of course. At this point, some of you are saying, "Whoah! This is extreme!" And it is. But these are issues that have to be thought out.

I manage this predicament this way: When I first see students in the office or in classroom presentations, I tell them that as part of their confidentiality, I don't acknowledge them in the hallways, in the main office, in the grocery store, or on the playing field unless they acknowledge me first. Unless they say hello to me first, they can expect that I won't indicate in any way that I recognize them, and they should understand that I am not being unfriendly but that I am waiting for their cue. I also tell them that I am not at all offended when students don't want to acknowledge me—because it is their choice.

When I wind my way through the lunchroom or courtyard, I hear, "Hi, Mrs. Newsam" from various students, whom I acknowledge by name with a wave or a smile. When students don't acknowledge me, I assume they don't want to be acknowledged, and I look through them or over them or whatever. This was a hard thing to establish at first, but now it works very well, and students understand that their feelings are being considered. If you have a dual role in the school (such as a teacher and an SAP person), this issue is much easier to handle because you could know students in different capacities. Student assistance program people who occupy only one role, however, need to work this out.

Some Final Words about Confidentiality

All aspects of the federal confidentiality regulations must be taken very seriously in this litigious age. Information that identifies a person as being an alcohol or other drug abuser (even in the past tense) can potentially prohibit him or her from getting certain scholarships, admission to the military forces, jobs, and even life and health insurance coverage.

However, rather than worrying about confidentiality and suffering silently, become informed. Call your state's attorney general's office and your single state agency that deals with alcohol and other drug abuse treatment (see Appendix B: "State Government Agencies for Drug and Alcohol Information.") Put your school lawyers onto the task. Not only will you feel better, but you will generate interest in this new area and you will gain support for your SAP. If your administration seems jumpy about the regulations, remind them that, historically, all aspects of schooling have come through a period of trial and refinement. What seemed cumbersome and frightening in special education, for instance, is now mundane.

The regulations were adopted and continue to change in the attempt to provide an opportunity for young people suffering with alcohol and other drug concerns to get well. As long as you are informed and do all you can to satisfy the regulations, you can operate within your collective conscience and within the law, providing essential services to students who need your assistance.

4

Starting a School-Based Student Assistance Program

CHAPTER 4

Starting a School-Based Student Assistance Program

Although you need a general philosophy which colors your practice, you must also have practical guidelines to follow when setting up a smooth-running student assistance program. You needn't go through this process without help. This chapter focuses on the practical procedures that a working SAP needs to direct its beginning operation, whether you are thinking of starting one after-school group or implementing a full range of SAP services. The checklists included in this chapter are helpful both in gauging the progress of the start-up phase of your student assistance program and in evaluating the health of an existing one.

The way your SAP operates will depend on a number of factors: the structure you've decided on (see Chapter 2), your current school climate, level of funding, quality of leadership, teacher and student morale, and the constraints of your particular logistics. There are, however, issues common to most SAPs. The way you meet these challenges and the creativity you apply to these beginning tasks will provide the personality and spark of your program.

Don't be afraid to challenge your own basic assumptions when designing your student assistance program. It's easy to put yourself on "autopilot" and forget to question your own motivations and subsequent actions. When setting up your SAP, think through every "obvious" answer to make sure it's not obvious just because it's what is usually done. Sometimes unusual perspectives and procedures get programs off the ground. There may be specific circumstances in your school that you'll need to work with—or around. You may have an enthusiastic faculty or one that needs to be won over. You may have a tremendously diverse student population, or a very homogeneous one, and your efforts will, of course, need to reflect these differences. What works very well in the school in the next district may need some adjustment before it works well in your school.

If you don't have the resources to do it all at once, don't be discouraged. Every little bit of effort toward helping students counts. Parcel it out; break it down; delegate. See what you *can* do given what you have. One interested teacher can get a grass-roots support group program off the ground; one administrator with vision can provide time for the faculty to participate in the planning phase of an SAP; an enthusiastic guidance department can get the necessary training to work in perfect concert with a recently hired SAP person. Each piece, though it may seem small alone, is part of a working system.

The very existence of an SAP can sometimes challenge the general assumptions the school community has had for a long time, so it can be rough at first for those invested and involved with the program. The start-up of an SAP sometimes rocks the precarious foundation of denial that some schools have been perched on for decades. In many school systems, the assumption has been, "Student alcohol and other drug use is a phase. If we ignore it for long enough, it will go away." Obviously, this isn't so. The start-up of an SAP collides with that worn-out rationalization while providing some new strategies for dealing with the reality of the situation.

Most school personnel will welcome an SAP, but be prepared for some resistance. Some school personnel will be genuinely discouraged that student assistance programming has become necessary, and they will swallow the idea like medicine—necessary, but unsavory at best. Student assistance programming is not without its outright critics, either. In varying degrees, some people believe that schools are overburdened enough already and that it is the job of parents and community agencies to meet students' personal needs. These people may even be angry at the inception of SAPs because they see referring students as another addition to their already lengthy job description. So while you endeavor to bring new ideas and procedures to school systems, you must tread gently and help those who are skeptical or discouraged to understand the mission, scope, and projected outcome of SAPs. You are there to help, but you may have to convince some people of that. Institutional denial is discussed in more detail in chapter 11, "Field Survival Guide for SAP Personnel."

SELLING THE REASON FOR SAPS

School departments must recognize the need for student assistance programming based on the educational merits alone, if they are to consider it an essential component of a state-of-the-art school plan. Student assistance programs encourage academic success by helping students with personal problems that preoccupy them and prevent them from reaching their academic and developmental potential. A working SAP provides a whole range of student services including prevention, intervention, and access to treatment, especially around the issues of alcohol and other drugs. These programs are drop-out prevention strategies as well because they encourage student retention. Superintendents, principals, parents, teachers, and support staff must eventually recognize that student assistance programming must be an integral underlying part of a successful educational system.

Without recognition of the primary educational goal of student assistance programming, it will be considered a frill and will be the first thing to be cut in case of fiscal crisis. Because budget crises are such a reality in school systems, you have to work on this component of your programming right from the start, not just hope against hope that nothing happens. Know from the start that eventually you will have to justify your programming with a good fight and hard data.

Students, too, know about precarious funding for school programs and will resist depending on programming that they believe might be there in their sophomore year but probably won't be there in their senior year. The school system must recognize SAPs as top priority and must make their *long-term commitment public* for the programs to operate effectively. Otherwise, student assistance programming becomes yet another temporary band-aid solution to the problem of student alcohol and other drug use. The effectiveness of your SAP suffers terribly when there are questions about whether it will survive the next budget crisis.

FITTING INTO YOUR SCHOOL'S CLIMATE

Take careful steps to ensure that the operating practices of the SAP fit comfortably with the climate of your school generally. If your school runs on Swiss-precision timing, and all students are required to have passes to get from one room to another, it won't do to have a seemingly "loose" student assistance program where students can stop by whenever they feel the need. Such a departure from the school's norm challenges the very philosophy of the school or district, and you will meet with mighty resistance. On the other hand, if your school is very loosely run, with an open-campus philosophy, for instance, it will do no good to run the SAP like a bootcamp. On all levels, even an atmospheric one, students and teachers alike should feel that the SAP is a part of, not apart from, the rest of the school.

The mission of the SAP is to do the best job possible given certain constraints. Changing those constraints is a measured process, and at the beginning, especially, you must *pick your battles*. Is it really so important that you get a certain speaker for a workshop? Or is it really important that you get the go-ahead to take students out of class when you need to? If the less important choice will preclude the more important one, drop it for now and pick it up later when you have gained the confidence of key people.

While an SAP can certainly encourage a change in attitudes, the structure must be consistent with the personality of the school, and you must be able to work within the confines of the political system (all systems are political) without becoming so discouraged that you feel that your program is worthless. After your program has been in place for several years, the school may sing the program's praises and give you carte blanche to do whatever you need to do to operate effectively, but at the beginning it is best to work within the confines of the system as much as you can, to avoid becoming an outlaw. There is truth to the saying, "You can attract more bees with honey than vinegar."

Denial about the magnitude of alcohol and other drug issues is strong in some systems, and your SAP may be the first voice to address these subjects explicitly. From a system's perspective, such pressure to change guarantees some resistance, either overt or covert. Expect it, accept it, and roll with the punches. You'll get more done with fewer gray hairs.

FITTING INTO THE ADMINISTRATIVE STRUCTURE OF YOUR SCHOOL

Where does the SAP director or SAP counselor(s) fit into the administrative structure of the school? A great deal of this decision will depend on the structure you have chosen for your SAP. Some SAP people work for the school district and report to a district office, some work for the state, some work for agencies hired by school departments, and some work for individual schools. All are reasonable situations, but some are more effective than others.

The SAP director and counselor(s) should fit into the administration of the school in the way that will give them the greatest freedom to intervene effectively with the largest number of students. That means entirely different things from school to school, and your school will have to determine what works best.

When you do have an SAP counselor serving a specific school, the first instinct is to put him or her in the guidance or student services department. Unfortunately, there can be significant difficulties with this arrangement. First, confidentiality regulations are vastly different for guidance personnel and student assistance programs, and the melding of the two functions can cause confusion. While SAP models encourage guidance personnel to be an integral part of programming, in some cases providing assessments, interventions, and follow-up care, the theoretical missions of SAPs and guidance departments are not one and the same.

Guidance departments are responsible for providing a whole range of academic advising, personal counseling, and crisis intervention to the entire student population and have very little additional time to devote to a specific group of very high-risk students. Student assistance programs seek to isolate this high-risk group of youngsters and meet their specific needs through identification, assessment, and referral. There is, of course, some overlap, as guidance personnel do have contact with every student who is involved in the SAP, whether for additional personal counseling or for academic advising. An analogy could be that while special education teachers teach English, for instance, they are not administratively in the English department because they teach English to a specific group of students who require specific expertise from their teachers. Student assistance program counselors can be similarly considered. "SAP Services vs. Guidance Services," on the following page, illustrates these differences.

When you do have SAP personnel serving a particular school, it is essential that they be treated like members of the school faculty, not visitors. Students and faculty alike need to understand that the school values and respects the SAP person and the job he or she does. Even if the SAP person is hired part time, he or she should be offered a competitive salary and have keys, a mailbox, photocopying privileges, access to teachers' lounges, phone privileges, and all the amenities offered to full-time faculty members. Denying SAP personnel basic symbols of respect and inclusion on the faculty creates distance and suspicion of the program and those who staff it. Who is going to refer a student if they can't find the mailbox for the SAP? Students understand that when an SAP person has to wait for the custodian to open a classroom for a group meeting, the custodian has more clout. Simply put, these kinds of arrangements do not speak well of the school's commitment to the program.

Probably the most desirable and effective set-up is for SAP professionals to work for the schools in which they operate and report directly to the principal or his or her designee. This way, the faculty can become accustomed to the SAP personnel and long-term referring relationships can grow. This means that, administratively, the SAP becomes its own mini-department and can operate effectively within the system, gathering information and technical assistance from other departments as necessary. Student assistance program core team members provide the link to other interschool departments, and the SAP is regarded as a part of the school, not an outside program imposed on the system.

SAP SERVICES

VERSUS

GUIDANCE SERVICES

DIRECT SERVICES FOR PERCENTAGE OF SCHOOL POPULATION

DIRECT SERVICES FOR ENTIRE SCHOOL POPULATION

Climatic change:

Legitimize "no-use" message

Resource for AOD questions/activities:

Education through guest spots in academic classes

AOD awareness

Some direct services:

Identification

Support group participation

Ancillary programs

Early intervention

Prevention efforts

Direct services:

AOD use/abuse/dependency

- Intervention
- Access to treatment
- In-school support
- Aftercare

Children affected by addiction

- Education
- Identification
- Intervention
- In-school support
- Access to protective services

Other students at extreme risk

- Crisis intervention
- In-school support

Lower-risk students

At-risk students

Extreme risk

Personal counseling

Academic advising

Career counseling

College counseling

Crisis intervention

FINDING THE RIGHT LEADERSHIP FOR YOUR SAP

Someone must be at the helm of the idea to start an SAP. It may be a guidance counselor or a drop-out prevention person, or a principal, superintendent, or district-wide alcohol and other drug professional. Perhaps a needs survey has been conducted and you have concluded that SAPs are the next step for your schools and community. The start-up phase and "personality" of the SAP will vary widely depending on who is in charge and how much the community is willing to invest, in time, money, and commitment.

An SAP director and/or SAP counselor(s) should be hired by the school, district, or community, and the people in charge should advertise the position at a competitive, professional salary range to attract qualified applicants. Full-time SAP people should make in salary what a commensurately qualified teacher or administrator would earn and should have an educator's (school-year) contract, unless other year-round arrangements are made and additional compensation is secured. As in most other things, you get what you pay for. If teacher unions require that people paid on contract have teaching certificates, every opportunity should be afforded for otherwise qualified SAP people to get the necessary certificate through alternative certification routes within a certain period of time. Student assistance programs are not necessarily looking for people who have been working in schools all along, so some allowances must be made for other, equally rigorous areas of training. These are new positions, so no one had the opportunity ten years ago to train in college, for instance, specifically to be an SAP director. There wasn't any such thing!

Try advertising the position(s) outside of your immediate geographical area to attract people who have the necessary combination of education and experience for SAP work. A number of people who will be working with the SAP director should be involved in the hiring.

Hiring Considerations

If you are in the position of hiring a student assistance director, there are a number of things to consider. Directing a student assistance program is a difficult job. It combines counseling, administration, diplomacy, public relations, and knowledge of educational systems and how they work. In an ideal situation, an SAP director is hired as well as one or two SAP counselors and clerical help. Obviously, this varies with the size of the school. The director then takes on most of the administrative duties of the program, perhaps providing clinical supervision for the counselors. At the beginning, however, it is more likely that one or two people will be hired to do what could be the work of four.

Who can do the work of student assistance programs? Alcohol and other drug abuse counselors will bring much-needed clarity to the issue of chemical dependency in the schools and can sharpen the focus on the magnitude of the alcohol and other drug problem while breaking down some of the denial. It is worth noting, however, that counselors with clinical backgrounds may be frustrated by the school setting. The sheer numbers of students referred to an SAP make for an unbelievable caseload. A clinician must also be careful to carry out the primary duty of the SAP, which is to refer student clients to other professionals when necessary. Some clinicians may be tempted to carry on long-term counseling or therapy, which most SAPs cannot do.

If the person being considered is not an alcohol and drug abuse counselor, it is imperative that he or she understand the disease of addiction and have clear principles on how to intervene in student alcohol and other drug use. People with experience in psychology, social work, crisis intervention, education, and counseling can all be effective student assistance directors provided that they are able to intervene effectively in a variety of student problems. All candidates should have specific additional training in the area of alcohol and other drug abuse, familial addiction, and surrounding issues.

Most traditional guidance counseling programs do not include enough emphasis on the alcohol and other drug issues to qualify individuals for this work without additional training or experience with addicted teens, children of addiction (COA) and their families. People who are themselves recovering from addiction may be a good choice, but personal recovery alone by no means qualifies people for this work. Most of all, a responsible SAP director needs to understand his or her strengths and weaknesses equally and know when to ask for help.

Clearly, in deciding on SAP personnel, an evaluation of a person's education and experience is vital. Some other points to consider are as follows:

- Will this person work effectively with administrators, teachers, parents, and students alike?
- Does this person have experience working with adolescents?
- Does this person have energy? (The job requires a lot of it!)
- Does this person understand the disease concept of addiction?
- Does this person have a working knowledge of self-help groups, including AA, NA, Al-Anon, Alateen, ToughLove, etc.?
- Is this person willing to seek more training in areas where needed?
- Can this person recognize when he or she needs to refer a case to someone with more expertise in a certain area?
- Will this person be able to create the kind of rapport that is necessary to build trust in the student community?
- Does this person represent our SAP's mission?
- Can this person build the necessary bridges into the community at large?
- Can this person provide the public relations element of student assistance programming?
- Will this person be comfortable working in an educational setting?

DETERMINING AN EFFECTIVE WORK SCHEDULE

Look at the hours the SAP director works. Is it really best for him or her to come in with the teachers and leave at the same time? In some districts, this is necessary to insure that SAP people are treated the same as teachers—usually this has to do with negotiated contract hours. In some cases, SAP people come in later and leave later to accommodate meetings with parents and individual appointments with students. Contract or agency-based SAPs have greater flexibility with time. If it is difficult to maintain confidentiality because of your location, perhaps seeing some number of students individually after school would meet the need, as long as the SAP person's safety is considered and provided for. If the SAP director is running any sort of groups *after school,* some arrangement should be made so he or she can come in later in the morning.

PROVIDING ADMINISTRATIVE SUPPORT FOR NEW SAPs

Administrative support is the single most important element for the successful operation of a student assistance program. The superintendent of schools must be behind the programs. Most importantly, though, the leading building administrator, usually the principal, must be wholeheartedly behind the SAP if it is to be effective and help students. It is the principal's job not only to tolerate the program, but to *sell it to the teachers, parents, and students.* Without public and vocal support, incoming SAP people are suspicious strangers in the school and will not be able to make the necessary inroads to help students. Student assistance program people should never have to feel that they are working against an administration. Supposedly, we are all in this together, and SAP people are hired to create much-needed change. Understandably, change makes people nervous, but it is essential.

Because of the strict federal confidentiality regulations governing SAPs, it is sometimes impossible for the SAP director to let other school personnel know the particulars of certain situations involving students. It is essential, therefore, that the SAP director and the administration of the school have a good working relationship and that the principal have confidence in the judgment of the SAP director. Student assistance programs end up dealing with some of the most delicate situations in modern school operation. They must be considered allies and work with the cooperation of the administration, not against a tide of arbitrary controlling measures and inflexibility.

If there is an adversarial relationship between the SAP and the administration of the school, not much will get done. If this exists, both "sides" need to examine what role they have in the conflict and how it can be resolved before going any further. We can't hope to help students settle their conflicts if we can't settle our own.

A proactive and responsible administrative office can smooth and speed the way so the student assistance program can begin to help students right away. As the old saying goes, you are either part of the problem or part of the solution. Erratic, reluctant, or controlling administrative support becomes part of the problem. See the handout, "Ways Administrators Can Support the SAP," provided.

Introducing the Program

One way the administration can kick off its support for the student assistance program is by writing and distributing two letters of introduction—one to the faculty and staff, and one to parents. School personnel often need to hear "from the top" before they are willing to accept a new program. These letters must underscore the administration's enthusiasm for the program. Samples of both have

WAYS ADMINISTRATORS CAN SUPPORT THE SAP

- Provide either an office big enough to hold group meetings or an office *and* a group meeting room.

- Make sure that the SAP has a confidential telephone line.

- Arrange for clerical support. Either hire a secretary, or have the SAP utilize another secretary.

- Become knowledgeable about the federal and state confidentiality regulations governing SAPs.

- Train all school personnel commensurately with their level of involvement with the program.

- Participate in the core team and encourage your teachers to get involved.

- Provide "staff development hours" to teachers who participate in trainings, workshops, or who are members of the core team.

- Provide opportunities for your SAP to train faculty and staff.

- Write a letter to all parents informing them of the student assistance program and the school's support of it.

- Provide needed information to the SAP director.

- Work on a chemical use policy for your school detailing the consequences for violations incurred.

- Enforce the adopted chemical use policy consistently.

- Do not minimize students' personal problems.

- Allow students to attend groups once a week during class time.

- Do not ask your SAP personnel to disclose confidential information to you.

- Introduce your SAP professionals to the school community at faculty meetings, orientations, parent–teacher organizations, etc.

SAMPLE LETTER OF INTRODUCTION TO PARENTS

Dear Parents:

This letter calls to your attention the new student assistance program being implemented this year at _____. The purpose of this program is to identify and
<u>(name of high school)</u>
help troubled students and their families who may be experiencing personal, school, family, alcohol, or other drug problems. These problems may be affecting the student's ability to perform at school.

Student assistance program (SAP) participation is completely confidential. Providing procedures for the early identification and intervention with students who are having personal and drug and alcohol-related difficulties in school, the SAP works closely with existing in-school services to make appropriate referrals so students can get to the help they need. Teachers, administrators, guidance staff, and parents can make referrals to the SAP, and students can refer themselves. The only mandatory referrals are made when a student violates the school's chemical use policy.

_____ has been hired to direct the operation of this new program.
<u>(Name of the SAP director)</u>
_____ has a Master's degree in Social Work or [Education, Psychology,
<u>(Name of the SAP director)</u>
Certified as an Alcohol and Drug Abuse Counselor, etc.], experience working with chemically dependent adolescents, and has spent the last two years working in a community mental health agency [hospital, school, etc.]. _____ will be working full
<u>(Name of SAP director)</u>
time, holding individual and group meetings with students, providing teacher training and speaking to parent and community groups. If you have any questions you'd like to ask or if you are concerned about your child, please call _____ directly at
<u>(Name of SAP director)</u>
the student assistance program, 555-1111.

We are very excited about this new program, and we are making a long-term commitment to its operation. Please don't hesitate to call if you have any questions.

Sincerely,

_____
Principal

SAMPLE LETTER OF INTRODUCTION TO FACULTY

Dear faculty members:

This year, our school is implementing a student assistance program to help students with a variety of personal problems that may be affecting their ability to perform academically and socially at school. My name is _____ and I will be directing the opera-

(name of SAP director)
tion of this student assistance program.

The student assistance program is currently forming a core team of teachers, administrators, and support staff to help guide policies and practices. We are looking for personnel from a wide variety of school departments to add their expertise to this team. The core team will primarily be responsible for

- ☐ developing and adapting a very specific chemical use policy for our school
- ☐ advising the SAP director in the policies and practices of the program
- ☐ providing promotion for the program by disseminating information to other faculty members in your department
- ☐ (in some SAP structures) providing assessments and referring students to helping services.

Core team members will receive training in the areas of alcohol and other drugs, dysfunctional family systems, identifying children of alcoholics and addicted persons, student adjustment problems, and intervention in student alcohol and other drug use. Members will also receive staff development credits for their participation.

If you are interested in serving on this core team, please fill out the bottom of this paper and put it in my mailbox. I look forward to working with you!

Sincerely,

_____   _____
Principal   Student Assistance Program Director

- -

☐ Yes! I am interested in serving on the core team.

_____   _____   _____
Faculty Member's Name   Department   Mailbox #

been provided. The letter can include a pamphlet describing the services of the student assistance program. (See chapter 5 for a sample pamphlet.) But by no means should the administration wait until there is a brochure available to introduce the program and its mission to the school community.

The SAP director must also have an opportunity to introduce himself or herself personally to the faculty and, ultimately, to the student body. This can be accomplished through faculty meetings, small classroom presentations, or general meetings with each grade level. Chapter 5 focuses on ways to promote the program.

FORMING A CORE TEAM

One of the first tasks for successful SAP operation is to form a core team. Once formed, this team will be trained in alcohol and other drug issues, will agree on a chemical use policy for your school, and will guide the policies and practices of the SAP. As discussed in chapter 2, the composition of your core team will vary widely depending on how the program plans to utilize it. If there is no SAP director and the core team will be responsible for providing assessments and seeing students on an individual basis, it is best for the team to include at least half of the guidance counselors at the school and perhaps contracted, outside alcohol and other drug services. If, however, there is an in-house SAP director, only those guidance counselors who are comfortable serving on the core team and express an interest should be involved. Mandatory participation frequently backfires.

Eliciting Membership for a Core Team

Choosing or appointing members for the core team is sometimes a difficult project. If an SAP director has the time, he or she can research the faculty and ask recommended people to join on an individual basis. Be very careful with this approach, however, because those you don't ask may feel angry or undervalued. You needn't walk on eggshells in your school setting, but you do not want to create more work for yourself by alienating people right from the start. Every teacher who feels alienated will have to be "won back" to get student referrals for the SAP, so it is wise to be careful with this process.

An SAP person or an enthusiastic faculty member can canvass the faculty to see who is interested in joining the core team. If you decide to canvass the faculty, you must have some equitable way of choosing between the candidates if more than one from a department shows interest in joining. To elicit teacher participation, a letter such as the one on page 58 can be sent to all staff through the in-school mail system, or can be handed out during a teacher workshop explaining the role of the SAP. Whether or not you have an SAP director, a core team must be established.

Consider the following things when deciding on the composition of the SAP core team:

☐ Are several points of view represented on your team?
☐ Are all school departments represented?

☐ Will the team be able to work together effectively?

☐ Is everyone involved a proponent of the programming, or is someone there to question the very existence of it?

☐ Are both women and men involved with the program?

☐ Do you have top-level administration represented so you can implement easily what you develop?

☐ Is everyone on the core team there voluntarily? (Mandatory participation is the kiss of death.)

☐ Did you get back to all faculty members who showed an interest?

An in-school SAP core team cannot operate effectively if it is so big that it becomes difficult to hold a meeting. Nor can it operate effectively if it is so small that it becomes insular and isolated. A manageable size for a core team is five to twelve members, including the SAP director. (Some progressive SAP professionals suggest, however, that small core teams like this encourage only partial ownership from school personnel and suggest "an SAP team composed of as many staff members as wish to participate, [which] grows each year to eventually include almost all staff.")[1]

Sample Core Team Composition (without SAP Counselor)

- Up to four guidance counselors
- School nurse
- Athletic director or coach
- Principal or assistant principal
- Two to four classroom teachers

Sample Core Team Composition (with SAP Director)

- Two to four guidance counselors
- School nurse
- Athletic director
- Principal or assistant principal
- Four teachers
- SAP director

Sample Core Team Composition for Small Schools

- All guidance staff (one to three counselors)
- Principal
- Four teachers
- Athletic director
- Specialists (special education, vocational education, etc.)

---

[1]Zimman, Richard N., *Student Assistance Journal,* "The Working Together Model: The SAP as a Whole-School Effort," May/June 1991, p. 36.

Very important people are often overlooked for membership on core teams. Carefully think through who might be helpful on your team. It might be someone you hadn't thought of before. Who is a really top-notch proponent of education? Who has access to students and a good rapport with adults and adolescents alike? As core team members, they will be doing the promotion for your program, so they should be positive, motivated, and professional. Consider other people you may not have thought of for membership on your core team. School secretaries (main office, assistant principal, guidance) may see students who come in late every day, or may have to deal with their parents who exhibit unreasonable or unusual behavior. Librarians may notice students who are extremely isolated or who display unusual behavior. Special education people or alternative program teachers (English as a Second Language, Young Parents' Programs, etc.) may have tremendous insight, as they see large numbers of students every day in a different way than most other school personnel see them. Depending on how your team operates, some members may be doing only promotion and referral, while others may be responsible for assessments and group facilitation. Of course, anyone who is involved in direct student services should be properly qualified through education and training.

Core team members should

- Have an honest desire to learn more about alcohol and other drugs and the way they affect students, staff, and the school climate
- Be able to maintain extremely high levels of confidentiality
- Have their personal lives in working order, especially where issues of alcohol and other drugs and familial addiction are concerned
- Be willing to look at new ways to help students
- Not be unduly uncomfortable with confrontation
- Be prepared to give quite a bit of time to the SAP core team
- Be committed to an alcohol and other drug-free school climate.

Training the Core Team

The necessity of training your school's core team is clear. You want the people who are going to be responsible for guiding the policies and practices of the SAP to understand the issues of adolescent alcohol and other drug use, familial addiction, and the other sorts of problems that arrive at the doorstep of SAPs. In situations where there is no SAP director, some core team members may be trained in providing very basic assessments and referring chemically dependent students for further treatment, and potential group facilitators must be trained in group techniques. An incoming SAP director must first assemble this group of dedicated people, then provide fill-in for any gaps in the collective knowledge about relevant issues, and then set these people to work. If there is no SAP director, this job falls to whoever undertakes it. But it is always good practice to train the core team first so its members understand fully the mission, scope, and resources of the student assistance program before they decide how it's going to work in the context of your specific setting. For instance, how you design your chemical use policy depends on what resources are available to you and your program. Chapter 6 focuses on core team and other staff training.

Developing the SAP's and Core Team's Mission Statements

One of the first tasks of a core team is to develop its role within the student assistance program. There is no set way for a core team to operate; it will depend completely on how your school program regards its mission. This is a two-step process because in programs with a counselor, the core team's mission statement is complementary but different from the SAP's mission statement. To decide how the core team will carry out its mission, you must first decide what the mission of the SAP itself is. This seems almost unnecessary at first, or so obvious that it can be overlooked, but it is absolutely essential. There are tremendous differences in scope, sentiment, and procedures. Be sure to leave some time in initial core team trainings for development of mission statements. The core team itself should always develop its own mission. Ask a few basic questions when developing your SAP's mission statement:

- Why do we have an SAP? (What is our motivation?)
- Who do we propose to serve? (target population)
- What do we hope to provide? (expectation of services)
- What are our specific goals? (expectation for change)

Sample SAP and core team mission statements follow.

DEVELOPING A WORKING CHEMICAL USE POLICY FOR YOUR SCHOOL

A school or school district needs specific guidelines about what will happen if a student is caught using alcohol or other drugs at school, at a school-related activity, or while not in school. Preferably, one of the first tasks a core team will undertake is the development or revamping of such a policy. This written policy must detail the consequences of possession of alcohol and other drugs, sale, distribution, and nonactive participation. Too often, the consequences of such violations are based on an arbitrary decision, depending on which administrator caught what kid doing which drug where. Perhaps the bright football player will be dealt with differently than the student who struggles in his classes if they are both caught smoking marijuana. Students understand this sort of discrimination as being punished for *who they are* and not for *what they did*. This takes the potency out of the consequences for alcohol and other drug use because the students believe that the consequences were levied unfairly.

The formation of your new chemical use policy sets in motion the mechanism of people working together in the school to decide how they will deal with infractions of the policy (and how they have dealt with them in the past). It gives core team members a chance to brainstorm and reevaluate their own ideas about student alcohol and other drug use and helps them process any previous experiences that concerned students' use of alcohol or other drugs. After training the core team in the relevant issues and developing a mission statement, developing the chemical use policy is usually the first task before the core team, administration, and SAP director. Even if your district already has a chemical use policy, it's time

SAMPLE MISSION STATEMENTS

For an SAP:

Central High School's student assistance program aims to identify and help troubled students and their families and encourage healthy coping alternatives. This policy is based on the conviction that school should be an alcohol and other drug-free environment.

The student assistance program has the following goals:

- To identify and help troubled students and their families
- To reduce student alcohol and other drug use
- To assist teachers coping with troubled students
- To develop an advisory team
- To encourage student retention
- To have a readily available place for students to bring personal concerns
- To work closely with existing services, especially guidance
- To be an informational clearinghouse/referral service
- To review and adopt a new chemical use policy for Central High School

For a Core Team:

The role of the core team is to support and promote the Student Assistance Program and its counselor through consistent communication with the school community. It is also the function of the team to review school policies regarding alcohol and other drug use. Regularly scheduled meetings will be conducted for these purposes.

Specific goals include the following:

- Ongoing support for students seeking assistance
- Regular communication via school newspaper, parent publications, and other media
- Developing an instrument to evaluate the program and policies
- Beginning cofacilitation of groups by individual core team members to use their training and skills more effectively
- Offering training for faculty members to help them better identify unusual behavior and to follow referral procedures
- Providing outreach to police departments, courts, and social services

well spent for the core team to review it and to add SAP participation as part of the consequence of a violation of the policy. A sample chemical use policy follows. You will note that it is lengthy and detailed. This is necessary for consistency and ownership of the policy. Every possible infraction must be covered so administrators can use it as a comprehensive tool.

Developing or reviewing a chemical use policy takes time. Although most chemical use policies come out looking almost the same, the *process* of developing them is essential for their proper enforcement. By canvassing the faculty for a core team, the entire school community has the chance to develop the policy. You needn't reinvent the wheel when looking for models, but specific consequences for violations must be hashed out by those people who will ultimately be responsible for enforcing the chemical use policy, especially top-level administrators. When a core team spends a good many hours working out the specifics of a policy, they feel that it is theirs and that they can use it. When administrators are faced with a student who has been caught with a controlled substance, they feel empowered to levy the consequences they have worked out in concert with fellow professionals.

SAPs and Identifying Violations of the Chemical Use Policy

Student assistance programs work with the disciplinary system to insure that students who are caught in violation of the policy get access to help as well as punishment. If your SAP will be tied in any way to the disciplinary consequences for violating the chemical use policy (as it should be), make sure that the SAP person is not the one designated to verify student use. This uses trained SAP people like trained police dogs, to sniff out using students, and it undermines student trust. *After* students are caught using by other school personnel, *then* SAP participation begins. Try to include the disciplinarians or a representative of them on the core team so a working relationship can be forged and expectations discussed.

If you are a trained SAP professional or alcohol and other drug counselor, you can probably spot students who are high, tripping, drunk, or under the influence of a number of other drugs with fair accuracy. This helps you to confront students who are in your office or in support groups. However, this training would be grossly misused if you were to go into the courtyard of your school and round up everyone you thought was under the influence for disciplinary purposes. Students would then equate the SAP with a "narc" operation, and all the hard work of setting it up would go down the tubes. So what can you do if you see a student in the hallway who you think is high? I try to find out from someone who the student is (if the student is unknown to me), and later I call the student into my office. There, I tell the student that I am well trained and that I'm pretty sure he or she was high yesterday in the hallway. At least then the behavior has been noticed and confronted. Surprisingly, many students respond well to this approach. Of course, if you are crossing the courtyard and see a student who is so obviously under the influence that to ignore it would be enabling, or you see a drug deal in progress, you are obliged to report such an occurrence to an administrator for disciplinary purposes (anonymously if possible). School administrations must recognize this fine line and respect it.

SAMPLE CHEMICAL USE POLICY

Policy Statement:

This policy is based on the convictions that school should be an alcohol and drug-free environment and that the abuse of mind-altering substances is a treatable illness. Effective identification of drug and alcohol problems begins with consistent consequences incurred for violations of the school's chemical use policy. Therefore, violations of the chemical use policy incur simultaneous disciplinary action and referral to the student assistance program, emphasizing both our adherence to the code of conduct, the interscholastic athletic code, and our commitment to help troubled students reach help.

The student assistance program is a school-based, short-term educational counseling and referral service for students and their families. The use of this program along with disciplinary action is part of the school's effort to address this widespread and dangerous problem.

The following policy will be enforced to encourage individual responsibility, to discourage enabling behaviors, and to send a clear message of wellness to students, staff, parents, and the community at large.

The following actions involving chemicals or paraphernalia will incur consequences:

1. Attempting to secure or purchase
2. Using or having used
3. Possessing
4. Intending or attempting to sell or distribute
5. Selling or distributing
6. Being knowingly present when used, possessed, or consumed

This policy refers to

1. Alcohol
2. Restricted drugs (misused prescription or over-the-counter)
3. Illegal drugs (including steroids)
4. Look-alike drugs
5. Pills or other substances which are misrepresented and sold or distributed as restricted or illegal drugs
6. Products misused for the purpose of mind-altering effect (aerosols, solvents, etc.)

SAMPLE CHEMICAL USE POLICY, *continued*

VIOLATION	CONSEQUENCES	
	Disciplinary	**Student Assistance**
Attempting to Secure or Purchase	One day internal suspension Loss of extra-curricular participation for sixty calendar days	Up to nine hours participation*
Using or Having Used	Two days internal suspension. Loss of extra-curricular participation for sixty calendar days	Up to twelve hours participation*
Possessing	Two days internal suspension; usually followed by two or more days of external suspension Loss of extra-curricular participation for sixty calendar days Referral to Police Department	Up to twelve hours participation*
Intending or Attempting to Sell or Distribute	One day internal suspension usually followed by four or more days external suspension. Loss of extra-curricular participation for sixty calendar days	Up to twenty hours participation*

One or More of the Following Options May Be Pursued

Referral to outside chemical dependency assessment counselor

Referral to Police Department

Referral to superintendent for action that might include extended suspension (up to fifteen days)

VIOLATION	CONSEQUENCES	
	Disciplinary	**Student Assistance**
Selling or Distributing	One day internal suspension usually followed by four or more days external suspension	Up to twenty hours of participation*
	Loss of extra-curricular participation for sixty calendar days	
	One or More of the Following Options May Also Be Pursued	
	Referral to outside chemical dependency assessment counselor	
	Referral to Police Department	
	Referral to superintendent for action that might include extended suspension (up to fifteen days)	
Being Knowingly Present When Used, Possessed, or Consumed	One day internal suspension	Up to nine hours participation
	Loss of extra-curricular participation for sixty calendar days	

Any student who violates the chemical use policy will be referred to the director of the student assistance program. The director or core team member will meet with the student and sometimes the parent to develop a remedial program to meet the student's needs. The remedial program may include group educational meetings, individual meetings, in-school or outside support groups, referral to a member of the core team, and referral to school counseling staff. There is no cost to the student or parents for participation in the SAP. After participation in the SAP or in conjunction with it, students and parents may choose to pursue treatment in private counseling or treatment programs. The cost of such programs is fully the parents' and students' responsibility.

Participation in the SAP by the student who violates the chemical use policy is based on our conviction that such violations can be indicative of serious involvement with alcohol and/or other drugs.

SAMPLE CHEMICAL USE POLICY, *continued*

NOTE: All consequences begin with at least one day of internal suspension. During that first day of internal suspension, the student should make contact with the student assistance program to begin a program plan. It is the intention of the policy to encourage *retention* by making that initial contact after a violation is confirmed.

Disciplinary Procedure

This policy applies to school and school activities or whenever students are under the jurisdiction of the school or are representing the school in any off-campus activity. This includes all school property (including athletic fields), the neighborhood adjacent to the school, and the sites of off-campus activities and surrounding areas.

When a violation has been confirmed, the administration of the school will attempt to contact the student's parents or guardian during the first days of internal suspension. If contacted, the parent/guardian will be informed about the disciplinary consequences and participation in the student assistance program. A brochure describing the student assistance program and the chemical use policy will be sent to the parent or guardian if it is requested.

The school administration will contact the coaches and advisors of extracurricular activities to alert them of the loss of privileges.

Second Violation: Multiple violations may be indicative of a level of serious involvement with alcohol and/or other drugs. Five days external suspension with SAP participation upon reentry will be the usual consequence, except in unusual circumstances. In some cases, the SAP team will deem it necessary to contact the superintendent's office concerning the case. The superintendent's office may extend suspension to fifteen days, and expulsion is a possible consequence.

Should Staff Be Included in Your Chemical Use Policy?

Some progressive school systems extend the coverage of the chemical use policy to students, faculty, and staff alike. For example, some colleges and universities are beginning to use the campus assistance program model, which provides services for both students and staff. Consequences for faculty and staff use would include participation in the district's employee assistance program, if there is one. This is a progressive step, and not without political risk. If this step is taken, it must be made clear whether the SAP person or team provides services for students only or for staff as well. Providing both is an extremely difficult role and places the SSAP (student and staff assistance program) person in a very isolated position. The benefits, which include positive role modeling and equal accountability, must be weighed carefully against the drawbacks. In addition to a chemical use policy for its students, every school system should have or be working on an employee assistance program for its employees (though this is not expressly the responsibility of the SAP).

Combining Discipline with Assistance

When developing the chemical use policy, it is essential to remember that punishment without help is useless. Similarly, help without consequences sends a message of nonaccountability to adolescents, who developmentally need to be held strictly accountable for their actions. The SAP model *combines* (it does not replace!) a disciplinary consequence with assistance. Every infraction of the chemical use policy must combine a disciplinary consequence (internal or external suspension, detention, demerits, or whatever) with participation in the student assistance program. This sends out a dual message: that alcohol or other drug use is wrong (disciplinary action) and that it indicates the existence of personal problems (student assistance program participation). While you are working out the chemical use policy, be sure to figure out how SAP participation will be verified. How will student attendance be verified while maintaining student confidentiality? How will parents be notified?

Any student who violates the chemical use policy will be required to utilize the student assistance program. Surprisingly, in a comprehensive, school-based SAP, there are not too many students caught using or under the influence, relative to the number who will refer themselves without being caught. Those who do get caught, of course, will be some of your toughest customers but also most in need of help.

A great percentage of students who violate the chemical use policy will be assessed and referred to the "challenge group," if you have one, to evaluate their personal relationship with alcohol or other drugs. There is a complete curriculum for a challenge group in chapter 13. If you don't have a school-based forum for students to assess their relationship to alcohol and other drugs, think about setting one up. If that's impossible, students who violate the policy should have an assessment of some kind, either through an outside alcohol or drug abuse counselor or through the school-based SAP. Core team guidance personnel, school nurses, or teachers can get specific training in chemical dependency assessment techniques to process these students if there is no SAP counselor or director. These assessments should be available to students and their families at no cost.

In certain cases, it will be necessary to refer a student who violates the chemical use policy directly to inpatient treatment so the challenge group experience will have to be either revoked or postponed. The SAP participation requirement attached to the chemical use policy must be kept flexible so students who are in a great deal of need can get help in a timely fashion. The whole idea is to facilitate, not hinder, students from getting help.

FINDING A LOCATION FOR THE SAP

Every school will have a different solution to the question of where the SAP should have its headquarters. The important thing to remember, regardless of where the SAP ends up being located, is that where a school places its SAP indicates loud and clear its commitment to the program. Therefore, the SAP director whose office is located in the boiler room can expect that his or her administration, while it may give lip service to its support of the program, really would like the program to stay underground. It is clear that the program is undervalued.

On the other hand, the school that places the SAP director in a small office, with access to classrooms to use for groups only when the rooms happen to be available, has an average commitment to the program and an administration that hopes the program will work, as long as it doesn't disrupt anything. This reduces the program to the level of an extracurricular activity, because it has no place of its own. Actually, some extracurricular activities have more administrative support than some start-up SAPs. Believe it or not, this mixed message is probably the most difficult situation to work under, because while the school thinks it is encouraging the efforts of the SAP, it is actually only tolerating the effort, making no allowances for sweeping change. The message here is, "We'll let you try to fix things. Just don't get in anyone's way."

Ideally, the school will recognize the importance of the program and house it in a room of its own. You need a room that is large enough to hold both an office (set off by dividers) and a space for groups to meet, or an office and a group room. (A converted classroom will work.) The best set-up would be to have an office that adjoined a group room, but successful programs have worked in less-than-perfect conditions. The room(s) should be in a place where students can get to them discreetly, but they should not be so isolated that anyone seen in that area of the school is immediately identified as participating in the SAP. The SAP does not necessarily have to be located in or near the guidance department, though many schools seem to do this automatically.

The SAP office or group room should do the following:

☐ Adequately represent the school's commitment to the program

☐ Be equipped with a confidential telephone line for the program

☐ Be equipped with comfortable chairs

☐ Be in a place so students can get to the room without the entire student body knowing where they are going

☐ Have adequate ventilation and lighting

- ☐ Have opaque curtains over windows that look out on school grounds or parking lots, etc.
- ☐ Be soundproofed enough so students can speak freely without fear of being heard outside the room
- ☐ Have locked file cabinets and a desk for program materials
- ☐ Be easy to find for a student who has never been there before
- ☐ Be large enough to accommodate comfortably a group of ten or twelve students
- ☐ Have posted schedules of meetings, group rules, posters, audiovisual aids, etc.
- ☐ Have access to a television and a VCR.

Don't be daunted by this list. Successful SAPs have started out with very little, provided that the long-term commitment is made to bring them up to standard quickly. When I started as an SAP director, I spent September of the first year stocking my office. I found a desk left over from the Special Education department, painted the walls of my office myself one weekend, and after school one day, my principal and I took a field trip to a used office supply warehouse to choose my first file cabinet. By the end of the year, two cardboard boxes gave way to file cabinets, folding chairs became sturdy chairs, and a temporary group room was transformed by my core team into a full-time group room.

OBTAINING ADEQUATE CLERICAL SUPPORT

It is essential that the student assistance program have clerical support in the school. As with teachers, if you don't provide clerical support, you are paying someone who is professionally educated to type letters, run the photocopy machine, and answer the phone. This clerical support must include staff with good secretarial skills trained in the highest levels of confidentiality. It is best to hire full-time clerical support for the SAP, but if this is not possible, a part-time position could be posted. The least desirable, but still workable, arrangement would be to have an existing secretary in the school take on some duties for the SAP. Unfortunately, it is impossible to use student helpers in the context of the SAP for all but the most mundane tasks (stuffing nonconfidential folders or folding pamphlets, for instance) because of the highly confidential nature of the paperwork. The efficacy of the program will be greatly hindered if there is no available clerical help.

Some Final Words about Starting Up

Starting a student assistance program, no matter how big or small, is difficult work. The sheer magnitude of the problems you're trying to address can leave you discouraged or cynical from the outset. Or, you may feel breathless when people show unprecedented enthusiasm or willingness to help. At other times, it can feel that the school system is hurling obstacles at you at exactly the same rate you're breaking them down. This rollercoaster ride can be exhausting. So the most important task in starting your program may be to make a realistic approximation of what you can expect to do, and accept those limitations.

On the other hand, keep your hopes high. All the dire warnings about picking your battles and pacing yourself are included because if you do those things, you *can* make tremendous progress quickly. If, in the first year, you train a core team, develop a chemical use policy, design a referral procedure, and start one or two groups, you have accomplished a great deal. Keep your sights on what you want, and consistent, positive, and professional action will get you there.

5

Promoting Your Student Assistance Program

CHAPTER 5

Promoting Your Student Assistance Program

When you decide to try to save the world, you may not expect to have to persuade the world it needs to be saved before you can get down to work. If you're in the SAP business, either at the beginning or on a continuing basis, a large part of your job will be to promote your program, to explain it and thereby elicit referrals. Promotion in the SAP business means getting information and instructions for referring out to faculty, students, parents, and community members.

Even if your program has been in operation for five or ten years, you'll find that you have to explain how your particular SAP works over and over again, and you'll need to use every vehicle available to you repeatedly to get the word out to faculty and staff about referring students. Even after you have explained it to people, some will still not understand, because they bring to this concept of an SAP a whole set of preconceived notions that they cannot abandon. You may get a lot of comments like, "Oh that's so sad! Do we really need this? Is this what the world has come to?" and they'll leave, shaking their heads. You have the opportunity to turn that discouragement into encouragement as you explain how SAPs can be a catalyst for whole-school change.

People are naturally suspicious of what they don't understand, so you will need both to guide their understanding of SAPs and to build trust quickly. If your faculty and administration don't trust you and the basic tenets of the program you are implementing, they will feel manipulated by it. Having the trust of your faculty and administration is paramount to getting your job done and, ultimately, to helping students. A great deal of thought should be put into how you will market your SAP effort to the faculty and staff, students and community so you can gain their participation, support, and enthusiasm.

GETTING THE WORD OUT TO FACULTY

If your SAP is new, it is *imperative* that information about the program reaches the faculty before it reaches other populations. At the beginning of the year, in the first-day faculty meeting, a newly hired SAP person needs to be introduced by the principal as a member of the faculty. The principal may have to outline briefly that the newly hired SAP person will be getting a program underway shortly and will be eliciting faculty participation.

Beyond that introduction, faculty and staff must also know who is directly involved with the program's implementation. The faculty gets a better sense of the administrative support if they can see the core team (if you have one yet), including a top-level administrator along with the SAP counselor(s) assembled together during a later, official meeting. A memo won't do the trick sufficiently.

When you have assembled a core team and developed basic procedures for the program, schedule a separate, full faculty and staff meeting to introduce the core team, the counselor(s), and the relevant information. It is best, however, to wait a few months into the school year, after your initial core team training, for this general meeting than to schedule it without knowing exactly how the SAP will function in the school or district. The staff will have questions, and you want to be able to answer them without hesitation.

For Continuing Programs: If your SAP has been in operation for a while, now would be a good time to have a faculty-wide evaluation of the progress of the program. A faculty survey like the one provided here can clue you in to faculty concerns. A faculty-meeting forum can be arranged, and the current members of the core team or the SAP director can reexplain present operating procedures, recent changes, and progress that has been made since the inception of the effort. Explain exactly how you've been following up referrals, how you handle disciplinary referrals, and share with your faculty and staff the numbers of students who are coming to the program under their own steam. You may wish to share total numbers of referrals from students themselves, faculty, peers, and parents.

Another way to report on the progress of the SAP is to prepare composite anecdotes to describe a typical student's journey through the SAP. (Make sure it really is a composite and doesn't correlate too closely with any one student's experience.) Faculty and staff can then bring up concerns or share their positive experiences with the rest of the faculty. You may want to provide a written survey for this purpose. Faculty members may have some great suggestions to help your SAP run more smoothly, too. An SAP walks a delicate fence: You want your program to be a part of general school operation and you are absolutely dependent on the cooperation of your faculty and staff for appropriate referrals, but you also want to maintain a subtle separation to maintain the highest standards of confidentiality.

MAKING CLASSROOM VISITS TO INTRODUCE THE SAP

The best way to promote your program to students is to go door to door—to classrooms, that is. Individual faculty members also get a much better idea of how the program really works if they get a chance to sit in on a few classroom presentations. Once the procedures for the program have been established and you have an SAP counselor, your program will be well served if that counselor can spend a couple of weeks going classroom to classroom to introduce himself or herself to the students and to explain how students can access the SAP. Particularly in the beginning or when there is turnover in SAP personnel, going personally into the classrooms is an essential process. Face recognition goes a long way to building trust within a school setting.

Choosing Classes to Visit

In a large school, where it is impossible to reach every student in a classroom presentation, you may have to choose strategically which classes to visit. If you can, visit classes which seem to fit nicely with a presentation on the student as-

SAP FACULTY SURVEY

The student assistance program would like to get your feedback on a number of issues. We are trying to evaluate our policies and procedures so we can make the program more effective. Please respond as honestly as possible.

How many students of yours do you estimate use the program? _____

_____

Do students tell you when they will be attending group? _____

_____

Do you suspect that any students are abusing the system? If so, how? _____

_____

Do students generally make up the work they miss from class? _____

_____

How many referrals to the program do you estimate you have made in the past year? _____

_____

What could the SAP do to make it easier for you to refer students? _____

_____

What concerns you about the student assistance program, and how could we answer

those concerns? _____

_____

_____

Additional comments: _____

_____

sistance program—classes in health, psychology, communications, "living skills" classes, or physical education (if your PE program has a "total wellness" theme). Once you have chosen which classes you'd like to visit, speak in person to the teachers about when would be a convenient time (rather than sending a memo) and work it out on an individual basis. Memos tend to give the impression that teachers have no choice but to let you use their class time. Letting you come to their classes is a favor the teachers do for you; if you treat it that way, you'll fare better. If you think it would be best to go through a particular department, speak directly to the chairperson about getting time in each class.

In your attempt to explain the SAP to a fair representation of the school population, you may choose to visit only one grade level—for instance, going to every sophomore English class—or you may choose to visit the classes of core team members. Be sure to make contact in all different types of classes, including special education classes and alternative programs. If your school has vocational, general, and college preparatory "tracks," make sure you market the SAP effort to all tracks. Participation in the SAP should be available to all students in a school or district.

Using Your Teaching Skills to Promote the Program

If you have a team-based SAP without a counselor, the teachers that comprise your core team can promote the program by devoting a day of their curriculum to explaining your particular program and how it works. If you do have a counselor-based SAP, and the counselor has had previous training as a classroom teacher, this is where that training will pay off. The counselor can make the presentations in person, giving the students both basic information about the program and a chance to become familiar with the person(s) who staffs the program. Counselors who haven't had much experience doing classroom presentations may feel nervous handling thirty students at a time, but remember that you do know more about your SAP than the people you're going to talk to. You don't have to be a brilliant public speaker to get the job done; you just need sincere concern for the population you serve. Some SAP counselors feel comfortable having the classroom teacher stay in the room during the presentation, and some would rather do the presentation without the teacher there. This will depend on your comfort level.

Gaining Referrals from Classroom Presentations

Classroom presentations often generate immediate referrals. During a classroom presentation, some students will distinguish themselves as being either extremely knowledgeable about alcohol or other drug use or extremely curious about the SAP. You must consider that the student who is asking a lot of questions during a classroom presentation may be asking for help, and it's worth following up. My experience has been that at least one referral is usually generated from each classroom visit, just because a student makes himself or herself so obvious to me.

After sending a call slip to the student through his or her homeroom, I'll usually start off my individual appointment with this student by saying something like, "I just called you down to thank you for helping me out during that presentation I did in Miss Smith's class about the student assistance program on

Tuesday. No one else was answering any questions, and you seemed to know a lot about what was going on." A lot of students will launch right into their experience with alcohol and other drugs with this simple invitation to do so. Others will require more prompting. However, my experience has been that students who draw attention to themselves during classroom presentations usually appreciate getting what they asked for.

PROMOTING YOUR PROGRAM THROUGH THE SCHOOL MAIL

One way of keeping faculty updated is to send brief, informational handouts through the school mail. Various faculty information handouts have been provided for you throughout this book; one on "Common Drugs Adolescents Use" appears on the following page. These handouts can be supplemented by copies of brief articles you may find in professional journals and magazines. Because this sort of information is not confidential, enlist the help of students to photocopy the articles and put them into mailboxes. This way of keeping in touch can also be extended to parents if you have the resources.

Creating a Newsletter

Distributing a newsletter is a good way to keep your faculty updated on current trends in student alcohol or other drug use nationwide, from statistics on everything from alcohol and other drug-related highway fatalities to new ways of identifying children of addiction in the classroom. Also, if your faculty is hearing from the SAP effort on a regular basis, they will feel more connected to the program and may contact you concerning students. Even if your newsletter is a one-sheet mimeographed copy, the effort you make creates room for dialogue with other faculty. In a small school, it might be feasible to distribute an SAP newsletter to the entire faculty and student body.

Producing a good newsletter is also a lot of work. There are a few commercial operations that will sell you a newsletter, ready-made for a price, and you can attach the name of your SAP and put it through your interschool mail. If you have the funds, this is a great idea. Another way to get a newsletter is to contact local colleges who may be looking for internship placements. They may have undergraduate students who are looking for semester-long projects. Having a college student compile a monthly newsletter could benefit both your program and your relations with your local community. See a sample newsletter on the following pages.

CREATING PAMPHLETS AND POSTERS

It's good practice to have a pamphlet describing the general operating procedures of your SAP and asking some very basic questions of the reader which might encourage him or her to seek help through the program. These pamphlets can be left in the nurse's office, the principal's office (kids have a lot of time to think when they're waiting to see the principal), the library, or wherever students will have access to them. If you have funding for only one type of pamphlet, make one that

Faculty Information Handout
COMMON DRUGS ADOLESCENTS USE

Alcohol: Alcohol is still the number 1 drug of choice of teenagers. Because of the way it is benevolently portrayed on television commercials and through other media, it is somehow deemed more acceptable than other drug use. While the recent campaign to reduce the incidence of drinking and driving has been somewhat successful, more and more teenagers are drinking. New products, such as wine coolers, have made alcohol more palatable to the inexperienced user. The dangers of alcohol include dependency, alcohol-related auto accidents, accidental death (drowning, fall, etc.), death by overdose, serious damage to self-esteem, and suicide.

Marijuana: Marijuana is still popular, but the drug itself has changed quite a bit since the 1960s and 1970s. Though it is still called "pot" or "weed," the average amount of the active ingredient (THC) has increased significantly. This means that one joint now might have the effect of five or six joints. Marijuana tends to make adolescents more lethargic and indifferent. Performance in school and athletic ability can be greatly decreased. Physical symptoms include red, glassy eyes, inappropriate responses, weight gain, and lack of proper hygiene. *Hash* is the resin collected from marijuana plants and has the same effects, though the concentration of THC is even higher.

Cocaine: Cocaine, once the drug of the rich and famous, is now widely available to teenagers. It can be snorted through the nose or shot intravenously. Crack, a less expensive and more powerful form of the drug, which is smoked, has made the drug easier to procure. The dangers of cocaine use include dependency, weight loss, inability to concentrate, paranoia, and cardiac arrest. Addiction to cocaine is difficult to beat.

LSD: LSD is back in circulation (some contend it never left). LSD is sometimes sold as liquid, but more often on small squares of paper that have been saturated with the liquid. The dangers of acid include bizarre behavior, hallucinations, paranoia, "bad trips," and dependency.

Other Drugs: There are almost too many drugs available to teenagers to list. Among them are speed, ice, mushrooms, heroin, anabolic steroids, PCP, amphetamines, and barbiturates. Students also misuse over-the-counter medications, prescription medications, and household products to get high.

Side One of a Sample Newsletter

Student Assistance Program Update
Keeping You Informed

SAP GROUPS

Thanks to all the teachers who made group participation possible for students last year. SAP groups will be starting up during the first week of October. In the meantime, we will be conducting individual appointments and screening interviews for groups. We appreciate your support for students who choose to participate in groups.

CORE TEAM

The core team for the student assistance program has been active for two full years, guiding the poli-

cies and practices of the SAP. This year, we will be eliciting continuing and new participation by Central High faculty. This dedicated group of individuals has facilitated the rapid progress the program has made. Thanks go to these people. A list of participants will be published once faculty participation is determined for the school year.

We want to encourage faculty to consider joining this hard-working team. We have made great progress without sacrificing a good time.

FRESHMAN FRENZY

This year, the student assistance program is trying to reach students earlier in their high school experience in the hopes of increasing their awareness about available in-school services.

To this end, the SAP will be presenting to all freshman English classes to elicit participation in SAP groups and to get the word out that help is available. Thanks go to freshman English teachers who rearrange their schedules for this purpose.

STOP BY!

I invite your comments to make Central's SAP operate as effectively as possible. My office is crammed full (those who have been there can verify this!) of materials about adolescent behavior, alcohol and other drug information, intervention, etc. You are welcome to borrow materials. My office is located at the left end of the guidance hallway. I look forward to working with you this year! Let's make it a good one!

Side Two of a Sample Newsletter

REFERRAL FORMS

Attached, you'll find two behavioral checklists to refer students
to the SAP. By no means should this
limit you to two referrals! If you
run out, the main office, the guidance office, and the SAP office
have plenty more. Forms can also be
found on the wall in the faculty
mail room.

Remember that students <u>do not</u> have
to be exhibiting alcohol and other
drug-specific behaviors to warrant
a referral to the SAP. Any unusual
behavior can be a legitimate cause
for concern. When you do refer students to the SAP, remember that you
are not "getting them in trouble"—
you are trying to get them the help
they need.

SYSTEM ABUSE

Now that the SAP has been established, some enterprising students
have begun to figure out ways to
misuse the privilege of SAP participation. If you suspect that this is
the case with one of your little
cherubs, please bring it to the attention of the SAP. We want students to get needed help, but not
at the expense of their education.
If everything is working as it
should, a student should not miss
more than one of your classes every
eight weeks. There will, of course,
be exceptions when things must be
rescheduled, etc., but not often.

INTERNAL AFFAIRS

Central's student assistance program welcomes two interns to the
program this year.

J. BurKe

Jon Donovan joins us from the Anti-
och Graduate School, where he is
pursuing a Master's degree in substance abuse counseling.

Deane Beman hails from Notre Dame
College, where he is pursuing a
Bachelor's degree in psychology.

Feel free to stop by the SAP office to say hello to our new re-
cruits. We wish them well in their
endeavors with the program this
year.

is designed for the students to be given out during classroom presentations. Both sides of a sample pamphlet (made by folding one 8½ × 11 sheet of paper twice) are provided here as a model.

Parents and community groups are also very appreciative of a simple explanation of the services available, and you may be able to leave some pamphlets at the juvenile division of the Police Department, the city library, the Boys' and Girls' Club, or wherever students in your community spend time. Leaving a pile of pamphlets at local malls and burger joints may also be helpful (especially if your students tend to hang out in one particular place). Once you have drafted the pamphlet on your typewriter or computer, do some research to see if your vocational or technical program can do the printing for you, to make it an in-house job. If you have a large school or district, you may need a lot of copies.

Another helpful informational tool is a rack full of pamphlets on issues ranging from alcoholism and children of addiction to sexually transmitted diseases and everything in between. Particularly popular are pamphlets describing the pharmacology of whatever drugs are widely used in your student population, as students are more curious about those things they are actively ingesting, smoking, etc. If you can, print informational pamphlets yourself, with information about the SAP included in each. That way, students who pick up a pamphlet on LSD, for instance, will simultaneously get information about helping services.

Local twelve-step programs (AA, NA, Al-Anon, Alateen, etc.) will provide you with meeting lists and pamphlets describing their philosophy and information about meetings. These pamphlets will cost you little or nothing, and many other agencies have pamphlets describing their services as well. Call your designated state agency for alcohol and other drug issues or the National Clearinghouse for Alcohol and Drug Information (NCADI) for help in securing free or almost-free pamphlets (see the Appendix, "Additional Resources").

Catchy posters can sell the program if they are well placed. Both commercial posters and home-made versions can advertise the program well. Make sure that they are put in places where students can see them clearly, and often. (Next to the soda machines is always a good spot.) One way to promote the program school-wide is to have a yearly poster contest for an SAP motto and logo. See if you can get a community sponsor to donate a worthwhile prize, or you may not get too many entries. Also consider having a panel of students judge the entries. Face it, most of us are just too old to know what appeals to students. Surely you have artists in your student population, and great talents can be unearthed. The illustrator for this book was found through an SAP poster contest!

MOBILIZING YOUR PARENT GROUPS

Never underestimate the power of a good PTA or other active parent group. They are usually well organized and accustomed to getting things done. Your PTA can offer you practical assistance as well as virtually take on your public relations effort for parents. If your PTA has regular meetings, offer to make a presentation about the SAP, or any related topic, such as "Signs and Symptoms of Adolescent Alcohol and Other Drug Use." Most PTAs tend to be in favor of support services for their children, and you can only gain support and affirmation from forging a

ONE SIDE OF A SAMPLE SAP PAMPHLET

Clear the clouds with the student assistance program!

aged to use the program for help with family problems, emotional concerns, alcohol or other drug abuse, and eating disorders. Many students become involved in the program because they are concerned about a friend. The program offers support and educational groups, information and referral services, and individual sessions up to a maximum of four meetings.

STUDENT ASSISTANCE PROGRAM GROUPS

Students are encouraged to participate in group meetings to share ideas, experiences, and friendship with peer support. When students participate in group, the absence is noncounting, but students are responsible for all class work missed. Groups meet on a rotating mod basis to avoid missing the same class.

GETTING HELP FOR PROBLEMS

Students: If you are concerned about yourself or someone you know, please contact the student assistance program. You may make an anonymous referral if you choose.

Your referral and your participation will be kept strictly confidential within the guidelines of the program.

The student assistance program office is located:

Parents: If you have any questions, please call the student assistance program directly at:

Community Agencies: The student assistance program wants to work in cooperation with your efforts. Please contact the SAP directly at:

STUDENT ASSISTANCE PROGRAM

The student assistance program aims to identify and help troubled students and their families and to encourage healthy coping alternatives. The program provides confidential services for students whose personal concerns may be affecting their performance or behavior at school. Students are encour-

---

GOALS

The student assistance program aims to help students develop healthy coping skills, make positive life-style choices, and avoid substance abuse problems. Services are also provided for students whose lives have been affected by their own or someone else's use of alcohol or other drugs. Some students who use the program are not involved with substances but are looking for help with a variety of other personal problems.

CONFIDENTIALITY

Confidentiality is the cornerstone of the student assistance program. If you contact the program, no one will know unless you tell them. No information will travel from the program to anyone else without your permission. Exceptions to that rule are that in cases where suicidal or homicidal behavior is evident, the appropriate people will be contacted. The counselor must also report cases of abuse and neglect.

THE OTHER SIDE OF A SAMPLE SAP PAMPHLET

All groups are informational, educational, and supportive in nature:

- Discussion Group: open discussion for any teen concerns (friends, dating, peer pressure)
- Friend's Group: for those students affected by the drinking or drugging of a close friend or relative
- Educational Group: for those interested in learning more about alcohol and other drugs, addiction, and recovery
- Recovery Group: for those interested in staying clean and sober at Central
- Special Topic Groups: for those interested in a specific topic (i.e., divorce, blended families, eating disorders)

All information shared in the groups is also confidential.

HOW THE PROGRAM WORKS

When you first meet with the program director or core team member, he or she will discuss your situation with you and tell you about services that are available in the community to help you. You may choose to see the

counselor again, up to four formal meetings before a referral to a program group, outside support, or community resource.

Your participation is completely voluntary unless you are referred for violating Central High School's chemical use policy.

Teachers may refer you to the program if your school work is slipping, or if you are frequently absent or tardy, because they care about you and want to help. Friends or parents may refer you if they notice a change in your behavior or mood.

Although the student assistance program can assist in providing the names of treatment professionals in the community, the decision to seek professional services is the full responsibility of the student or family seeking treatment.

COULD THE STUDENT ASSISTANCE PROGRAM HELP YOU?

1. Do you feel overwhelmed and simply don't know what to do?
2. In spite of all your accomplishments, do you

ever feel that you're not any good?

3. Do you have a parent, relative, or friend whose drinking or drugging bothers you?

4. Have you ever felt that you should cut down on your drinking or drugging?

5. Are you increasingly concerned about your body weight or size? Are you involved in crash dieting, binge eating, skipped meals, or vomiting?

6. Do you continue to date people who have personal problems, abuse alcohol or other drugs, or treat you badly?

7. Do you find that you can't remember parts of what happened while you were drinking or drugging?

8. Do you feel alone and depressed and that no one could possibly understand?

Every yes to the above questions means that you are troubled by something. When problems aren't taken care of, they tend to get worse. The student assistance program can help you help yourself.

strong relationship with this group of vocal and concerned parents. If your PTA is involved in arranging orientation nights for incoming students, try to become a part of these as well, because it is good to let parents know about SAP services even before their children attend your school.

Never turn down a PTA's offer to sponsor a speaker or workshop series, or an offer to volunteer clerical help. Conversely, offer to help the organization in any capacity you reasonably can. Your relationship with the PTA may save your program someday during a school budget crisis.

HANDLING OPEN HOUSES AND ORIENTATIONS

The science fair in the cafeteria will certainly be a bigger draw at an open house than the SAP booth. At open houses, your SAP people may especially feel that subtle separation from the rest of the school, as academic advising staff and classroom teachers are overrun with parents wanting to find out about this or that grade or deadline or college entrance exam.

At the high school level, especially, students are understandably reluctant to drag their parents to the SAP table and exclaim, "Mom, this is the counselor I had to talk to after I got caught drinking at the dance" or "This is the counselor that runs my Children of Addiction group, Dad." So while it may be uncomfortable or seemingly unnecessary for the SAP counselor to be present at such events, it is important for the SAP to be represented when the school is on display to the community, because it underscores the need and the commitment the school is making. If there is no SAP counselor, members of the team should staff the SAP booth or table throughout the evening, handing out pamphlets and explaining basic SAP services, confidentiality, and the chemical use policy. Think of open houses and parent nights as a way to transmit information to parents you wouldn't otherwise see, and as a way to get to know your community better.

SCHEDULING APPROPRIATE ASSEMBLIES

Most schools have a schedule of assemblies to be presented during the school year. It is usually someone's job to schedule different presentations to the school community at large either several times a month or several times a year. The more often assemblies are scheduled, the more likely that you can get your SAP a slot (or two). If assembly slots are rare, choose your assembly program carefully. Do you want to piggyback with Students Against Driving Drunk (SADD) around prom time? Do you want to be part of the national Red Ribbon Campaign, a drug awareness week in October? Do you want to hire one of the many theater groups that do presentations on alcohol or other drugs? Do you want your school's drama club to present a series of vignettes depicting alcohol or other drug situations? Or do you want to keep the focus on your SAP and how to access it? A great deal will depend on the size of your school and the way assemblies are usually handled. For instance, a small student theater group performance may be inappropriate in an auditorium or gymnasium full of 1,000 students, but it may be a perfect presentation in a health class.

If you are hiring someone to do a big presentation—maybe a "clean and sober" rock band, or a local celebrity telling his or her story of alcohol and other drug use and his or her subsequent recovery, make sure that you preview a videotape of the performance or presentation. It is one thing to be personally embarrassed by someone's performance; it is another thing altogether to have chosen the program yourself without previewing it and to be embarrassed in front of 1,000 of your colleagues and potential clients. Sometimes presenters who tout themselves as having a "no-use" message actually have a "responsible-use" message, so listen carefully for this.

Consider assembly presentations in terms of whether or not they are in accordance with the fundamental philosophies of your SAP. For instance, consider whether the "Don't Drink and Drive" campaign really complements your SAP's admonition to really take a look at drinking patterns or instead concentrates on damage control once students are too impaired to drive. Consider the message students may get from having an older person who is recovering from addiction tell his or her story. It may be, "Yeah, when I get as bad as she got, I'll definitely quit!" There is room for this kind of programming in the school setting, but think carefully whether you want the SAP anchored to it or whether it would be more appropriate to have sponsorship from another school-based group such as SADD, the student council, or various parent groups.

MAKING PRESENTATIONS ON STUDENT ASSISTANCE PROGRAMMING

If your marketing efforts are successful, chances are that you'll be asked to describe your school's student assistance programming to parents, perhaps the school board, and community groups. Someone, either your SAP counselor or core team members, will be asked to serve on panels for conferences and community education.

Any presentation about your SAP to students, faculty, or community groups should include explanations of the following elements:

- Justification for programming
- The mission statement of the program
- The population the program serves
- How to access the program
- Who staffs the program
- Where staff can be located (include office phone numbers)
- What is expected of students who use the program
- Detailed explanation of the confidentiality rules (including exceptions to the rules)
- A description of how behaviorally based referrals are made
- A description of what an individual session would be like
- A description of the availability of groups.

Consider these presentations free publicity. Although they are not incredibly exciting, it serves your program well to get the information out to the people that can support your program in the community.

MARKETING YOUR PROGRAM TO YOUR COMMUNITY

However insular schools may seem, they are ultimately supported by their parent communities, and it makes good public relations sense to let the community know what is going on in the hallowed halls. Most people in the community will be especially pleased to hear about a new SAP operation because it is a positive step in a direction almost everyone agrees is necessary. Making allies in the community can also help your program when budgets are cut. Marketing your program in the community is as simple as making your program visible. Serve on community task forces that concentrate their efforts on alcohol and other drug issues. Participate in community prevention efforts, even if they have no formal ties to your school. Elicit help from community sponsors, and when you get the help, make it well known who provided it. When possible, have core team members share this responsibility so you are not saddled with the whole public relations package.

As soon as the community knows that the SAP is the designated vehicle in school to deal with alcohol and other drug issues, be prepared for the reality that all mailings, information seekers, and people who want you to disseminate information for them will descend on the SAP, and you will be responsible for making a large percentage of the alcohol and other drug-related decisions for your school. Your only defense will be to delegate, delegate, delegate. In my school, I must wade through piles of advertisements for various groups that arrive in my mailbox weekly and then send off a small selection to the student council officers. Then, they narrow it down further for promotion through homeroom delegates of the student council.

Some Final Words about Promoting Your SAP

Because of the confidentiality concerns inherent in SAP operation, it is easy for the faculty and school community to misinterpret your program (or you personally) as clandestine, suspicious, or aloof. This misinterpretation can become a tremendous obstacle when you are trying to create a system to help students. One task in promoting the program is to dispel these myths, and to be visible and available to teachers and students alike. Depending on your program's structure, you are probably not at liberty to discuss specific student cases, but you are at liberty to discuss general operating procedures and to answer general questions. Promotion means making yourself and your program approachable, so when people need the program, they can assess it with confidence.

6

Training Faculty and Staff

CHAPTER 6

Training Faculty and Staff

Since student assistance programs rely a great deal on student referrals from faculty and staff, it is important to train your school personnel right away to use the program. A primary objective of the training is to explain the purpose and target population of the program. If you don't explain the program well initially, your faculty and staff may be suspicious and perhaps uncooperative, and your program will suffer a slow start. Invest in good initial training for your core team, administrators, additional faculty and staff; it will go a long way to guarantee wide faculty participation in the program, and it will save time in the long run.

DECIDING WHO NEEDS WHAT TRAINING

In the context of SAPs, training means giving people the information they need to do their part and then asking them to take specific action. You can do this in a variety of ways, from presenting brief informational spots at faculty meetings to taking personnel off-site for days at a time to hear outside experts present on their areas of expertise. It is always important to remember that each population you serve requires training that meets its own special needs. For example, administrators may need information about the school district's code of conduct or may need to hear from a top-level administrator from another district who has implemented student assistance programming successfully. Teachers, on the other hand, may need very specific information about how attendance can be taken while students are involved in the program or how to send a crying student out of class and to the SAP office. Parents need to know their specific rights and responsibilities in the program, and they need to know how to access it. Each population needs different information so they can refer students and feel good about it. Taking the time to train each group encourages ownership in the program and helps people feel that they are a part of the process rather than apart from a new structure that has been imposed on their system. It is not unusual for start-up SAPs to spend the majority of their time during the first year training people (including students) to understand and use the program.

In deciding what training each group will need, first identify what it is the program needs them to do and then design the training around those tasks. For instance, while it would be nice if teachers and other staff who are not on the core team were trained in basic alcohol and other drug-related issues, they absolutely *must* be extensively trained in using the referral procedures for the program. Design your training for them around how to access the program, how to make referrals, how to notice high-risk kids, and how to intervene themselves. To delve into deeper, peripheral issues at the beginning might only cause confusion.

Core team members, on the other hand, should be trained in family issues, adolescent development, chemical dependency and related issues, recovery, and confidentiality, so they can bring an educated perspective to guiding the policies and practices of the SAP and offering technical assistance to the SAP director, if there is one. If the core team will be involved in providing direct services, including informal assessments, its members will require even more intense training.

DESIGNING A LOGICAL TRAINING SCHEDULE

Your training schedule is going to depend completely on where you are in the process of implementing an SAP and who you are in the scheme of things. If you are at the very beginning of the process, your first step may be to present a proposal to the school board, the principals' association, or the superintendent of schools about the possibility of starting a student assistance program. If you are part of a community task force, you may be presenting a proposal to a political body or, in private education, to a board of trustees. Even this first proposal can be considered training, because you are giving people information and then asking them to take specific action.

The training schedule should follow a logical progression, from gaining support for implementing a program, to educating the faculty and staff about utilizing the program, to continuing education for the school community once a student assistance program is implemented. (As goals are met, training responsibilities may shift from one person to another. For instance, a concerned faculty member may instigate a task force that makes the initial recommendation for a counselor-based student assistance program and may then present the school board with the needed information. After a program is started and the coordinator hired, the remainder of the training may be arranged by the coordinator.)

Depending on the structure you choose to implement, some groups must be trained before others. It doesn't make sense to train faculty members to report students under the influence of alcohol and other drugs before core team members have developed a chemical use policy that determines what is to be done when such students are identified.

Following are some groups worth training and advice on training them. Only you can determine what order is best for your particular setting, however, depending on the structure you have chosen for your program and how far you have already come.

TRAINING SCHOOL BOARDS OR BOARDS OF TRUSTEES

If you are just beginning, you may be in the business of convincing a school board that the district needs an SAP (or several). It is important, when you are addressing school boards, to keep the focus on the educational benefits of student assistance programming. Members are obligated to search for better ways to educate the young people under their supervision. They need to know the extent to which students are affected by personal problems and the numbers of students who seek help in other districts. It may help to involve community agencies. For instance, the police can report on the number of alcohol and other drug-related arrests they are seeing in the juvenile division, or a child protective agency can report on the number of child abuse cases where alcoholism and addiction are obvious. It may help to have teachers report on the magnitude of personal problems they see affecting students' ability to do their schoolwork. If there is funding involved in the proposal, make sure you have a budget and that you can justify every item. Practice answering questions before you get to the meeting.

In an ongoing program, you may be required at some point to report to the board about the efficacy of the program to maintain both financial and administrative support. Although this may seem intimidating, it is a great way to garner support for the program. However, because these folks work with a bottom line in mind, they will need specific information about the costs of the program and the numbers of students who use it. Be sure to mention any internships or community volunteers who make "in-kind" donations to the program, as this serves to show community support and visibility of the program. It also helps to have reports of other SAP operations in "competing" states or cities, as boards generally like to keep up with one another.

Some school board members may want to be more involved in the SAP operation and may want additional training. It can be very helpful to have school board members on an advisory core team, and if this is the case, they should be involved in training designed for the core team. The more a school board member knows about SAP operation and the range of services, the more information he or she can disseminate to others on the board. In a budget crunch, proactive and well-informed school board members can champion for the SAP cause. If you provide intense training for your school-based core team, consider inviting a school board member along for the experience (though he or she would not be responsible for intervening with students the same way core team members would). In some cases, the alliance you foster with the school board may have lasting benefits.

TRAINING PRINCIPALS, ASSISTANT PRINCIPALS, AND OTHER ADMINISTRATORS

This group must be trained in the confidentiality regulations. Building-level administrators should also be part of the team that guides the policies and practices of the SAP. (Make sure your superintendent also understands the confidentiality regulations and the procedures of the SAP.) Without top-level participation, progress will be slow. Principals are for the most part captains of their ships, and they like to know what is going on in all quarters. This is appropriate, as they may be called on to explain the specific programs in their schools or to deflect any difficulties arising from their operation. If at all possible, include either the principal or an assistant principal on the core team. In the long run, it is so much easier to work with administrators than around them.

Because administrators often handle school discipline, it is also essential for them to be involved in the drafting or redrafting of the chemical use policy. If they are going to levy consequences to students, they must have a hand in developing the consequences and they must have facility with the policy. If your core team is responsible for drafting a new or updated chemical use policy and your administrators in charge of discipline are not members of the core team, invite them to the chemical use policy drafting sessions to gain their input and their assurance that they will enforce it consistently.

My experience has been that administrators are concerned about school climate for both students and faculty members, about educational directives, about liability, and about relations with parents. Have these issues in mind when you design training for them, keeping the focus on the educational underpinnings of SAPs. If you can, have a legal expert do a brief workshop on the confidentiality regulations so administrators can feel more comfortable with them. Also, invite other SAP directors who have fully operational programs to come to your training to explain their procedures. You don't have to adopt the whole package they present, but it can give you and your administrators good ideas and can put them at ease about the feasibility of programming.

TRAINING THE CORE TEAM

Core team training is going to vary widely depending on the structure you have chosen for your SAP. Some core teams will be fully responsible for implementing a student assistance program and will be involved in cofacilitating groups and conducting assessments. Obviously, these folks need to be well trained before they embark on such an expedition into uncharted territory. Other core teams, which act in an advisory capacity only, need comprehensive training that focuses on the theoretical foundation of SAPs. The sample "Core Team Training Agenda" provided here can be used or adapted for any core team group.

Using the Core Team Member's Self-Evaluation

Use the "Core Team Member Self-Evaluation Checklist" (which follows the sample agenda) at the beginning of your core team training or at any time during a meeting to help core team members evaluate gaps in their knowledge. Do not use it as a process-of-elimination tool, separating those who know a lot from those who don't. Often, it is those who have the least amount of training who are willing to learn the most. Every yes to the fifteen questions indicates the need for more training. The questions indicate common misconceptions about alcohol and other drugs and the ways of dealing with student use. You can use this tool as the beginning of a training, or as a way to generate discussion.

When choosing workshop topics for any training, especially for the core team, remember what it is that they are going to be asked to do. In certain cases, their only task is to understand what is going on; in others, the task is to be an active participant. Here is a list of topics that you might cover in an initial core team training (see also the sample three-day training schedule):

- Student assistance programming—the theoretical basis
- Student assistance programs—how you can work with them
- Confidentiality concerns
- Disease concept of addiction
- Adolescent development
- Chemical dependency in adolescents

SAMPLE CORE TEAM TRAINING AGENDA
Year 1

Day 1

7:30–8:00   Coffee, tea, fruit, and goodies

8:00–8:15   **Introduction and Overview of Training**

- SAP coordinator, principal, or core team coordinator

8:15–8:30   **Getting to Know Each Other**

Some of us have been working together for years and still don't know much about each other. This exercise will help us know one another better so we can work as a team.

- Any member of the core team or SAP coordinator

8:30–10:00   **Overview of Student Assistance Programming**

This workshop will introduce members to the basic components of a student assistance program and the student population we hope to reach. Confidentiality will also be discussed.

- SAP coordinator or outside consultant

10:00–10:15   Break

10:15–10:30   **Group Energizer**

10:30–12:00   **Adolescent Chemical Dependency**

The disease concept of addiction, as well as the progression of the disease and early warning symptoms, will be covered by an expert in the field. Special attention will be paid to the disease as it appears in adolescents.

- Alcohol and other drug professional from the community or SAP coordinator

12:00–1:00   Lunch

1:00–2:30   **Identifying High-Risk Students in the Classroom Using a Behavioral Checklist**

Our SAP coordinator introduces our referral procedure and explains behavior which indicates that students are at high risk.

- SAP coordinator

2:30–3:00   Wrap-up and impressions of the day

Day 2

7:30–8:00   Coffee, tea, fruit, and goodies

8:00–9:00   **Current Trends in Adolescent Drug Use**

A professional from our community helps us understand current levels of alcohol and other drug use in our young people.

- Alcohol and other drug professional from the community or hospital

9:00–10:00   **Pharmacology and Paraphernalia**

This workshop will briefly explain the effects of alcohol and other drugs. Drug paraphernalia will also be on display.

* Hospital, chemical dependency treatment facility, or police

10:00–10:30   Break

10:30–12:00   **Enabling Behaviors**

Sometimes when we think we are helping someone, we are really making it easier for them to stay sick. This workshop focuses on enabling behaviors in general, and, specifically, on how school systems enable students.

* Expert on codependency and/or enabling from an agency, hospital, or other community setting

12:00–1:00   Lunch

1:00–2:30   **Chemical Use Policy Workshop**

This team is responsible for the school's chemical use policy. We will begin reviewing any existing policy and using our new information to create a new policy or update the existing one.

* SAP core team

Day 3

8:00–8:30   Coffee, tea, fruit, and goodies

8:30–10:00   **Children Affected by Addiction and the Roles They Play in Adolescence and Adulthood**

This workshop will focus on children who grow up with addiction and the various roles they play in the classroom and ways we can identify them and intervene. Some attention will be given to the roles these children play in adulthood if they are left untreated.

* Expert on addiction as a family disease or SAP coordinator

10:00–10:15   Break

10:15–10:30   **Group Energizer**

10:30–12:00   **Role-Playing Intervention Techniques**

We'll get a chance to role-play some difficult situations with students, parents, and administrators.

* SAP coordinator or outside alcohol and other drug professional

12:00–1:00   Pot-Luck Lunch

1:00–2:15   **Policy and Procedures Brainstorming Session**

This time is set aside to talk about policy and procedures for our SAP. We may work on the chemical use policy, or we may work on a system for students to attend groups.

* Core team and SAP coordinator

2:15–2:30   **Wrap-up and scheduling next core team meeting**

2:30–3:00   **Evaluations**

CORE TEAM MEMBER SELF-EVALUATION CHECKLIST

		YES	NO
1.	Do you believe that alcohol use is less dangerous than drug use?	☐	☐
2.	Do you believe that every student will go through a phase of experimentation with alcohol and drugs?	☐	☐
3.	Do you think that if students were just smarter, they wouldn't use alcohol and drugs so much?	☐	☐
4.	Do you believe you can tell who uses alcohol and other drugs by the way they dress or talk?	☐	☐
5.	Would you encourage a kid who was using alcohol or drugs to "cut down" or "take it easy"?	☐	☐
6.	Do you believe that students talk about alcohol and drug use more than they actually use alcohol or other drugs?	☐	☐
7.	Would you be uncomfortable "turning a kid in" to the administration because he or she was under the influence of alcohol or other drugs?	☐	☐
8.	Do you believe that most students who come from alcohol or drug-addicted homes are obviously neglected and easily identifiable?	☐	☐
9.	Do you believe that students whose parents are strict about alcohol or other drugs will "go crazy" after graduation or at college?	☐	☐
10.	Do you believe that students who learn to "drink responsibly" with their parents are less likely to develop alcohol or other drug problems?	☐	☐
11.	Do you believe that alcohol and other drug use is a moral issue?	☐	☐
12.	Do you believe that peer pressure is the most common reason that students use alcohol or other drugs?	☐	☐
13.	Do you believe that students could quit using alcohol or other drugs if they really wanted to?	☐	☐
14.	Does the thought of evaluating your own or someone in your family's use of alcohol or other drugs make you anxious, nervous, or uncomfortable?	☐	☐
15.	Do you find yourself making nervous jokes about alcohol and other drugs after workshops or around SAP professionals?	☐	☐

- Current drugs of choice—pharmacology and effects
- Mental health issues in adolescence
- Identifying high-risk students
- Children of alcoholics and addicts in the classroom
- Roles that traumatized children play
- Adolescent recovery and relapse
- Enabling behaviors
- Confronting students who use
- AIDS and student assistance programming
- Fundamentals of group work
- Duty to report child abuse and neglect.

Core team trainings should also include time for the team to discuss general operating procedures for the remainder of the year: when they will hold meetings, who will be responsible for coming up with an agenda for the meeting, who will be contacted in an emergency if the SAP counselor is not in the building, and so forth. In later years, core team trainings can review these basic issues and add new, or more advanced, training. It is also wise to remember that issues for adolescents will change, and that your trainings must reflect those changes.

Special Points to Cover in an Initial Training

The huge task in initial core team trainings is determining the actual procedures for your SAP, and you should leave plenty of time for that. Some points to consider are as follows:

- What is the core team's role?
- What is our policy for taking students out of class to attend groups?
- How many individual appointments can a student have before a referral is made to an outside agency or inside group?
- Under what circumstances are parents contacted?
- What are the procedures for students who are under the influence in class?
- What precautions have we taken to guarantee student confidentiality?
- What are we doing to encourage faculty referrals?

Even a highly motivated and well-organized core team may need quite a bit of time and an agenda to answer all the policy questions in an initial core team training. (A great deal more is said about getting underway with a core team in chapter 4, "Starting a School-Based Student Assistance Program.")

TRAINING OTHER FACULTY AND STAFF

After core team training, your most important training will be that of the faculty at large. (The larger your faculty, the larger the challenge!) In these trainings, you want to focus on the teachers' part in gaining help for their students—

namely, noticing unusual behavior in students and reporting it, using a behavioral checklist or another SAP referral form. Another issue that causes a lot of confusion is the difference between referring a student to the SAP out of concern versus noticing that a student is currently under the influence and reporting it to the administration for necessary disciplinary action. Teachers need to get this distinction clear from the start.

If you have a coordinator, he or she would be the logical choice to present such workshops, although you can also use an outside "expert" to great advantage at these types of trainings. Such a basic full-faculty training could be completed in an afternoon session, during an in-service day, or, if there is absolutely no other way, even in half an hour of a whole-school faculty meeting. Obviously, the more complete the training, the better response you will get in terms of student referrals. Your promotion work also functions as training, to some extent. See chapter 5, "Promoting Your SAP," to see how handouts and newsletters can get the word out to faculty.

Managing the Logistics of Training

Training can mean anything from holding a brief, informal afterschool workshop for a handful of interested personnel to taking a group away from school for a week at a time. Obviously, the afterschool workshop is a breeze, while the week-long session seems to be a logistical nightmare. Don't be discouraged! The logistics of all trainings can be cut up into manageable bites, and the overall experience can be successful and satisfying.

Because designing a training package can be an intimidating task, there is a brisk business in training packages from outside consultants; if you have the resources, this might be the way to go. Just make sure that the consultant really knows what it is you want and that the company is expert in implementing student assistance programs. Also, understand from the outset that some agencies set up SAPs to gain the referrals from the school, so make sure this is the arrangement you want if you choose to work this way. There are some conferences which are advertised through journals and the mail at which a core team could glean a great deal of the important information needed to set up a program. If you go this route, however, supplement the conference with a day or two of your own training, to fill in any gaps and to provide your team the time to develop policy for your particular program.

Setting Up Your Own Training

Setting up a training is like planning a wedding. You think the details really don't matter until someone gives you a choice. A question like, "Do you want coffee or soda at the break?" or "Do you want blue or green napkins?" can send you into a tailspin, so if you are floundering, ask someone for help. If you are working with a conference center or restaurant, they usually have someone who can help you set things up conveniently. If you are putting together a training on a shoestring—holding it at a school building and providing your own meals, for instance—delegate responsibilities to others so you don't feel overwhelmed. Ask certain core team members to be responsible for bringing or keeping track of equipment or training materials. Have a core team member organize a pot-luck lunch for the last day of training, or have someone meet with the school food service to see if you can get snacks.

SURVIVAL TIPS FOR SUCCESSFUL TRAININGS

Trainings can be memorable, enjoyable, and educational if they are set up correctly. Your training sets the tone for how your faculty and staff, core teams, and administration will view your program. The advice that follows will help you make training a positive experience for all involved. The more meaningful and informative and respectful the training, the more likely that school personnel will refer students, which is the ultimate goal of all SAP trainings.

Tip 1: Gain Administrative Support for Training

Most administrators understand that if new programs are to succeed, the people involved in them must be sufficiently trained. While most administrators are in favor of such training, they are likely to be daunted by the imagined cost or the exaggerated fear of messy logistics. If you want training and you want your administrators to be reasonably happy about approving it, your job is to be calm and cool and to have the logistics worked out in advance. Then, your proposal can't be countered with "That's a great idea really, but it simply won't work because there's no place we could hold it." When you cheerfully respond that you have already checked and a local college will let you use its classrooms during spring break, that only four substitutes are needed for three days, and that you've identified five or six speakers from the community who are willing to volunteer their time, the picture brightens considerably.

True administrative support is evident when administrators choose to go to the trainings. So while verbal approval of training is necessary, participation is a real vote of confidence. You may choose to provide training for administrators first to gain their cooperation with later trainings. However, many teachers report that it is beneficial to have administrators trained with them so they can feel more like a team.

Tip 2: Find Funding for Training

The level at which faculty and staff can be trained will, of course, depend to some degree on the resources of your school or district. If you are responsible for designing or proposing a budget for your SAP operation, think ahead and include funds for training faculty, core teams, and other staff. Training can cost a lot of money, or it can be an honest bargain. You can sometimes do things for a lot less than you fear.

If you want to propose training and you need additional funds, write a proposal and present it to whoever holds the purse strings. Be sure that you include line items that are being donated so you show that you have done all you can to save a little money. If you can't afford a training in the current year, maybe the training can be worked into the budget for the next year. Many people are needlessly intimidated by coming up with a budget, but the process is simple. Think about what you want for training, and then spend an afternoon making phone calls asking for ballpark figures. Note on your budget that these are approximate costs. See the brief sample proposal and budget on the next pages. The worst they can say is no.

Tip 3: Schedule an Appropriate Time for Training

It is always preferable for training to take place during the school day to underscore the school's commitment to the success of the program. With advance notice, the number of substitute teachers needed can be kept to a minimum, and if the group does not include teachers (primarily guidance people and administrators, for instance), no substitutes at all will be necessary. Schools that have times set aside for faculty meetings and so on may utilize some of that time for training relevant to the SAP. For whole-school workshops, in-service days may be used, or some schools let the students out before lunch so the faculty can meet for an afternoon. Training may take a few hours or a few days, depending on whom you are training and what is to be covered. Training non-core team members about basic SAP functions and how to use a basic behavioral checklist usually takes anywhere from two to three hours to a whole day. Initial core team trainings are far more comprehensive and can take from three to five full days, in the most ideal situations.

Tip 4: Find an Appropriate Site for Training

Your site must be comfortable for the number of people who will be trained. From experience, I advise you to secure the very best accommodations you can, given your resources, because when people are treated respectfully, their willingness to work increases immensely. If your school district has a conference room that will hold the numbers being trained and you can operate without interruption, that can be a workable and extremely cost-effective solution. On the other hand, if there is an affordable conference center, restaurant with a function room, or local college, or church with empty classrooms, the change of scenery can energize your people. Your life becomes easier if there are overhead projectors, chalkboards, easels, and so forth available, but you can take those things to a site if you get a real bargain.

Some hospitals and chemical dependency treatment facilities offer training sites at little or no cost; however, there is often the hope that such hospitality will generate referrals from the school. As long as it is a hope and not a contract, this arrangement can work well. One way to make this sort of arrangement more comfortable is to make sure that you do have respect for the facility and would feel comfortable referring students there anyway. One benefit to holding a training at such a site is that it gives school personnel, who are often unfamiliar with the very idea of treatment, an up-close look at what it is like.

For brief trainings, try comfortable places within your school or district. If your training is going to take place after school hours, libraries often have room for twenty people or so, and it is a change of pace to be out of the classroom setting. Also, you might try a lunch-time training, at which school people "brown bag" their lunch, or a drop-in training day, when anyone who has a "prep" period can drop in to get a brief half hour or so of training on some specific topic.

Sample Proposal for Training, with Budget
CENTRAL HIGH SCHOOL STUDENT ASSISTANCE PROGRAM CORE
TEAM INITIAL TRAINING
November 13-15, Any Year

Purpose: This training is designed to educate the core team in issues relevant to the operation of the new student assistance program. The core team functions to create and/or guide the policies and practices of the student assistance program and must therefore have a current understanding of alcohol and other drug use and additional issues that young people face.

This group of individuals has volunteered to serve in this capacity and has met several times to discuss this proposed training. Please see attached training schedule.

Participants:

(List participants by name and title)

_____, Principal

_____, Assistant Principal

_____, SAP Director

_____, SAP Intern

_____, Guidance Counselor

_____, Guidance Counselor

_____, School Nurse*

_____, Classroom Teacher**

_____, Classroom Teacher**

_____, Classroom Teacher**

_____, Specialist

*Health Department will provide substitute coverage
**Need substitute teachers for dates listed

Budget for Proposed Core Team Training, November 13-15
Eleven Participants

Substitute Teachers
    $_____ per day × 3 days × 4   _____
Rent for Conference Center
    $_____ per day × 3 days   _____
Speaker Fees
   Three volunteers, two at $_____ a piece   _____
Snack food for participants   Donated
Lunch for participants   on own
Training materials
   Folders, newsprint, overhead transparencies   _____
Total: $_____

Tip 5: Find Terrific Presenters

If you have little or no funding, rely on in-school experts and volunteers from the community to present to core team and faculty trainings. Call around to hospitals and chemical dependency treatment facilities, almost all of whom now have public relations and marketing departments, and try to get some of the basic alcohol and other drug information from them. Ask agency counselors to present on their areas of expertise, emphasizing that this will help the core team get to know them and their area of expertise for referral purposes.

Your SAP coordinator may be a good presenter, in which case you can rely heavily on him or her to share expertise. However, in longer trainings, make sure you break up the training by having different people speak. Also, for some reason, people tend to believe "outside" experts more than they believe "inside" experts. Arrangements with other SAP people can be beneficial: You volunteer to run one part of their training, and they volunteer to run one part of yours. This helps break things up while keeping costs to a minimum.

Tip 6: Make the Training Special

Spend small amounts of money to make the training feel very special instead of spending huge amounts of money on a one-time celebrity speaker. Things like T-shirts or baseball hats with the core team's nickname go a long way in making people feel appreciated for giving their time. Some businesses can even be persuaded to donate such things.

Try ahead of time to secure approval for staff development hours for people who participate in trainings, and if forms or signatures are necessary, have those things ready for people to fill out when they get there. Your attention to participants' needs will be appreciated.

In general, try to treat people at trainings as well as you can given your circumstances. Small things can make a big difference: pitchers of water and glasses on tables, nametags, simple food at breaks, taking the doughnuts out of the box and putting them on a plate. The get-to-know-you exercises and energizers during trainings may seem like the easiest thing to cut from the schedule, but they are the flavoring to a potentially bland day. Treat trainings as special days; treat the people there as special people who are willingly there to help do an important job. People will remember the effort you put in to make the days memorable, and they will respond with positive effort of their own.

PLANNING WHOLE-SCHOOL WORKSHOPS

Whole-school workshops designed to explain the purpose and scope of an SAP are tremendous logistical undertakings, but they can be the push that you need to gain momentum when a program is new or just gaining recognition. Such whole-school workshops usually take place during days that are set aside for workshops by the district or town. You may need to propose such a workshop the year before it is to happen. One format calls for the entire faculty and staff to listen to a series of large workshops (this can get tedious but is easier to plan). More complicated, but usually more successful, is having a large keynote address followed by smaller concurrent workshops for the remainder of the day. These whole-school trainings are best arranged after a core team has already been trained and you can count on them for enthusiasm and assistance.

The same kinds of workshops can be offered to the whole school during concurrent workshops, but schedule to insure that everyone has a basic training on the student assistance program and what it hopes to accomplish. Also, make sure everyone hears how to use the referral procedure and about the confidentiality issues. A sample "Whole-School Workshop Schedule" is provided on the following page.

Occasionally, an ambitious district will plan a district-wide training. My district recently completed a "Wellness Training" for 1,200 school department employees. Alcohol and other drug prevention, education, intervention, as well as student assistance programming, were highlighted topics. This tremendous undertaking was a complete success. (It took months to plan.)

OFFERING ADDITIONAL TRAINING

There will be people among your ranks who will be inspired by your training and your efforts and who will want to hear more. There will also be others who weren't so inspired but need to fulfill their staff development hours, so if you offer something convenient and painless, they'll take you up on it. One of the easiest ways to offer additional training is to hold a simple afterschool workshop series. These can take place in the school library or a comfortable classroom. You can often find people who are willing to volunteer to present for an hour at a time. Also, since this is additional training, you can offer workshops about more peripheral issues that smaller groups of people may be interested in. Topics like adult codependency, eating disorders, and process addictions (gambling, spending, etc.) tend to do well with an adult audience.

You can hit several points at once by offering such additional training to the community at large. While you may not get wide community participation, your advertising effort serves as a public relations effort. Parents and community people may be interested in attending such trainings. As for cost, if you do the trainings yourself or can get your speakers to volunteer, you may be able to offer the training for the cost of the refreshments.

ONE-ON-ONE TRAINING

While SAP personnel do not have the time to train many people one-on-one about the basics of SAP operation, when you must, you can be encouraged by the ripple effect. Sometimes, a half hour well spent with an individual faculty member who has initially been resistant or reluctant can result in a number of referrals, especially if the faculty member is well connected to others in his or her department.

Some faculty members will need to "check you out" one-on-one to see whether they trust you (as a person or as a team) before they will refer a student. Remember that most teachers who refer students truly care about the students

SAMPLE WHOLE-SCHOOL WORKSHOP SCHEDULE

7:30–8:00   Coffee, tea, fruit, and goodies in the cafeteria

8:00–8:15   **Introductions to Workshop Day**
- Principal or SAP coordinator

8:15–9:00   **Keynote Address**
- Principal or SAP coordinator or speaker

9:00–10:00   **Student Assistance Programs: How They Work**
- SAP coordinator or outside expert

10:00–10:30   Break (snacks in the cafeteria)

10:30–12:00   **Concurrent Workshops***

12:00–1:00   Lunch (on your own)

1:00–2:30   **Concurrent Workshops***

*Attend one workshop each session

Concurrent Workshops

I (Room 423)   **Identifying High-Risk Students in the Classroom**
- Alcohol and other drug professional

II (Room 502)   **Chemical Dependency in Adolescence**
- Alcohol and other drug professional

III (Room 611-A)   **Children of Addiction**
- Alcohol and other drug professional

IV (Room B-13)   **How to Identify and Change Enabling Behaviors**
- Alcohol and other drug professional

and want to reassure themselves that what they are doing is the right thing. They may need to sit in your office, talk for a while, go over exactly what will happen if they refer, and get a sense of you before they are comfortable making the referral. While you may be frustrated going over what you feel you've been over three times before in memos and faculty meetings and workshops, these individual sessions may be the "convincer" for the teachers sitting across from you.

7

Reaching High-Risk Students

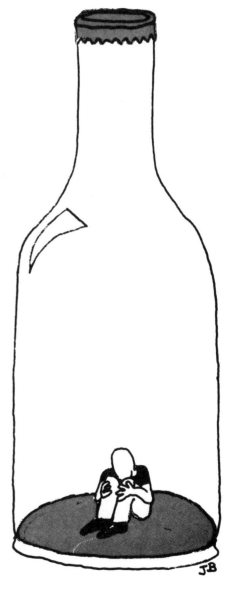

CHAPTER 7

Reaching High-Risk Students

WHO IS A HIGH-RISK STUDENT?

Motorcycle racing without a helmet is a higher-risk activity than taking a drive in the country in a sturdy car, but, unfortunately, it doesn't mean you can't get into an accident in the sturdy car, no matter how carefully you've prepared. We in education are conditioned to think of high-risk students as those who are failing academic subjects, who come from poverty, who have dropped out of school, or who are involved in the disciplinary systems of our schools. These students are figuratively careening through our hallways without helmets, tragedies waiting to happen. And, obviously, these students are at tremendous risk for being in trouble already and for developing problems down the road. They are the ones who are wearing their risk where we can see it and respond to it. It would be a big enough job for SAPs if these were the only students in need of attention.

Unfortunately, there are a lot of other students we hadn't previously considered high risk because we couldn't detect their pain and distress as easily through empirical data like grades, attendance, and so forth. With the prevalence of addiction and the variety of people it affects, students we didn't previously label high risk may be at very high risk indeed. Our basic task as educators has broadened to include identifying students who are at high risk of developing difficulties associated with alcohol or other drug use to get them services.

The National Drug-Free Schools program lists the following criteria to define who is at risk of becoming an alcohol or other drug abuser (under age twenty-one).

- Children who are at risk for dropping out of school
- Children who experience school failure
- Pregnant students
- Children of an alcoholic or drug abuser
- Children who are economically disadvantaged
- Children who have been physically, sexually, or psychologically abused
- Children who have committed a violent or delinquent act
- Children who have mental disorders
- Children who experience long-term physical pain
- Children in state detention facilities

This list is fairly comprehensive, and a lot of students will fall into these parameters. Clearly, students experiencing the aforementioned troubles are statistically at risk for experiencing more trouble in the future. But, even our students who aren't "officially" at risk may be dabbling in behavior which is very dangerous indeed. Without diminishing the seriousness of the students who are officially at risk, questions must be asked about those who aren't: How far is the sexually active teen from the pregnant teen? How close are children of problem drinkers to children of alcoholics in terms of their risk? When reports indicate that childhood and adolescent depression and suicide are on the rise, how far are the depressed yet silent, undiagnosed students from those with established psychiatric diagnoses? If you work in an economically depressed area, for instance, the whole student population is statistically at risk for developing problems with alcohol and other drugs.

Adolescent culture nationwide is streetwise; it accepts the overuse of alcohol and other drugs and other problem behavior. It's just a part of their lives. It's not considered too cool to drink and drive in some communities, perhaps, but it's perfectly okay to turn your car keys over to someone (maybe even a parent) and get completely sloshed. In some areas, other drugs are "out" but alcohol is definitely "in," and kids are running into serious problems, including dependency at an early age. In some urban areas, murder is the leading cause of death for young men aged sixteen to twenty-one. And unfortunately, even students who have none of the "high-risk" strikes against them can still head off to a party, drink ten or twelve beers, and die in a car accident, a diving or boating accident, or simple alcohol poisoning. While these statistics might frighten or depress you, do not let them paralyze you. There is a lot that can be done.

How a Student Assistance Program Helps Students in Trouble

School-based programming cannot solve these huge problems alone, but it can help in the effort, and it must. Because we, as educators, have daily contact with those students we can keep in school, we must monitor their behavior to screen for potential problems. Under all that bravado, and leather or gold or hairspray or denim, lurk the spirits of children, and while we have to respect their sophistication, we also need to keep them safe. Keeping them safe means watching them closely and responding to the signals they send us, even if they deny they are sending us any. (That is the very nature of adolescence.) This is how referral-based student assistance programming has developed, by utilizing the observation powers of well-trained and dedicated teaching personnel. Add to that an SAP team, or staff trained in the issues of adolescent alcohol and other drug use and surrounding family issues, and you have a tighter net with which to save, not trap, students who are in trouble.

Referrals to SAPs are based on directly observable behavioral changes that a concerned person notices. Some of these students who are referred to the SAP will turn out to be drug users, some will be the children of alcoholics or addicts, and some may have school adjustment problems. The referrals are not based on a diagnosis of the underlying problem, only on the fact that problem behavior exists. Regardless of your SAP's structure, the process of eliciting referrals is essentially the same.

BUILDING A REFERRAL SYSTEM THAT WORKS

Three kinds of referrals are usually generated in a student assistance program: students refer themselves for help, others refer students out of concern, and some students are referred as a result of violating the school's chemical use policy. In the case of concern referrals, which can be provided by teachers, staff, peers, or parents, the troubling behavioral changes that are reported do not necessarily indicate chemical dependency or depression, for instance, but do indicate the possibility that the students referred are experiencing personal problems. The referral source's primary job in this process is to record and report behavior, and it is the job of the SAP to get to the bottom of the trouble.

The more communication the SAP has with the other sources that serve students, the better it can reach the students who need assistance. Student assistance programs are part of the tremendous effort schools and communities are making to insure that students don't get lost in the shuffle.

Identifying and Overcoming Enabling Behaviors

Teachers are accustomed to watching students' academic progress and reporting it to the guidance staff, but they are not as accustomed to reporting less measurable behavioral changes that they find troubling. An SAP asks teachers both to record those aspects of behavior that they find disturbing and to use their gut reactions about students. Teachers, guidance counselors, and staff may be initially hesitant to follow through with referrals to the SAP. Part of this reluctance stems from the fact that teachers believe that they are "turning kids in" if they report the behavior to the SAP. They would rather "give the kid a break" and say nothing.

"Giving the kid a break" usually prevents the student from getting the attention he or she desperately needs. Trying to "help" students by not talking about it, or letting them off the hook is the result of a set of beliefs and behaviors that constitute "enabling," on which whole volumes have been written recently. Enabling is the process whereby well-intentioned people actually diminish another person's chances of getting help or helping themselves. Though customarily a benevolent notion, in this context it means enabling the person to stay sick and can be tantamount to assisting that person with his or her own demise. A three-page information handout on "Enabling Behaviors" follows; it can be used in core team trainings, teacher workshops, and even student groups. Without a clear understanding of the concept of enabling, many teachers, counselors, and administrators will be reluctant to refer students to the SAP.

For example, imagine that a student (we'll call him Joe) comes to a teacher's class stoned, and a significant portion of the students know he's under the influence (which, by the way, they usually do). When the teacher does nothing, and says nothing, the students think one of several things:

> You mean to tell me Mr. Jones can't tell that Joe is stoned? What is this guy, blind?

> Mr. Jones knows that Joe is stoned, but he doesn't care if people come to his class stoned, as long as they don't act up.

Faculty Information Handout
ENABLING BEHAVIORS

What Is Enabling?

When we talk about alcohol and other drug problems, we often accuse the person in question of "being in denial" and "not wanting to deal with the problem." Unfortunately, this part of chemical dependency is contagious, and people who are involved with a person who has an alcohol or other drug problem tend to take on some of the following behaviors. These behaviors are called "enabling" because they enable the person to stay sick longer. These behaviors are certainly prevalent in school systems. When we in schools quit our enabling behavior, our students have a better chance of getting well.

Denying That a Problem Exists

School Level: Some school personnel deny that there is an alcohol and other drug problem in the school (or district). They simply don't believe it or they think the reports are so grossly exaggerated that it doesn't even warrant their concern. This is easy to do, especially if you avoid students who use and don't listen to what students are saying. School personnel who deny that there's a problem wonder, "What is everyone talking about? *I've never seen a drug deal here.*"

Individual Student Level: This is simply denying that a student uses alcohol or other drugs because we'd rather not believe it than have to deal with it. "John is not drinking. I know it. He's just not the kind of kid who'd drink."

When we deny the existence of problems, we don't have to work on their solutions.

Minimizing the Problem

School Level: In this case, school personnel admit that there may be a problem, but they minimize it in their minds so it's not too important. Then they don't have to deal with it. Minimizing a problem in a school system sounds like this. "OK, sure, there's some drinking and drugging going on here, but our basketball team is ranked second in the state. We must be doing something right." What does one have to do with the other? In this way, we eliminate the urgency of dealing with the alcohol and other drug problem by soothing ourselves with other successes.

Individual Student Level: When we minimize an individual student's use, we diminish the student's chances of getting the help he or she needs. Minimizing use can mean calling the use a "phase" or saying, "Sure, she's had a few beers in her life, but that can't be what's affecting her grade."

When we minimize problems, they seem so insignificant that we can overlook them.

Rationalizing the Problem

School Level: When we rationalize behavior, we try to think up reasons or excuses for it as though that's part of the solution. In school systems, we say, "Increased alcohol and other drug use is a product of the breakdown of the family." While this may or may not be true, it doesn't help solve the problem, but it helps us to feel that we have put some thought into it. We still haven't affected the problem at all.

Individual Student Level: When we rationalize a student's use of alcohol or other drugs, we think we have figured it out. We make excuses for the behavior and say, "He's going through a hard time right now. That's why he's smoking so much pot." Or, "Her parents got a divorce. That's why she's drinking."

When we rationalize a problem, we find excuses for it and therefore don't have to deal with it.

Blaming the Problem on Someone or Something Else

School Level: Blame is just another rationalization, but it is so often used that it deserves special attention. When we blame the problem on someone or something else, we relieve the affected person (or system) of his or her responsibility to do something. In school systems, if we blame parents for their children's alcohol and other drug use, it relieves us of our responsibility to try to address the problem.

Individual Student Level: When we blame someone or something else for a student's alcohol or drug use, we are conspiring in the student's own denial. When we say, "It's his girlfriend's fault because she introduced him to the wrong crowd," we essentially tell our affected student that he has no say in whether he uses—it's up to his girlfriend.

When we blame problems on other people or situations, we don't have to deal with the real problem.

Avoiding Discussion of the Problem

School Level: When we avoid discussion about alcohol and other drug-related problems, we don't have to acknowledge them and we don't have to create policies and practices to deal with them.

Individual Student Level: When we avoid discussion about alcohol or other drug use with individual students, we insure that they won't bring up anything we'd have to deal with. In this way, we are hoping that if we don't talk about it, it won't exist.

Avoiding discussion about alcohol and other drug problems makes us believe that we won't have to deal with them.

All enabling behaviors ultimately guarantee that *we* don't have to deal with the problem.

Enabling for School Personnel Includes the Following:

- Looking the other way when you know that students are using or have used alcohol or other drugs

- Laughing at, or minimizing, students' talk about alcohol and other drugs in the classroom

- Lowering your standards in class for behavior, level of attention, and quality of work

- Allowing students to sleep in class

- Believing that a student is a "lost cause" and therefore not referring him or her to appropriate services (or assuming he or she has already been referred)

- Believing that a student is "above" being involved with alcohol or other drugs

- Wanting to give every student a break, seeing yourself as Mr. or Ms. Niceguy

- Not asking students about their chemical use in counseling sessions

- Thinking that all alcohol and other drug use is attributable to underlying causes

- Trying to handle violations of the school's chemical use policy by yourself

- Being reluctant to confront a student about alcohol or other drug-related issues because you're afraid the student will be "mad at you"

- Being reluctant to report alcohol or other drug-related suspicions because you're afraid you'll push the student "over the edge"

- Trying to make consequences easier for some students

- Correlating alcohol and other drug use to intelligence or morals ("John's too smart, or too good a kid, to use drugs")

- Thinking that some level of adolescent alcohol and other drug use (which you've determined) is acceptable and even amusing

Joe's been stoned every day since the eighth grade, and nobody's done anything. This kid's got a real problem, and no one cares.

Joe's getting away with it. Why not give it a try?

Many teachers do not want to be put in the position of accusing a student of doing something he or she did not do. Teachers may say, "Well, I don't know if Susie is drinking. I'd hate to accuse her." However, in a well-functioning SAP referral system, teachers will not, in fact, be accusing students of anything. When teachers are not sure, they are encouraged to write a referral out of concern. *They will only be taking note of that behavior which is of concern.* In Susie's case, maybe the behavior is that she's sleeping in class, or that her words are slurred, or maybe that she talks openly about her hangovers in morning classes. These are all behaviors that arouse concern for the student, regardless of the reason for them.

Enlisting Your Faculty's Cooperation

While adopting workable referral procedures in consultation with the administration and core team, take care not to alienate teachers and counselors in the process. Unfortunately, there are still territorial issues between different departments in school systems. Teachers and especially counselors may feel that they would like to have more time available to help students themselves and may resent SAP people who are encouraging them to relinquish this part of their job to SAP professionals hired for this purpose. Encourage teachers to build on their existing relationships with students to make a referral to the SAP. Don't encourage teachers or guidance personnel to give up their relationships with students; rather, ask them to stretch them by telling the student about their concerns and asking the student to consider going to the SAP.

Start-up SAPs must work very hard at establishing practices which make it comfortable for teachers to refer students and must disprove the notion that teachers are doing something mean or underhanded to students when they bring the unusual behavior to the SAP's attention. Only an SAP's proven track record of helping students will encourage teachers and other staff members to refer students to the program. Teachers' and counselors' confidence is earned individual by individual, and it would be unusual indeed if SAPs garnered the unanimous support of the faculty right from the start, without any successes to their credit. Some faculty and staff may have fundamental reservations about SAP services in the school and, try as you may, your efforts may not change their minds.

There are others, though, who will applaud the new SAP because they have recognized the need for a long time. In your promotional efforts, you want to underscore that student assistance programming is designed to make the jobs of teachers and guidance counselors easier, not more difficult.

Using Referral Forms and Checklists

Student assistance programs use different methods to encourage teachers, guidance counselors, and staff to record behaviorally based observations, some using exhaustive checklists of problematic behavior for teachers and staff to fill out. Listing all the behaviors in a checklist format reminds teachers to be inclusive and jogs their memory about important information they might have left off a simpler form. Other SAPs find checklists intimidating or cumbersome and choose to use a simple form which asks teachers to describe those behaviors which are of concern to them. Your core team can decide which method will go over best with your faculty. Two very different referral forms are included here.

Always encourage your faculty to look for directly observable behavior to back up their concern. An SAP referral depends solely on directly observable data, and a teacher makes no accusation when he or she reports, "I'm concerned about Ralph because yesterday he left to go to the bathroom, which he does every day at the same time, and I happened to see him in the hallway putting eye drops in his eyes on the way back from the bathroom." On the other hand, it is accusatory to say, "I think Ralph's smoking pot because he's shifty and he looks like the kind of kid who's into drugs anyway." You can assure faculty members that there's absolutely no accusation in the former statement, only concern.

There will always be some faculty members who prefer to make their referrals in person, letting the SAP counselor scribble down some notes during a brief meeting. Take your referrals any way you can get them. You will want to train your faculty to be aware of behaviors which indicate the problems your SAP screens for. Checklists and trainings for teachers should include training to detect problems in the following areas.

EIGHT MAJOR INDICATIONS FOR REFERRALS

1: Problems with Grades

This includes students who are continuously experiencing academic difficulty, or students who are experiencing a sudden downturn in otherwise good grades. If this is the only indication, guidance should be notified first to see if the problem is academic in nature. There are indications, however, when it is not purely an academic matter. For instance, students who do very well on assignments *when* they turn them in, or who report that they can't do their homework because of problems at home, may well be living with addiction, abuse, or neglect. Students who are perfectionists, who become unduly distressed because of a less-than-perfect grade, may be under tremendous pressure from home and may be acting out the "hero" role in alcoholic or addicted families. For students whose grades are a first priority, a change can mean a change in friends or values, or the onset of hopelessness or depression. For students whose grades are a last priority, we have to ask—what else are they taking care of?

2: Problems with Attendance

This includes truancy, tardiness, sporadic attendance, inability to make it to early-morning or late-afternoon classes, and students who come to school but leave soon after. These problems can all be indicative of a chaotic family life where older siblings are required to care for younger ones, even if it means missing school. It can also be indicative that the student is experiencing the various illnesses that are associated with being a child affected by addiction. Studies

STUDENT ASSISTANCE PROGRAM REFERRAL FORM

Person referring: _____ Date _____

Student: _____ HR: _____

Please check one:

☐ I give my permission to show this form to the student.

☐ The student may know that I made this referral but cannot see the form or know its content.

☐ I wish to remain anonymous as the person referring.

Please check the characteristics appropriate to this student. Use the reverse side for any additional information or concerns.

GRADES:
☐ Achieving below potential
☐ Failing class
☐ Attitude affecting work
☐ Always behind in class
☐ Overreacts to less-than-perfect grade

ATTENDANCE:
☐ Frequently absent
☐ Frequently suspended
☐ Frequently tardy
☐ Frequently asks to see the nurse
☐ Cuts classes and/or has been truant from school

BEHAVIOR/SYMPTOMS:
☐ Defiant/requires disciplinary attention
☐ Irresponsible/loses everything
☐ Hyperactivity/nervousness
☐ Cries in class
☐ Argumentative/defensive
☐ Frequently teased or "made object of fun"
☐ Wears drug-related clothing/jewelry
☐ Withdrawn/loner
☐ Change in friends
☐ Frequently/easily upset
☐ Older social group
☐ Inappropriately displays affection

☐ Personality/emotional changes
☐ Sleeps in class
☐ Lethargic/blank stares
☐ Frequently asks to leave room
☐ Police/court involvement
☐ Frequently exchanges money with others
☐ Poor hygiene/signs of neglect
☐ Sudden change in weight or appearance
☐ Smells of alcohol and/or other drugs
☐ Bloodshot eyes/wears sunglasses indoors
☐ Makes inappropriate comments/jokes
☐ Denies problems despite evidence/lies

STUDENT ASSISTANCE PROGRAM REFERRAL FORM, *continued*

SPECIFIC CONCERNS:

☐ Talks about home problems
☐ Has run away
☐ Talks freely about alcohol and/or other drug use
☐ Other students talk about this student's abuse of alcohol and other drugs
☐ Student talks constantly of parties
☐ Student lives with someone who is chronically/terminally ill
☐ Friend or relative has died
☐ Student has been raped*
☐ Student has been abused**

☐ Student has difficulty making friends
☐ Student or student's girlfriend is pregnant
☐ Student is a teen parent
☐ Student talks about hurting him/herself**
☐ Student talks about hurting others**
☐ Contacted by concerned person about student: _____
☐ Current/past hospitalization for drug or emotional problems
☐ Alcohol or other drug problem in the family

*All cases of child abuse must be reported to the Division of Children and Youth Services (D.C.Y.S.).
**Cases involving suicide, threat of harm to others, or sexual assault must be reported to the parent and in some cases D.C.Y.S. or the police.

If a faculty member suspects that a student is impaired in school, this needs to be reported to an administrator.

PLEASE RETURN THIS FORM TO _____. This sheet will not be placed in the student's office folder.

Form used with permission of Mary-Jo Bourque, Memorial High School, Manchester, New Hampshire.

Student Assistance Program
REFERRAL FOR SERVICES

Name of student _____ Grade ___ HR ___ Date _____

Referring faculty member's name _____

May I use your name when telling the student that someone is concerned? Yes ___ No ___

Please describe in as much detail as you can the behaviors that concern you:

_____

_____

_____

_____

_____

_____

_____

What is your relationship to this student?

_____

_____

Have you made this student aware of your concerns?

_____

_____

Additional comments (anything that would be helpful for the SAP to know):

_____

_____

_____

_____

show that children of addiction complain of far more physical ailments than other children.

Very spotty attendance can also indicate that the child is completely out of control—that the parents no longer even attempt to keep track of him or her. This sort of neglect usually indicates a lengthy history of problems in the family. The parents may be simply exhausted, or they may need help in understanding their responsibilities to the child.

3: Disruptive Behavior in Class

This includes sleeping in class, disciplinary problems, fighting, cheating, dramatic attention getting, acting out, crying, sullenness, negativity, paranoia, and being the class clown to the point that the student's antics distract the rest of the class. All these behaviors can be indicative of budding chemical dependency or can be the characteristic screens under which children of addiction hide their pain, or they can be indicative of learning disabilities. Clearly, some of these behaviors must be dealt with using the traditional disciplinary system, because teachers cannot set a standard of allowing negative behaviors to go unchecked. To do so invites mayhem. Where disruptive behavior in the classroom is evident, encourage teachers to make multiple referrals—to the administrator in charge of discipline, the guidance department, and the SAP team or counselor. When students are responded to this way, their attention needs can be met more appropriately.

4: Involvement with the Disciplinary System of the School

This includes students who are found over and over again in internal and external suspension, detention, and the specific disciplinary consequences of your school or district. Administrators in charge of discipline can be great referral sources to the SAP. Students can be acting out their pain in very inappropriate ways, which lands them in trouble again and again. For some, the missed class time resulting from disciplinary action puts them even more behind and provides the final incentive for dropping out altogether. Especially for students who are disadvantaged because of addiction or other serious dysfunction in their homes, a timely referral to the SAP can sometimes turn the tide.

From experience working with recovering students, I can also say on good authority that some students "use" the disciplinary system because it is the path of least resistance, especially if a student is stoned, nursing a hangover, tripping on LSD, or coming off a high. It is easier to mouth off to a teacher first period and spend the rest of the day in suspension than it is to face every class and every teacher all day long. For the student who is experiencing the despair of chemical dependency, it seems an easier choice. So, if you carefully comb the disciplinary system of your school, you are likely to find students who are in trouble with more than just the principal.

5: Legal Problems

This includes possession of alcohol or other drugs, vandalism, DWI, involvement with the police for assault, breaking and entering charges, student being subject to a restraining order or issuing one, and involvement in school violence. (Minors' police records are protected by confidentiality laws—so be careful with this information if you happen to come across it.) Teachers are most likely to come across information that one of their students has been involved in legal problems through the student, parents, or other students talking about the situation. Rarely do police make contact with schools because of the complicated confidentiality concerns. (However, students can sign releases of information through the police department and police can make contact with the SAP. This might be an alliance you want to foster.)

Any kind of legal problem indicates that the student is experiencing difficulty of some kind. When police are summoned to a student's home, it is often because of violence. Many students become involved with the police because they are runaways. My personal experience has been that, frequently, runaways are either chemically dependent and therefore can't put up with the rules of the house, they are being physically or sexually abused, or they are children of addiction, fed up and scared. All these situations merit a referral to the SAP. Clearly, possession charges and DWI are good enough reasons for a referral to the SAP.

Legal difficulties that are not school related may be tricky in terms of the school's authority to intervene. Some may argue that legal difficulties which have nothing to do with school should not be followed up by a school-based program. However, a very good case can also be made that legal troubles indicate high-risk status for a particular student, and that such behavior should be followed up. Your core team must determine how cases outside of school will be handled when drafting your chemical use policy.

6: Problems with Extracurricular Activities

This includes sudden lack of interest in an extracurricular activity or loss of privileges because of unacceptable behavior. In particular, pay attention to good and promising athletes, musicians, writers, and so forth who give up these demanding activities completely. It can mean that practice time is cutting into party time.

Extracurricular activities are the little families that emerge out of school communities in which students identify themselves socially. When a student begins to withdraw from his or her chosen school "family," we should take the same notice that a real family would. Of course, there are good reasons why students sometimes drop out of activities; for instance, they may be overcommitted, or get a job, etc. But often, students who are beginning to get into trouble reject their old ways for new ones. On the other hand, children of addiction are often needed at home to care for younger siblings or to take care of the addicted parent, and they are forced to give up extracurricular activities. Encourage teachers, coaches, and advisors to try to catch up with kids who have dropped out of extracurricular activities, to get a feel for what is going on.

7: Problems at Home

This includes a student living away from home, or a student fired from a job, or any other situation at home that could be affecting a student's ability to perform at school. A teacher's knowledge of any of this or about parental alcoholism or addiction, or a chaotic or abusive family life, is also good reason to refer to the

SAP. It is interesting to note that most of the other "signal" behaviors, at the source, may indicate problems at home. Often, a student who has problems at home may also display one or all of the other indications for referral to the SAP.

When an adolescent moves out of his or her house or goes to live with a relative or friends, the situation is rarely a good one. (Although it is occasionally a healthy, well-thought-out response to irreconcilable differences.) However, these situations often indicate real family dysfunction, including the biggies: alcoholism, addiction, abuse, and neglect. Also pay attention to students who move out of their houses on the very day they turn eighteen. Even though most of these eighteen-year-olds are seniors, there is still time to intervene so they can get some of the self-help they need and deserve.

8: Alcohol or Drug-Specific Behavior or Indications

This is where there seems to be the most confusion about referrals to SAPs. Teachers, counselors, and administrators who catch students in the act of using alcohol or other drugs or being under the influence need to make immediate referrals to the *administration* so students receive both a disciplinary consequence and automatic referral to the SAP, with their parents' knowledge (because it is a disciplinary referral). Entreat your faculty to remember that they are not the ones getting the students in trouble. The students are getting in trouble because of their alcohol or other drug use.

Students who are caught using or having used alcohol or other drugs should receive both a disciplinary consequence and participation in the SAP. One without the other doesn't do much good. Discipline is needed so students get the message that it's not okay to use at school. Participation in an SAP is needed so students get the message that we think their use at school or school-related functions is indicative of a problem.

Student assistance programs underscore that it is not acceptable for students to be at school under the influence of alcohol or other drugs, and we're not going to make a dent in student use until we begin to address that subject explicitly. When teachers strongly suspect that a student has been using alcohol or other drugs, and are currently under the influence, they need to respond to that, and call an administrator. The discipline half needs to be handled right there and then. Otherwise, enabling is going on.

On the other hand, teachers who notice unsettling behavior changes, have gut feelings that something is wrong, or who are made aware of alcohol and other drug use by students (without catching them) should make referrals to the SAP out of concern. These referrals are made in the spirit of concern, not accusation, and in some SAP structures students are not even required to respond to an SAP referral made out of concern. So, a student who is overheard in homeroom reporting to her friends that she can't remember getting home from a party on Saturday night merits a concern referral to the SAP. A student who is currently under the influence in homeroom merits a disciplinary referral to the school administration. As part of the consequence for violating the school's chemical use policy, she will be involved with the SAP as well as spending a day or two in internal suspension.

The aforementioned behaviors do not necessarily indicate that a student is seriously involved with alcohol or other drugs, but the behaviors do indicate that something is amiss in the student's life. In the beginning of SAP operation, referral procedures must be explained over and over again. Teachers will have questions and fears that must be answered by an unflappable and very patient SAP staff. Three information handouts for faculty follow.

HELPING TEACHERS MAKE APPROPRIATE REFERRALS

Most teachers will want to make nonanonymous referrals because the straightforwardness helps to build an honest atmosphere. One guidance counselor I work with has developed such a good and honest relationship with his students that he fills out the SAP checklist for referral in consultation with the student in question, asking the student which things he ought to check off. After the student has approved the completed checklist and added any appropriate additional comments, the two of them together deliver the referral to the SAP. You can bet that his referrals seek SAP participation in greater proportion than anonymous referrals, because they have already had a part in the process and there's no mystery and less anxiety. They are not as likely to feel that the SAP has been imposed on them. Also, they have not been accused of anything. Work toward an atmosphere in which all referral sources can feel as free to share the concern they feel with their students.

As much as possible, encourage teachers to leave their names with concern referrals, especially when their cause for concern is based purely on observation, because it makes the SAP's initial session with the referred student so much easier. When a student is referred anonymously, the potential is there for the student to spend most of the first session trying to figure out who referred him or her. There is also some question as to whether the name of the referring teacher should appear on the referral form, in case you ever have to relinquish records. If you are concerned about this, have the referring person's name on a tear-off section of the referral form and simply record the name in your personal notes.

There are bound to be some cases, however, when a teacher will not want to leave his or her name at all, and an SAP should allow for that in the planning. It helps those teachers who genuinely want to contribute to the SAP effort, but simply don't feel able to jump in with both feet yet.

Handling Anonymous Referrals

When teachers leave anonymous referrals concerning a particular student, I usually approach the student in this way: After introducing myself, reassuring the student that he or she isn't in any trouble with me, and going over the rules of the program, I usually start with this short speech:

> The way you got here to my office is that someone, probably one of your teachers, was concerned about some of your behavior in class. This person could have made a mistake, but you tell me. Is there any reason you can think of why someone might be concerned about you and would want you to come in to see someone like me here in the student assistance program?

Even with this pretty lame introduction, it is surprising how often students respond without hesitation, "Yeah, I'm sorta into drugs, and everybody knows it,

Faculty Information Handout
INDICATIONS FOR REFERRAL TO THE SAP

There are a great number of behaviors which indicate that a referral to the SAP might be helpful. Here are eight of the most basic, but feel free to refer students who display other, troubling behavior which is not listed here.

Grades: Pay attention to sudden changes in grades for students who have done well previously. Their sudden lack of interest in academic subjects may signal trouble. Also watch for students who give you clues like, "I can't get work done at home, everyone's always yelling." They may be asking you to get them some assistance. Sometimes, students who are overly concerned about getting good grades are under tremendous pressure.

Attendance: Students with attendance or tardiness problems may be experiencing real difficulties at home. Pay special attention to students who can't make it to early-morning classes, or who always cut the classes after lunch.

Disruptive Behavior in Your Classroom: Think of the two or three students who cause the most trouble in your classroom, and jot down a quick referral to the SAP. Often, students who play the class clown, who are disruptive, or who command all of your attention are masking real emotional pain. Make referrals both to the appropriate disciplinarians and to the SAP.

Involvement with the Disciplinary System: Students who keep getting in trouble may, in fact, be troubled. If you have repeatedly thrown a student out of class, and it doesn't seem to be getting you anywhere, try a referral to the SAP as well.

Legal Problems: If a student tells you that he can't make your test on Tuesday because he has to go to court for his assault case, you may choose to make a referral to the SAP. Many legal difficulties begin or are exacerbated by alcohol and other drug use. Angry students who are troubled often work out their anger by rebelling.

Problems with Extracurricular Activities: If you are an advisor and have watched a student's interest and participation dwindle, consider making a referral to the SAP. Such declining interest may signal trouble.

Problems at Home: If you know that a student is dealing with a difficult situation at home, make a referral to the SAP. Often, there are other students who are dealing with the same issues, and your student can be reassured by speaking with them.

Alcohol or Other Drug-Specific Behaviors or Indications: If a student talks freely about his or her alcohol or other drug use, or you overhear that student telling friends about how messed up he or she got on Friday, make a referral to the SAP. The student may be giving you that information in the hopes that you'll respond.

Faculty Information Handout
WHERE ARE THE CHILDREN AFFECTED BY ADDICTION?

Children who live with or are affected by someone else's addiction are sometimes difficult to identify in the school setting. However, some of them may be right in front of you, in places you may not have thought about. The following are places where children affected by addiction may spend their time:

- The school nurse's office. Children affected by addiction report more physical complaints than other children and may be frequent visitors to the school nurse.

- In the guidance counselor's office. Some children affected by addiction constantly seek help for academic or school adjustment problems without letting the counselor know about the drinking or drugging going on at home. This is their way of asking for help without letting the "secret" out.

- In the band, sports teams, drama club, newspaper office, language club . . . any extracurricular activity that gives them a legitimate reason to get away from home. Pay special attention to students who are extremely overextended.

- Working long hours after school. In some homes where there is alcoholism or addiction, the children are depended on for income. In others, the teenagers are simply "on their own," expected to earn their keep, stay out of the way, and help care for the younger children.

- Staying with other people. Often, children who are affected by addiction will move out to stay with relatives or friends. Even though the student has left the situation, he or she may need help dealing with his or her feelings.

- Involved in the disciplinary system of the school. Chaotic home lives may make it difficult for some students to navigate school rules successfully. Truancy, skipping classes, and acting out may land these students in trouble.

- In honors classes, winning awards, or playing on varsity teams. Many children affected by addiction are overachievers, hoping to gain much-needed recognition for their efforts.

- The streets. Some children affected by addiction drop out of school. Keeping up in academic classes is sometimes too much to think about when there's a family member suffering from addiction.

Faculty Information Handout
USERS' TECHNIQUES TO AVOID BEING IDENTIFIED

Students who are very invested in protecting their alcohol and other drug use utilize some very interesting strategies to avoid being detected.

- Be ingratiating: Get on the good side of teachers and "butter them up."
- Stake your bets: Never use in school, but use heavily after school and on the weekends.
- Stay stoned: Some kids are under the influence so much of the time that adults are accustomed to their lethargic and detached manner and consider it part of the student's personality.
- Act dumb: When students can't keep up with school work because of alcohol and other drug use, they act dumb to get help from teachers. If they do this long enough, they will eventually get transferred into less demanding classes.
- Lie low: A good ploy is to never ask questions, never act out, never come to the attention of adults in any way.
- Have an arsenal of explanations: Excuses for drug-induced symptoms can range from "I'm just tired" to "I'm having problems with my new contact lenses."
- Be a fast talker: Some kids are really good at thinking on their feet. They can come up with believable stories for teachers, coaches, administrators, etc.
- Find a weakness in the system: Many students go to the nurse's office to sleep off the effects of drugs.
- Take advantage of department isolation: Students recognize that teachers from different departments can't communicate often, and they use this information to advantage.
- Forge passes.
- Be compliant. Sometimes doing everything agreeably wards off confrontation.
- Lie and tell half truths: Outright deception still works well.
- Write your own excuses: Older students get away with writing their own notes for absences.
- Elicit sympathy: Some students rely on teachers' sympathies to insure that no one holds them accountable for their behavior.

Adapted from *One Step Ahead,* by Joseph A. Muldoon and James F. Crowley, © 1986 by Community Intervention, Inc.; used by permission.

even most of my teachers" or "I guess so; last week my stepfather beat me up and I came into school crying. Probably my math teacher noticed. She's really nice and she notices things like that." Some students respond that they have no idea why they would have been referred, and then the SAP person and the student can collaborate on solving the mystery at hand. Usually, the student volunteers a number of difficulties he or she is having in trying to figure out who could be at the root of the referral. "Um, let me see . . . I'm getting a D in biology. Could that be it? Or, there was the fight in the courtyard last week. I didn't start it, but I wasn't going to back down."

Every once in a while, a student does become hostile about an anonymous referral, thinking that he or she has been "ratted on" (which of course isn't the case, because in concern referrals, the student isn't in any trouble). Leaving room for exceptions, hostility is usually an indication that there is something going on for this student. Students who "protest too much" are probably keeping something from other people, maybe even from themselves. It is worth trying to soothe the squashed egos of these students long enough to gain their trust. I have found that one way to do this is to tell them (without sounding patronizing) that it looks as if there really isn't a whole lot to be concerned about and whoever made the referral was just overreacting. Then engage them in a conversation about something—anything else—and let them go. Next time you get a referral on that kid, it may not be anonymous and you will have an established rapport. Of course, if the referral indicates serious trouble—suicidality, for instance—you can't let the student go as a way of "winning him or her over."

Survival Tip: When you know who left an "anonymous" referral, don't tell students that you know. Then the SAP becomes the bad guy, withholding information. Just pretend that it's a mystery to both of you.

ENCOURAGING FACULTY REFERRALS

Some faculty members will refer students to the program—others will not. It is far better to have a number of enthusiastic referral sources than grudging, mediocre participation all around. Eventually, you will win over some of the more reluctant teachers as they realize that student assistance programming is here to stay and that it can help them do their work more effectively. My experience has been that the teachers and counselors you meet in the lounge or those that are geographically near your office will become your best referral agents because they have the opportunity to build up trust in the SAP personnel individually. Staff members who meet you in the context of core team trainings will also tend to be more supportive than others. This serves as a reminder to all SAP personnel to try to wear an approachable expression as you travel the hallways and eat lunch in the teachers' lounge. Without encouraging probing questions or gossip about students, you want to encourage referrals by becoming approachable to faculty and staff.

On the other hand, you can't spend too much time worrying about whether each and every teacher is invested in your program; you can reevaluate your procedures to insure that they aren't in any way prohibiting teachers from participating. If some still don't refer students, don't lose sleep over it; it detracts your energy from the very important work you do. If you keep up the good work, you will be surprised by some formerly reluctant faculty members who will eventually become star referral sources.

HANDLING ADMINISTRATIVE REFERRALS

If you have a fully functioning chemical use policy, your SAP will doubtless receive administrative referrals of students who are found in violation of the policy. There are questions about requiring students to utilize the SAP as part of a disciplinary consequence, but you can troubleshoot most problems by making sure that parents get to see a copy of the policy once it is drafted. Send it home in the beginning-of-the-year informational packet, through a parent-group publication, or in the next mailing of report cards after it has been drafted or refined. Most parents are happy to see a disciplinary consequence for alcohol and other drug-related violations supplemented by the educational and counseling components that the SAP adds.

The SAP's referral relationship with administration can be much more comprehensive than simply receiving chemical use policy violation referrals, if you are willing to work on this relationship. Often, school administrators are faced with unusual circumstances that could benefit from SAP consultation. Student assistance program personnel may be able to offer technical assistance or an "educated opinion" to administration in dealing with certain cases of pregnancy, school violence, suicidality, school phobia, etc. Administrators in charge of discipline can be great referral sources if they recognize students "in trouble" as "troubled students." Student assistance program services should never replace traditional discipline, but they can supplement it. Perhaps participation in the SAP may head off more involvement with the disciplinary system.

ENCOURAGING SELF-REFERRALS

If you have an easily available, counselor-based student assistance program, and things are working as they should, the numbers of students who refer themselves to the program for assistance will keep pace with the referrals that are sent by others out of concern. This will obviously not be the case if your program primarily performs interventions on chemically dependent students. However, if you do have a counselor-based, broad-brush SAP and students are not approaching the counselor of their own volition, you should take a look at what is preventing them from doing so and make the appropriate adjustments. Use this checklist during a core team training or meeting to generate discussion, troubleshoot potential problems, or to informally evaluate the health of your current SAP operation.

SAP TROUBLESHOOTING CHECKLIST

☐ Has your "marketing campaign" for your SAP been successful? Do students know about the SAP and how to access it?

☐ Do students have to get into trouble before they can have access to SAP counseling? (This can encourage trouble.)

☐ Do students know where the office is, or where team members can be located?

☐ Are your procedures for locating students adequate?

☐ Is your program voluntary or mandatory? Is this a factor for students?

☐ Does your program have a reputation of letting confidential information leak?

☐ Do your students think of the program as only being for "losers"?

☐ Have you inadvertently created an atmosphere of secrecy and shame rather than one of confidence and trust?

☐ Is your program seen as a "narc" operation—students who go to talk about their drug use mysteriously get busted within a few days?

☐ Do students take the program seriously?

☐ Is your SAP counselor able to communicate effectively with adolescents?

If you suspect that any one of the preceding questions exposes a problem in your SAP, take some corrective action. Situations left alone don't change.

Making the Program Available

Students should be able to access the SAP during as large a percentage of school time as possible. Crises in adolescence can come and go in a matter of hours, and sometimes those hours count. Student assistance program people should have mailboxes, telephones, and a place to check for messages every day. Students should know where the SAP office is located and how the counselor can be contacted. While running groups is important, a full-time SAP counselor should never have so many groups scheduled that he or she can't find one class period during the day to spend with a student in crisis.

You will know that your SAP is filling a need when students begin to show up wanting to join groups and wanting to see the SAP counselor without behaviorally based teacher referrals. Still, just because students begin to come on their own doesn't mean that your SAP can stop eliciting referrals from teachers. You must always encourage referrals from teachers and staff because it is the students who *aren't* coming to the office by themselves who may be in the dangerous phases of denial that characterize chemical dependency. And other students just don't know that it's all right to ask for help, though they are just aching for someone to ask them what's the matter.

ENCOURAGING PEER REFERRALS

Students know, better than we adults can ever hope to, the differing shades of tragedy that affect their own generation. If asked, they can tell you which kid in their particular crowd "sorta has a drug problem" and who "really has a drug problem." They know when a friend is being abused, when he is sexually active, when parents leave for the weekend, when a fellow student sells drugs, and which door is left unlocked to the storage rooms in the gym. Somehow, we adults are left in the dust in this regard, and we have to depend on the kindness of these young people to fill us in. That is why it is essential that your SAP person(s) is accessible to adolescents and that all your policies and procedures reflect deep respect for the student body you serve.

Peer referral is a central part of a student assistance program, because rarely will students break a friend's confidence unless they have their finger on the pulse of a potential tragedy. Because peer referral is so important, we must make sure students know that they can come talk about a friend who's in trouble. Make this part of your message on posters, pamphlets, and especially in classroom presentations. Present different scenarios in which a referral to the SAP would be appropriate and when it would be absolutely necessary. Even if your SAP is team based, you'll want to insure that students can contact someone when they know a friend is in serious trouble.

It is common for groups of young people to refer a friend who they feel is "headed into the deep end" to the SAP counselor. This friend might be changing in any number of ways, perhaps becoming involved with a new, older boyfriend or girlfriend, using alcohol or drugs, or talking either vaguely or specifically about suicide. Particularly where suicidality is concerned, peer referrals must be taken seriously, and it is imperative for the SAP person to make contact with the student, the student's parents, and guidance staff without delay. Students will sometimes bring in notes that their friends have written that seem to be saying goodbye, and these situations must be taken seriously as well and handled immediately.

Handling Anonymous Peer Referrals

Students, too, need the option of leaving a referral anonymously. In fact, a good percentage of peer referrals are left anonymously, because in some settings students may still worry about what will happen to them socially if they express concern about the way a friend is drinking or drugging. Sometimes, it is practically impossible to keep a referring student's anonymity if he or she has information that couldn't be obtained elsewhere. Try to convince these students to take the leap of faith and leave their names. Sometimes it even works to have the referring student go and get the other student. When they both arrive back at the office, keep them both for a few minutes, explaining the referral procedure and reassuring them both that it was a good thing that the friend cared enough to make the referral. Try to make them both comfortable with the arrangement, and thank the referring student before sending him or her out so you can talk one on one with the other.

When students can't or won't leave their names, respect that decision. It probably wasn't arrived at easily in the first place. In those cases, you may have to do some research, look at the student's grades and attendance to give yourself some plausible reason for calling the student to the office.

When handling an anonymous peer referral, I often tell the student that it was a teacher who made the referral, because adolescents will ferret out who left the referral if they know it was a peer. Particularly in sensitive referrals involving alcohol or other drugs or physical or sexual abuse, I protect student confidences as much as possible, while encouraging the referring student to tell the friend that he or she was the concerned person who left the referral, but in his or her own time.

ENCOURAGING OUTSIDE REFERRALS

Community referrals to your SAP are great, because it means that the school and the community are beginning to work together, and this is what we're going to need in the years to come. Your core team can decide how it is feasible to network with your community. For example, one way our district has worked with the community is to have some appropriate alcohol or other drug offenses that come through the police department make their way to city SAPs. In one case, a student committed a "minor" alcohol-related offense, and instead of going through the courts, the police department referred this student to the SAP. His "sentence" was to participate in the SAP as the director saw fit for up to twenty hours of direct participation. This particular student eventually went to treatment, and once he'd treated his chemical dependency, he didn't get in any more trouble with the law. In this particular case, it was clear that the SAP could do more to help this student than the fifty-dollar fine the courts would have levied. The goal is to encourage community referrals that seem to benefit the student, the SAP, and the referral source. Student assistance programs have received referrals from Boys' and Girls' Clubs, Scouts, employers, neighbors, outside sports leagues—the list could go on forever.

Handling Agency Referrals

If a student is seeing a counselor on the outside and that therapist recommends that the student join an SAP children of addiction group, for instance, this can be a wonderful arrangement because the student will get support both in and out of school. Participation in an SAP can supplement the treatment of any student who is involved in ongoing care through an agency, hospital, or day-treatment program.

Care must be taken, however, that your SAP doesn't become replacement therapy for students who really need continuous and comprehensive care. Student assistance programs simply cannot be part of a primary treatment team for young people who have ongoing psychiatric diagnoses, and SAPs cannot be expected to take over with the same concentration of resources when insurance runs out, because we are not set up to do a lot of individual work. We can, however, provide support and referral to other agencies. Working relationships with agencies who understand the SAP's mission are a real asset to your program.

Relationships with outside agencies are built essentially by meeting with the people who staff them so you can be sure they understand the services available and the limitations of the program. At the beginning of SAP operation, and on an ongoing basis, try to meet with agency people. Go to their informational open houses. Ask to meet the staff. Ask a staff member to come to the school to describe their services to you. Since these are all promotional efforts, most agencies are more than willing to do it. When meeting with agency people is impossible, try to at least develop a "phone friendship." Call up to ask about the staff—educational background, specialty, and clinical orientation or style. Ask about fee structure, insurance, and usual timeframe for getting an appointment. Be wary of therapists who claim to be expert in everything from children to geriatrics, sexual abuse to alcohol and other drug concerns. Most good therapists have a relatively narrow focus and a wealth of experience in a particular area.

ENCOURAGING PARENTAL REFERRALS

Two kinds of SAP referrals come from parents. The first is when a parent discovers that something is amiss with his or her child, talks with the adolescent, and then refers the student to the SAP with his or her knowledge. Because parents talk to the guidance counselors, the student's guidance counselor is also aware of these referrals, and the student comes to the SAP, perhaps grudgingly, but with a pretty good idea of what has been reported to the SAP. In some cases, the parent brings the student in personally to talk with the SAP person, which indicates good commitment on the part of the parent. It may take a while to "win" these students, but once the SAP has, you have a great chance of guiding them to appropriate services because their parents have been involved from the start, are aware of the difficulties the student is experiencing, and, as evidenced by the referral, are willing to take steps to insure that their child gets help. These are manageable referrals and the kind you want to encourage.

An unmanageable referral occurs when a parent suspects the child of something, especially alcohol or other drug use or sexual involvement, but hasn't confronted the student and wants the SAP to check up on the student and then check back with the parent. They want the whole thing to be on the sly. I won't accept such referrals anonymously, but I will talk to a student whose parents refer him or her, as long as the parents allow me to tell the student who made the referral. This is not designed to discourage parental involvement, but consider how it looks from the viewpoint of the students: Now the SAP is taking calls from our parents and using the counselor to check up on us! Whose side is the SAP on, anyway? Parents usually respond positively to the policy once they understand it.

For the most part, parental referrals are positive and very helpful because there are a lot of students who hold things together pretty carefully at school but really display symptoms of chemical dependency or other problem behavior at home. The mood swings, temperament, new unfamiliar behavior, isolation, etc., plays itself out more clearly in the context of the family than the schoolyard. It is also not unusual for an SAP to get a call from parents who have returned from an emergency room where they have had their child's stomach pumped after the student " . . . who we never dreamed even drank at all . . . " had pounded down twelve or fifteen shots of liquor.

Headway can be made with students from a parental referral once you assure the student that you are not on anyone's side and that you won't be getting back to the parents without the student's knowledge. The same confidentiality regulations apply to parental referrals, although parents will know that the student is involved with the program.

Some Final Words about Reaching High-Risk Students

Intervention in student alcohol and other drug problems begins when students begin to realize that people are noticing their behavior, and they're going to keep on noticing. There's great strength in having school, family, and community simultaneously keeping an eye on a student's behavior.

Connecting students to helping services using a behaviorally based referral system is the basis of student assistance programming. *Behaviorally based* means that you are paying attention to the signals that adolescents send and are responding appropriately with an offer of services. The good news is that if you answer their first behavioral call, some may never need to call any louder.

8

Assessment and Referral

Jim Burke

CHAPTER 8

Assessment and Referral

This chapter provides practical advice on the ongoing, inside workings of a student assistance program—what actually happens in the office once a student arrives, from initial individual sessions to referring students to a group, an outside agency, or inpatient treatment.

Obviously, an SAP's basic structure will affect your assessment and referral techniques. For instance, if your program is closely tied with the disciplinary system in your school, you will see a lot of students who come to the SAP initially against their will, and your procedures must accommodate that initial resistance. If your SAP is purely voluntary, you may have the vastly different difficulty of students who are in denial not showing up for appointments. However, there is something in this chapter for every situation, whether your SAP is counselor based or team based, whether you have been in the SAP business for a decade or you are currently implementing one.

If your marketing efforts are successful, sooner than you expect, teachers will begin referring students to the program. And, as those students have a positive experience in the SAP, they will encourage their friends to seek assistance there. The first procedures you need to work out, therefore, are those for individual sessions with newly referred students.

THE NEED TO MOVE QUICKLY

Generally, an SAP's mission is to identify troubled students, assess the presenting difficulty, and refer the student to appropriate services. In the context of a broad-brush SAP, therefore, individual sessions should be designed primarily for assessment purposes. Many SAPs have a limit on how many individual sessions a student can have before he or she makes a move to an outside counselor, treatment facility, guidance counselor, or SAP group. (A reasonable limit is four sessions, but this may vary depending on the SAP staff and the number of students involved in the program.) Obviously, these limits can be bent if need be, but they are there because most comprehensive SAPs simply can't become a school-based clinical practice with a small number of students who are seen individually every week: the need for services is far too great.

The broad-brush SAP's purpose is to build trust with individual students fairly rapidly to get enough information to move to an appropriate referral, all within two to four sessions. This can be frustrating, particularly for SAP people who have come from clinical settings and who are accustomed to smaller caseloads and more individual time spent with each client. Of course, there will always be a few students for whom you stretch the rules just a bit in the hopes that it will make a difference. Perhaps this is the direction SAPs can move toward in the decades to come; however, for now, your procedures must reflect the urgency of the problems at hand.

MAKING NEWLY REFERRED STUDENTS COMFORTABLE

When students are called to the SAP office for the first time, they are understandably nervous. If they did not refer themselves, they are going to suspect that they are in some kind of trouble. Even if your SAP enjoys a relatively benevolent reputation at your school, students are still apprehensive when they come in to see the counselor or core team member for the first time. Many of them have never been to a counseling session. In some cases, their apprehension is appropriate, because you will eventually be presenting them with some of their behaviors which may indicate that there's a problem. This may be a problem that they didn't have any intention of telling anyone about, so they may feel "caught." Student assistance program personnel have the difficult responsibility of making these students comfortable.

In individual appointments, children who live with addiction or abuse, especially, may experience a conflict between desperately wanting to tell you what is going on for them and literally having no idea how to do so. Most students have also never dealt with an SAP counselor or a member of the SAP team in this particular capacity; if you are a teacher of theirs or their coach, for instance, they may not know what they can "safely" tell you. You must guide the way, helping the student understand that this is a different kind of meeting—the student is not getting a "talking-to" by an angry teacher, nor will he or she get the third degree. The appointment with the SAP is in a new category; you are going to be giving the student some options that could make life better for him or her. You may also have to gauge a student's willingness to talk and may have to schedule another one or two appointments before you feel that you have gotten to the real issues.

Unless the student is a mandatory referral, getting help is up to the student. Unlike most things in schools, students really do have the choice whether or not they want this assistance. Making this absolutely clear from the outset is one way that we can show our student clients respect and increase their comfort with the process.

SCHEDULING INDIVIDUAL APPOINTMENTS

If you have a counselor-based SAP or an outside contract with an agency, your SAP person is going to see students individually during the school day for the purposes of assessment. Murphy's law of SAPs is that the number of students who urgently need to be seen will expand to fit the number of hours the SAP person is available, so your SAP person will almost always be busy.

The way you schedule individual appointments will vary from school to school, but continuing care must be taken not to remove students from classes they cannot afford to miss. Besides, it's bad public relations with teachers. On the other hand, a resistant student is much more likely to come to an appointment that is scheduled during class time than one that is scheduled during free time.

One way to manage this dilemma: When you can't get a student during one of his or her free, study, or lunch periods, take the student out of the class of the teacher who referred him or her. That way, when the teacher is making the referral, you can ask right then and there, "If you don't have a test scheduled or something he'll really need to be there for, may I take John out of your class on this Friday, period 6 for his initial appointment?" Then the teacher knows that the referral is being followed up right away and knows whether the student goes to the appointment because the student will be leaving class. (Anytime you can keep teachers informed without breaking a student's confidentiality, you are keeping ahead of the game.)

Depending on how reliable your system and student body are, you may have to schedule more than one student into a time slot to insure that your time is not wasted waiting for an appointment that never shows up. The drawback to this is that sometimes two students arrive at the same time. Because the student population of SAPs is generally very high risk, exhibiting spotty attendance, it is worth your while to explore calling two at a time. If, on occasion, both show up, you may have to ask one of them to wait.

Of course, you'll need the administrative go-ahead to take students out of classes for individual appointments. This may be one of your hardest battles, and it may be one that you continue to fight at various stages of SAP development. A few SAPs operate without any authority whatsoever to take students out of classes, instead scheduling groups in common free periods and after school, but I would not recommend this approach. It reduces the SAP to an extracurricular activity, and it indicates weak administrative support. There can be strict guidelines on how many classes a student can miss, but some allowances must be made for SAP people to do their work during the school day.

Calling Students to the SAP Office

You want a way to contact students individually which is neither intrusive to students nor exhausting for the people who have to orchestrate it. Student assistance program counselors can't go around in person tapping students on the shoulder in homeroom period; it is clearly a breach of their confidentiality, and it puts them on the spot. If your program is broad brush, it wouldn't break their confidentiality legally, but it could backfire as students might feel self-conscious about talking to you where others can see them. However, if you have a team-based SAP, team members who also have other recognizable roles within the school setting can be used to make contact with students and to tell them that they have an SAP appointment scheduled, or to give them an SAP call-slip which gives them the details. Guidance personnel can also be instrumental in directing students to SAP appointments. If the SAP has access to a secretary with a dual role, he or she could perform this job without compromising student privacy.

Student assistance programs have generally tried to work their correspondence with students through the regular operation of the school because it is so cumbersome and time-consuming to do otherwise. For the most part, schools have some way to conduct a headcount everyday, whether that happens in first-period classes or later in the day through a homeroom period. Most school-based SAPs contact the students they need to during this check-in period.

Students can be contacted about individual appointments by sending a slip to the "headcount" teacher, if this is common practice throughout the school. These slips should blend in with all the other slips of paper going out to various students. If, however, these slips are obviously identifiable as coming from the SAP, you may be sacrificing confidentiality because others students will notice who is being called to the SAP. If this happens, you'll have to rethink your procedure. Make sure the slips are either stapled closed or in envelopes.

You can use a call-slip like the one that follows for calling students to the office.

Homeroom _____

Dear _____ :

Please come to the Student Assistance Program office (*include directions to the office*) for an appointment scheduled on _____ (date) _____

Mon Tues Wed Thurs Fri   Period: 1 2 3 4 5 6 7 8

Teachers: This is a pass to the SAP office only. A verification pass will be issued to students when they leave the office.

Some schools use generic call-slips to call students to the main office throughout the day. If this is the case, you can "code" (write them in a different-colored ink or put some discreet symbol on them) these generic slips so a trained main office secretary or administrator can direct the student to the SAP when he or she arrives at the main office. Another solution is to have core team guidance personnel call-slip the students and have them direct students to the SAP. If you use either of these procedures, monitor it closely to make sure that students are being treated respectfully throughout the journey from homeroom period to your office.

Some schools use an intercom system to call students to various offices throughout the day. In intercom systems, SAP referrals are usually called to the main office, where a designated person gives them a slip which directs them to the SAP. This can only work if other students are called to the office regularly for other reasons as well; otherwise, it identifies students as participating in the SAP. If neither of these methods appeals to you or would work within your school setting, brainstorm with your core team new ways to get students to the SAP office discreetly.

BUILDING TRUST WITH ADOLESCENTS

An adolescent you've never met before presents herself at the office door through her own decision or perhaps through a teacher's, friend's, or parent's concern. This student may be angry, defiant, depressed, chemically dependent, sexually abused, working too many hours at an afterschool job, flunking algebra, or some combination of these things. You have essentially one class period to get enough information from a student to begin to discern what the trouble could be. Student assistance program people are dependent on reliable referral sources, good intake techniques, and instinct.

Getting the Rules on the Table

First and foremost, make sure that students are aware of the rules of the program before they so much as open their mouths. If they misunderstand what is to be held in confidence and then, for some reason, you have to break their confidentiality, they will be mighty upset, and they'll tell all their friends that the SAP cannot be trusted. You don't need that kind of publicity, because there may be a student somewhere who was gathering her courage to come tell you about how it is at her house when her mother drinks, and now she's not going to come.

Your rules will vary depending on how your district interprets the laws governing student assistance programs, but whatever the rules and regulations are, they should be posted visibly in your office. Some SAP directors ask students to sign a statement underscoring their understanding of what is to be held in confidence and what needs to be followed up. This is a good step. You can use a sheet like the following to help students understand the program rules, but make sure you alter the sheet to be consistent with the laws of your state and your program's interpretation of the federal regulations. For instance, if parental permission is required, you might briefly describe services available through the SAP and add

---

Welcome to the Student Assistance program at _____.

We're glad you came here.

You should understand the rules of this program before you speak to a counselor. One of the staff will go over these rules with you.

Rule 1: What you tell us is confidential. We don't tell your teachers, your guidance counselors, the principals, the police or your parents what you tell us.

Rule 2: There are exceptions to rule 1. If we believe that you are going to harm yourself or someone else, we will break your confidentiality. If we believe that you are being abused or neglected, we'll contact someone who can help.

Your signature here indicates that you understand these rules:

_____, _____
Student signature   Date

a parent's signature line. Although it may feel contrived or formal to restate the confidentiality rules at every initial meeting, it sets a tone of deep respect for what the students are going to tell you. It also assures students that you aren't going to worry about petty details like whether they like their chemistry teacher or not. That is not the sort of information you are bound to report. Another aspect of respect for the student is to point out that he or she does not have to be there. If the appointment was made on a concern referral (rather than one tied to the disciplinary system), I make it very clear from the start that the student is in my office of his or her own volition and can leave at any time, that he or she is not required to talk to me, but that no one has ever dropped dead as a result either. I have never had a student leave the office after I told him or her that it was his or her choice to go. I take this as proof positive that adolescents need a place to discuss their lives where all the cards are on the table, the rules are on the wall, and they know just what to expect out of the person sitting across from them.

Students respond well to respect. We can't assume that we know what the problem is already, because often we don't. A student may have resigned herself to the fact that her father is alcoholic, but she is now experiencing anguish anew because her favorite older brother is developing chemical dependency. We can't know these things unless we give our students the room to discuss it. Students won't offer that a parent drinks unless you ask—they also won't volunteer that they're feeling suicidal unless you ask. These are questions that must be asked in an atmosphere of trust. Even if your program is very defined, catering only to those who are displaying symptoms of chemical dependency, these questions must be asked. Suicidality and chemical dependency are very closely linked. Your intake procedures must reflect your commitment to facing problems head-on.

Letting the Student See What You Are Doing

When administering an assessment interview of any kind in the context of the SAP, it lessens suspicion to show the student exactly what you are doing, sometimes even moving to a table side by side so you can fill out the questions together. There is no sense in presenting information about a student to that same student in an intimidating, reproachful, or condescending way. You can also collaborate with a student by asking him or her the questions and letting the student record the responses.

STRUCTURING YOUR INTAKE INTERVIEW

The first hour your SAP spends with a student makes or breaks whether that student is going to accept help from the program. You must ask consistent questions in each and every initial interview to screen for potential problems. Some SAPs choose to use standardized interview outlines, while others use specific intake forms for the first meeting. The whole idea is to make sure you ask all the appropriate questions without leaving any out. A basic intake interview and intake form will be structured depending on what you are screening for and who will be administering it. An intake form should flow in the natural direction of an interview you are comfortable giving, and you must allow room for your own notation (sounds easy, but it isn't!). If you use intake forms, be extremely aware of the confidentiality regulations surrounding an SAP's intake form; decide early on how these will be handled. If intake forms contain information that identifies students as alcohol or other drug abusers, the forms will have to be kept completely confidential.

Some programs handle intake questionnaires by having students fill them out themselves prior to an appointment with the SAP counselor. While this approach may expedite the process, it eliminates a good trust-building exercise. A student and counselor working together to complete an intake form can break a lot of ground in building basic trust. However, if you are pressured for time, a good compromise is to split the task; have students fill out a form with all the "easy" information such as name, address, who they live with, etc., and have an additional intake form with the more difficult questions that the counselor asks. It's helpful during an intake to tell students that you're writing only the information they tell you, that you're not making any sweeping diagnoses and scribbling them in the margins. This helps to take some of the mystery out of the process and helps students feel comfortable with the answers they're giving.

Creating a Working Intake Form

A good SAP intake form includes questions about the following aspects of a student's life:

Academic Performance: Ask about grades for the current semester and usual academic performance. A sudden downturn can signal trouble, while consistent difficulty indicates that the student is at higher risk for alcohol or other drug problems. On the other hand, you can't assume that simply because a student has good grades everything is fine.

Problems or Conflicts with Teachers: A student who can't get along with one specific teacher may indeed be experiencing a basic personality clash. On the other hand, a student who can't get along with *any* teacher may be having more serious problems with people in general, which can indicate anything from a learning disability to alcohol and other drug-related difficulties.

Consistent Involvement with Discipline: Adolescents always push the limits of the rules, and one or two detentions probably don't indicate serious trouble. However, students who are in consistent trouble with the disciplinary system of the school may be acting out their pain or rage about a family situation in the schoolyard. Pay close attention to students who turn up in the disciplinary system time and time again.

Social Life at School: Loneliness can make a student want to drop out of school or join an alcohol or other drug-using peer group. A colleague conducted an informal study of dropouts at her high school over five years and concluded that a significant number of students dropped out simply because they didn't have any friends at school. Another thing to watch for is that students who hang out primarily with older students may be more involved with alcohol and other drug use than their own age group. Ask whether students feel fearful in any school situation and whether they like being at school.

Guidance Counselor to Which Student Is Assigned: Make sure you find out who is the guidance counselor assigned to this student and what their relationship is like. You may want to make a referral to the guidance counselor, or you may want to gain permission from the student to pass some information along.

Extracurricular Activities: Diminished interest in activities can signal a change in attitude and may be related to alcohol or other drug use or a variety of other problems. Children who live with active addiction in their homes are often so overextended at home or so worried about what will happen if they aren't at home that they do not participate as fully as other students in extracurricular activities. On the other hand, some "hero" children of addiction will become involved in more extracurricular activities than most students in the attempt to stay out of the house while simultaneously winning much-needed praise. Clearly, problems in extracurricular activities such as getting cut from the team should be looked into.

Free Time: It's important that your intake interview pay as much attention to what goes on outside of school as what happens on the inside. Students reveal a great deal about themselves when they tell you their hobbies and habits. For instance, a student who likes to go four-wheeling or mountain climbing may be adventurous, while a student whose favorite activity is watching television may be very isolated. Pay attention to students who say they don't enjoy anything, students who say their hobby is partying, or kids who seem incredulous that you're asking them about "free time." The answer "*what* free time?" should send up a red flag that this student may be under a tremendous amount of pressure.

Employment: While working a part-time job can provide experience, skills, and self-esteem, it has to be balanced with the business of being a teenager. Working becomes a problem when it becomes impossible for students to perform other necessary developmental tasks and academic assignments. If students are forced to work, it could indicate poverty or sometimes an antagonistic relationship between parents and the student, though not always. In some work situations, students have contact with an older, more independent social group and may therefore have access to alcohol and other drugs.

Previous History of Counseling: Always ask whether a student has been in counseling before and whether he or she is in counseling now. Find out the circumstances surrounding previous counseling. First, a previous history of counseling can tell you a great deal about the family's situation. If the counseling is current, try to find out the name of the agency and the therapist, and if you can, persuade the student to give you the permission to contact the therapist. Students who are being seen for outside counseling generally should not be seen in the SAP except in a group setting, because the primary purpose of the SAP (referral) has already been accomplished and the student has a primary therapist.

Family Situation: Ask about parents' marital/living situation status. Find out where the student resides, and for how long he or she has been there. Try to find out where the student's biological parents are and where the siblings are. Ask whom they live with; do they spend the week at one place and the weekend at the other? These are all very important questions in the assessment process. I usually include these questions in the middle of an intake interview so students get the impression that I'm interested in them first, and their families take second place. However, this is really primary information. Sometimes it is helpful to ask if there's one significant person in the student's life who is not in the immediate family, as you get some interesting and telling responses.

I like to ask students if they like being at their home. Sometimes I ask students to describe what it's like there—is it busy, quiet, loud, chaotic, depressing, etc? "Is it a great place to be, an okay place to be, or do you wish you didn't live there? Do people yell a lot there? Does anyone ever get hit? Have you ever been hit there?" At this point you also want to screen for neglect by asking about the basics: food, heat, clothing, medical care. I also ask them several questions which have proved telling in my experience: whether they ever have people over, whether they have any privacy, whether they feel respected there, and whether they have a place to study.

Personal History of Alcohol and Other Drug Use: It is often difficult for adolescents to be honest with this information, especially since they are giving it to an adult. I usually acknowledge this difficulty and say, "I know this is unusual for you to be telling an adult about your alcohol and other drug use, and it might be hard to be honest, but really try." A good intake interview should include, for each drug (including alcohol and prescription drugs), the following:

- A history of first use (what age and what happened)
- How often used (daily, weekly, monthly)
- The most ever used
- Last use (and how much used that time)
- Usual use (how much of what substance is usually used)
- Experience of blackouts (how many times).

A few other questions to consider are the following: Do the student's parents know about the extent of alcohol or drug use? Is the student comfortable with his or her level of use? Adolescents are looking to you for cues in this process. When asking about alcohol, for instance, if you say, "You've never drank more than a six pack, have you?" they will answer "no, never," because that is the way you stacked the question. So if you are seeking honesty about quantities, aim high. Ask, "How much do you usually drink on a weekend night, a case of beer?" Your answer will likely be, "Oh no, I can't drink a case. I'd say more like nine or ten beers. Once I drank fourteen, but I got really sick." Also remember that many people do not know the proper definition of blackouts, for instance. You may have to change your question to read, "Have you ever forgotten things you did while under the influence and other people had to tell you later?"

Family History of Alcohol or Other Drug Use: For each immediate family member, including all four blood grandparents, take a history of alcohol and other drug use, including prescription drugs. If there are stepparents in the home, include them in the questions. If a student indicates that there is a problem with alcohol or other drugs in a family member, try to gain an understanding of the progression, whether the family member has been to treatment or acknowledges the problem, and other family members' response to the problem. This also helps you assess what role the student plays in the family.

An efficient and helpful way to do a family history of alcohol and other drug use is to use a genogram as part of your intake. A genogram is a symbolic representation of the student's family, and its use is explained in detail later in this chapter.

Sleeping Patterns: Include specific questions about whether the student has trouble sleeping or waking up in the morning. Sometimes, you will not unearth insomniacs, but students who live in chaotic situations. For instance, a student might volunteer, "I can sleep during the week at my Mom's house, but when I'm at my Dad's, they're always yelling." Students who have difficulty getting up in the morning may be experiencing depression, or may be staying up late to hold a job or to use alcohol or other drugs.

Weight and/or Food Issues: Ask if the student is comfortable with his or her weight. Some will clearly indicate that it is not much of a concern. If students indicate it is a concern, ask whether they would like to lose or gain weight. You can then ask specific questions about bingeing, purging, and compulsive overeating. If a student looks very underweight yet reports that he or she is concerned about weight and would like to lose some, you may be dealing with an anorexic or bulimic. Both these conditions are potentially life threatening, and you must get treatment for them immediately.

Physical Health: Ask if the student has any conditions, hospitalizations, operations, or diseases that you should know about. If the student identifies a condition, ask if the school nurse has been alerted to the fact. Often, they haven't. Encourage the student to make contact with the nurse.

Long-Term Goals: Ask the student what he or she plans to do; does the student plan to finish school or leave school early, learn a trade, go into the service, go to college, go into business? You get a good idea whether the student has realistic goals and sense of self.

Feelings: Include specific questions concerning suicide, thoughts about it (called *ideation*), means, plan, opportunity, and previous suicide attempts, to assess a student's risk. Clearly, a student who has expressed a desire to die, who has either the means, a plan, and/or an opportunity is at tremendous risk and must be responded to. Previous attempts put the student at statistically higher risk for a successful one. Any student who is in immediate danger needs to be kept safe with a call to parents and a referral to a therapist, mental health center, or hospital. If you have any questions about your skill in assessing suicide risk, ask for help from a colleague or clinical supervisor. Above all, do not be afraid to address the issue explicitly. Asking a student about plans to harm himself or herself will not "give the student ideas." Those who are suicidal have reached that state before arriving in your office.

Sexual Activity: You include questions about sexual activity to screen for dangerous practices and to refer students for more specialized counseling if they need it. Ask if they have ever been molested, raped, or sexually abused. If they report sexual abuse, you are under obligation to report it through your division of Child Protective Services. You should be aware that a student who reports very early sexual activity may actually be reporting sexual abuse.

A lot of today's teenagers are sexually active. Students who are engaging in unprotected sexual activity can be at risk for pregnancy, AIDS, and other sexually transmitted diseases. If, in the intake process, it becomes clear that a student is making dangerous sexual choices, a referral to the school nurse or an outside clinic may be appropriate.

In all questions dealing with sexuality, use a non-gender-specific word such as *partner* instead of *girlfriend* or *boyfriend* to include those students who are gay or lesbian. Alcoholism and addiction are prevalent in the homosexual population, so pay special attention to questions concerning alcohol and other drug use when doing an intake interview for a student who identifies himself or herself as gay or lesbian.

Anything Else: Include in your intake form an invitation for the student to bring up anything that hasn't already been asked about specifically (for instance, the recent death of a loved one or a friend, bad drug experience, etc.). A colleague of mine asks, "Have you ever experienced anything that changed you, so that from that day forward you were completely different?" or "Is there something in your life you think no one really understands?" Questions like these bring unexpected but relevant information about car accidents and near-drownings, avalanches and psychic experiences.

Gaining Consistency by Using Intake Forms

Giving each student the same intake interview or questionnaire insures that you will have exactly the same information about each student at your fingertips. If you are dealing with a large caseload, as many SAP people are, this is very helpful. Even the best counselors can sometimes forget to ask the right questions, and a well-designed intake form jogs your memory and insures that you ask those important questions every time. A sample intake form is included; note, however, that you may need to change it to accommodate your intake style. During the intake period, it may also prove helpful to the SAP team and/or counselor for students to write down a copy of their homeroom and class schedule to keep with the rest of their material.

There will be times when the intake will not be completed during the first session. It doesn't make a great deal of sense to sit down with a student who is very upset and ask a battery of questions that don't have much to do with the crisis at hand. Often, in crises, students will simply tell the SAP person what is going on that day, and the formal intake will be scheduled for later. There may even be cases where you never get to the formal procedure, but it is best to make it a prerequisite of SAP participation. Otherwise, you run the risk that you could

SAP INTAKE FORM

Name _____ Parents' names _____

Age _____ Grade _____ Address _____

Referred by _____ HR ____ Phone (h) _____ (w) _____

School Functioning

Grades: Disciplinary system:

Social life at school: Guidance:

Extracurricular: Conflicts with teachers:

Physical Health   **Free-time Interests, hobbies**

Long-term Goals   **Legal Troubles**

Employment   **Previous Counseling**
                                         Type:
                                         Duration:
                                         Current:
                                         Therapist:

Living Situation   **Relationship with Parents**

What's it like at your house?

quiet chaotic lonely busy   Is your mom or dad employed? Do they
depressing happy violent   have health insurance?

Feelings

angry ____ sad ____ happy ____ frustrated ____ out of control ____ violent ____

Suicidal:

ideation ____ plan ____ means ____ opportunity ____ previous attempts ____

Drug History

Tobacco: Caffeine:

Alcohol: Marijuana:

Cocaine: Acid:

Other drugs: Drug of choice:

Family History of Drinking and Drug Use

Mother   Father

Brother   Sister

Grandparents   Stepparents

Relationship with Family   **Love Relationship**
                                   Sexual activity:

Sleeping Patterns   **Weight or Food Issues**

Additional Comments

Recommendations for Referral

be seeing a student who is potentially suicidal, but without having solicited that information, you could miss important clues and not be able to intervene when appropriate.

In some strictly defined SAP structures, those students who have no alcohol or other drug-related issues apparent after the intake interview will be referred directly from the SAP counselor to the guidance department for further help. School guidance counselors may be working directly with the SAP as either team members or direct-contact personnel, depending on how your school has designed the program.

GOING FROM INTAKE TO THE NEXT STEP

The intake interview usually indicates what the next step must be. For some students, it is obvious—they need a formal chemical dependency assessment and referral to treatment. For others it will be clear that they could benefit from SAP group support to help them cope with an alcoholic or drug-abusing family member. In all these cases, you are now in the position of convincing these young men or women to take the next courageous step in helping themselves—either moving into an SAP group, a referral to a therapist, an assessment, or perhaps even hospitalization. In other cases, you may suspect that there is more going on than meets the eye, or you may know that the student still has a story to tell, though you don't know what it is yet. In these cases, schedule another individual appointment, try to build more trust, and try to find out more about what is going on.

Assessing Children from Addicted Families

If your intake interviews are properly designed, familial addiction will present itself early on and you can get these students into support groups or at least into some short-term educational group right away. However, some students will hang on to the "secret" for a long time, so assessing a problem in the family with addiction may take perseverance, patience, gentleness, and good interpretive skills on the part of the SAP. One tip: Don't ask students if they live with an alcoholic or addict, because they are loathe to label their loved ones so. I usually ask the questions in this order: "How much does your mom/step mom drink? Have you ever seen her drunk? Can you tell when she's been drinking? How does her personality change when she's been drinking?" The student who reports that he saw his mother drunk once three years ago on New Year's Eve may not be a COA. On the other hand, the student who responds that he's seen his mother drunk "millions" of times is living with a problem, no doubt. Included on the following pages is a tool, the C.A.A.S. (Children Affected by Addiction Screen) that can be used to help screen for familial addiction. Using such a tool can be relieving for some students because the piece of paper makes the decision about whether there's a problem, and then they don't have to.

Assessing for Chemical Dependency or Harmful Involvement

There are a number of very good assessment devices (questionnaire types) available which lend themselves to formal assessments of chemical dependency or

C.A.A.S.: CHILDREN AFFECTED BY ADDICTION SCREEN

Please check (✓) the answer below which best describes your feelings, behavior, and experiences related to a parent's (or a person living with you) alcohol or drug use. Take your time and be as accurate as possible.

YES NO   QUESTIONS

☐ ☐ 1. Have you ever thought that one of your parents had a problem with drinking or with drugs?

☐ ☐ 2. Have you ever lost sleep because of a parent's drinking or drug use?

☐ ☐ 3. Did you ever encourage one of your parents to quit drinking or quit using other drugs?

☐ ☐ 4. Have you ever felt alone, scared, nervous, angry, frustrated because a parent wasn't able to quit drinking or using drugs?

☐ ☐ 5. Did you ever argue with a parent when he or she was drinking or high on other drugs?

☐ ☐ 6. Have you ever threatened to run away from home because of a parent's drinking or other drug use?

☐ ☐ 7. Has a parent ever yelled at you or hit you or other family members when he/she was drinking or using other drugs?

☐ ☐ 8. Have you ever heard your parents fight when one of them was drunk or under the influence of any drugs?

☐ ☐ 9. Have you ever protected another family member from a parent who was drinking or using other drugs?

☐ ☐ 10. Have you ever felt like hiding or emptying a parent's bottle of liquor or his/her supply of other drugs?

☐ ☐ 11. Do many of your thoughts revolve around a parent's drinking or drugging or difficulties that arise as a result?

☐ ☐ 12. Do you ever wish that a parent would stop drinking or using other drugs?

☐ ☐ 13. Do you ever feel responsible for and guilty about the way a parent uses alcohol or other drugs?

☐ ☐ 14. Did you ever fear that your parents would separate or divorce because of the drinking or drug use?

☐ ☐ 15. Have you ever withdrawn from or avoided outside activities because you were embarrassed or fearful about a parent's drinking or drug use?

☐ ☐ 16. Did you ever feel caught in the middle of an argument between a parent who was using alcohol or other drugs and the other parent?

☐ ☐ 17. Did you ever feel that you made a parent use alcohol or other drugs?

☐ ☐ 18. Have you ever felt that a parent who drank or used drugs did not love you?

C.A.A.S.: CHILDREN AFFECTED BY ADDICTION SCREEN, continued

YES	NO	QUESTIONS
☐	☐	19. Did you ever resent a parent's use of alcohol or other drugs?
☐	☐	20. Have you ever worried about a parent's health because of his/her alcohol or other drug use?
☐	☐	21. Have you ever been blamed for a parent's drinking or drug use?
☐	☐	22. Did you ever think your father was an alcoholic or drug addict?
☐	☐	23. Did you ever wish that your home could be more like the homes of friends whose parents didn't have a problem with drinking or drugs?
☐	☐	24. Did a parent ever make promises to you that he/she did not keep because of drinking or other drug use?
☐	☐	25. Did you ever think your mother was an alcoholic or drug addict?
☐	☐	26. Did you ever wish that you could talk to someone who could understand and help with the alcohol or drug-related problems in your family?
☐	☐	27. Did you ever fight with your brothers and sisters about a parent's drinking or other drug use?
☐	☐	28. Do you ever stay away from home to avoid the drinking or other drug-related problems?
☐	☐	29. Have you ever felt sick, cried, or had a knot in your stomach after worrying about a parent's drinking or drug use?
☐	☐	30. Did you ever take over any chores and duties at home that were usually done by a parent before he/she developed a problem with alcohol or other drugs?
☐	☐	31. Do you ever worry that your parent will get into trouble with the law as a result of his/her drinking or drug use?

☐ **Total number of "yes" answers**

"Yes" answers indicate that this child has been touched in some way by addiction. Score of 6 or more indicates that more than likely this student is a child of an alcoholic or an addict.

Jones, John W., from Black, Claudia, *It Will Never Happen to Me*, Ballantine Books, New York, 1981, pp. 199–201. Adapted and printed with permission.

harmful involvement with chemicals in adolescents on those occasions when you want to augment your intake interview or want "objective evidence" to persuade a student. One I have found to be useful in my practice is the "Youth Diagnostic Screen for Problem Drinkers" (provided here), which breaks its questions into four groups indicative of attitudes, evidence of pathological style (the disease of addiction), evidence of problematic consumption, and evidence of negative consequences because of drinking. Because of the current prevalence of multiple drug use in junior high and high schools, questions must also be asked about the other drugs when using this tool. The "Drug Use History Tool" provided can help you do this.

What is helpful about the "Youth Diagnostic Screen for Problem Drinkers" is that it doesn't concentrate too much on the consequences of drinking to determine if a problem exists. I find this approach helpful because although a small but significant number of adolescents who are harmfully involved with chemicals have experienced serious negative consequences as a result of their drinking, a lot of young users have not experienced too many consequences yet and therefore feel that there's simply no problem. In scoring this particular device, you can explain to a student that though there don't seem to be too many consequences yet, there is evidence of the presence of the disease of addiction, or evidence of problematic consumption. This is part of the prevention effort; students can be made aware of dangerous drinking and drugging patterns long before they experience obvious negative consequences as a result of their use.

Most chemical dependency assessment tools ask essentially the same basic question: How is drinking or drugging getting in the way of the rest of your life? Because of the existence of denial, however, we are compelled to ask that question in various wrappings, and then present the answers to students who already know the truth about themselves and their drinking/drugging somewhere under all the rationalizations. Experience has shown that assessment tools can be used to motivate students, because they ask all the hard questions all at once and hand back an informal diagnosis, just like that. Students can be told, "If you have a question about your drinking or drugging, an assessment can answer it." Some students really respond to that kind of objective announcement of their condition, and then they can go on either to treat their chemical dependency, or they'll let that seed of information become uncomfortably planted somewhere in their consciousness, both of which are ultimately desirable outcomes.

Using Assessment Tools to Motivate Parents

Assessment questionnaires can also be particularly useful in convincing parents who are in denial that their youngsters need treatment, because they seem very official and can cut through parents' wishes that it "simply isn't true." Those of us in the field know that social users don't worry about their drinking or drugging—they moderate it, or eliminate it. So an assessment is usually going to legitimize what has previously been informal common knowledge.

The only danger in using some formal assessments is that younger and perhaps less experienced alcohol and drug users may come out of a chemical dependency assessment with a clean bill of health, convincing the counselor, the parents, and the student that there's no need for concern. In some cases, the

YOUTH DIAGNOSTIC SCREEN FOR PROBLEM DRINKERS

Non Drinking Items, Questions 1–8

1. Are you male or female?	No score _____
2. How old are you?	No score _____
3. Do you use or have you ever used drugs?	Score 1 _____
4. Have you been busted for possession of an illegal drug?	Score 1 _____
5. Have you had a drink of beer, wine, or liquor *more than two or three times in your life?*	Score 1 _____
6. Do you consider yourself a person who drinks?	Score 1 _____
7. Do you favor pot over alcohol?	Score 1 _____
8. Do you and your friends think sex and drinking go together?	Score 1 _____

Total score for this section: _____

Pathological Style Items, Questions 9–30

9. Do you sometimes hang out with kids who drink?	Score 1 _____
10. Do you prefer to be with friends who drink?	Score 1 _____
11. Do you sometimes drink because it makes you feel more at ease on a date?	Score 1 _____
12. Do you sometimes drink because it makes you feel more relaxed with the opposite sex?	Score 1 _____
13. Do you sometimes drink because it makes you feel better around people?	Score 1 _____
14. Do you sometimes drink because it helps you forget your worries?	Score 1 _____
15. Do you sometimes drink because it helps to cheer you up when you're in a bad mood?	Score 1 _____
16. Do you sometimes drink to change the way you feel?	Score 1 _____
17. Do you sometimes drink because it makes you feel stronger?	Score 1 _____
18. Have you ever borrowed money or done without other things to buy alcohol?	Score 1 _____
19. Have you ever skipped meals while drinking?	Score 1 _____
20. Do you sometimes gulp down a drink rather than drinking it slowly?	Score 1 _____
21. Do you sometimes drink before going to a party?	Score 1 _____
22. Do you ever notice that your hands shake when you wake up in the morning?	Score 1 _____
23. Have you ever taken a drink in the morning?	Score 1 _____
24. Have you ever felt guilty or bummed out after drinking?	Score 1 _____
25. Do you ever have times when you cannot remember some of what happened while drinking?	Score 2 _____
26. Have you ever stayed high drinking all day?	Score 2 _____
27. Do you ever get mad or into a heated argument when you drink?	Score 1 _____
28. Have you ever gotten into a fight when drinking?	Score 1 _____
29. Do you sometimes get drunk when you didn't start out to get drunk?	Score 1 _____
30. Do you sometimes try to cut down on your drinking?	Score 1 _____

Total score for this section: _____

Problematic Consumption Items, Questions 31–36

31. Do you sometimes drink until there's nothing left to drink?   Score 2   ____

32. Would you say that you get high when you drink more than half the time?   Score 2   ____

33. Would you say that you get drunk or bombed at least once a month or more?   Score 2   ____

34. Have you had anything to drink in the last week?   Score 1   ____

35. When you drink, do you usually end up having more than four of whatever you're drinking?   Score 2   ____

36. Would you say that you have a drink of beer, wine, or liquor at least once a week or more?   Score 2   ____

Total score for this section: _____

Consequence Items, Questions 37–40

37. Have you ever missed school or missed a class because of drinking?   Score 2   ____

38. Have you ever gotten into trouble at home because of your drinking?   Score 1   ____

39. Have you ever gotten into trouble outside your home because of drinking?   Score 1   ____

40. Have you ever gotten into trouble with the police because of drinking?   Score 1   ____

Total score for this section: _____

Total score for test: _____

Score all items 1 for yes response unless otherwise indicated. Scores will range from 0–44. An *alcoholic* scores at least 3 on the nondrinking items (3–8), at least 5 on the pathological style items (9–30), at least 4 on the problematic consumption items (31–36), and at least 2 on the consequence items. A *problem drinker* scores at least 3 on the nondrinking items and scores the same as that required for an alcoholic diagnosis on *two of the three* problem-drinking components. A *potential problem drinker* scores at least 3 on the nondrinking items and scores the same as that required for an alcoholic diagnosis on *one of the three* problem-drinking components.

From *Young Alcoholics,* by Tom Albrandi, © 1978 by Compcare Publishers; used by permission.

DRUG USE HISTORY TOOL

Below on the left is a list of sixteen types of drugs. On the right is a key in which ten different experiences with drugs are described. Please give us your personal history by circling the appropriate number or numbers that describe your experience with each drug. Please read the key carefully, as more than one number may apply to you. This is confidential, of course.

Caffeine	1	2	3	4	5	6	7	8	9	10
Tobacco (cigarettes)	1	2	3	4	5	6	7	8	9	10
Tobacco (chewing)	1	2	3	4	5	6	7	8	9	10
Wine coolers	1	2	3	4	5	6	7	8	9	10
Beer	1	2	3	4	5	6	7	8	9	10
Liquor	1	2	3	4	5	6	7	8	9	10
Marijuana	1	2	3	4	5	6	7	8	9	10
Inhalants (things you sniff)	1	2	3	4	5	6	7	8	9	10
PCP (angel dust)	1	2	3	4	5	6	7	8	9	10
Cocaine	1	2	3	4	5	6	7	8	9	10
Crack cocaine	1	2	3	4	5	6	7	8	9	10
Amphetamines (speed, uppers)	1	2	3	4	5	6	7	8	9	10
Barbiturates (downers)	1	2	3	4	5	6	7	8	9	10
Hallucinogens (acid, mushrooms)	1	2	3	4	5	6	7	8	9	10
Heroin	1	2	3	4	5	6	7	8	9	10
Anabolic steroids	1	2	3	4	5	6	7	8	9	10

KEY

1—I have never used it.
2—I tried it once.
3—I have used it 2–5 times.
4—I have used it 5–10 times.
5—I have used it 10–20 times.
6—I have used it more than 20 times.
7—I use it daily.
8—I have friends who use it.
9—Someone in my family uses it.
10—I would like to try it.

By Jennifer Bouchard; used by permission.

assessment is "right" and there's reason for relief. However, even students who have had only one experience with alcohol, for instance, may be at incredibly high risk for future problems because of the combined disadvantage of family history, school, and home situation. Relying solely on one assessment tool for chemical dependency can miss these very high-risk students and send them off thinking they can drink and drug in safety. More questions must be asked.

Some SAPs do formal assessments at school, and others refer students to outside alcohol and other drug counselors. More and more state and city agencies are keeping a person on staff who can perform such assessments. Referring out can sometimes be a positive move, however, because it usually requires that the student's parents be contacted to have it done. Then the parents get both the information that the SAP believes that the student needs an assessment and the formal results of a chemical dependency assessment administered by an alcohol and drug abuse counselor. The more professional people concur on the outcome of such an assessment, the more likely that the student will get the help he or she needs.

USING GENOGRAMS IN INDIVIDUAL SESSIONS

Genograms are a visual representation of a family made by using symbols for male and female members and different symbols to represent the relationships these people have to one another (see the example on the following page). These simple tools really help you visualize a student's family situation while, at the same time, allowing you and the student to concentrate on a common task and thereby build trust. Use genograms to get a sense of the players in the student's life. Ask the student to indicate somehow which people in the genogram are the most important to him or her, who is deceased, who lives far away, etc. If you are screening a student for chemical dependency treatment, a COA group, challenge group, or recovery group, make a genogram shading in relatives with alcohol or drug problems, gambling problems, obesity, and/or other compulsive behaviors. This "picture" can give both you and the student insight.

At times, you get insight even before you begin a genogram. Often, when I tell very troubled students that, as an exercise, we're going to make a symbolic representation of their family, they say something very telling like, "Good luck! It's such a mess it'll take you about ten sheets of paper. My father's been married three times, just for starters." Already you have a very good sense of how these students perceive their families.

Start genograms at the bottom of the page by drawing the symbol for the student in question and work your way up the paper and back through the generations. The purpose is not to have a perfect product but to engage the student in the process so he or she feels that you understand the players in the family.

You can say the following things to students when using genograms:

- Shade in all the people you know here who have alcohol or other drug problems.
- Shade in all the people here who are more than fifty pounds overweight.

GENOGRAMS

Using the sample genogram, try to see how a complicated family is represented fairly simply. See if you can follow along, looking at the genogram.

Sam is the student you are seeing in the SAP. He is seventeen. He has a sister Rachel, who is twelve, and a half-brother Peter, who is five. Sam's parents are divorced. His father is remarried to Peter's mother. Sam's mother is not remarried, but she has a boyfriend who is a significant part of their lives. Sam's father is an alcoholic, or has those tendencies, according to Sam.

Sam's mother has an older brother, Marty, and a younger sister, Elaine. Both have developed alcoholism and/or addiction. This is not too surprising since their mother also had addiction of some sort. She is dead now and Sam only knows that his mother's childhood "wasn't good," but he is not sure what went wrong. He knows that his grandmother drank a lot in her later years.

Sam's father has an older brother who doesn't display any symptoms of alcoholism or addiction. However, their father (Sam's paternal grandfather) is in the later stages of alcoholism.

If you were using this genogram as part of an assessment for Sam, you could tell him that he is at greater risk for developing problems with addiction than some of his friends might be. Because his father is an alcoholic, Sam would be a great candidate for a friends' group. Make a note to yourself to contact Rachel when she comes up from the junior high school.

Both of Sam's parents are adult children of alcoholics as well, so their parenting skills may be erratic. Sam has addiction on both sides of his family and a direct link through his father (which is the strongest: Male children of male alcoholics are at greatest risk of developing the disease themselves).

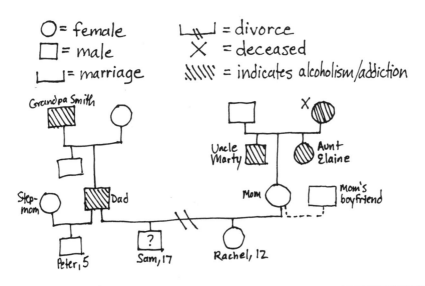

- Shade in all the people who kind of "disappeared" and your family doesn't talk about very much.
- Shade in anyone who you know is or was abusive to other family members.
- Who are the positive role models in this picture?
- Whom do you wish you could spend more time with?
- Whom do you trust in this picture?
- Who takes care of you?
- Whom are you responsible for taking care of in this picture?
- Who would you most like to be like?
- Who would you least like to be like?

If you are unfamiliar with using genograms, the technique is very easy to learn. You don't have to be a great artist to help students see their families this way. After spending even half a session with a student and his or her genogram, you'll have a very good picture of how this student experiences life.

MAKING REFERRALS TO OUTSIDE AGENCIES

Because an SAP's main mission is to identify students who are experiencing trouble, assess the nature of the problem, and then refer the students to appropriate help, one of the most important services an SAP can provide is a current list of available resources. Your team coordinator or counselor(s) needs to know of agencies in the community that can deal with a wide range of student problems and must know enough resources so he or she can give the family of the student a choice of people to see.

Giving students and their families *choices* of people to see in the community is very important. If the SAP recommends only one counselor/hospital, etc., a fair argument could be made that the SAP and that agency have created some kind of monopoly. If the student is treated badly by the agency, for instance, the parents may come back to the school demanding an explanation (or, in the worst case, reimbursement). Depending on the socioeconomic health of your community, many students will need treatment but won't have adequate insurance to pay for it, so you must keep track of how flexible certain agencies are when it comes to terms of payment. Make it very clear that while the SAP may suggest outside counseling, it is fully the responsibility of the family to seek it out and pay for it.

Compiling a List of Resources

This will be a difficult task, but the following list should be completed by your SAP counselor or team. Don't hand out this list to students, parents, or faculty members, but use it as a resource yourself. Be aware that if community agencies know that you are compiling such a list, and it is official, they will butter you up to get on it. While this is not necessarily bad, check out resources before you put them on such a list. Call trusted colleagues to ask what their experience has been with certain agencies, private therapists, hospitals, and the personalities there. Try to stay on top of changes in personnel, turnovers in management, and the like, so you have a realistic picture of what kind of treatment is available at any given time. This may seem like a poor use of your limited time, but your work will pay off tenfold when you have a desperate student and his or her parents in your office and you need a referral in a hurry.

You should have a few sources (either in-school or in the community or, preferably, both) who can provide counseling in the following areas. These sources may include volunteer services, private therapists and counselors, hospitals, psychiatrists, psychologists, pastoral counselors, etc. Remember that the final decision for outside treatment always lies with the student and his or her parents and that they are responsible for the payment for such services.

Areas for Referral:

Alcohol and other drug abuse (both inpatient and outpatient)

Adoption

Adult children of alcoholics

Anabolic steroids

Anorexia nervosa

Bulimia

Codependency

Compulsive overeating

Depression

Domestic violence

Family therapy

Gang violence

Grief/loss

HIV/AIDS

Homosexuality

Incest

Mediation

Nutrition

Physical abuse

Pregnancy

Prenatal care

Rape

Satanism and the occult

Self-help groups

Sexuality

Sexual identity

Sexual abuse

Stealing

Suicidality

Truancy

A given SAP counselor probably has expertise in many of these areas, but no one can know it all. Any SAP counselor should have very strong backgrounds in adolescent chemical dependency, and, in particular, children of addiction. While this list may seem to fall well out of the boundaries of alcohol and drug-related issues, anyone involved with SAP knows that they can be all sadly interrelated in myriad ways. For instance, COAs are more likely than other students to have been sexually abused, which can manifest itself in serious depression and suicidality. Realistically, students experiencing any of these various difficulties are at much greater risk for developing alcohol and other drug-related difficulties.

MAKING REFERRALS TO CHEMICAL DEPENDENCY TREATMENT FACILITIES

Some SAPs are set up with the singular purpose of intervening in well-established student drinking and drugging problems and motivating these very ill students into inpatient chemical dependency treatment facilities. If your SAP team acts as a formal intervention team, contacting parents and setting up interventions, you already have an established mission. This is an aggressive and effective policy. Teams that operate this way generally elicit very specific, alcohol or other drug-related concern referrals and then gather more information from other teachers, friends, and parents which indicate that this particular student is without question in serious trouble with alcohol and/or other drugs.

Laws governing confidentiality don't go into effect until the student has been contacted, so this method of intervention[1] tends to require a lot of time before the initial contact with student, for coaching teachers, parents, and friends of the student in loving confrontational techniques which may motivate the student into seeking treatment. If you have limited resources and no counselor, this approach may be the way to go. Take care, though, because if it is implemented poorly, your team can come to be regarded as a SWAT team of sorts, trying to clear these "nasty drug users" from the hallowed halls of your school. This method also serves a very small, needy segment of the school population. There are many good books which you should have on hand in your SAP library that discuss specific intervention techniques. Student assistance program counselors should be comfortable and familiar with caring confrontation of students.

A more complete approach is to include formal intervention techniques and referrals to chemical dependency treatment facilities within the context of a more comprehensive SAP. Participation in a challenge group through the SAP, for instance, can be the first step to motivating a student to seek treatment. Of course, you will probably be called on to facilitate the transition from school to treatment and from treatment back to school. These are primary and necessary functions of an SAP.

In a comprehensive, counselor-based SAP, the option of inpatient chemical dependency treatment is most apt to come up after the student has been unsuccessful staying clean and sober using less intrusive means. For instance, the student may have been unable to complete a challenge group or may have been unable to stay sober in a recovery group or may have been involved with the disciplinary system of the school. Usually, by the time you are considering inpatient treatment for a student, his or her parents are involved somewhere in the process. If they aren't involved, they should be. Most states allow students to seek this sort of treatment without their parents' consent, but it just makes sense to enlist the parents' help. Almost without exception, parents love their children and want what is best for them. In some states, you must get a written release from the student to contact the parent, but if the student is considering treatment, this probably won't be too difficult.

In referring students to chemical dependency treatment facilities, care must be taken to insure that the parents and student make the final decision about where, when, and whether the student wants to go. Parents and schools can make the argument to go to treatment pretty convincing (forcing the student to choose, for instance, between going to treatment or living on the streets instead of at the parent's home), but there must be an element of choice. Schools can also make the

---

[1]Based on the Johnson Institute Intervention Model described in Johnson, Vernon E., *I'll Quit Tomorrow,* Harper and Row, © 1980.

treatment option more attractive by assuring students that they will not flunk out simply because they go to treatment.

The school can recommend to parents that a student seek treatment, and should, if it is necessary. The safest policy is to have several treatment centers on your list of resources that you can give to parents who want inpatient treatment for their children. Be careful not to endorse a treatment facility officially, lest you be held responsible for the bad experience of a student there. School-based programs cannot get into the business of *requiring* students to go to treatment as a condition of their enrollment—in public schooling, that is against the law, unless the school district is willing to pay for it. Don't make a lot of work for yourself by setting up a procedure you can't follow through.

Every once in a while, a student will drop exhausted onto your doorstep from out of the blue, very sick with the disease of addiction, and tell you that he or she needs to go to treatment immediately. Clearly, these students' requests for help must be honored as quickly as possible. In other, more typical cases, motivating students into treatment may take a long time and a lot of frustration. It is not unusual for the process to take a year or more as the student tries to cut down, gets in trouble, goes to counseling, goes on a binge, is confronted with his or her behavior, gets in more trouble, and so on. Some of these students will eventually get "clean and sober" partly as a result of having services available to them in school. (And, unfortunately, some of them won't.)

EASING STUDENTS' RETURN FROM TREATMENT TO SCHOOL

Some treatment centers are very good about getting all the correct authorizations and contacting school personnel when students are in their facilities. Some facilities, however, haven't worked out this aspect of the treatment plan, and you will have to chase them down with numerous phone calls. Most adolescent treatment centers have a modified "school day," and if the communication is open, students can at least keep up in the classes they are missing at school, making promotion to the next grade possible, for instance. Even if they can't keep up, they are certainly aiding their education ultimately by choosing treatment over their continued use of chemicals. Teachers who are irate because students are in treatment can be reminded that while it is difficult to do homework at a treatment center, it is even more difficult to do it from the grave.

Try to insure that someone from your SAP becomes part of the team that will monitor a student's progress during and after treatment. There are cases when the SAP will have been instrumental in getting that student to treatment and will be the school contact person, and there will be cases when a parent calls the SAP on Monday morning and announces that she admitted her daughter to a treatment center on Saturday morning at four A.M. There will also be cases when the SAP is informed in the eleventh hour that a student has been in treatment and that he's returning—tomorrow. If communication is stilted in your setting or if you work in a large school or district, there may even be cases when the SAP is not informed of some students who go to treatment, for whatever reason. Be prepared for all eventualities.

Student assistance program group participation should be a part of aftercare

planning for a student returning from treatment. However, if the treatment center doesn't know about your program, it may not think to include SAP participation in the aftercare plan. You can help both the student and the treatment facility by letting them know what services are available at school through the SAP. Try to strike a balance, though. An SAP cannot provide the entire aftercare plan for a student, and the hospital should not be led to think that it can fully relinquish its responsibility to follow up on that student's progress.

MAKING REFERRALS TO SAP GROUPS

Your own in-school SAP groups will quickly distinguish themselves as a readily available, reliable, and effective place to intervene with students who would otherwise "go it alone." Group participation, while cost-effective and time-effective from the administration's point of view, seems also to be in the best interest of the students themselves. There is no other age (twelve to eighteen) when it is as appropriate and helpful to harness and regulate that heavy reliance on peer interaction and create a supportive atmosphere for students experiencing stress in similar situations. An adult can tell a student that she's really OK, and it's not her fault that her mother drinks the way she does, but it means infinitely more coming from another student who has come to terms with the same situation. Students who are experiencing difficulty in school because of a family situation may also be having trouble making friends, and groups can carry support out of the group room and into the classroom and schoolyard. Lasting friendships can be made in group as a result of not having to worry about the "secret" of the family situation getting out. Establishing the rules of honest interaction and trust in the group setting helps students extend those rules to the relationships they forge at school. For adolescents who are growing up in highly dysfunctional families, this kind of training may help them to understand the elements of healthy relationships.

The number and types of your groups will vary depending on whether you have SAP counselors and whether your SAP is broad brush in nature or narrowly defined. In an SAP with a defined audience, it is important to have available, at the very least, a group for children who are affected by someone else's addiction, a recovery group, and some sort of group in which students can evaluate their own use of chemicals in a supportive but straightforward atmosphere. Even if there is no SAP, and no plan to implement one formally, an interested and qualified teacher or guidance counselor can begin a group program using the three groups discussed in chapters 12 through 14. (Of course, whoever runs these groups should either have, or get, some training in group counseling, chemical dependency, and children of addiction.)

Some students are excited about joining groups. They self-refer to the SAP and tell you that they want to join "that group" they heard about in health class: they can't wait to meet other kids and share their experiences. Others are predictably less excited; in fact, some may be terrified about sharing their experiences with others. Children of addiction, in particular, tend to latch on to those they trust, and if your SAP is structured so you can't see students individually long term, it must be made clear to these COAs at the outset that an outside referral to a therapist or the in-school SAP group is available to them and is the ultimate goal of individual appointments. Many would rather just stay with the SAP counselor individually, and indefinitely.

Convincing students to give an SAP group a try can be challenging. Sometimes your job is made easier because a friend may have encouraged another friend to join the group. Obviously, your SAP will have to "sell" group to some reluctant youngsters by concentrating on what seems to make them most comfortable. More information about screening students for groups and encouraging them to participate can be found in chapter 9, "General Guidelines for SAP Groups." We must give credit for the tremendous courage it takes for young people to walk into a room full of students they may or may not know and share what they have been previously taught to conceal.

Screening Students for Groups

Most adolescents can benefit from group participation. Even some whose behavior seems disruptive at first will settle down considerably once the group experience is underway. More is said in chapters 12 through 14 about screening students for particular groups. However, for groups in general, consider the following:

- There are all kinds of people in the world, and a group provides a microcosm of the world for students. There probably should be all kinds of people in groups, too, even people who are difficult.

- In groups, the rules of conduct are very explicit. If a student is unable to operate within the rules, that student and the group may be better served if he or she does not attend.
- Students who are currently suicidal do not belong in groups. Do not try to treat suicidality in the context of a group. Refer the student to emergency treatment.
- Try to prevent students from becoming "groupies." A student should probably never be in more than two groups at a time.
- Remember the purpose of in-school groups: to help students manage their lives more effectively so they can succeed academically, developmentally, and socially. If group participation is not working this way for a particular student, it may not be appropriate.

Understanding SAP Group Participation

Using groups as a way to offer the motivation for change in adolescents was born of both necessity and experience. We know that adolescents respond much more willingly to their peers than they do to adults. This is developmentally appropriate. The idea of SAP groups is to harness that positive peer interaction to provide support and education for students with similar concerns. Ultimately, this has a calming effect on students individually, and students can begin to concentrate better in school. Groups also make an inestimable contribution to the general climate of school wellness, making it okay to try on new behaviors and to share your concerns with small groups of trusted people. Also, there is the consideration of cost-effectiveness. With the sheer numbers of students who will show up on the doorstep of your SAP if it is implemented properly, groups are the only way to "hold" these students. An SAP's mission is not to provide long-term, in-depth therapy, but rather to provide for as many students as we can, to keep them in school so they can accomplish developmentally, academically, and socially what they need to do.

9
General Guidelines for SAP Groups

CHAPTER 9

General Guidelines for SAP Groups

> Our grand business of life is not to see what lies dimly at a distance, but to do what lies clearly at hand.
>
> *Thomas Carlyle (1795–1881)*

Why Groups in Student Assistance Programming?

Groups for troubled adolescents are an efficient and effective way to channel developmentally appropriate behavior in a positive and manageable direction. Why not utilize the unique synergy of shared experience and adolescent energy? Group participation can save lives, and where it doesn't *save* lives, it can make the quality of lives infinitely better. Cost shouldn't be our only concern, but the serendipity with adolescent services is that the most do-able and cost-effective option—groups—also seems to be the most effective in helping this population.

Groups in the context of the school-based SAP are fundamentally educational in nature and serve the educational directive of both public and private schooling to educate the whole person. The objective of having students in groups is to increase student effectiveness in school and to give students who have one or more strikes against them the opportunity to manage their anxiety so they can survive their schooling, their families, and their adolescence.

This chapter is all about SAP groups and contains most of the logistical directions that you need whether you are starting one group or a spectrum of different groups. It includes advice about group facilitators, administrative support, and all the things that will make running groups not only effective, but enjoyable. If your school doesn't have groups of any kind yet, don't be daunted by what looks like a lot of footwork. It can all be done, step by step, if you break it down. It also doesn't have to be perfect the first time around.

GAINING ADMINISTRATIVE SUPPORT FOR GROUPS

You must have administrative support to run groups in the school. Without at least administrative tolerance, there will be no SAP groups, and perhaps no SAP at all. If, at first, groups during the school day seem impossible, true administrative support means finding a way to make them work, knowing that it will be awkward at first. For the group component of the SAP only, good administrative support consists of the following elements:

- **Allowing and arranging for students to miss a class once a week on a rotating basis to attend group.** This is the most important part of administrative support, because it underlies the basic functioning of

SAPs. Although this seems like an educational risk, it is time well spent out of class. The whole purpose of group participation is to allow students to deal with their anxiety so they can concentrate on their schoolwork when they *are* in class. For some students, group participation is a last-ditch dropout prevention effort, because by the time we identify some students, they are already in serious trouble. The hope is that group participation and the support students get there is one more reason for them to stay in school. Students are, of course, responsible for any work they might miss in class.

- **Providing technical assistance to develop an attendance policy for group participation.** Working within the regulations surrounding confidentiality, school personnel must come up with a way of accounting for students' whereabouts during group. If your program serves a broad-brush population, students can get passes from the group leader, because their participation is no comment on whether they are alcohol or other drug users. If mere participation labels a student as an alcohol or other drug user, the attendance must be handled delicately, usually through an administrator who is trained in SAP confidentiality issues. A list of students participating would be sent to the administrator, who would intercept "cut" slips sent by teachers so these absences would not be counted against the total number of absences allowed by your school or district.

GAINING TEACHER/COUNSELOR SUPPORT FOR GROUPS

While teachers and counselors don't need to give SAP people "permission" to operate the way the administration does, not having the support of your staff can make a difficult job of scheduling groups seem downright impossible. So, it is important to win teacher and guidance counselor support for groups from the outset.

Teachers may have problems with the idea of students being taken out of classes for group participation. The idea is to have students out of class once in seven or eight weeks so the time they are in class will be better spent. If the truth be told, however, this practice may actually make a little more work for teachers because they have to be willing to help students catch up on missed work. But if both sides of the argument are presented clearly and nondefensively, most teachers will agree to withhold judgment until there are some results to be evaluated.

FINDING YOUR PLACE IN THE SUN: A GROUP ROOM

A working SAP needs a room large enough to accommodate a dozen students and two facilitators. Ideally, this room will be used for no other purpose and can therefore be used throughout the school day. Comfortable chairs are a plus (chairs of any kind are a must), and this room must be in a place where students can find it but where there will be few distractions. Students should not be able to be identified through windows, doors, etc. From the perspective of the students, your group room displays the school's commitment to the program, so stand in their shoes and evaluate the accommodations. They needn't be luxurious, by any stretch, but they must be respectful.

FINDING TERRIFIC GROUP FACILITATORS

There are several ways to draw good group facilitators into the operation of the SAP (and even more good reasons for doing so). Some group cofacilitators can be drawn from the pool of other school personnel, some may be outside professionals or paraprofessionals, and still others may be volunteers from the community or self-help programs.

The structure of your program will dictate the way you elicit help. One word of caution: Try to get help in your SAP right from the start. If you don't take this step, people will believe that the SAP is handling it all—and no one will feel compelled to offer his or her services. This is dangerous policy for the SAP, as it leaves you professionally isolated. Community-wide efforts are usually more effective than individual ones.

Having more than one group leader for each group is beneficial for all involved. It helps ward off burnout, for adolescents require the exhausting trio of structure, confrontation, and sometimes discipline in groups. Two people can hold the attention of the group better than one. If students have trouble warming up to one of the leaders, or have transference issues, they will have a fall-back position with the other leader. Another reason is that in schools, teachers, counselors, and SAP people are called on all the time to field crises, attend staff meetings, and intervene with distraught families. Having two people leading each group insures that if one of these crises arises, the other can take the group for that week.

At the root of the argument for cofacilitation is the knowledge that two people can help each other become better counselors, pointing out room for improvement and giving each other encouragement and validation. A good working relationship with another adult helps you feel connected to your workplace, and you are less likely to feel overwhelmed by the chaos and tragic situations that often characterize students' lives. Having two personalities leading a group also wards off any potential power struggles that may arise. While one interacts with students, the other can watch the interaction and provide feedback to the other. In addition, two counselors can keep each other in check about their personal boundaries when dealing with students, ensuring that all counselor/student relationships remain professional and appropriate.

If you find that you are reluctant to cofacilitate with others, check your own control issues to see if you are not falling victim to the erroneous and dangerous assumption that you're the only person who can do this work "right." Not only will that attitude tire you out, but it will take your program with it. It is right, however, to be careful about whom you choose to help you. As in other counseling or support situations, facilitators must have their own issues treated before they attempt to lead a group of adolescents to their self-discovery. Potential group facilitators who are in recovery themselves (from addiction, codependency, or "adult children" issues) should have a firm grasp on recovery and should be involved in a recovery program to prevent relapse. Though there are no hard and fast rules, it is recommended that a cofacilitator have at least a few years in recovery and in a self-help program as well before embarking into the field. The worst-case scenario is to have a person with an untreated issue leading a group. Not only does it set a bad example for the students involved, it creates anguish for the group leader.

Draw potential group leaders into the system by asking them to run a group in their area of expertise, where they will feel most comfortable. If a counselor has experience working with children of addiction individually, for instance, encourage him or her to colead a group. If the school nurse is willing, have him or her help run a young parents' group. (This group is at risk for alcohol and other drug use, physical and sexual abuse.) Ideally, these leaders will become invested in the group and in the program as a result and may eventually end up running two or three groups or expanding their section of the program to include more education and prevention.

Recruiting Guidance Counselors as Cofacilitators

Guidance people can be great group facilitators because they have experience working with adolescents and may also have extensive experience and training working with groups. They are also available, and they are certified school personnel, which means that from a legal standpoint, it is perfectly appropriate for guidance people to be working with groups of students in the context of the SAP. From the students' perspective, guidance counselors are usually well known and accessible. In some cases, your SAP will comprise some subsection of the guidance department plus a handful of concerned teachers. In other structures, the SAP will be completely separate from the guidance department, and having guidance counselors cofacilitate SAP groups may require some coordination between the SAP and guidance departments.

Any potential problems that having guidance people as SAP group facilitators may create can be averted with planning and talking through potential scenarios before they happen. Try to form a positive and cooperative relationship from the start. Having SAP groups facilitated by guidance personnel may help to smooth some of the tensions that start-up SAPs tend to experience. The first thing to troubleshoot is that most traditional guidance training has not focused on chemical dependency and surrounding issues. This makes sense because guidance people have traditionally serviced the entire school population, at least half of which has no alcohol or other drug issues. Student assistance programs provide information and resources to this less-affected half and additional services to the other half. It is imperative that guidance people who want to work in alcohol and other drug-related groups get additional training in the area of alcohol and other drug issues before they cofacilitate a related group. Some of this training can be provided at your initial and continuing core team training so guidance people who are also core team members will be encouraged to colead groups. Never *require* guidance people to run SAP groups; not all of them are prepared or willing.

It has been my experience that some guidance people would love to run groups but are a little unsure of themselves, particularly where alcohol and other drug issues are concerned. If you sense this, work on them, bit by bit, and ask them to run one group with you, "as an experiment" or to "help you out" by acting as a consultant on the group activities. The more people who are trained and invested in the operation of the SAP, the more students can be identified and helped. That's the bottom line.

Recruiting Teachers as Cofacilitators

Teachers, by definition, have experience working with groups of students, even if the setting has not been formally therapeutic (though I have been in some class-rooms that felt therapeutic). Creative strategies to release teachers from classes can provide a fleet of willing group facilitators, as long as you provide training for these folks and make sure that they are paired with someone with more extensive counseling experience and training. There will also be teachers who are internally motivated to start a group of some kind, though they lack extensive training. As long as these people understand their limitations and know when to pass a prob-lem along, they may do well and will garner experience along the way. Many orig-inal SAP efforts began as insightful teachers across the nation noticed that their students weren't performing to their true academic potential due to pressing per-sonal concerns. These programs helped many students who wouldn't have other-wise been helped. Now is the time to take those efforts further by hiring SAP help or by releasing these teachers from other duties so they can pursue these helping programs and additional training full time.

While some teachers may be more able to commit to becoming a cofacilitator if groups are held after school, it is important to stress SAP group participation as an integral part of the school curriculum, not as an extracurricular activity. Whenever possible, insist on having groups held during the regular school day, underscoring that group participation is educational in nature.

Minimizing Role Conflict for Teachers and Guidance Personnel

The largest problem with non-SAP school personnel cofacilitating SAP groups is the potential for role conflict and the resulting difficulties, which can get messy. Think through these potential problems thoroughly in the context of your partic-ular school or system, and read carefully about confidentiality in chapter 3. Stu-dent assistance program people occupy a strange gray area—being members of the faculty, but being bound by the federal regulations governing drug and alco-hol abusers and any information that identifies them. Student assistance pro-gram counselors who have no other duties are in a position to study these strict regulations and settle into practices which are consistent with them. Other school personnel do not have the luxury of this singleness of purpose, and the roles may be too difficult to merge while doing equal justice to confidentiality, respect for parents' rights, and dedication to their primary duties.

If guidance people, for instance, are working in the context of a challenge group and are privy to details about students' alcohol and other drug use, one interpretation of the regulations forces them to compartmentalize and withhold this knowledge even in meetings with the student's parents, unless they have written consent from the student to divulge this information. In some cases, even the information that a student was interested in being part of a challenge group or recovery group is protected. This can be anxiety-producing for guidance person-nel and teachers. Students may also guess or intuit this role conflict and be reluctant to share honestly within groups, knowing that guidance personnel and teachers are likely to meet with their parents to discuss different aspects of their lives. They will be understandably nervous about whether the teacher or counselor will be able to honor the confidentiality rules while discussing something else with the student's parents.

Guidance people and teachers work with the student's permanent school file, so there is more potential that identifying information will reach the school file than if an alcohol or other drug issue is being handled only through the SAP, separate from the guidance department. This is not only confusing for guidance people and teachers themselves, but it is confusing for students. It can be construed as a mixed message if students are encouraged to talk freely about alcohol and drug use in the context of a group, when the same teachers and counselors occupy a disciplinarian role outside of group. Imagine that a student talks about his alcohol use in group and then, at the next school dance, shows up under the influence. Now this teacher or guidance counselor who cofacilitates his group and who is also a chaperone at the dance is in the worst of positions: If the use is ignored, the student gets absolutely the wrong message. If the student is confronted, he is going to believe that it was the information divulged in group which got him "busted"—which may in fact be true.

Another potential conflict is that the writing of college recommendations can be affected by the knowledge that a student is struggling with alcohol and other drug issues, and not everyone recognizes addiction as a "no-fault" disease. What do you say as both the guidance counselor and the cofacilitator of a recovery group when you know that the student has great test scores, fair grades, all the academic requirements, a varsity sport, and an addiction to cocaine? How do you grade a paper in class if the student tells you in group that she was high when she wrote it? Another potential problem is that students who are working in a teacher's class may attribute the assessments of their academic performance to something they have divulged in group. After getting a D on a paper, for instance, a student may argue, "She gave me that grade because I told her that I drank over the weekend." Of course, there are people who are going to be able to manage these conflicts successfully, but the potential for disaster must be recognized, and cofacilitators should go into these situations with their eyes wide open.

One solution for this potential conflict is to have teachers and guidance personnel cofacilitate groups for children of alcoholics and addicts, general discussion groups, and special topic groups, but steer them away from recovery groups and challenge groups. These use-oriented groups can be co-led by the SAP person with the help of outside professionals, volunteers from self-help groups, etc. This solves one of the problems. If counselors and teachers *are* going to be involved in groups that ask students to discuss their use (recovery groups and challenge groups), the different roles inside and outside of group must be clearly explained to students and adhered to by all group leaders consistently. Teachers and counselors must understand the distinction between what happens in group and what happens in the hallway, classroom, parking lots, and playing fields.

Even in groups that don't discuss student use, potential cofacilitators must search themselves for prejudices. Will they feel differently about a student if they know her mother deals drugs? What about the student whose father is in prison, or who has sexually abused his son or daughter? Are they going to be able to carry out their primary duties without letting the new information affect their performance? Will the exposure to tragic situations depress them terribly? The most important question for potential group facilitators, however, is, "Are you going to be able to maintain the very strictest standards of confidentiality?" Some people will be able to manage these conflicts, but others will have other aspects of their professional lives which will be more important to them.

Being a group cofacilitator is not for everyone; nor should an SAP effort convey that message. Not everyone wants to or should work with adolescents on this intense a level, and that is perfectly okay. Adolescents need people to meet them on all levels, and people can become involved without leading a group. Some very good one-on-one counselors are ineffective as group leaders and recognize these limitations. Some are great group facilitators but choose not to exercise those group "muscles" for various reasons. Student assistance programs need group leaders, but they can also use the help of people who do not want to lead groups. These people can become involved by offering to serve on the core team, making more referrals to the program, asking the SAP person to do a presentation in classes, becoming part of a planning committee for ancillary programming, or becoming involved with a newsletter, workshop series, or some other informational component of student assistance programming.

Utilizing Outside Professionals as Group Facilitators

There are great ways to utilize outside professionals within the context of the school-based SAP. The first is to refer students for further treatment after assessments because SAPs cannot do it all. The second way to involve outside professionals is to invite them to cofacilitate groups with the SAP person or team. If you have any funds available, these can be paid positions, and it is actually very cost-effective to pay a professional with specific expertise for a special topic group. The positions are paid on a consultant basis, and since the group is run only once a week, you pay only for an hour a week. (A small grant can also be written to secure these funds, if necessary.) In a school system without an SAP counselor, a certified alcohol and other drug counselor could be hired to run a recovery group or challenge group with a guidance counselor or teacher.

In a school where there is an SAP counselor, the program can hire someone with special expertise in grief, trauma, sexual abuse, the occult, etc., to run a special topic group—thereby providing training to the other cofacilitator and expertise to the students.

Some SAP people have made arrangements with outside treatment professionals who come to specific topic groups at no cost to the school. These generous professionals consider this time a gift of their expertise to the community. For arrangements like this, it is often necessary to schedule the group at the same time every week (which may be a logistical hurdle) to accommodate the schedule of the outside professional.

Because adolescents are so vulnerable to adults, you will want to make sure that any outside people conduct themselves according to the highest ethical standards. No matter how trustworthy outside people are, school-based SAPs should take care to include a cofacilitator who can make sure the practices of the professional are consistent with the practices of the SAP and the school. If the outside professional in question is unwilling to work with a school-based person, you need to wonder why.

Try to forge a relationship between your school and city and state offices such as your state Office of Alcohol and Drug Abuse Prevention. Most of these agencies employ certified alcohol and drug abuse counselors to do outreach work and would be happy to make contacts in the school system. It's great to have these folks come to a school-based SAP meeting to share some of their expertise, though they may not be able to offer ongoing participation. Also look into your local office of Youth Services or Child Protective Services. Many of these offices, while over-burdened, are making attempts to come into the communities to do prevention work. There is no better audience for prevention efforts than high school and junior high school students.

We have had tremendous success in utilizing counselors from the Office of Youth Services to conduct chemical dependency assessments and to intervene with families in crisis—particularly families with limited means. In some cases, personnel from these offices can become group cofacilitators. Conflict of interest is less of a concern because there is no potential for profit. Not only does this arrangement help school-based SAPs, but it creates a needed bridge to services in the community. Agencies may want to count the group members as contacts for the agency, which provides them with higher numbers statistically. However, before asking a person connected to any agency to be involved with group on an ongoing basis, make sure that the agency is willing to maintain the same strict level of confidentiality that the SAP adheres to.

Avoiding Role Conflict for Outside Professionals

Most of the potential role conflict with outside professionals stems from money. If a professional comes from a private agency and is volunteering time, will that agency expect referrals to the agency in return? If this is the case, then the time is not really volunteered at all and there is an unwritten agreement about "payment." Such arrangements are dangerous policy. Outside professionals should not be in the schools drumming up business for their private agencies. The roles are far too muddled and the ethical concerns too great. Volunteers should be volunteers with no strings attached—preferably people who have personal convictions about sharing expertise and want to keep up with what is going on with adolescents in school environments. My experience has been that many positive relationships with private agencies can be forged, and many do volunteer their time with no strings attached.

Using Self-Help Group Volunteers as Group Facilitators

Seasoned members of AA, NA, or Al-Anon may be good group facilitators, if they are willing to volunteer their time and if the school understands that self-help volunteers are not professionally trained. Self-help volunteers can share their own experience, strength, and hope with members of the group, which is the very nature of self-help. School-based SAPs should contact the public information bureaus of any of the twelve-step programs for further information. (Call the main number in your local phone book.)

Another way to utilize this valuable resource is to ask twelve-step group members to be guest speakers at group. It is particularly effective to have young recovering people come to speak to either challenge groups or recovery groups, perhaps creating a bridge for students to get to a meeting themselves. Adolescents respond to peers, so whenever possible, ask another adolescent or young adult to share his or her story of recovery from addiction.

Avoiding Role Conflict for Self-Help Volunteers

School-based SAPs are not school-based twelve-step programs; their missions are similar but separate. Self-help volunteers must be willing to recognize the differences, particularly if they are going to help cofacilitate a group. One-time guests may represent the twelve-step programs in the area and may try to attract new membership, but ongoing group cofacilitation must be more balanced. The measure of success for SAP participants is not whether they eventually join twelve-step programs but whether they make positive changes in their day-to-day lives, including a positive change in their school performance. Volunteers from twelve-step programs must keep their roles separate if they are to work in the school on a long-term basis.

PROMOTING STUDENT PARTICIPATION IN GROUPS

Student assistance programs generate referrals for participation in groups in different ways. Some SAPs wait for students to be referred to them because of behaviorally based observations from teachers before they try to assemble groups. Originally, this group approach came out of need; students were referred for assessments and, sooner or later, SAP people had more of them than they could handle individually. Because outside resources were limited, in-school groups were born. The time it takes to gather a group of students with similar concerns who could benefit from the group experience depends on how active your faculty is in making referrals and what the "lag" is before core team members or SAP people can make the appropriate assessments and referrals to groups. Waiting for appropriate referrals to fill groups is still a good plan in systems where there is no SAP counselor, because the process of advertising groups is a massive logistical effort and most core teams will have their hands full simply keeping up with teacher referrals. If your structure is narrow and elicits very few referrals annually, you may not have sufficient numbers of students to run groups. However, because groups have proved so effective, group participation for a good percentage of referrals should be your aim.

In systems where there is an SAP counselor or a dedicated individual with time who can take on the task of promoting groups, a call for group participation can be made by making a pitch classroom to classroom, or sending out some sort of sign-up sheet. This pitch can be delivered in the context of a larger presentation to introduce the SAP person and to explain the procedures on how students can access the SAP. Participation can also be elicited through any number of ancillary programs or from distinct subsets of students: return visitors to the disciplinary system, students on academic probation, freshman study groups—any group that presents itself in your particular system.

If your SAP group effort is starting up, the personal appearance of the SAP person is essential in these presentations to get students to sign up for groups. Presentations should include a description of the groups, and an individual sign-up sheet should be distributed to every student. (See samples on following pages.) Adolescents won't sign a paper if they don't have any inkling of who will be sorting through this stack of sign-up sheets and eventually handling the group. On the other hand, in systems where the SAP person(s) is known and well liked, sending individual sign-up sheets out to homerooms and asking students to return them to the SAP person if they wish to join is a workable solution. You can also put a call out for groups during regular school announcements through an intercom or television system. Include a time limit for initial group sign-ups and start scheduling groups right away so the anxiety-producing wait for groups to start is shorter.

Creating a Safe Environment for Students to Join Groups

In classroom presentations where you are eliciting participation in groups, you will want to take great care to insure that students who want to sign up can do so safely, without other students ridiculing them. One way of doing this is to pass out sign-up sheets to all students and to require that everyone fill out their name and homeroom, regardless of whether they want to sign up or not. That means that all the students will be similarly occupied with reading over the sign-up sheet. Some sign-up sheets include a spot to check off "Do not want to join" buried somewhere among all the other options. This keeps those who are not interested in group participation occupied while those who are fill out their sign-up sheets. Ask students to turn their papers over as soon as they are done, and collect them one by one. Do not ask students to pick up the papers or "pass them to the right," etc. In your presentation, appeal to students' maturity and ask that they keep to themselves whether they are signing up for group. If you don't do this, an influential student can make a disparaging comment that would inhibit others from joining. If Joe Popular exclaims, "Only a geek would join something like this. I'm not joining!" chances are that participation from that class will be low.

CONDUCTING A "TEST MARKET SURVEY"

The only potential danger is that you will get more students to sign up than you ever imagined, so if you choose to elicit group participation, it may be advisable to try a "test market" of sorts to see what kind of response you'll get. In my first year as an SAP director, we canvassed only one quarter of the high school population (400 of 1,600) and received requests from fifty students who wanted to be a part of various groups. This seemed like a good return on our investment of time and a feasible number of students for the first time around. I can only assume that if we had canvassed the entire population, we would have received 200 requests, and, at that time, we weren't prepared to manage those numbers. It might have been a disaster. Remember that there is self-selection at work in this method; older students (juniors and seniors in high school) seem to be more willing to sign up from surveys and sign-up sheets, so take that into consideration when eliciting participation.

There are philosophical questions inherent in any kind of "selective test

STUDENT ASSISTANCE PROGRAM GROUPS

Confidential groups that deal with the following issues are available to students through the student assistance program. Please check off those issues that apply to you, fold the paper, and return this sheet to your homeroom teacher or to the student assistance program office.

This Sheet Will Be Kept in Strict Confidence.

☐ Dealing with a divorced family/stepfamily

☐ Coping with an alcoholic parent, guardian, or close relative

☐ Coping with a drug-addicted parent, guardian, or close relative

☐ Educational group about alcohol and other drugs

☐ Challenge group to take a look at *your own* drinking or drugging

☐ Recovery group for students who want to stay clean and sober

☐ Girls' discussion group

☐ Boys' discussion group

☐ Co-ed discussion group—"Peers, Parents, and Partying"

☐ Dealing with a pregnancy or a child while finishing school

☐ Stop-smoking group

☐ I'd like an individual appointment to discuss my options.

☐ I have a suggestion for another group _____
(write in your suggestion)

_____

_____

_____

_____

_____

_____

_____

_____

_____

Name _____ **Homeroom** ___ **Grade** _____

ATTENTION   *ATTENTION*   *ATTENTION*

Student Assistance Program

The student assistance program offers discussion groups for the spring semester. This is a great way to address problems you might be having while at school. Groups meet on a rotating basis so you do not miss the same period each time. Absences are noncounting.

1. Discussion Group—Discuss those issues close to your heart—parents, pressure, and partying—and get some healthy tips on coping. *You do not have to be having any problems to join this group!* (Maybe you can avoid some by joining!)

2. Friends' Group—For those concerned about the drinking or drugging of a close friend or relative. Learn about the disease called addiction and how to help yourself deal with a friend or relative who drinks or does drugs.

3. Recovery Group—Are you staying away from drugs and alcohol and would like some support? There are a lot of you out there! Join this recovery group that deals with the issues of being clean and sober while in high school.

4. Educational Group—Do you ever wonder about yourself or someone you love? Learn more about drugs and alcohol. Learn about the signs of addiction and how to help yourself or someone you love get straight.

If you are interested in any of the above groups, please complete the bottom portion of this handout and put it in the student assistance program mailbox. The office is at the left end of the guidance hall. Mrs. Newsam will contact you concerning meeting times. All participation is confidential.

- -

Name _____ Group number _____

Grade _____ Homeroom _____

Alternative Sign-Up Sheet

Name _____ Age ____ Grade 9 10 11 12

Homeroom _____

Check off all of the groups that apply to you or interest you.

1. ☐ Adjusting to high school
2. ☐ Coping with the illness of a loved one
3. ☐ Living with chronic illness
4. ☐ Communication problems at home
5. ☐ Adjusting to a stepfamily
6. ☐ Alcoholic/drug-abusing family member
7. ☐ Remaining free of alcohol and/or other drugs
8. ☐ Quitting smoking
9. ☐ Identifying an alcohol/drug problem
10. ☐ Recovering from alcohol or drug problems
11. ☐ Study skills
12. ☐ Coping with death
13. ☐ Making friends
14. ☐ Do not want to join
15. ☐ Coping with divorce
16. ☐ Teen parents
17. ☐ Coping with pregnancy
18. ☐ Healthy relationships
19. ☐ Other

Student assistance program support groups are confidential except in cases of child abuse or when you are a threat to yourself or someone else.

STUDENT SCHEDULE

MOD	SUBJECT	ROOM	TEACHER	
A				
B				
HOMEROOM				
C				
D				
E				
F				
G				
H				

This paper will be held in strict confidence.

———————————

Used with permission of Mary-Jo Bourque, Memorial High School SAP, Manchester, New Hampshire.

marketing" because you might ask yourself, "Shouldn't every student have the same access to SAP services?" Ideally, they all will have access to services through the observation of teachers who will refer to the program those students who are displaying maladaptive behavior in the classroom. These students should end up in groups anyway. Eliciting wide participation through canvassing the entire student body is the role of fleshed-out, counselor-based SAP services (unless you are in a very small school). You cannot offer services to every student if you cannot provide them.

DESIGNING A WORKABLE GROUP SCHEDULE

Scheduling groups may be one of the SAP's most difficult challenges because nailing down the schedule requires complicated logistical feats. The things to consider when scheduling groups are (1) will the schedule give you sufficient time with the students to cover issues appropriately? and (2) how can the schedule minimize disruptions to the students' academic schedules? Your core team can brainstorm the best way to run groups during the initial training. If you have an existing group schedule, don't be afraid to reevaluate whether it is working or needs fine-tuning (or a complete overhaul). If you are just starting out running groups, begin with two or three for a semester to gauge how the school community responds. There are several ways to manage group schedules.

Scheduling Groups throughout the School Day

This is the ideal working model for successful SAP group operation. Each group meets once a week in the same place, on a rotating schedule so students work through missing their classes one by one. Because of the rotation, the same teacher is not always being inconvenienced by having students taken out of class. Two versions of a sample rotating group schedule follow. The samples include five rotating, one-period groups, plus a challenge group (two class periods per session, group 5), and one nonrotating group (group 7). This sample group schedule should not be regarded as definitive; depending on the SAP structure, many SAP counselors run fewer groups while heavily group-oriented programs run many more. Our program has run as many as fourteen groups at a time, utilizing the skills of the SAP personnel, outside professionals, community volunteers, student interns, and interested guidance counselors.

One extremely helpful tool for scheduling groups is at least one large "write-on/wipe-off" calendar that you can keep posted outside the group room or office with the current month's group schedule. If possible, get two, and post them in convenient places in the school so students and faculty alike can prepare a few weeks in advance. Various organizations (the Armed Forces, colleges, class ring distributors) give out large calendars on a fairly regular basis, so if you can't get the write-on/wipe-off variety, use your charms to secure a couple of these for group schedules. It helps your own organization to be able to see at a moment's glance the commitments for the following month. Be sure to list the groups by numbers, colors, or codes on this large posted schedule, because the point is to make it accessible to everyone without compromising individual students' confidentiality. The posted schedule definitely breaks students' confidentiality if it

SAP GROUP SCHEDULE*
ANYMONTH, 199__

	MONDAY	TUESDAY	WEDNESDAY	THURSDAY	FRIDAY
Week 1	Group 1–P1* Group 4–P4 Group 6–P5	Group 2–P2 Group 5–P4&5**	Group 7–P7***	Drop-in lunch†	Group 3–P3
Week 2	Group 1–P2 Group 4–P5 Group 6–P6	Group 2–P3 Group 5–P6&7	Group 7–P7***	Drop-in lunch†	Group 3–P4
Week 3	Group 1–P3 Group 4–P6 Group 6–P7	Group 2–P4 Group 5–P1&2	Group 7–P7***	Drop-in lunch†	Group 3–P5
Week 4	Group 1–P4 Group 4–P7 Group 6–P1	Group 2–P5 Group 5–P3&4	Group 7–P7***	Drop-in lunch†	Group 3–P6

---

*P denotes class period. Notice that the groups are always listed by number only. That way, the nature of particular groups is kept confidential.

**Group 5 takes two class periods because it is a challenge group.

***Notice that group 7 (topic group) is fixed, assuming that an outside professional is helping with that group and can commit to one time during the week.

†Drop-in lunch is a once-a-week lunchtime meeting for children of addiction (members of groups 1, 2, and 5) who want to meet during their lunch period.

MONTHLY SAP SCHEDULE*

SAMPLE WEEK 1

	Monday	Tuesday	Wednesday	Thursday	Friday
Period 1	Group 1			Clinical Supervision	
Period 2		Group 2		Clinical Supervision	
Period 3			Paperwork and/or Ancillary Programming		Group 3
Period 4	Group 4	Group 5	Paperwork and/or Ancillary Programming		
Period 5	Group 6		Paperwork and/or Ancillary Programming		
Period 6			Paperwork and/or Ancillary Programming	Lunch-Time Meetings	
Period 7			Topic Group	Lunch-Time Meetings	

SAMPLE WEEK 2

	Monday	Tuesday	Wednesday	Thursday	Friday
Period 1				Clinical Supervision	
Period 2	Group 1			Clinical Supervision	
Period 3		Group 2	Paperwork and/or Ancillary Programming		
Period 4			Paperwork and/or Ancillary Programming		Group 3
Period 5	Group 4	Group 5	Paperwork and/or Ancillary Programming		
Period 6	Group 6		Paperwork and/or Ancillary Programming	Lunch-Time Meetings	
Period 7			Topic Group	Lunch-Time Meetings	

SAMPLE WEEK 3

	Monday	Tuesday	Wednesday	Thursday	Friday
Period 1				Clinical Supervision	
Period 2				Clinical Supervision	
Period 3	Group 1		Paperwork and/or Ancillary Programming		
Period 4		Group 2	Paperwork and/or Ancillary Programming		
Period 5			Paperwork and/or Ancillary Programming		Group 3
Period 6	Group 4	Group 5	Paperwork and/or Ancillary Programming	Lunch-Time Meetings	
Period 7	Group 6		Topic Group	Lunch-Time Meetings	

SAMPLE WEEK 4

	Monday	Tuesday	Wednesday	Thursday	Friday
Period 1	Group 6			Clinical Supervision	
Period 2				Clinical Supervision	
Period 3			Paperwork and/or Ancillary Programming		
Period 4	Group 1		Paperwork and/or Ancillary Programming		
Period 5		Group 2	Paperwork and/or Ancillary Programming		
Period 6			Paperwork and/or Ancillary Programming	Lunch-Time Meetings	Group 3
Period 7	Group 4	Group 5	Topic Group	Lunch-Time Meetings	

shows, for instance, that the COA group meets period 4 in room 12 and then their friends see them going there. Even though most kids are freer with their confidentiality than you are, you must set the standard for respect. It's always better to be safe than sorry, lest we unknowingly break the trust of adolescents who desperately need someone to count on in their lives.

Accommodating Student Needs in Scheduling

In certain cases, one class period will not be enough for a group to cover what needs to be covered in a session, in which case a creative solution will be required so students get what they need without sacrificing academic classes. Always plan for this in advance; don't wait for the bell to ring and then decide to extend group right on the spot. Of course, there are going to be extreme cases when this will be necessary, when you may have to run over for a few minutes, but it's bad policy to let this happen often. Students who are late to the next classes again and again are the ones who have to deal with the consternation of their teachers when they arrive. Better to anticipate that some groups simply need more time per session. A case in point: It is recommended that challenge groups run for six weeks for two consecutive class periods each, making a total of twelve class periods missed. This is appropriate for short-term groups because the time out of class is limited. However, there may be situations when a group regularly requires more than one class period. In this case, schedule the group every two weeks for two consecutive periods. If the periods in your school are extremely short, you may want to make this the standard for all groups. In most schools, though, one class period per week is sufficient for group participation. Proven effective in many school systems, this one period per week seems a small price to pay to address long-ignored problems that keep students from reaching their academic and social goals.

Scheduling Groups during Free Periods

Some student assistance programs have successfully used this approach, particularly in structures that do not include an SAP counselor, where cofacilitation is dependent on teachers also having a free period to run an SAP group. One concern about this approach is that in schools where everyone has the same free time every day, participants in the SAP are easily identified, compromising their confidentiality. This approach can also punish students who need their free periods for studying. Asking students to give up a free period every time group meets may discourage some students from joining. One could also argue that this approach indicates weak administrative support and that some students will be missed because of full schedules. If you must run basic SAP groups during free periods, do so, but work toward a policy that recognizes the importance of groups as an integral part of the total curriculum. When you use a rotating group schedule, students have to give up free periods as well as class time, balancing the commitment of the students and the school.

There are good reasons to run some types of groups during free periods. These would be less formal groups, perhaps lunch-time drop-in discussion groups or group meetings *in addition* to regularly scheduled meetings. In a larger school, you may have four or five children of addiction groups (friends' groups) that meet on a rotating class schedule. You might design a lunch-time program for any students from those groups who want to drop in at a specific time for a "pick-up" meeting with whoever shows up. "Rap" groups or general discussion groups are also good candidates for free periods, because they offer the group experience to a larger group of students.

Scheduling Groups Before and After School

There are some ancillary programs that are appropriate for after school—for instance, extra activities for recovery groups or perhaps an Alateen or AA Young People's meeting housed in a school building. Similarly, having a before-school drop-in program or more structured meeting for recovering or reentering students or disciplinary referrals can be a creative response to the need for especially high-risk students to have daily contact with caring adults. These extra components are successful and worthwhile but are not part of the core functions of a working SAP. To have all SAP groups after school is like asking the school nurse to come in after school for those students who want to stay after to discuss a health problem that is bothering them. Eventually, basic student assistance programming must be part of the general operation of the school. However, some start-up efforts will only be able to manage afterschool groups, in which case it is a fair start.

REMINDING STUDENTS ABOUT GROUP

An issue that requires a fair amount of consideration by SAP people is how to remind students about group participation. Is it our responsibility? Should we "enable" students to forget, knowing that we will remind them later? Some SAP people believe that the responsibility is shouldered fully by the students and that no reminders are necessary. Some believe that nonattendance or "forgetting" group is psychologically motivated and indicates that students are not ready for group. My experience has been that how often students do not show up for group has a great deal to do with how rigid the system is. If students are kept track of consistently throughout the school day, they will probably come to group fairly regularly, because they can't be anywhere else without drawing attention to themselves. If it is a more open system, students are more likely to "forget" group, especially during lunch and free periods, when they can blend in with their friends.

There are probably a thousand reasons why students sometimes forget to come to group, and some of them definitely are psychologically based, but the pragmatic question for SAP people is whether they are going to take on the task of reminding students in some way. Reminding students may never even cross your mind as a possibility until you have scheduled a guest speaker who pushes aside all professional duties to come by for a group session and only two students show up for group because there's a field trip they forgot to tell you about. Unfortunately, this happens more often than you'd think. Here are several options for reminding students about group, listed from the easiest to the most time-consuming.

- At each group meeting, announce when the next session will be. If students don't show up, it's their loss.
- Give students the list of dates and times of the next meeting.
- Post the schedule in a couple of visible places, and leave it at that.
- Institute a "buddy system." Each group participant is paired with another. They must exchange class schedules, and if one doesn't show up, the other one has to go get him or her. Both are counted as tardy if this process disrupts the group. (Be careful not to create a monster by pairing two mischief-makers.)
- Announce groups by number over the intercom system at the beginning of the day.
- Announce groups by number over the intercom system immediately prior to the meeting.
- Send reminder slips to all participants through their homerooms. (One benefit of this approach—although there are significant drawbacks as well—is that you can also make changes in the group schedule to accommodate unforeseen events.)

A sample reminder slip follows.

Group # _____

Please note that your group meets on: _____ (date)

Mon, Tues, Wed, Thurs, Fri   Period: A, B, C, D, E, F, G, H

☐ This is a regularly scheduled meeting.
☐ This is a change in schedule because of unusual circumstances.
☐ This week's meeting has been canceled.

Teachers: This is only a note reminding students! They will return with a verification pass if they came to group. Please ask for verification.

Experiment with these methods to see what works in your system. You may come up with very creative ideas to insure almost perfect attendance. A great deal will depend on whether you are working in a large or small school, whether groups are open or closed, and whether your group composition is cohesive or scattered. Unfortunately, my experience has been that the number of students who show up for group is directly related to how much effort the SAP person puts into reminding them.

KEEPING TRACK OF GROUP ATTENDANCE

If I could give only one piece of advice to new or even seasoned SAP people, it would be to keep accurate attendance records of group participation. Teachers relinquish some control to SAPs when they allow their students to attend group and expect that you will at least keep track of their students when they are not in class. The very nature of adolescence is to test boundaries; some students will report to their teachers that they were in group when they were not. You win deserved credibility from teachers when they mention to you that a certain student has been in group often lately, and you can check attendance records immediately. Sometimes a student who has been telling a teacher that he's at group has actually been meeting his girlfriend in the cafeteria or hiding out in the library with his friends.

If your program structure is broad brush in nature and participation does not identify students as alcohol and/or other drug abusers, encourage teachers to check on attendance and keep in touch with you, because it creates alliances and keeps the lines of communication open. Abuses of group participation and group passes should be dealt with quickly and strictly. Tell teachers that you are more than happy to confirm that passes are genuine. Also, be sure to tell students up front that any tampering with passes is very serious business that will result in disciplinary action. The credibility of your entire program is jeopardized when other staff see group participation as a way for kids to get out of their responsibilities. Figure 9–1 illustrates the process of keeping track of students in groups.

One way to handle passes is to utilize a two- or three-step system. First, remind students about their group meeting using a reminder note like the preceding one. Then, when students actually come to group, they get another pass which verifies their attendance. That way, students have something to show their teachers on the way out of the classroom, and something to show them the next day that verifies where they were. If you only use a reminder, students can leave the class but never show up to group. Have students fill out everything but the authorizing signature on the verification passes (in ink) first thing as they file in for group. Then, you can supply the authorizing signatures. If you deal in large num-

This pass verifies that _____
                                              (student's name)
was in the student assistance program office on _____Time _____
                                                                (date)
Class period _____

Authorized Signature _____
                                              (SAP personnel)

Figure 9-1.
SYSTEM TO ACCOUNT
FOR STUDENT PARTICIPATION
IN GROUP

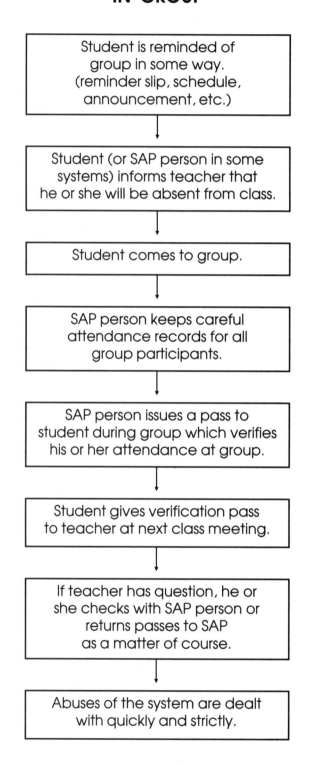

Student is reminded of group in some way. (reminder slip, schedule, announcement, etc.)

Student (or SAP person in some systems) informs teacher that he or she will be absent from class.

Student comes to group.

SAP person keeps careful attendance records for all group participants.

SAP person issues a pass to student during group which verifies his or her attendance at group.

Student gives verification pass to teacher at next class meeting.

If teacher has question, he or she checks with SAP person or returns passes to SAP as a matter of course.

Abuses of the system are dealt with quickly and strictly.

bers of students, invest in a signature stamp which, if kept extremely secure (like in your pocket), will reduce the number of falsified passes. An additional step well worth taking is to ask teachers to return verification passes to you. That way, you can check that students are using them properly, while keeping communication with teachers open.

Keep group attendance records in your personal files, and never indicate what kind of group it is on the record itself. Identify the group by a number or color code only, to protect the confidentiality of the students. Even without any identifying information on the card, do not tell others who else is in the same group because they will speculate about the issue common to participants—"Oh, Bob and Sam are in that group together; it must be for kids who have alcoholic parents."

DEVELOPING PROCEDURES FOR STUDENTS WHO MISS GROUP

Some programs will approach group attendance and participation much like classroom attendance—with a certain number of absences creating some consistent response. That response usually can't be the same one students would get if they missed classes, because, for the most part, group participation is a choice while class participation is not. For instance, after a student has missed three group sessions in a row, I call him or her in to discuss what's going on and whether the student wishes to continue with group participation. Usually, they're pleasantly surprised that the group leaders noticed, and you may discover that there is in-fighting among group members or that someone's confidentiality has been compromised. In those cases, students should be encouraged to come back to group to make the appropriate confrontations in group.

For mandatory group participation (a challenge group for chemical use policy violators, for instance), your programs may choose to devise some disciplinary action for nonattendance. Be careful not to make your SAP into an enforcement agency. Attendance rules should be outlined in the beginning sessions, and students can always use a reminder here and there. If the student does not fulfill his or her attendance contract, the administrator who will levy the disciplinary consequences should be notified.

ESTABLISHING GROUP GROUND RULES

Rules are most closely adhered to when students have a hand in making them, adjusting them, or amending them. Experience has shown that students understand the need for rules and can work within their confines as long as they are outlined from the start, and as long as they have a chance to question them before they are cast in stone.

Student assistance program adults are responsible for enforcing the rules, not just presenting them and hoping against hope that no one violates them. This is the one area in which SAP people need to act like other school personnel and must concentrate on constancy and consistency. Not enforcing rules is easier in the short run, but agonizing in the long run, as you end up having to "put your foot down" in an uncharacteristic move which catches students unaware and frightens some. Children of addiction, in particular, need SAP people to act like adults—if we don't, we repeat the same dysfunction they experience in their families and they legitimately wonder, "Who's in charge here? Am I safe here? Are they giving me a mixed message—here are the rules, but it's okay if you break them? Since they're not handling the problem, should I?" Leaders should not try to *control* the group or the particular outcomes of students' lives, but, in the context of the group, students need to know that someone will handle enforcing the rules consistently, and it shouldn't be the students.

If a troublesome issue presents itself in group, which it invariably will, it can be helpful to bring it up to the students for discussion. In one of my COA groups, for example, students were filing in late for group sessions, making both the leaders and the students who had arrived on time feel cheated out of group time. Our school counts "tardies" against absences, which eventually affects a grade in a class, so to count tardies wouldn't have helped in the least. When the situation was brought up to the whole group, the offending students themselves offered a solution. Three minutes after the bell rang, it became a leader's job to close (and lock) the door to the group room. Anyone left outside for the duration of the group either had to go into class tardy or be counted absent from both group and class. Here is a great example of students having a hand in creating a rule, with the leaders taking responsibility for enforcing it. How difficult it was to close that door the first week! (But how quickly the problem was rectified!) Remember, too, that students will rise to meet the expectations you have for them, if it is possible for them to do so. An example of student assistance program group rules can be found on the next page.

Making Group Rules Consistent with School Policy

Managing group rules and school rules is an issue to which you should give a lot of thought. Some school rules may seem arbitrary, and you may not believe in all of them, but to not enforce them alienates your SAP operation from the general operating procedures of the school. Your program becomes a subversive operation. Following are a few of the seemingly insignificant, mundane issues that can become problems if not thought through:

Eating or Drinking in Group: If students aren't allowed to eat or drink in classes, should they be allowed to eat and drink in group? Our groups run through lunch periods, so we answer this question affirmatively. We've recently purchased a small carpet sweeper, and students are responsible for throwing out all their trash, putting bottles into the recyclables bin, and sweeping up under their chairs at the end of each group session. If you don't run through lunches, this is something you'll have to decide. While at first you may be tempted to offer this as incentive for students to join groups, students will join anyway, so don't let this affect your decision.

Use of Profanity in Groups: I allow a modest amount of profanity in groups at the outset because it is the language some of my students speak and they can't at first seem to express their feelings in any other way. But I encourage students to express themselves in language that will offend no one so everyone

SAP GROUP RULES

Name _____ HR ____ Group # ____ Date _____

Participating in a group here at school brings both rights and responsibilities. Your initials by each right or rule indicate your understanding of what is expected of you.

_____What you hear here, stays here. Confidentiality is the cornerstone of a working group.

_____You are encouraged to share your experience. Please also support other members of the group as they share theirs.

_____You are expected to attend group free of alcohol and other drugs. *Do not* come to group under the influence.

_____Your confidentiality will be broken by the counselor(s) if there is reason to believe that you are suicidal, homicidal, or if there are indications of abuse or neglect.

_____Absences due to group participation are noncounting. This privilege must not be abused. *You are responsible for all classwork missed.*

_____You are expected to attend group on time every week. If you do not attend group on your lunch or free mods, and are not on the absent list, a cut-slip will be sent. This rule has been adopted to insure that all participants are committed to group participation, not to missing classes.

_____You have the right to withdraw from group participation at any time, but you *must* inform the counselor.

These rules have been set down to insure commitment to the SAP and to one another. Your input is always appreciated.

I have read the following rules and have initialed each one. I understand that they are necessary, and my signature here indicates my willingness to follow them.

_____,   _____
Student's signature   Date

can "hear" them. After establishing trust, challenge them to try to say it another way. If swearing gets out of hand, or students begin to swear for the sake of swearing, I may say, "I need to have you stop swearing because it's distracting me from what you're trying to tell me." Adolescents are looking for the limitations, and once they've found them, they tend to be a little more comfortable. If profanity makes you uncomfortable, insist that students refrain from using it, and couch the rule positively in your ground rules or preamble.

Dress Code in Groups: Certain schools have dress codes, and students are expected to dress appropriately for school. You may avoid unnecessary trouble by staying consistent with these policies. More murky are issues such as the following: If a student has gym right before group, can he or she come to group in gym clothes? Or, for instance, in my district, young men are not allowed to wear hats in the school building, though many do. Use your judgment in determining these things, but any insignificant departure from the rules that can draw unnecessary negative attention to the program should be avoided. A good rule of thumb is to imagine a student telling your principal the rules and procedures of group. If one particular issue makes you squirm, you had better look into it.

DETERMINING WHETHER A GROUP IS OPEN OR CLOSED

One of the things that you must establish right away is whether a particular group is open or closed. This is a decision that is usually made by the group leaders, but in special cases, students can decide whether to keep a group closed or to open it to general membership. I have tried keeping a group open until a certain date (that student participants determine) and then closing it to new membership thereafter. A closed group consists of the same students each week from the beginning to the closure of group. This is sometimes a good format for educational COA groups, particularly those of short duration. Challenge groups should always be closed, and most discussion and special topic groups, if they are educational and time-limited in nature, should be closed. You have such a short period of time in the first place that it doesn't seem to make much sense to have the introduction of new members upsetting the careful balance you've achieved. If new students come to the attention of the SAP while a short-term closed group is in session, this student should be encouraged to hang on until another group can be assembled.

Ongoing support groups are good candidates for open membership. Using this format, a student who has just come to terms with an alcoholic parent, for instance, can join a group consisting of students at various levels of acceptance of their problems. Newer members can benefit from the wisdom of more experienced members. There are challenges with this format, especially since underclass students (freshmen and sophomores) are very different developmentally from upperclass students. Sometimes, however, these differences work to advantage. Older members can serve as role models to younger participants, and older students can identify with the feelings of younger members as they move into adulthood. I have seen incredible interaction between students from seventh grade to twelfth grade; it can work well.

Recovery groups for students recovering from addiction should always be open, in my opinion. Recovery group depends on the accumulated experience of students who have successfully negotiated school without using alcohol or other drugs. That experience should be made available to all who need it, particularly students who are just returning from treatment and reentering school. Special topic groups could be developed from a base of recovering students. For example, single gender groups can discuss issues in recovery which they might have trouble discussing in a co-ed environment. But general recovery group participation should be open to all who want it—because it provides not only in-school support but access to a life-sustaining group of alcohol and other drug-free friends which is so essential to adolescent recovery and relapse prevention.

TROUBLESHOOTING GROUP PROBLEMS

One of the best ways to troubleshoot problems in groups is to be willing to examine leadership practices as a possible contributor to problems. To say, "It's those darned kids, they don't have any respect," etc., denies the possibility of working on the problem from the leadership end. To balance the scale, however, there are some problems which will exhaust every trick in the SAP bag and still go unsolved. As in most circumstances in life, we must endeavor to accept the things we can't change and find the courage to change the things we can.

Maintaining Regular Attendance

If attendance is uncharacteristically poor in a particular group and good in others, it would make sense to look at the group in question and evaluate the composition, the leadership, the timing, and see if there is a problem that can be resolved easily by making minor adjustments. There also might be confusion about the rules, or there might be a conflict between group members that you don't know anything about. How could you know that one member dated the other member's older brother, that they just broke up over the last weekend, and that group members took sides?

Usually, poor attendance in a particular group indicates that the group has not bonded well initially, or that it has fragmented into factions and you might want to reevaluate your start-up or screening procedures. You may want to send reminders to students (even if that's not your usual practice) and, when you have the group assembled, ask them what's going on. Sometimes these sessions are pretty electric as students communicate honestly for the first time in group about the concerns that kept them away on previous weeks. Sometimes this is when the group experience really starts.

In a group with spotty attendance, alter your leadership style to see if that has any effect on participant attendance. If you are unable to get students to come to group, you may have to see students individually to get to the bottom of the problem. There may have been some experience in group which traumatized students—for instance, someone interrupting group during a sensitive period or a perceived betrayal of trust of some kind.

If, on the other hand, attendance is poor across the board in most or all of your groups, you may have to look at more fundamental questions:

- Are the groups scheduled so students have access to them? What prevents them from attending?
- Do students understand the attendance requirements? Were they sufficiently outlined?
- Is the start-up of group too slow, leaving students frustrated and bored by the third or fourth session?
- Is the start-up of group too fast, so students feel overwhelmed by too much information or feel too vulnerable?
- Are teachers or administrators giving students trouble about group participation, either making it difficult to keep up with assignments or broadcasting a student's participation?
- Is group participation misperceived as being only for "losers" or "druggies" or some other stereotype?
- Is the leadership style too controlling—students feel unable to focus on what is important to *them?*
- Is the leadership style too lax—students feel that the leadership commitment is not there, and they feel vulnerable and dissatisfied at the same time?
- Are screening procedures insuring that participants are ready for group?

It's important to remember that group participation for students is, for the most part, voluntary. Students should not be punished in word or deed for not coming to group unless they are required to be there because of some disciplinary issue. Students who choose to leave group should not be made to feel that they have failed, but rather encouraged to think that the timing may not have been ideal and that they may want to come back to an SAP group next year or join another group later in life. Take extreme care not to shame students who are at various levels of dealing with very sensitive issues in their personal lives, lest they feel unable to ever deal with them. Student assistance program people represent "helping services" at large to students. Where we can offer no help, let us not harm, either. Unless there are unusual circumstances, recovering students who leave group are in a slightly different category because the likelihood that they are in grave danger is good. Student assistance program people should make a reasonable effort to get recovering students back into group and should monitor the students for relapse. Leaving group may be a significant indication that relapse is imminent or may have already begun.

Dealing with Students in Group Who Are under the Influence

Students who are under the influence of alcohol and/or other drugs should never be permitted to stay in a group of any kind. Their presence is unfair to other students. When people are in this state, they are unable to make rational observations about their own behavior. They are distracting or detached at best, erratic and potentially dangerous at worst. Decisions about how such situations should be handled should be made in conjunction with the core team and school administration. Group cofacilitators should be in agreement. These questions constitute treacherous philosophical terrain because they define how your SAP interfaces with the disciplinary system of the school and how your efforts will be perceived by both faculty and student populations. Don't make this decision alone! If something backfires, you'll want to know that others were in agreement with you. Several solutions are possible, though all have potential drawbacks.

Decide ahead of time what constitutes "under the influence." Some experienced SAP people can detect the odor of day-old alcohol on heavy drinkers and can sometimes tell when a student has smoked marijuana within twelve hours or so. Decide ahead of time how you'll respond when you ask a student if he's high and he tells you that okay he got high on the way to school, but now it's five hours later and he's not high anymore. My rule is that if I can detect it consciously, then others can notice it unconsciously.

I have also made mistakes and have thought students were under the influence when they weren't. However, observations made nonjudgmentally are not accusations and are usually valid. For instance, I once smelled alcohol on a student's breath and discovered that he was legitimately taking cough medicine (I say *legitimately* because over-the-counter medicines are rapidly becoming a drug of choice for students, particularly in the younger grades). So the observation was correct, but my hypothesis surrounding it was faulty. I have noticed red eyes that have turned out to be legitimate contact lens problems. The simple way to find out is to ask. "I notice that you smell like beer. Have you been drinking?" Sometimes just saying "I notice you smell like beer" is sufficient. No one can fault you for your observations. If you accuse, you have to retract it later. If you observe, your observations stand. Ways to confront students in group follow.

Confronting Students in Group Using the One-Chance Method: In this scenario, the group leaders confront the student in group and tell him or her their observations and that they believe the student is under the influence. If the student admits that he or she is under the influence, the group leader asks the student to leave and explains that there will be a follow-up appointment scheduled as soon as possible. Other participants may want to join the confrontation, but care must be taken here to keep the confrontation short and nonjudgmental—otherwise students get the message that they have access to a lot of attention and power through using. At all costs, avoid sarcasm. The message needs to be, "It's not okay to come to group under the influence of alcohol and other drugs. You'll have to leave." The message is *not,* "Boy, are you a stupid so-and-so for using. We're so disappointed in you . . . haven't you learned anything?" After the student has left, leaders should give the group the chance to process what has just happened. Some will be angry at the leaders, and some will be frightened simply because they have witnessed a confrontation.

During the follow-up appointment, the leader explains that that was the student's "one chance." The next time the student comes to group under the influence, a disciplinary referral will be made immediately. Keep track of who has used their one chance; it lasts for the entire relationship you have with the student. A student who cashes in his or her one chance as a freshman doesn't cultivate another one for use in junior year. Say what you mean and mean what you say (and don't say it mean!).

The one-chance method encourages students who may be experiencing difficulty in quitting to come to the SAP. Word gets out that students have one chance to talk to the SAP person, even if they are under the influence, without being "caught." Several students who are now clean and sober in my recovery group used that one chance to come into the office when they were finally sick and tired of being sick and tired. Some students use this set-up to ask for help nonverbally. It also encourages honesty about use; if students know they have one chance and they're confronted, they can answer honestly. Giving students one chance means that if you have an SAP person with heightened sensitivity to alcohol and other drug use, this skill will not be perceived as being used to unfair advantage. To a certain extent, however, this system enables the student to use, if only once. Also, leaders have to be fairly confident about the detection of use. This method also requires some room for flexibility. If a student is unable to function because of the use, then parents and at least the school nurse need to be involved. It can also send out a double message to faculty—okay, you are supposed to "catch" students, but when the SAP does, we give them a break.

Making a Disciplinary Referral Immediately: In this case, when current student alcohol or other drug use is detected in group, the student is asked to leave and a referral to the disciplinary system is made immediately. When you have more than one group leader, one leader can immediately take the student to the administrative office in question, leaving the disciplinary consequence to the school administration. The chemical use policy adopted by your school or district will dictate how the administration responds to the violation. That's why your core team put in the time to develop it or amend the existing one.

This method sends an unequivocal message of no use in the school, which is what we ultimately want to convey. Teachers will feel that the SAP is practicing what it preaches. On the other hand, students can become confused about the role of the SAP and may be reluctant to share information in group, thinking that talking about past use can get them into trouble. Having a no-chance policy can unintentionally encourage dishonesty because when confronted with suspected use, students knows that to admit the use will bring a disciplinary action, so they insist that they didn't use. Because SAP people generally have better training in detecting alcohol and other drug use, their skills can be perceived as an unfair advantage. The SAP person can be perceived as a "narc," and self-referrals to the program may suffer.

Making a Private Confrontation: If, logistically, you can get to a student you are fairly sure is under the influence before group starts and make the confrontation individually, this would seem to blend all the best possible solutions. This has happened to me a few times—while students were filing in, I've been able to say very casually, "Joe, I need to see you for a second" and, walking directly into the hallway, make a quick and private confrontation. From this point, you either continue with your one-chance policy or with the immediate disciplinary referral, whichever is your usual method. Talking to the student after group, while seemingly more comfortable for some people, cheats the other students out of the leader's attention throughout group. Only a superhuman counselor could endure group with a student under the influence without going over and over what to say to the student later. In some cases when you are truly unsure if a student is under the influence, let it go so it doesn't occupy your attention, and wait to process it with your cofacilitator. When two facilitators concur that a student appeared to be under the influence, it is extremely likely that he or she was. In this case, even though you haven't "caught" the student, a follow-up appointment should be scheduled.

Doing Nothing: Unfortunately, this option sometimes tempts us. However, to do nothing repeats the same dysfunction and denial that has allowed students to get in as serious trouble with alcohol and other drugs as they already are. Student assistance program people must deal with these issues, awkward as it feels at first, falter as we may.

Group Interfering with Schoolwork

Occasionally, a student will have serious trouble juggling group participation with the rigors of an academic schedule and asks to drop out of group. Whenever possible, try to get a release of information from the student to work with guidance personnel and teachers to make group participation feasible. It is usually hypervigilant students who are concerned. Sometimes their anxiety is legitimate; at other times it indicates perfectionism. Children of addiction, children who have been sexually abused, bulimics, and anorexics tend to display this sort of behavior, so it's wise to take a second look at this type of request, just in case. Some kids will just outgrow the need for services and move on—and that's what we want, eventually. The goal is not to have students in groups for the rest of their lives, or even the rest of their schooling.

There is also the possibility that the student simply wants out of the group and has the need to describe it as academic troubles. Except in the case of recovering students who may be relapsing, this request should be respected, but it is worth calling the student to the office and asking the student what is going on. Sometimes it pays to ask the question in a very nonthreatening way—making sure that you have already taken the request seriously. "Since you've left group, Janet, I thought I could pick your brain a little bit about it. What did you think of the experience? Is there anything we could change or anything that you think is bothering the group members?" Since they are no longer group members, some students feel free to discuss their concerns. Some rejoin group at the closure of the discussion, or at least leave the door open to joining again at a later time.

Students Who Monopolize Group Time

Students who monopolize the group time are trying to secure the attention that they don't get elsewhere. And they probably need it. If you don't kill them first, you may have a fair shot at providing them with the appropriate attention.

A distinction can be made clearer here: SAP groups are not group therapy, though therapeutic things happen in their context. In group therapy, one conceptualizes the group as a microcosm of the world, and interaction within the group mimics interaction outside. The intent of group therapy is that participants confront one another about maladaptive patterns and it is deemed a therapeutic breakthrough when a person recognizes for himself or herself those patterns which have caused the self the most discomfort. If we were in the business of running group therapy, we would want our attention seekers to discover that this behavior is backfiring for them and we would hope that other people would support them in trying on a new behavior which is more adaptive. Of course, elements of this process happen in an SAP group, but you are more likely to have to take charge to insure that others get the "air time" they need. This may mean talking to the student in question privately or being very directive in group. "Bob, we need to get around to everybody." You can also include a reminder in your preamble or group rules that participants must give everyone an equal time to share. However, it has been my experience that just as you are about to confront a student who monopolizes group time (and have worked out a brilliant intervention), his or her behavior becomes more appropriate.

Dealing with the "Dead Group Syndrome"

Even with appropriately trained counselors, great screening procedures, administrative support, and a freshly painted group room, you still may have a group that just doesn't seem to work. I call this the "dead group syndrome." Rigorous evaluation leads me to believe that leaders are uncomfortable with groups in which they have to do a lot of work—perhaps where there is an unruly faction, or a silent membership—and they have to take on roles which are unfamiliar or uncomfortable. Like writing with the hand you're not accustomed to, it can be done, even if it is uncomfortable, barely decipherable, and exhausting. Luckily, most "dead" groups eventually come to life, usually through the very last thing you can think of to try.

The emotion to resist is anger. If our base natures could speak, they would say to students in "dead" groups—"Hey! you're making this too damned hard! What the heck do you guys want to talk about anyway?" Your best defense against anger is to talk to other people about your experiences without compromising anyone's confidentiality. If the three rules in real estate are location, location, and location, the rules for SAPs should be cofacilitate, cofacilitate, cofacilitate. Sharing the burden of a "dead" group diminishes its power to sap your self-confidence and energy for other groups.

Remember that groups that aren't working don't know how to work. Members are counting on leaders to facilitate the process. Try anything. Try games. Try humor. Try showing a film and then asking for reactions. Try using handouts. Try getting students to talk to each other in brief assignments. Add structure. Remove structure. Try taking them outside. After each student shares something, ask each student individually if he or she can identify with what the other has said. Resist the temptation to say something like, "I've run a lot of groups, and this one is the worst!" That punishes people for not doing what they don't know how to do. By the time you've tried everything, it's likely that the group will be almost over.

Surprisingly, while the leaders may chuckle about how dreadful the experience is, the students experience it very differently. For example, I had been running the same one-day-long ancillary program for two years with the same cofacilitator. Every Monday, eight to ten adolescents we had never met were delivered to us to learn something about alcohol and other drugs, and this particular week, the group was just awful. They never laughed at the jokes, they didn't respond to interactive activities, and they moaned and groaned at our every suggestion. That day was the longest on record. As we handed out the final evaluations, we were sure these were going to be the worst evaluations we had ever received. Shaking our heads in disbelief, we read the glowing evaluations; how we had listened to them, how we had answered questions they had had for a long time (though they never asked any!). The lesson here is that if you treat every group with respect and resist the temptation to compare them to other groups, students may have a positive experience, even if it is a lot of work for you.

Some Final Words about Groups

If you work on it, group participation can become the main thrust of your entire SAP operation. You can offer general discussion groups, friends' groups, recovery, parenting—the list goes on forever. Through general discussion groups, your SAP staff can identify students who may be at higher risk than others, and through groups for children of addiction, recovery groups, and challenge groups, you can create a safe place for those whose lives are touched by alcohol and other drug use. Special topic groups may provide enough positive identification and appropriate contact with professional counselors that students may avoid serious trouble later on or will know how to access the system later if they need it. A heavily group-oriented SAP is really the ideal, because it effectively channels the natural resources available in schools. It combines the energies of SAP personnel, additional interested cofacilitators, and the developmentally ideal component of peer interaction. With a variety of SAP groups and a broad-brush philosophy, great numbers of students can be reached. If you don't yet have any groups in your school, now is a great time to start!

An information handout you can use to explain groups to faculty follows. You will also find complete curricula, with worksheets, for friends', challenge, and recovery groups in chapters 12 through 14.

Faculty Information Handout
UNDERSTANDING SAP GROUP PARTICIPATION

When students take time out of your class to attend an SAP support group, you may legitimately wonder what goes on there. Is it important enough to take time out of class?

Why Groups in School? Some of you may wonder why we use school time to run groups through the SAP. The reasons are based in education. We have found over the years that some groups of students, particularly those who are dealing with very serious home situations, have very little concentration left for their studies. Taking them out of class every once in a while may make their time in class more productive. For those students who are at risk for dropping out of school completely, SAP group participation may be added incentive for them to even come to school. Because a lot of these students have responsibilities before and after school, we use school time to contact them. We use a rotating group schedule to minimize the inconvenience to each individual teacher.

Reasons for Groups: Counselors have found over the years that one of the best ways to support teenagers is to put them into a group of students who share their particular concerns. This combines adolescent energy with the students' need for peer identification. Add to that a trained group leader, and you can make some real progress. Children who live in families where there is addiction, for instance, can benefit greatly from sharing their concerns with others who can identify with them.

What Goes on in a Group Session? In most groups, there is a brief welcome to remind students about the rules of group (confidentiality, consideration, support, and sharing.) In some groups, there are structured educational activities about specific topics. For instance, in a "children of addiction" group, students might learn about the disease of addiction and the various symptoms, so they can feel less alone when they witness these symptoms. In other groups, students share their experiences from the previous week. For instance, in a group for students recovering from addiction, students might share how they resisted the temptation to use. In some cases, they may share that they need additional help. Group sessions are generally educational and supportive in nature, but we do have specific rules of conduct.

What Can I Do? Your cooperation in letting students attend groups is greatly appreciated. There will be a few students who begin to abuse the system if we don't keep an eye on them. If you have any questions about whether students are actually showing up, please let us know. If a student says he or she is going to the SAP office, you have every right to check up on that. If you think that a particular student is missing too much class, please let us know immediately. Chances are, the student is not with us as much as he or she claims. We want to nip this sort of thing in the bud so you will be comfortable with students using the program and attending groups.

10
Additional Programming

J. Burke

CHAPTER 10

Additional Programming

This chapter focuses on additional alcohol and other drug-related efforts in school systems nationwide, but it by no means provides an exhaustive list. There may be ideas for you here—ways your SAP can expand to work in conjunction with other, already existing programs in the school and community. Ancillary programs may fall partly under the jurisdiction of the SAP, or these programs may be run by other people in the school and simply complement the SAP general operation. Your program can decide how to expend your energies, but there are some extremely good adjunct programs or facets of programming you may decide to undertake. Even if there is no official connection to the SAP, ancillary programming of the sort briefly outlined in this chapter makes an impact on the climate of the school system, perhaps increasing referrals or educating subsets of the population.

SETTING APPROPRIATE LIMITS

In the realm of ancillary programming, SAPs need to take care that they do not become the "obvious solution" to every alcohol or drug-related effort in the school system. The designated SAP person or team member cannot become the one person who takes over the leadership role in every promotional effort, community awareness project, or educational endeavor. That leaves the total responsibility on a few people—and SAPs need the help of the wider community to enact any real change in attitude about alcohol and other drug-related issues and personal problems that affect students. An SAP person cannot hope to orchestrate the fundamental SAP referral process *and* head up six or seven offshoot programs, and shouldn't try to. The effort will not only burn out your SAP people, but will send the wrong message to the students and community alike. Students' personal problems, including the alcohol and other drug-related issues, cannot be compartmentalized and entirely managed by the efforts of a few. Schools need to embrace the magnitude of the issues, roll up their sleeves, and get involved by pitching in on some of these adjunct programs. One thing the SAP counselor and/or team *can* do is suggest to other faculty members that they get involved in some of these ancillary efforts, and then step back and let them go at it.

SAPS WORKING WITH OTHER SCHOOL-BASED PROGRAMS

There is a good likelihood that some of these programs have been underway in the school systems for a significantly longer time than the SAP effort, in which case the advisors/creators of these programs need to work closely with recently hired or trained SAP people to see how their efforts fit in to the advantage of everyone involved, and into the total picture of alcohol and other drug-related services.

These adjunct or related programs cannot serve as replacements for referral-based SAP services, nor do SAP services replace the specific efforts of these programs—rather, they have distinct but complementary missions. Most programs outlined here attempt to aid specific student populations by providing activities for at-risk students or general information for students at lower or average risk. The programs represent the spectrum of services available, from education and prevention to intervention and direct services. School personnel may not even be aware that some of these programs are considered alcohol and other drug prevention strategies.

Following are brief descriptions of offshoot or ancillary programming for students that some school systems are including or could include as part of a larger SAP effort.

PEER EDUCATION

(Also known as peer outreach, peer counseling, peer leadership, and any number of acronyms.) Peer education is a term that describes educationally based programming that imparts knowledge about alcohol and other drugs and other problems and helps student participants feel good about themselves. The hope is that they won't feel the need to use alcohol and other drugs themselves in their teenage and young adult years. These efforts are prevention programs, although early peer education efforts trained students to recognize dangerous patterns of behavior in fellow teenagers. The student participants were encouraged to bring warning signs to the attention of professionally trained adults, specifically teachers and guidance counselors, giving the programs intervention elements.

In the process of learning about early warning signs of alcohol and other drug abuse and other problems students may be having, participants glean a healthy dose of self-esteem and self-knowledge. The now-famous and highly successful "Teen Institute" is one such program. It trains its students during week-long camp experiences during the summer, and some school systems continue some variation of the summer experience throughout the school year. Other systems concentrate the trainings in the school year, and still other peer education initiatives are headed by community agencies (YWCA, Girls' and Boys' Clubs, etc.). In some peer education programs, student participants, who are generally in high school, travel to communicate about high school life to junior high and elementary school students. Role-modeling positive behavior, these high school students can exert a little positive peer pressure to offset a little of the negative the younger students might come across later.

Some peer counseling programs have designed drop-in programs for students to stop by with different concerns. Others have paired themselves with incoming freshmen to make the transition to high school life easier for the younger students. All these undertakings are commendable and worthy of notice. Peer leadership members should be good role models for other high school students as well as younger students, and should definitely help in legitimizing the "no-use" message for alcohol and other drugs to the student body at large.

My experience has been that peer education programs tend to attract a very involved and active element of high school students, many of whom are academically successful and socially popular. As such, these peer counselors can really effect major changes in the collective thinking of a high school population, so the "payoff" on the investment can be immeasurable. Peer educators can be an invaluable resource during awareness campaigns and alcohol and other drug-related undertakings that require a lot of enthusiasm, people power, and promotion.

It's important for the peer education advisor(s) and the SAP people to have a clear understanding of the differences between the programs and to use each other as referral resources. Students with experience in SAP groups can make great peer leaders, especially recovering students (usually with a year or more of sobriety), and peer education advisors who notice problems arising for students can make the appropriate referrals to the student assistance program. Participation in a peer education program cannot constitute in full a student's recovery program, and peer education advisor(s) should be wary of that situation. Screen potential participants to be sure they are relatively stable and healthy themselves. Because of confidentiality, it is virtually impossible to use peer counselors in the context of SAPs for student-to-student counseling. This function is best served by SAP groups facilitated by trained professionals.

Though these programs can be highly successful, it's questionable whether an SAP person ought to be in charge of such a program, as the roles between counselor of the SAP and advisor to a fleet of fledgling counselors can become muddled. Legal confidentiality is also a concern, as is the time needed to devote to such a program. Some number of these students who become peer leaders are "hero" children of addiction who are beginning to gravitate toward helping others before they help themselves. If the SAP person becomes the advisor to the group, he or she may be cutting off access to helping services for these students as they become locked into the helping role and can't see their way clear to asking for help for themselves should they need it. A training arrangement would be ideal—one in which SAP people help train the peer leaders and make them aware of SAP services without taking on responsibility for the program as a whole.

STUDENTS AGAINST DRIVING DRUNK (S.A.D.D.)

S.A.D.D. was originally established to reduce the number of alcohol-related motor vehicle fatalities, and this is the purpose to which S.A.D.D. has remained dedicated. The message originally promoted by S.A.D.D. is that when people drink, they shouldn't drive, and indeed, they shouldn't, because alcohol-related motor vehicle fatalities constitute the leading cause of death for people between the ages of fifteen and twenty-four. The "Contract For Life" is designed so students who have been drinking (or whose rides have been drinking) can call their parents and get a ride home, with no questions asked immediately. Both parents and students sign the contract, explaining the details of this life-saving arrangement. S.A.D.D. deals with the reality that students do use alcohol—lots of it—and that some of them do drive under the influence of alcohol and other drugs as well. This program has years of experience in getting the message out and underscoring the dangers of intoxicated adolescents getting behind the wheel. Their efforts, through dances, promotional activities, and charter memberships, have touched a good percentage of schools nationwide and have probably saved innumerable lives. Having an active S.A.D.D. chapter is part and parcel of a comprehensive alcohol and other drug effort.

Unfortunately, it may send a mixed message for SAP people to be directly involved with S.A.D.D. simply because S.A.D.D. originally promoted a responsible-use message while SAPs promote a no-use message. (S.A.D.D. has since changed and adopted a no-use policy, but there may be lingering confusion, both for students and advisors.) S.A.D.D. provides a perfect illustration of how some alcohol and other drug-related programs are good and are necessary and also need to be completely separate from the SAP. Driver's education teachers, especially, as well as school nurses, guidance people, and teachers are good candidates for S.A.D.D. advisorships. For more information about starting a S.A.D.D. chapter in your school, contact

S.A.D.D.
P.O. Box 800
Marlboro, MA 01752
1-800-481-3568

ADVENTURE PROGRAMMING

Community agencies, such as the Boy Scouts, Girl Scouts, and Boys' and Girls' Clubs, sometimes offer programming that is "adventure based"; it encourages self-esteem as a result of students overcoming obstacles in the wilderness or simulated wilderness experiences. Camping, mountain climbing, ropes courses, and the like are usually included in this exciting programming. The object is to have students transfer the ability to overcome obstacles in the wilderness to overcoming obstacles in their personal lives. This is particularly appropriate with children of addiction and recovering students, as their very survival requires getting over personal hurdles. In addition, adventure programming takes students out of the house after school and for overnights, etc., so students can gain some relief from the chaos at home. If such programming is available through a community agency, the SAP should know about it and should make referrals to the program whenever appropriate.

If at all possible, network with the adventure programming agency to provide even a day-long adventure experience for existing SAP children of addiction and recovery groups. Taking a group into the woods to do some trust-building exercises can speed up group process immensely. When you have such short time to give to these students, this sort of accelerating experience is well worth the effort. If there is no such programming available in your community, it is a great prospect for which to compile a grant. Even a field trip to a campground would be new territory for a lot of these students, and perhaps the Boy Scouts or Boys' and

Girls' Clubs would offer technical assistance, a tour guide, or even the sleeping bags. Make sure, however, that you have appropriate personnel and that the school's insurance would cover any accidents.

SUMMER STUDENT ASSISTANCE PROGRAMMING

Summer programs are designed to help students who have made personal gains through the SAP during the school year to sustain them throughout the summer months. The summer is particularly difficult for recovering students and students who live in homes affected by addiction. For recovering students, alcohol and other drugs are more widely available and supervision is generally looser. For COAs, school has often provided a haven; without it, they are left home all day to care for younger siblings, or, in the worst case, the addicted parent. There are several types of summer programs available, from week-long camp experiences to extended SAP services.

In my school district, we have secured grant funding in recent years for basic, bare-bones student assistance programming throughout the summer months. Always working two at a time (because we are the only people in the school building over the summer), the SAP directors from our three city high schools and SAP personnel from our junior high schools run a children of addiction group, a recovery group, and have time for individual appointments for students in crisis over the summer.

This is certainly not comprehensive, as we staff the office only one day per week, but it is available, free to students who use it, in a familiar spot, and the SAP people are familiar to the students who use the services. This format has worked well and perhaps should be considered when designing basic SAP programming for schools working on a traditional school calendar.

There should be a link between junior high school SAP services and high school SAP services, especially for children of addiction and recovering students who have been involved in group support in the junior high school or middle school or who have been identified by guidance as high risk. High school SAP people can make contact with junior high school people (who will need to get releases of information if the students are over the age of twelve) to inform the high school of any participation in the junior high school SAP. Another way of providing this link is to encourage junior high school students who will be entering the high school in the fall to become involved in the summer SAP groups. The summer between eighth grade and high school can be a crucial time in a student's development. To make the transition smoother, an SAP counselor can travel to the junior high schools to make the student body aware of the summer programming (through an assembly) or visit specific junior high SAP groups. In this way these especially vulnerable ninth graders come to high school with a ready support system.

If you cannot provide summer programming for students, at the very least provide a ready resource list of what will be available during the summer in your community. Agencies should be encouraged to advertise their efforts through the student council or some other student-based organization (SAPs cannot promote every program to students). Student assistance programs can certainly keep track of what is going on so students already involved with the SAP can get any necessary information.

INTERSCHOOL RECOVERY CLUB

With recovering students, there is definitely safety in numbers. It is one thing to know that you are a part of a group of, let's say, twenty students in your high school who have made the choice to stay clean and sober. It is another thing entirely to know that you are part of a group of one hundred or so students city-wide who have made the same choice. Developing interschool programs for students with like concerns can be very effective, especially for recovering students. Start small. The first year we tried an interschool effort, our city's three high school SAPs brought together approximately forty recovering students for pizza and a meeting. Missing only three class periods including a lunch period, students were bussed to one school, where the recovering kids ate donated pizza and sodas and held an hour-long meeting that was chaired by the student with the longest amount of sobriety (two years). They were back to their own schools before the end of the school day, with very little disruption to their academic schedule but a great experience to add to their memories. This is the best kind of ancillary programming because it costs practically nothing and the payoff is so great.

Recovering students in my district look forward to the city-wide meeting every year. In future years, we would like to have a "Recovery Day" where we treat these students to a day full of self-discovery and fun while staying clean and sober. This idea could be expanded to include a recovering students' outing club, a meeting club (going to twelve-step meetings together), or some sort of exchange program in which recovery groups travel to "sister" schools twice a year or so. Be creative with your design, or put the notion to the students and see what they come up with.

INTERSCHOOL COA ACTIVITIES

Children of addiction can benefit from this sort of interschool experience as well, although they are bound to be more comfortable if the thrust is educational in nature, at least at the start. A COA workshop could be arranged and students from various schools could attend. The difference between recovering kids and children of addiction is that a lot of the recovering kids will have been to treatment facilities where they were taught to talk about their feelings and were taught that they should depend on other recovering kids for their social interactions, so they may be more comfortable interacting with unfamiliar people. Children of addiction do not have to depend on other COAs for their social lives (though many of them gravitate to each other almost instinctively), so the networking element is not quite so crucial; it is still important, however, for these students to recognize that they are not alone.

AWARENESS CAMPAIGNS

High schools usually wage the alcohol and other drug awareness war right around prom time. This effort primarily in May and June seems to be a plea to students to not mess up graduation and the gleeful end of school with a tragedy. Principals knock on wood when another graduation passes without problems. In junior high schools, the effort seems to be concentrated around the transition from junior high to high school, but this appears to be too little too late, since reports currently indicate that the average age of first use of alcohol or other drugs is twelve. Judging by the levels of use in junior high schools and high schools, students need alcohol and other drug awareness campaigns year round, and such campaigns shouldn't simply concentrate on the dangers of drinking and driving. How about the connection between alcohol and other drug use and violence, unwanted pregnancy, sexually transmitted diseases, AIDS, physical risk taking, date rape, vandalism, crime, decrease in school performance, poor family functioning, etc.?

Take every chance you can get to raise student awareness about alcohol and other drugs. Your system can either concentrate the awareness effort into one day or can stretch it out over a week or month. Awareness campaigns are essentially massive advertising efforts, so in a large school they cannot be effectively promoted by one person or program only. A school-based SAP can be heavily involved in an awareness campaign or can simply offer technical assistance or act in a consulting capacity, depending on how the system works. Generally, awareness campaigns require a lot of footwork, because they are massive logistical undertakings. Some suggested activities for awareness days, weeks, or themes include the following:

- Assembly program about drinking and driving
- Play or skits put on by community theater or school-based drama club depicting alcohol or other drug situations
- S.A.D.D. (or similar organization)-sponsored dance
- Chemical-free carnival
- Poster contest for alcohol and drug-free logo and motto
- Pep rally for Red Ribbon Week
- School-sponsored video about alcohol or other drug use
- Breakfast workshop for faculty and staff to explain the awareness week.

Tragically, awareness campaigns are often begun after the alcohol or other drug-related death of a student. These campaigns are often zealous, as students and faculty alike try to work out their grief and helplessness in the process. Try to present awareness campaigns with this sort of earnestness without getting morbid, in the hopes that you can avert such a tragedy in the first place.

Red Ribbon Week

In October every year, there is a nationwide community awareness program called Red Ribbon Week, in which people of all ages are encouraged to wear a red ribbon to indicate their support for a reduction in drug use. This existing campaign can provide a framework for a school-based awareness campaign at the beginning of the school year, just as prom time creates a natural opportunity to talk about alcohol and other drug-related issues. Red Ribbon Week is sponsored by the National Federation of Parents for Drug-Free Youth. For more information or assistance, contact

> National Red Ribbon Week
> National Federation of Parents for Drug-Free Youth
> 9551 Big Bend Rd.
> St. Louis, MO 63122-6519.

PROGRAMS BEFORE AND AFTER SCHOOL

Any program which does not fit into the regular school day can be called an afterschool program. Regular SAP duties should not be carried out before or after school; general operation of an SAP should not be squeezed into extracurricular time unless absolutely necessary, because it indicates weak or nonexistent administrative support.

There are, however, many possibilities for both before- and afterschool programs. These time slots can be a very convenient way for SAP people to make contact with students who seem to need just a little more support than others. In particular, recovering or reentering students could have a before-school check-in every day (or every other day) if it could be worked into the schedule and would not overcommit the SAP people. Students at high risk for dropping out of school could be encouraged to come to school every day using this positive peer pressure check-in system. For SAPs without a counselor, before-school check-in might be a workable solution for recovery groups in general, as it is difficult for teachers (rather than SAP people) to work out a rotating time-out-of-class schedule. Interschool groups can meet after school, as can recovery clubs, and so forth.

It is unfortunate to have to mention this, but SAP people should not stay after school with students if they are going to be the only people remaining in the school buildings. The safety of SAP people must be considered when setting up these programs. Also, people who staff before- and afterschool programs should be compensated with "comp time" or some other recognition of their extended effort.

DAY-LONG EDUCATIONAL WORKSHOPS

There are circumstances when it is most beneficial for everyone to involve students in day-long educational workshops. This has long been the realm of teacher workshop days. But we have to ask, if we choose the workshop format for ourselves, why don't we give our students the same options? Issues pertaining to alcohol and other drugs lend themselves well to a workshop format because there is information that needs to go out to a certain percentage of the population. It could be argued that a workshop format is really less disruptive to a student's schedule, all things considered, because it is just like being absent from school for a day, and the work can be made up.

Identified children of addiction, for instance, make up an extremely appropriate group for a day-long workshop. The subject of "family dynamics in alcoholic or addicted homes," for instance, is vaguely interesting to approximately three quarters of the student population, who have no experience with it. But it is intensely interesting to those who live in alcoholic or drug-addicted situations. It's especially important to have them with other COAs during this experience so they can feel comfortable identifying with the information presented.

Clearly, the ideal would be to have these programs running as part of your regular curricula or on an ongoing basis, but that might not be plausible in your system right now. Some effort is better than no effort, so where there are populations that can be served by one-day workshops, try to arrange them. Student assistance programs can either run these, administrate them, or offer expertise and technical support. How about self-esteem trainings for students who have dropped out of school the previous year but are currently trying to make a comeback? How about alcohol and other drug training for young parents—students who have their own children and are trying to juggle parenthood and school? The possibilities are endless.

SCHOOL SUSPENSION ALTERNATIVES/DISCIPLINARY ALTERNATIVES

Many schools and districts have archaic disciplinary and suspension procedures. No one is really satisfied with the way school discipline is working nationwide, and staying with a failing system is not the answer. In traditional disciplinary programs, for instance, when students are truant, they can be suspended from school as punishment. What an irony! Many recovering students tell stories about planning certain infractions of the rules right around the time they wanted to be out of school anyway, thereby creating their custom "vacations."

Even more wasteful, in my opinion, is the practice of having students in internal suspension, where they sit in a single room all day, doing nothing. I know of at least four students who dropped out of school because they couldn't bear the thought of making up two or three days of internal suspension that they "owed" the school. It's hard to blame them, when you think about it. As we head into the next century, a measure of a school system's success will be the effectiveness of its disciplinary system.

Progressive school systems are beginning to reevaluate their disciplinary procedures as they begin to understand that a significant percentage of students who are fixtures in the disciplinary system are experiencing school failure or extreme difficulties at home. Moreover, the recidivism rate illustrates clearly that this traditional discipline is not working. My personal opinion is that a great number of the students who crop up again and again in the school disciplinary system are children of addiction and those who are experiencing the middle-late stages of adolescent chemical dependency. When you come at school discipline from this angle with a counselor-based SAP, it takes on a whole new dimension and exciting possibilities occur.

Students who would otherwise be in school suspension provide a ready, high-risk population that would do practically anything to avoid having to serve suspensions, so they're ready to try the creative alternatives you design. I have designed an in-school suspension alternative program (called the SSAS—School Suspension Alternative Series) which provides a day-long workshop-type experience for repeat offenders in the school disciplinary system. The subject matter? Alcohol and other drugs and surrounding relevant issues. Remember, though, that the screening criteria for this program has *nothing* to do with alcohol or other drugs; the student need only be involved repeatedly in the disciplinary system of the school to qualify for participation. The student can only do this alternative *once*; otherwise it can become an incentive to get into trouble, because, like challenge group participation, the group experience itself is not a punishment. In fact, we endeavor to make the day as comfortable as possible for students so they will have good associations with the helping services and might choose to utilize them in the future.

Tremendous numbers of referrals are generated from this sort of program. Not surprisingly (for me, anyway), a significant percentage of these students turn out to be experiencing very serious symptoms of chemical dependency (67 percent report alcohol-related blackouts, for instance) and even more report living with addiction of some kind in their families. In the first two years that we ran the program through the SAP, more than half of the students who participated subsequently sought out services through the SAP, either in group support or in individual sessions.

It is questionable whether programming such as this, which is so closely tied to the SAP, can even be considered ancillary, because the main purpose of the program is to introduce these very high-risk students to the SAP and let them gain access to it comfortably. Not every SAP can provide a specific program to "tap" this particular population. However, the success of these programs shows that when SAPs are looking for referral sources, they need look no further than the disciplinary systems of their schools. Counselor-based efforts may be able to design some sort of program for these students, while team-based programs should consider "frequent flyers" in the disciplinary system good candidates for referral and assessment.

TRADITIONAL EXTRACURRICULAR ACTIVITIES

Remember that strong traditional extracurricular activities are alcohol and drug prevention tactics as well. A band, team, or club that creates a stable environment where students are closely monitored and challenged both intellectually and socially constitutes the best sort of prevention strategy. Coaches and advisors of drama, sports, newspapers, yearbook staff, spirit clubs, language clubs, and literary magazines are all in the position to monitor students closely both in school and during extracurricular hours, can make contact when they notice changes in a student's behavior, and can make referrals to the student assistance program, if appropriate. Classroom teachers who spark spirit, reinforce intellectual curiosity, and encourage students to pursue their dreams can combat some of the emotional precursors to chemical dependency, namely poor self-worth and hopelessness. Administrators can provide a positive and nurturing school environment, ensuring that consistent discipline is linked with access to available in-school helping services. Reframe what school personnel already do in terms of alcohol and other drug prevention, remind them that they are already pros at this, and enlist their help in more specific efforts.

PARENT PROGRAMMING

Inherent in basic SAP structure is the possibility for expansion. Student assistance program operation can branch out through various avenues to educate, inform, or even directly serve parents. Existing parent groups in schools can also take some initiative to become more aware of what is going on with a start-up or continuing SAP effort, and parents can become involved in some of the ancillary student programs as volunteers, chaperones, and technical help. Some SAP advisory boards include parents, to get wide representation from the community at large. This is a wise political move as well as a help to SAPs. Because of the stringent confidentiality regulations, which can alienate SAP people from the parent population, it is wise to encourage parental involvement whenever confidentiality is not a concern, as in the case of advisory boards. As in student programming, SAP people can either be directly involved in these adjunct programs, making them part of general SAP operation, or serve in an advisory capacity only. Following are several programs which rely heavily on the participation of parents and which can support both the parent population and efforts of the SAP.

PTA/PTO Activities

The PTA or other "official" parent group in your school can be the SAP's best ally. The PTA is responsible for getting the word about any school business out to fellow parents, so this organization can serve as a good vehicle for SAP information. If possible, SAP people should attend PTA meetings to get to know how the operation works and to see what the SAP can do for the PTA and vice versa. On a personal note, it's also refreshing to meet with a group of concerned and active parents, because SAP people often find themselves up against uncooperative or very dysfunctional parents in their daily work. This is not to suggest that joining the PTA insures one against familial dysfunction, but parents who are out there trying to learn all they can and who are trying to effect change in the school system may have a leg up on those that aren't. For SAP people, it is just comforting to be among supporters for an hour or two a week.

A start-up SAP should always schedule an informational presentation for the PTA so the organization understands the intentions of the SAP from the start. Explaining the confidentiality regulations without apology is one way to avoid misunderstanding later. Luckily, however, there is rarely much trouble from PTAs about the confidentiality regulations, mostly because these concerned parents are enthusiastic about having SAP services available to students. The referral process should be explained thoroughly as well as the procedures for group participation.

Some PTAs publish monthly newsletters to keep parents informed, and some present monthly workshops or informational programs. If they have an established avenue to get information to parents, don't reinvent the wheel; hop onto their cart and utilize their established methods. Most newsletters welcome editorials or simple informational articles, even advice on when parents should call the SAP because of a potential problem with their children.

Most PTAs head up major projects every year. Whether they are fund-raising initiatives or participation drives, the members are well versed in methods of drumming up parental involvement. Many take part in running the open houses or orientation nights for the entire school. If this is the case, SAPs ought to be in communication with PTA members so they can set up a booth or a table during the orientation night to be staffed by the SAP person or core team members. There are often other parent groups concerned with specific issues—for instance, a parent group that supports athletics or the band, or that is interested in curriculum change. These highly motivated and concerned parents provide a great place to start when you need to disseminate information to the parent population at large.

Parent "Home" Programs

These prevention programs are designed to generate a list of parents who agree to abide by certain agreed-on rules when dealing with both their children and other children. Usually, these programs include a training component in which parents are alerted to the various types of alcohol and other drugs currently popular in the local student population. Training concentrates on early warning symptoms of alcohol and other drug use and signs to be aware of. The culmination of this training is the generation of a list of parents who take a pledge not to allow alcohol or other drugs to be served to minors in their homes. They also agree to supervise all parties in their home and to inform other parents if alcohol or drug use is suspected in their children or anyone else's. Some Home programs then publish a list of participating parents. In this way, parents who are concerned about alcohol and other drug issues can rally with others who are similarly concerned, and parents will know what to expect in terms of supervision, etc., when their children are invited to a party at one of the participating homes.

Such a program can expand to include a newsletter, promotional activities, fund raising, and awareness. Some progressive programs of this nature are enlisting the help of local police, insuring that the parents of adolescents who are picked up for "minor" alcohol or other drug-related offenses are contacted immediately. Home programs may wage awareness campaigns to remind parents of their criminal liability in serving alcohol to minors, and may remind businesses of their legal responsibility to refuse to sell alcohol to minors. These programs, which require enthusiasm and perseverence but don't require much in the way of funding, are sometimes preliminary efforts to get the alcohol and other drug efforts moving at the school level.

Parent Awareness Events

Awareness events are designed to attract large numbers of parents and to impart certain knowledge about alcohol and other drug issues, other personal problems of teenagers, and available in-school and community resources. These days, since parents are sick of hearing about the dangers of alcohol and other drug use, it is sometimes best to couch the alcohol and other drug element in a more comprehensive format (for instance, the concept of "student wellness"). Though they can be huge logistical undertakings, parent awareness events can promote the SAP while at the same time promoting a general understanding of alcohol and other drug-related issues community-wide. If at all possible, garner support from several agencies, student groups, and parent groups before undertaking a large parent awareness event. Your best bet is to cosponsor such an event with the student council, PTA, or even varsity athletic teams.

Parent awareness events can piggyback on any existing forum, or new ones can be developed for the awareness purpose. Too many systems have tried huge advertising campaigns, only to have a pathetic showing on the night of the big event. Try to link the awareness event with something else that has a big draw anyway, so your significant efforts will not be in vain. In suburban areas, try a junior high school dance in the gym while there is a parent awareness night in the cafeteria. Parents have to drive their kids to the dance anyway and are therefore more likely to attend the awareness event, even for a few minutes on their way in or out. Utilize existing open house and orientation schedules to promote understanding of alcohol and other drug-related issues. Try a mock block party at school in which there are workshops for both parents and students. In our area, sixth graders attend a workshop day with parents, who are encouraged to take the day off from work to attend with their children.

In one school I know of, attending a parent awareness night with one parent is a requirement of being on a varsity team. This gives coaches a chance to tell parents to be proud of their student athletes *and* what can be expected of them in terms of practice schedules, away games, and training. It also gives coaches the chance to underscore the interscholastic code concerning alcohol and other drugs, including anabolic steroid use, and what the procedures will be for anyone caught using alcohol or other drugs, including SAP participation. Student assistance program people can introduce the program and can give presentations on alcohol and other drug use and/or on the services available through the SAP. Such collaboration benefits athletic departments, students, and SAP efforts. Such an arrangement could be made with virtually any other extracurricular activity, including band and chorus, student council, or the drama department.

School-Based Parent Support Groups

Certain factions of the parent population may respond to parent support groups. Parents of recovering students, for instance, may be having trouble dealing with the changes that students are undergoing (and the entire family as a result), and can benefit from talking out their emotions with others who have gone before them. There is a lot to adjust to when an adolescent enters recovery: AA and NA meeting schedules, new relationships, new vocabulary, Al-Anon participation for family members, new styles of communication, watching for signs of relapse, and what to do in the case of a relapse. The formats for these support programs can be short term and educational, something like the family components of treatment programs, and facilitated by SAP people. Or, they can be ongoing support programs. An ongoing support group is a wonderful resource for the bewildered, frustrated, and frightened parents of a student who has recently entered inpatient treatment.

Make sure that SAP people have the resources to handle this extracurricular undertaking. If the program is to be organized and administrated by an SAP person or other professional, perhaps this is another candidate for grant funding or comp time for the professional in charge. These ancillary programs take a tremendous amount of time to organize and administrate, and SAP people have other, primary duties. Another way to manage this sort of support program is to enlist the help of enthusiastic parents who have been down this road before and who are already involved in Al-Anon and other such self-help fellowships. They could lead such a group themselves, encouraging other parents to share their experiences. The SAP person or core team can act in an advisory capacity to such a group and offer educational presentations on adolescent recovery and relapse issues, family recovery and codependence.

Postprom/Preprom Committees

Recently, there has been a movement for concerned parents to manage the time before and/or after the spring proms to reduce the likelihood of an alcohol or other drug-related disaster. Technically speaking, all school events should be "chem free," so identifying a certain event this way illustrates that the job is not getting done the rest of the time. Usually, these pre- or postprom strategies include a parent and/or teacher-supervised party with lavish refreshments, sports events, movie marathons, and so forth. These chem-free events are highly successful in some communities and fall flat in others. Not surprisingly, these efforts are usually successful in communities where the student body is as excited about the prospect of such an event as are the parents, and where student groups have had a large part in the preparation. So, if you are planning this sort of event, mobilize the forces of student groups as well, and let them do your promotion. The last thing teenagers want to do is to attend a party that their parents have designed for them, without their input.

Toughlove

Toughlove is a national organization which helps parents to summon the courage that's required to "put their foot down" and regain control of their house, at least, and maybe gain some control of the adolescent who is driving the parents to an early grave. Toughlove is a nonprofit, parent-based support program primarily for parents who are living with teenagers who refuse to obey the rules, who are harmfully involved with alcohol or other drugs, involved with the courts, or who are generally uncooperative. Parents meet to strategize and give support to one another to offset the stress of living with a teenager hellbent on destruction. Chapters of Toughlove meet in localities in community buildings, the basements of churches, and sometimes in schools, though they are not customarily associated with one school only. Parents involved in Toughlove are great panel speakers at parent awareness events, and SAP people should have familiarity with the local chapter so they can refer distraught parents. Some chapters even have outreach volunteers who will come to talk with parents, sharing their own experience of life with an uncooperative child. Let your local Toughlove chapter know about your SAP operation; your programs may be able to help each other. For more information about Toughlove, contact

> Toughlove International
> Box 1069
> Doylestown, PA 18901
> 1-800-333-1069.

M.A.D.D.

Mothers Against Driving Drunk is a highly vocal victims' assistance organization, many of whose members have lost loved ones to drunk-driving tragedies. M.A.D.D. concentrates its efforts on supporting victims of drunk driving and creating awareness of drunk driving in order to curtail it (and preferably one day eradicate it). Its awareness and advertising campaigns have been very successful. The message to adults is, When drinking, refrain from driving. M.A.D.D. is not a temperance movement. However, for adolescent populations, M.A.D.D. has a decidedly no-use message. Its recent awareness campaign for adolescents has centered around the "celebrate sober" theme.

M.A.D.D. is a large national organization with approximately 400 chapters in various localities. These local chapters may represent themselves at school parent awareness nights, community panels, and the like. Members may be able to help in a chemical-free prom effort or awareness campaigns. For more specific information or to find the M.A.D.D. chapter in your community, contact

> M.A.D.D.
> 511 East John Carpenter Freeway, Suite 700
> Irving, TX 75062-8187.

WRITING GRANTS

Some of the very best alcohol and other drug strategies currently operating were started with a good idea and grant money, either from the federal or state government, their designated agencies, or private benevolent foundations. Some of these programs still receive partial or full grant funding for their continuing operation. The Drug-Free Schools and Communities Act of 1988 required schools to implement K–12 alcohol and other drug education, and, more recently, the bounds of such entitlement money have expanded to include SAP initiatives. This is good news for SAP people and school systems alike. If you don't have an SAP counselor, there may be money available for you to get one through the Drug-Free School and Communities program. School systems then need to figure out how to keep the programs going once the grant money runs out. It may not run out in the near future, but the directives will be repositioned slightly and salaries may not be allowed as expenses. School systems need to get ready to shoulder the salaries and benefits of SAP counselors/coordinators/directors, recognizing their permanent and important role in the regular school curriculum.

SAP teams or those interested in getting an SAP underway can easily write grants. Some grants will ask for funding of whole programs; others ask only to fill a very narrow and specific need. If you see a need that can be appropriately filled with some money, and you'd like to take a crack at writing a grant, go for it.

Finding Funds

The first order of business if you're interested in writing a grant is to find some available money. Contact your state governor's office and ask to speak to the Drug-Free School and Communities contact person there. While school systems are allocated a certain amount of this money every year (which is called *entitlement money*), governor's offices are allocated another portion (which is called *discretionary money*) to disperse by an application process. If your SAP is not on their mailing list, you won't be informed of their calls for applications.

In each U.S. state and territory, there is a state agency which is responsible for coordinating alcohol and drug prevention and treatment services (see the Appendix, "Additional Resources"). In New Hampshire, this is the Office of Alcohol and Drug Abuse Prevention, which has been instrumental in getting different SAP structures off the ground statewide. In other states, the office can be found in the state mental health office or in the Health and Human Services department. This single state agency can provide information, technical assistance, and sometimes even financial support for SAP initiatives and adjunct programming. Make phone calls, and don't get discouraged.

The National Prevention Network is a network of state alcohol and drug abuse prevention coordinators and others who are dedicated to comprehensive and effective programs to prevent the abuse of alcohol and other drugs. Members of the network focus on promoting good health and supporting, developing, and enhancing national, state, and local efforts to reduce the incidence and prevalence of alcohol and other drug-related problems. Since SAPs and their adjunct programming fall so directly into this definition, the National Prevention Network is a good resource for SAP people nationwide. For more information, write to

National Prevention Network
444 North Capitol St., N.W., Suite 642
Washington, DC 20001.

Other places to call are large corporations in your immediate area (especially if you are looking for a small grant—a thousand dollars or so). Some corporations will give you that kind of money simply for the publicity. Other corporations will donate food, office supplies, or even office furniture. Though it may take a lot of footwork, different companies can be depended on for small parts of the whole package.

Don't Be Intimidated

Grant writing has been misrepresented to the public as a mystifying process that only a person "in the know" can navigate successfully. This notion is simply nonsense. Gather your gumption and pick the brains of people who have written grants before; special education and vocational education people tend to write a lot of them, so find a comrade in these departments.

Writing a grant is very much like cooking; if you can read, you can do it. Most grant applications contain elaborate instructions, and this is what usually scares people off. You have to "jump through a thousand hoops," come up with twenty or thirty different documents assuring this or that or certifying that your elevators work, that you have the requisite fire exits, and that the board of health has passed your school's kitchen. It's all written in jargon that is barely decipherable. By the time you finish reading the application, you're exhausted. But, don't be discouraged—this is all eminently do-able. It is just time-consuming and picky.

A grant application is simply an exercise in following instructions. Part of the reason grant applications are designed this way is to insure that people who apply for the money are serious about it. The difficult application process weeds out those who would "take the money if they could get it" but don't really have fleshed-out plans for its use. The process also necessitates that you get authorizing signatures from principals and superintendents, so writing a grant application can be a worthwhile endeavor even if the program is not funded, just in terms of getting to know who's in charge in your system and letting them know what type of programming you would like to implement if you could. Sometimes, this process plants a seed of an idea that will eventually be funded. If your efforts for grant funding are not out of balance, no one can fault you for trying. If you do receive the funding, more power to you.

Look Before You Leap

If you are an SAP counselor or director, remember this: Time the SAP person spends at the computer or typewriter writing grants is time spent away from students. If you're pressed for time already, think it over very carefully before you decide to write a grant, because it does take a lot of time and running around. One way to manage the time dilemma is to have student interns work on the grant applications under the supervision of SAP people, or a core team can write a grant as a team effort. Remember that writing a grant and getting it means that you will also be embroiled in the process of writing requisitions, perhaps hiring additional personnel, and accounting for the way you spend the money. The check doesn't usually come to the SAP—it goes to the school department, and the SAP person acts like a department head and requisitions needed supplies.

With all these discouraging caveats, it's also important to remember that there can be tremendous benefits to applying for grants. First, you may be able to do some things with your program that you previously couldn't, things which may make a real difference for some students. Though it may be extra work, it is very satisfying to receive grant funding for a pet project and to see an idea become a reality.

11

Field Survival Guide for SAP Personnel

J.Burke

CHAPTER 11

Field Survival Guide for SAP Personnel

This chapter is slightly different in tone because it addresses the difficult role the SAP director plays in a school community and speaks directly to the unusual challenges that the SAP director, counselor, or coordinator faces. The word *survival* in the chapter title was chosen carefully, because SAP people do need to concentrate on their day-to-day survival—and since no one else may be looking out for it, they need to secure it for themselves and their programs. While this chapter's intent is to assist SAP directors, counselors, and coordinators who work directly in schools, team-based SAP efforts may find some advice and insight in these pages as well. An SAP coordinator is often in a very delicate position politically, administratively, and socially; if nothing else, this chapter is intended to soothe those of you who serve in these positions and wonder whether you are alone in your impressions.

Student assistance program work is hard work. While school systems may welcome student assistance programming as a concept, they can have a funny way of showing it, and students and faculty alike may be unsure how to react to whoever leads the effort. This may leave the SAP director feeling isolated and can eventually lead to early burnout. Some of the solutions can be found in these pages. Whether you are a formal SAP director, or a teacher who leads your SAP effort, you can identify with some of the challenges and utilize some of the advice. This is not to suggest that *anyone* working in a school system has an easy job. This chapter merely isolates those challenges that are unique to SAP personnel.

UNDERSTANDING THE EXPECTATIONS OF SAPS

Student assistance program people are hired in a number of different ways and are assigned disparate duties, depending on the budget and the understanding of the school administration and faculty. Different school systems have varying expectations of their SAP people (or lack of them), and it is up to the newly hired SAP person to figure out or to establish what is expected of him or her. To an extent greater than with most other positions in schools, many SAP people come on board to *create* their own positions, policies, and procedures.

For example, newly hired English teachers may at least be given last year's syllabus, a list of available textbooks, a box of chalk, and general instructions to cover this and that during the year. Having been an English teacher once, I might add that I wish my instructions had been a little clearer, and that the list of textbooks had been a little longer. As I remember, I was told to "teach" American Literature, start to finish, by the end of the year. So off I went, at least headed in the expected and established direction.

But these cryptic instructions were lengthy and detailed compared to the instructions I got during my first year as an SAP director! What I learned during the first year of being an SAP director was that there were no syllabi, no state mandates to cover, no real formulas for success. In my particular school, there really wasn't even an established direction, because the school was looking to the new director to define the direction. They were looking for an expert to give them advice about what to do about the personal problems that make it practically impossible for some students to experience success at school. In SAPs that are originally team based, the newly hired counselor/director must also meet the expectations of the entire team.

If you are the director of a new SAP, you have the opportunity to create a position and guide the school's reaction to it. You educate both students and faculty in the SAP's areas of expertise, which you may determine with the help of a core team. Typically, you find that the school is not telling you what to do by a set of established rules and regulations; rather, the school is looking for answers—from you! This challenge can be exciting and overwhelming, too. In most school systems, the bulk of the work will be exciting, with only minor snags. In other systems, the challenges will be greater, the resistance to change deeper, and your feeling of being overwhelmed more pronounced. This chapter tries to make the overwhelming part more manageable by explaining some of the potential pitfalls and obstacles and providing some suggestions for making the job a little easier.

FINDING A TITLE FOR YOURSELF

Your first task will be to decide what you want to be called. Your school or district may have already decided this for you—but even so, this may be your first battle, because you may need to change it to insure the success of your program. If you can avoid it, don't name yourself the "Drug and Alcohol Counselor" or any variation thereof. Drug and alcohol counselors in school are like the Maytag man—they don't get any business. Because I was formally called the "Drug and Alcohol Program Coordinator" during my first year, I was informally called "The Drug Lady" by the students for the same length of time, which I'm sure reduced the number of self-referrals and kept teachers from referring students they had already decided couldn't possibly have an alcohol or other drug-related problem. However, students do need to know that you can talk about alcohol and other drugs, so emphasize that in your classroom presentations. Don't leave them in the dark about your area of expertise, but fairly represent your range of program services in your title.

Also make sure your title accurately represents what you plan to do or what you already do in your position. Are you a coordinator of existing services? In that case, call yourself a coordinator. Are you a counselor? In that case, call yourself a counselor. If you are the director of a program, by all means call yourself the director of the program.

Survival Tip: Contractually, "Alcohol and Other Drug" should appear in your official job description because it helps save your position when budgets are being trimmed and school board members and others are perusing the budget for positions to cut. So, in the best of all possible worlds, you would be called the

"Student Assistance Counselor" or something like it at school, but your contract will read, "Drug and Alcohol Program Coordinator (or Counselor, or Director)".

COPING WITH ISOLATION

Back when I was a teacher in a high school, I enjoyed the camaraderie that characterizes school systems. I ate lunch with teachers (mostly from my department), socialized with them, spoke in the hallways and generally felt comfortable and a part of the school, even in my first few weeks there. When I got my additional training and became an SAP director in another school, I felt a real change in the way the faculty perceived me. And I hadn't changed at all (though I wondered if I'd developed bad breath or something). Finally, I talked to a lot of other SAP directors in my state and my impressions were validated by theirs. Following are a few reasons for our potential isolation.

Most people who are not in the alcohol and other drug field just don't know how to deal with people who are. They are unsure whether we are prohibitionists, ex-hippies, or simply fanatics. If the whole truth be told, they don't know where we stand on *their* drinking and other drug issues. They are nervous. They don't know whether we are going to try to abolish the December holiday party or wage a campaign to start a mandatory drug-testing program for city employees. They don't know what it is safe to tell us. And, with the complicated confidentiality issues surrounding SAPs, they don't know what is safe to *ask* us, either. This leaves the SAP person in a very isolated position in the school. Some of this is real, not simply perceived. As an SAP person, you are not at liberty legally to discuss a student the way you could if he or she was in an English class. The way you come to terms with this will determine how comfortable you will be in your workplace.

School personnel are no different from other people, which means that a great number of them have been affected by alcohol or other drug issues, and, statistically, a lot of them have never dealt with it. So, added to their uncertainty about what to talk to you about, some wonder if you will be able to somehow tell about their aunt Edna who was addicted to valium or their ex-husband who is an alcoholic, or their own weekend marijuana habit. I think of a friend of mine who went to a dinner party and was having a great conversation with an attractive man. When she asked him what he did for work and he replied that he was a psychiatrist, the first thing she thought was "Oh dear! I hope I didn't say anything weird," and she felt a lot less comfortable sharing with him. This is how some people, unfamiliar with the language of SAPs, will feel when talking with you. They hope that their conversations don't "give away" any secrets about their own drinking or drug experience or any naive or "wrong" opinions about student use. One way faculty members avoid this potential embarrassment is to avoid the SAP person(s) altogether.

For a lot of people, alcohol and other drug issues are just one more thing to think about, and they occupy the same amount of time in their minds as any other social problem. For SAP people, alcohol and other drug issues are a constant. You have opinions about them. You read the latest research, talk to other professionals in the field, take courses. You may become the "lone voice" about alcohol and other drug issues and how they should be handled, and sometimes being the only audible voice about such a large issue can make you feel hoarse from straining. It can also make you feel very alone—you may sometimes feel that you are one of the only people working against the tide. As school systems become more sophisticated, you will no doubt be joined by others who choose to concentrate their efforts in a similar direction.

COPING WITH INSTITUTIONAL DENIAL

Denial is a process by which people, institutions, and whole societies protect themselves from painful realities. We all do this, and some amount of denial is practically required to operate in the world. If we paid attention to every loss we'd ever experienced or chose to confront every painful reality twenty-four hours a day, we'd all be emotionally spent.

However, in the case of alcohol and other drug issues, institutional denial is rampant. Like an individual alcoholic or addict, the system itself displays characteristic denial, and those beliefs and behaviors are very closely allied with enabling. School systems enable students to use alcohol and other drugs in a variety of ways, from lowering academic standards to actually looking the other way when students use (see chapter 7). And because you may be more aware of denial and enabling, you may be more frustrated by it. So while you want to personally avoid behaviors which are characteristic of denial, and while you want to gently lead others to the place where they can understand these concepts, you cannot expect to wipe them out singlehandedly. When thinking about institutional denial, it's important to keep in mind that it is essentially an unconscious process. If you attach volition and consciousness to it, you get so angry you can't concentrate.

Identifying Types of Institutional Denial

Following are some of the ways institutional denial can be identified. You will notice that these are the same types of denial common in individual alcoholics and addicts, listed on page 309. They are listed here to describe characteristic denial in schools.

Simple Denial: In simple denial, the system simply denies that there is a problem. This can apply to the whole system (school) or any subsystem, like a team, honor class, etc. If top administrators deny there is a problem, students can wait a long time before the issues are addressed.

Minimizing: In the case of minimizing, the school admits that there is a problem, but that perhaps it has been exaggerated. This reduces every student's drinking or drugging to a "phase" and aligns alcohol and other drug problems along with problems like students running in the hallways. Another way to minimize these problems is to set up a scale of what's good and bad, loading the good side to offset the alcohol and other drug issues. "Here at Eastman High, we have quite a problem with parties where alcohol is served, it's true. But we also have eight National Merit Scholarship finalists and tremendous school spirit."

Rationalizing: When we rationalize as school systems, we try to find reasons why the current use of alcohol and other drugs by students and their families is okay. "Well, she's still getting a B in history, so it can't be too bad." Or, as a system, we say, "Our kids come from such high-pressure families, they really need a chance to be *kids,* to unwind." What we really mean is that it's okay for them to drink and drug.

Intellectualizing: Intellectualizing is a real trap for school systems because that is what we are all good at. That's why we became educators. Intellectualizing is puzzling over reasons and theories, and, by so doing, usually blaming others and questioning statistical measurements. "Don't you think kids report that they use more drugs than they really do on those surveys?" is a classic case of intellectualizing. (Even if the statistics were cut in half, we'd still have a problem on our hands.)

Blaming: Because school people have been blamed so much lately for everything from hyperactivity to poor test scores, we are ready and waiting to blame someone else for something. Blame is really easy, but it doesn't get us anywhere. To say as a school system that "this all started at home" may be true, but it doesn't help us one iota in helping students. To blame the police for the proliferation of street drugs may be easy and may make us feel better initially, but *we* still haven't gotten to the issue: to have the courage to change what we can.

Diversion: Diversionary tactics are a great way to avoid dealing with alcohol and other drug issues. "At least there's little school violence here" is a textbook case of diversion, as it diverts the attention (here, positively) to another issue. Less positive, but more common diversionary tactics include statements like, "Drugs? Who cares about drugs? Let's talk about attendance! Or doing homework. I mean really, let's get down to basics here." Such basic diversionary tactics are often heard at faculty meetings.

Hostility: Hostility is simple and effective. If the system, or any subset of it, blows up every time the subject is broached, it doesn't take long for us to understand that we're not supposed to bring it up. If, every time a faculty member brings up the issue of alcohol or other drugs, an administrator lambastes the faculty for not doing their jobs, people quickly learn to keep quiet. We put up and shut up.

Bringing institutional denial to the attention of school personnel is a worthwhile pursuit. Often, awareness is the beginning of the end of denial.

Survival Tip: The problem for SAP people may be that they are the lone voice in identifying institutional denial. Not only is this isolating and exhausting, but if you're not careful, you come off to the rest of the school sounding like a fanatic, undermining your greatly needed credibility. Elicit help! Schedule a workshop, and ask an outside expert (who always has more impact than an inside expert) to present the idea of institutional denial.

WORKING ON A POSITIVE RELATIONSHIP WITH ADMINISTRATION

A positive relationship with the administrators in your school can save your program and your sanity. If at all possible, include a top-level administrator on your core team and make sure that your initial training concentrates on the confidentiality issues so there is someone in the administration who has a working understanding of the meaning of confidentiality as it relates to SAP operations. If this is not spelled out clearly from the outset, administrators may feel that the SAP is willingly keeping information from them, and this is a bad foot to start off on. (Also read about confidentiality concerns in chapter 3.)

Cases of suicidality, abuse, or neglect might have to be reported to the administration, if that is the protocol in your system. Most schools do this to insure that they have documentation through the school of the report. In my system, I report to the principal that I have made an outside report of physical or sexual abuse or suicidality, and he documents it in his personal notes, but I do not make the report through anyone else.

Keeping Communication Open

Conversations with the school administration can be very difficult because of confidentiality. I've included a few samples here to give you some ideas of how to deflect inappropriate questions while answering as much as you can. Most administrators are not trying to "pump" you for information; they are just unaccustomed to working within these strict guidelines.

If your program is alcohol and other drug specific, you cannot divulge that a student is even participating (or has participated) without his or her written consent. Following is a sample conversation between an SAP person and an administrator:

> *Administrator:* I've called you in to talk about John Doe. He's been in quite a few fights here at school lately, and I wondered if he'd been in to see you.
>
> *SAP person:* (Whether or not you've seen the student) Anyone who's been involved in a lot of fights would make a good referral to the SAP. I'd recommend you refer him. Do you need a referral form, or do you have one?

If your program is broad brush in nature, you can divulge a student's participation, but not the nature of his or her difficulties.

> *Administrator:* I've called you in to talk about John Doe. He's been in quite a few fights here at school lately, and I wondered if he'd been in to see you.
>
> *SAP person:* Yes, I am familiar with John. His recent involvement in fights certainly warrants another referral.
>
> *Administrator:* Is he involved with drugs, do you think?
>
> *SAP person:* I can't answer that question, but I think his involvement in

fights is certainly something we should follow up regardless. I'll get you a referral form.

Dealing with Disciplinary Referrals

Because school administration is involved from the outset with referrals based on violations of the chemical use policy, you do not have to protect the information that the student is involved with the program, but you do have to protect any information the student divulges about his or her situation or alcohol and other drug experience.

> *Administrator:* I'd like you to meet Jane Doe. She was drunk yesterday in biology class and was sent to the nurse, and then I called her parents and sent her home. She'll be in suspension today and tomorrow, and she'll also have to participate in the SAP with you.

> (later)

> *Administrator:* How's Jane Doe doing? Was that an isolated incident, or do you think this young woman has a problem with alcohol?

> *SAP person:* Jane's doing what's required of her through the chemical use policy we set up. If there's any change or any reason to let you know anything, I'll contact you right away.

Using a Release of Information

With a release of information, you can tell the administrator what he or she needs to know, but there is no reason to divulge information which is peripheral to the issue.

> *SAP person:* I have a release of information from Jane Doe to talk about her situation with you. I've already talked to her parents and her guidance counselor about this. Through her participation in the challenge group, she decided she wanted more help, so she's going to a treatment facility on the day after tomorrow. Of course, we'll need to see to it that she gets the proper work sent to her so she doesn't have to forfeit this whole school year. Her guidance counselor is working on that, but we may need your help on the attendance policy.

> *Administrator:* Well, we can see to that. Tell me, is it just alcohol, or does she have a problem with cocaine as well?

> *SAP person:* I'm sorry, but I'm not really comfortable answering that question. Maybe when she comes back from treatment, she'll want to talk to you about it if you're still curious.

Fielding Questions about School-Wide Patterns of Use: This is another example of a difficult conversation with administration. The administrator is understandably concerned about the level of use in the school and would like to use the SAP as a resource in this regard. Student assistance program people can be good sources of information, but they can't be sources of specific information.

Administrator: Tell me, is there a lot of cocaine use among our student body?

SAP person: I'd say about one quarter of the students that I've interviewed through the SAP have used cocaine.

Administrator: Can cocaine be bought here at school?

SAP person: Yes it can, as far as I know.

Administrator: Do you know who is selling it? Is it students or adults?

SAP person: I know of one student who used to sell it and another one who still does, but I can't tell you who they are. I've never heard of an adult selling right here at school, though I know they sell off-campus. Suffice it to say that cocaine can be bought here. You work on the supply end, and we'll work on the demand end.

Administrator: Can you at least offer us some advice?

SAP person: Encourage the faculty to report suspicious activity to you and guarantee them your back-up. Keep good relations with the police, and don't disregard obvious signs of dealing.

Administrator: Like what?

SAP person: Like exchanging money, or students who seem to be doing extremely well financially for no apparent reason. Students who are very popular all of a sudden should be watched carefully.

Survival Tip: Without becoming condescending, try to explain the confines of confidentiality in as much detail as you can—as often as you can. They are very confusing, so don't become exasperated too soon. There is also always the possibility that these regulations will change, and then you must be in the position to change with them. Stay current and make faculty and staff aware of the changes as you become aware of them.

Survival Tip: Be aware of how your relationship to the administration looks to the students. If you are always seen with administrators, students will begin to wonder whether you are telling them about their situations. Also, never discuss one student's situation in the presence of other students.

CREATING POSITIVE RELATIONSHIPS WITH FACULTY AND STAFF

Adherence to the confidentiality regulations may set you apart from the rest of the faculty on one score, but it doesn't have to set you apart on all scores. As a school person, an educator, and a counselor, you have a great deal in common with these people and you don't have to feel alienated from them. But it will take hard work on your part, because it is completely up to you to guide them through learning what they can discuss with you and what they can't.

You will meet a great deal of your faculty through referrals. Following are some suggestions to troubleshoot difficult conversations with faculty members. (Bear in mind, of course, that these are only examples of the *difficult* conversations. Many conversations with teachers are productive and don't pose any problem at all.)

The "Almost" Referral

In the "almost" referral, the teacher wants to add to the information he or she is certain you already have about a student. These teachers don't really want to leave a referral, but they do want to make sure the SAP is aware of the situations. These attempts are both goodhearted and seemingly halfhearted. Many first referrals from teachers are made this way, and if you can help the teacher feel comfortable and helpful, you may get many more.

> *Teacher:* I just want to make sure someone has told you about John Doe. I mean this kid is out of control. I'm sure you have a million referrals on him already. (Here, the teacher looks at you for confirmation of the last statement. In a broad-brush program, you can tell the teacher that you do have other referrals on the student. If it is a narrow-focus program, you cannot. These examples are written as though it is a narrow-focus program, because these are the more difficult situations.)

> *SAP person:* What concerns you about his behavior?

> *Teacher:* Everything. He's been smoking pot since the sixth grade and God knows what else. I'm sure you know him.

> *SAP person:* Would you like to leave a referral?

> *Teacher:* No, no. I don't even have him in class this year. I just thought you ought to know about him, if you didn't already.

> *SAP person:* Well, thanks for bringing him to my attention. The more we know about a student, the more likely it is that we can help. It would be really helpful for me if you could fill out this referral form; leave it anonymously if you want. It just helps me to have a better idea of what's going on for a kid from a number of different sources.

> *Teacher:* But I don't want to accuse this kid of anything. He's the type that would slash your tires or something.

> *SAP person:* That's just why we have anonymous referrals. You won't be accusing him of a thing, and besides, he'll never know that you referred him.

The "Surprise Attack"

In the "surprise attack," faculty members use the direct-hit approach to see if they can fluster you into giving up information. They may also direct some frustration about the alcohol and other drug situation at the SAP person.

Teacher: Hey, I've been meaning to ask you, have you seen that kid John Doe?

SAP person: I can't answer that, sorry. Why? What's your concern?

Teacher: My concern is that the kid's a menace. I mean, he's out of control. He's stoned all the time, and if we're going to have a program like this in schools, he's just the kind of kid you ought to see.

SAP person: Would you like to leave a referral?

Teacher: The kid is a totally lost cause, believe me. I'm sure he's one of yours already.

SAP person: If he isn't already, I'd sure like to get ahold of him, from what you've said. Thanks for bringing him to my attention. Let me get a referral form and we can fill it out right here and now, anonymously if you want. How do you know him?

"Playing the Nice-Guy" Referral

These are perhaps the most difficult situations to handle because these teachers are trying to bypass the disciplinary system to maintain a friendly relationship with the student. You know that students need consequences and help for their alcohol and other drug issues and that help without consequences is an impotent stab at the problem. Also, you are in the position of chiding the faculty member for not going through the proper channels. In addition, the teacher is feeling like he or she did a heroic deed, while we feel that the teacher has done the student and the system a grave disservice.

Teacher: I'd like to refer Jane Doe to you. I'm sure that she was drunk today in biology class, but I didn't want to get her into any trouble, so I thought I'd just let you know and maybe you could talk to her.

SAP person: Being drunk at school is pretty serious stuff. If you're pretty sure that a student has been drinking, the proper procedure would be to contact your building administrator, and make sure that it gets dealt with right away.

Teacher: Well, like I said, I didn't want to get her into any trouble. We have a good relationship and I didn't want her to be mad at me. She has a lot of problems. Plus, this way, I thought she could see you.

SAP person: Seeing me would have been an automatic consequence of being drunk in class. Thanks for bringing this to my attention, but now we need to work together on this situation. I know you think you did Jane a favor, but you really didn't. This way, she's getting a really mixed message. It's important for her to understand that it's not okay to be drunk in class, and getting a day or two of suspension is really the only way we can officially tell her that. Remember—you wouldn't be getting her in trouble, her drinking would. Also, I'm concerned that Jane is at school (or left school!) under the influence of alcohol and that, as adults, we didn't intervene.

Teacher: But what can we do now? I mean, she has left my class already.

In the preceding case, there are two courses of action that can be taken, depending on the situation. If school is still in session for the day, try to get permission from the teacher to call an administrator. Have the administrator find the student's schedule and pay her a visit in the next class. The administrator should call the student out into the hallway or to the office (whatever is the regular procedure for speaking to a student) and pay close attention to the gait, speech, eyes, and odor of the student. If the administrator believes the student is under the influence, the student should be escorted to the nurse's office where another administrator and the nurse can verify the situation. It is always best if the student admits to the use, but if three or four adults (who are essentially untrained) concur that the student is under the influence, he or she probably is. Sometimes these are false alarms, but that is okay. This is one case where it really is better to be safe than sorry.

If school has already been dismissed for the day, it is an entirely different story. Then, the SAP's best defense is to try to persuade the referring teacher to at least call the student's parents to report his or her suspicions and to tell them that he or she has made a referral to the SAP. When the appropriate procedures are followed, and the administration is notified, the student gets the attention of his or her parents, the school administration, and the SAP. When teachers try to bypass these procedures, the student gets entirely the wrong message. The faculty information handout provided here can help you get this across to teachers.

FORGING POSITIVE RELATIONSHIPS WITH GUIDANCE PERSONNEL

Relations with the guidance department (or student services, or whatever your counseling department is called) are potentially the trickiest area of SAP operation. If the relationship with guidance is good, a great deal of work can be done in a short time, and troubled students can get the help they need. In some cases, the SAP is made up of guidance people. Guidance counselors can be tremendous referral sources and can smooth the way for SAP people with faculty and students alike.

If, on the other hand, the relationship with guidance is strained or competitive, the resulting tension will absorb a great deal of your badly needed energy and will adversely affect the operation of both the SAP and guidance services. There may be tension between the SAP and the guidance department for a number of reasons, several of which are discussed next.

Managing Territorial Disputes:

While most guidance people recognize the need for SAP services in this day and age, some have territorial misgivings about who should be handling the alcohol and other drug problems and feel that some of their authority and perhaps even job security has been usurped by the hiring of SAP people. If you're involved with an SAP and you are feeling an amorphous sense of tension, it's probably real. I know of one case where a state guidance association tried to sue a school department for hiring nonguidance personnel for an SAP position. Although this case

Faculty Information Handout
Making a Disciplinary Referral

Making a disciplinary referral is perhaps one of the most difficult aspects of being a teacher. Because you often know and like the student in question, you may be reluctant to "blow the whistle," but there are several reasons why you should.

What IS a Disciplinary Referral?

A disciplinary referral is one in which you are fairly certain that a student is currently in possession of, under the influence of, selling, or distributing alcohol or other drugs. Here are a few examples:

1. Anita has her head down on the desk. When you walk by to remind her that sleeping in class is inappropriate, you can smell liquor on her breath. As she starts to offer an explanation, she slurs her words and has trouble making sense.

   Yes. This is a disciplinary referral. Call, or send a student down, to get an administrator. Try not to let Anita out of your sight, because she could be a danger to herself or someone else if she leaves. The administrator may take the student to the nurse's office and will contact the parents to get Anita. As part of Anita's disciplinary consequence, she will be asked to participate in the SAP in the coming weeks.

2. Paul is in homeroom talking to his friends. They are rehashing the weekend's events, and you overhear Paul laughing that he'll never drink twelve beers again.

   No. This is generally not a disciplinary referral, unless Paul is bound by an off-school code of conduct like an interscholastic athletic code or an agreement not to use. Make a referral out of concern to the SAP.

3. Sam and Ralph are passing notes, and you have repeatedly asked them not to. At the next note's "send-off," you confiscate it. Inside the note are two hand-rolled cigarettes and four tiny squares of paper.

   Yes. This is either two joints and four "hits" of acid, or something fabricated to look like them. Either is a violation of most chemical use policies. Call or send for an administrator or walk the students down to the office yourself. Sam and Ralph will likely be suspended, and they will participate in the SAP as part of their disciplinary consequence.

Faculty Information Handout, continued

Making a disciplinary referral is hard, because you may feel that you are getting the student into trouble. Here are some important points to remember.

- You are not getting the student into trouble: his or her drug use is.
- Adolescent alcohol and other drug use is often dangerous. Because a student gets into trouble, he or she may decide to take a look at his or her use. (Try to remember any of the difficult lessons you had to learn as a teenager.) The student's serious look at his or her own use may curtail a potential problem.
- If you don't respond to the use, other students may feel that it's okay to come to your class (or your practice) under the influence. "Oh, Mr. Smith doesn't care. He lets everyone come to class messed up."
- It's our job as adults to make sure these students are safe. We can't let a student who is under the influence leave the building. He or she could get hurt in a car accident, crossing the street, or could have ingested enough alcohol or other drugs to put him or her in a serious medical condition.
- Often, students who use blatantly enough to get caught are asking for your help, or they are so out of control with their use that they can no longer choose when to use.
- Most disciplinary referrals result in a student's participation in the SAP. Through a disciplinary referral, you are providing them with the appropriate message: that alcohol and other drug use is unacceptable at school or at a school function. Further, you are underscoring that alcohol and other drug use can indicate problems, and you are securing help for them at the same time.
- If you don't report the use, the student may get the wrong idea and may believe that you simply don't care. If he or she is looking for your help, this may be a real slap in the face. The student also may get the idea that you think that using drugs at school is perfectly all right.

It is also all right to be wrong. If you make a disciplinary referral, you have reasons for doing so. If a student can explain away all the symptoms, then you might be wrong. However, you might be right, and a student in real trouble might get the real help he or she is looking for.

was lost, which set the precedent, it illustrates how some guidance people feel about SAPs. Some feel that the functions of SAPs come under the umbrella of guidance services and will resent the SAP person(s) even though the issue is really philosophical in nature.

Most schools split students into (more or less) manageable caseloads for guidance staff, either by alphabet, by grade, by homeroom, or whatever so counselors each have a group of students which they consider "theirs." It is understandably difficult for guidance people to see "their" students traipsing down to the SAP office to talk about "who knows what." They may feel that they are being kept in the dark, or that the students don't trust them. This is a difficult position for guidance people, and only the most secure could weather this without an occasional pang of wonder or self-doubt. These issues become even more muddled when the SAP is seen as an "arm" of the guidance department rather than a separate entity. It also provides a good argument for housing the SAP and guidance in separate areas of the school.

As an SAP person, remind guidance people that you are dependent on them in part for referrals and that you are working on the problems of the student population together. There are plenty of problems to go around, so there should be no competition for numbers. Be aware of your own limitations, and refer students back to their guidance counselors whenever their expertise could benefit the student more than yours.

Whenever you can, encourage students to sign releases of information so you can keep guidance abreast of what's going on with one of "their" students. This is particularly important in situations where the student may be going for treatment in the near future or when a student has returned from treatment and is reentering school. In all cases of suicidality, inform guidance and parents immediately. Work hard on developing good relations with guidance, encouraging collaboration, particularly in coleading groups. It may be up to the SAP people to reach out, even if they are the new kids in town.

Survival Tip: Never allow a student to spout off at length about a problem with a guidance counselor, and never get involved in helping a student change guidance counselors. The most the SAP can do is encourage the student to bring up the problem with the chairperson of the guidance department or the principal. Student assistance programs are not the "pinch-hitter" extra guidance person for every student who doesn't get along with his or her guidance counselor. Also, never overzealously involve yourself in career planning, suggesting colleges, arranging schedule changes, etc. These are all clearly guidance functions.

Some guidance people perceive the very inception of student assistance programs as an indictment that they couldn't handle the alcohol and other drug situation. While some are relieved to have someone on board with the alcohol and other drug expertise, others experience the posting of the position as a direct hit to their professional abilities. Student assistance program personnel can reassure guidance people that alcohol and other drug-related problems are so pervasive that guidance staffs can't handle all of them, not because of their lack of knowledge but because of their lack of numbers and time. Student assistance programs need to emphasize that SAPs were born out of burgeoning awareness of the extent of the alcohol and other drug problems, not out of the awareness of the inability of guidance people to meet the need.

Survival Tip: Never intimate that your position was created because other school personnel "didn't know what the heck they were doing." First of all, it isn't true, because if they really didn't know what they were doing, they'd still be doing it and they wouldn't have hired you.

Coping with Others' Job Dissatisfaction

A lot of people got into the guidance or student service business to do what SAPs are now doing. They didn't become guidance counselors to do scheduling, postsecondary school planning, testing, contacting parents, etc. They hoped to do a lot of personal counseling with students, unfettered by administrative duties. In most systems, guidance people are sadly overburdened by paperwork, and some are resentful that SAPs seem to have escaped that fate. (In actuality, SAPs have only escaped that fate because of the current confidentiality regulations. If those change, we'll be up to our eyeballs in paperwork as well.) There are no quick solutions to this that SAPs can provide. We need to understand the frustrations of guidance people and work toward positive relationships with them.

Gaining Acceptance

Respect is won, not given as a condition of employment in a school system. Guidance people have the right to question the training and practices of SAP people, and some will. Because traditional school counseling training does not concentrate on alcohol and other drug concerns, traditionally trained guidance people without additional training are not a first choice for SAP directors. As a result, candidates with disparate training and backgrounds will be considered and perhaps hired for SAP positions.

People are naturally suspicious about things they are not familiar with, so SAP people need to explain their training and prove to the guidance staff that they are knowledgeable, reliable, and worthy of referrals. You can't afford to be insulted if someone asks you to indicate what qualifies you for this work, because they may not be familiar with your certification, Master's program, or previous employment history and you may have to explain it. Consider your whole first year a final interview, and expect to *earn* the confidence of those you work with.

Survival Tip: If there are gaps in your training, fill them by taking courses and attending workshops. Don't talk much about it. Just do it.

DEALING WITH ROLE CONFLICT

Working in an SAP means you must work at managing the conflicts between who you are as a person and what you do for a living. If you have previous work experience in a chemical dependency treatment facility, hospital, or other clinical setting, you will probably have an easier time managing the potential role conflict SAP work brings. If, on the other hand, you worked in a school previously in another capacity, it may be difficult for you to adjust to your new role and responsibilities.

If your only role is that of the SAP director and you are not a guidance counselor or a teacher, you must deal with some dilemmas for yourself before you start. Should the SAP director, for instance, also become a coach of a team? Or an advisor to any school activity? It is not recommended, as there is too much potential for role conflict here. It is likely that a student on the team would want to use the services of the SAP, *unfettered by the relationship the student has with the coach.* In this example, let's say the star player has a problem with cocaine. Is she going to come to the coach/SAP director with the information? Is the SAP director going to be able to be a counselor one moment and a coach the next? These may seem like contrived questions, but in schools, faculty members are asked to do a number of things, some of which could create extreme cases of role conflict for SAP people, who really should have a single purpose.

Following are a number of situations which could potentially cause role conflict for SAP directors/counselors and coordinators. The advice here is to avoid these situations if you can. However, if you *do* choose to do these things, go into them with your eyes wide open, taking into consideration the potential pitfalls.

Chaperoning Dances: This is simply asking for it. There is never a greater likelihood that the SAP person is going to be in a position to point the finger at a student who is using or has used alcohol or other drugs. Particularly if the student is familiar to you, you run a great risk of being labeled the school "narc," and your program may suffer. I am sure that some people do not understand the inherent conflict here, but it is like having drug and alcohol counselors present when police pull motorists over to check for DWI. We are not in the enforcement business, and to put yourself in that position creates a lot of confusion for students and faculty members alike.

Chaperoning Overnight Field Trips: Field trips can be alcohol and other drug situations waiting to happen. You must decide ahead of time what the result will be if you happen to catch students using or having used alcohol or other drugs, or if some other personal crisis presents itself. Never chaperone alone, and make sure your co-chaperones understand where you stand on these issues and that you have their support. Be careful that your co-chaperones are reliable in terms of their own alcohol and other drug use.

Of course, there may be situations in which you make a decision to chaperone a field trip or something like that. Before going, think through a couple of possible scenarios and your planned reactions to them. Discussing them with a co-chaperone can be helpful in two ways: first, you can enlist your co-chaperone's help in thinking a solution through, and, second, you can screen for potentially disastrous co-chaperones.

MANAGING WORK AND YOUR PERSONAL LIFE

If you're a computer operator, no one wonders about your personal life, as long as you come in and do your work and get it done in a timely fashion, and as long as your personal life doesn't seem to be affecting your ability to do your work. The same is not true for politicians and SAP personnel. Students and faculty *do* care what happens in your personal life, as well they should. As an SAP person, your personal life and your job are somewhat interconnected. Students see you as a role model for healthy living, a counselor, and an educator. If you live near where you work, you are going to be under constant scrutiny; don't be afraid of it, but be aware of it.

Handling Your Own Use of Alcohol or Other Drugs

Be prepared to answer questions from students and faculty alike about your own use of chemicals, because they will ask. If you are a social drinker, students and faculty alike will wonder about it, and they may tease, or ask you about it, or even challenge your use. It is an understandably awkward feeling to meet a student or faculty member in the beer aisle of the grocery store, or at a local restaurant or lounge. If you work in an SAP, you'll need to be prepared for these feelings and think about how you will respond.

If you choose not to drink at all at school-related functions, expect questions and comments about that too. It is okay to drink socially, and it is okay not to drink at all in this business. *However, working in the addictions field if you have not treated your own addictions and codependence is unethical practice. Moreover, working in the addictions field as a means of treating your own addictions or codependence is unethical practice.*

Disclosing Your Own Recovery

If you are recovering from addiction yourself, think carefully before making self-disclosures. Some people believe that recovering people are the only people who can do this work successfully. Others believe that hiring recovering people for these positions is like going to dentists with bad teeth. Their rationale is, This person couldn't manage to stay out of trouble herself. How the heck is she going to help students stay out of trouble? Especially if you are coming from a treatment or agency background, remember that schools do not necessarily have the same sort of benevolent view of recovery as the treatment industry does. Your glowing admission of ten years of sobriety may be met with dull stares, fear, disdain, or even hostility. For some people, however, being open about their recovery is worth the potential risks. Self-disclosure is a personal decision.

Addressing Other Compulsive Behaviors

We cannot provide good role models for students struggling with compulsive behaviors if we have not managed our own codependence, eating, spending, gambling, raging, or sexual behavior. If our lives are unmanageable in any of these areas, we need to get these behaviors treated, not only for the sake of the students but for our own sakes as well. Denial is a painful plane in which to operate, and it saps our energy while making us less effective counselors. Remember that most of what we communicate to each other is nonverbal; if our lives are unmanageable in any area, students can sense it.

Some Final Words about Personal Lives: Make sure that you *have* a personal life. Take care to maintain interests that have absolutely *nothing* to do with your work. Student assistance program work can increase to fill any space because there are potentially so many students in need of assistance. If you are finding that you are losing your personal life to your job, you need to make some adjustments, or soon you won't be able to do your job effectively.

IDENTIFYING AND AVOIDING UNETHICAL BEHAVIOR

While some behavior is in a gray area of ethics and may depend on the situation, there are a few issues which are unequivocally unethical, and very dangerous, to the school, the student, the SAP, and the adult(s) involved. It is *never* okay to engage in the following behaviors:

Socializing with Students: This is just plain dangerous and unethical. Don't do it under any circumstances. Don't have students who are involved in your program over to your house, and don't "hang out" with students.

Adolescents count on adults to be adults. The last thing they need is another adolescent in their lives.

Confiding in a Student Like a Friend: Students cannot be used to meet our needs. It is never okay to use a student as a counselor, to divulge inappropriate information, or to ask a student to be a shoulder for us to lean on.

Sexualizing a Relationship with a Student: Inappropriate sexual relationships don't begin with physical contact. That's how they ultimately end. Inappropriate and unethical sexual behavior toward students includes the following:

- *Wearing provocative clothing:* When you're involved in individual counseling behind closed doors, make sure that what you wear gives no seductive suggestion. If you are trying to look sexually attractive to your students, get a different job.
- *Using touch in a seductive or suggestive way:* Don't touch students at all unless you are absolutely, 100 percent positive that the touch cannot be misinterpreted.
- *Not setting appropriate boundaries:* Your home, your personal life, and your sexual relationships are not a student's domain. Students shouldn't call you at home or hear details about your relationship with your spouse or partner, but it is up to the SAP person to set those boundaries, because students will test them. Many adolescents don't know how to set such boundaries and are counting on the adults to do it.
- It is also the responsibility of an SAP person to set straight any suggestive comments or actions students might make, even inadvertently. I am reminded of a time when an eighteen-year-old male student came up behind me and put his hands over my eyes in an attempt to be funny. I had to tell him on the spot that his actions made me very uncomfortable and not to do it again. If I hadn't, I am sure that this particular student would have tried

to connect with me over and over again in this fashion and, though it was unintentional, the physical contact was very inappropriate.

- *Making suggestive comments:* Saying something like, "Your girlfriend/boyfriend sure is lucky to have you" may seem innocent enough, but in the wrong context it can belie the counselor's feelings toward the student. "Possessive" statements are also very abusive. Saying "Oh, so I'm not good enough for you, huh? You're taking Dan to the prom instead of me?" coming from a counselor may sound fairly innocent, but it isn't. This comment pits the counselor against the boyfriend in a competitive, sexual stance and is inappropriate.

Survival Tip: Any counselor–student relationship that is flirtatious in nature should send up a red flag because it is potentially dangerous. If you find yourself unable to deal with a student in any way but a flirtatious one, refer the student to someone else and talk it over in clinical supervision.

OBTAINING CLINICAL SUPERVISION

Because the issues dealt with in the context of SAPs are so complex and difficult, SAP directors need to secure clinical and/or peer supervision so they can get feedback on cases and general support from colleagues. This aspect of programming is so important that it should be pursued as early as possible.

A clinical supervisor is a person with more extensive clinical background than you have with whom you can discuss cases and bounce off questions. The relationship of clinical supervisor is usually not administratively supervisory in nature; in other words, your clinical supervisor shouldn't be your boss, although this is the case in some hospital and agency settings. The clinical supervisor you choose should have supervisory experience, advanced degrees, extensive clinical experience, and thorough understanding of adolescent issues, including alcohol and other drugs. Principals are inappropriate clinical supervisors because their clinical experience is not extensive enough.

Our district hires a clinical supervisor on a consultant basis; her only dealing with the school is clinical supervision for the SAP directors. This sort of arrangement insures that there are no conflicts of interest. Generally, clinical supervisors meet with SAP people once a week for an hour or so. If needed, group supervision is acceptable.

Clinical supervision is a long-term investment in the sanity and professionalism of your student assistance program people; it ultimately reduces turnover and burnout. Without this weekly formal exchange of frustrations, strategies, and solutions, SAP people are left to absorb the often tragic situations of students by themselves. It should be the aim of every counselor-based SAP effort to provide clinical supervision. If you don't provide clinical supervision, you can expect to replace your SAP people every three or four years.

Survival Tip: Clinical supervision is not a luxury, but it requires a sophisticated school administration to understand the necessity for it. Start-up SAP efforts should include clinical supervision for the SAP director and counselors as part of the long-range plan. Clip any articles you come across which talk about clinical supervision and begin a file on it so you'll have plenty of back-up when you request the funding for it.

UTILIZING PEER SUPERVISION

If clinical supervision cannot be arranged because of budget constraints, the next best thing is peer supervision. In our district, we utilize both clinical and peer supervision, recognizing their disparate benefits. During peer supervision, SAP directors from different programs meet to discuss troubling cases and issues of concern, changing or eliminating all identifying information to protect the confidentiality of the students. Peer supervisory groups should be small (maximum of four, I'd say) and should be conducted according to the wishes of the group. Don't underestimate the need for this sort of arrangement. Particularly in counselor-based SAP efforts, SAP people can become very isolated. Schedule such a meeting at least once every two weeks, or it loses its original intent. If you get together only once a month, chances are you'll use the time to discuss issues common to your SAP operation instead of specific cases.

It is important that these meetings take place during the school day. This is not an "extra" thing that SAP people ought to do for themselves, but something SAPs need to build into their general operating procedure. Schedule your supervision (clinical or peer) on the same day every week, and don't run rotating groups on that day. Plan to rotate the location every week so you all get to see one another's different accommodations. Several formats are possible, depending on the makeup of the group and how well they work together.

- *Informal:* Peers get together with no agenda and no plans. They talk about whatever comes up, and whoever needs the time to share takes it.
- *Semiformal:* Peers get together, but they have an agenda which has been either sent to them or was adopted at last week's supervisory meeting. Participants bring issues of concern or cases to share. An appointed person takes notes.
- *Formal:* Peers meet with an appointed chairperson for the week and an agenda for the meeting. In some cases, participants take turns presenting cases or making didactic presentations in their area of expertise. Notes are taken and minutes distributed.

Survival Tip: Though formal peer supervision may seem stilted or prohibitively stuffy at first, it definitely has its benefits. Participants come ready to talk about the real issues and, because there is no clinical supervisor present, this format provides some structure and may actually prove more effective. When meeting with other SAP people, it is so easy to get swept away in the sheer pleasure of being with people who share your experience that you can lose track of time.

BECOMING A NETWORKER

Networking is so important because it makes you feel so much better about doing what you do, and ultimately your networking may pay off big when you need to refer a student or are looking for a cofacilitator for a group or a therapist to volunteer to do a brief guest spot in a teacher workshop. As you get to know the other people in your community, you reduce your own isolation and invite new ideas to your program.

Before the SAP people in my district acquired clinical supervision, we were already networking. We were going out for coffee and attending regional SAP network meetings, and stopping at each other's offices to borrow books and handouts. If you are new to the SAP business, try to meet with therapists in your community, visit treatment facilities, and visit other SAPs. Invite other SAP people to see your operation, and ask to see theirs. If you can get permission from a particular SAP group, ask another SAP person to sit in on a group, and then go to his or her school for a day and sit in on one of the SAP groups. This is how we learn from one another.

Meeting Community Responsibilities

As an SAP director, you will probably be asked to serve on five or six different community task forces, projects, special committees, and subcommittees. While you may be interested and invested in all the pursuits of these various boards, it is wise to "share the wealth" in this regard and have a core team member or other designated SAP representative serve on some of them. It is wise politically to draw others into the process and it is wise personally, as all these different projects can take up a lot of time and energy. Serve on the ones that really interest or recharge you.

KEEPING OFF THE PEDESTAL

You may wonder why I've included this. When people hear what SAP people do for a living, they tend to have one of two reactions. The first reaction is to say, "Better you than me, pal." Although this might take you aback, this honest, albeit brusque response is pretty healthy all around.

The other kind of reaction you can get is a lot more dangerous to you. Some people will want to put you on a pedestal and knight you for good measure while you're up there, as they congratulate you for "saving" all these students. Clearly, the people who give you this kind of feedback are complimenting you and showing you support, but avoid this kind of feedback. While it sounds flattering and seems innocent, it endows you with superhuman qualities and really diminishes the permission for you to be human. This sort of labeling gives an illusion of control to SAP people that we simply don't have and gives the false impression that we have ultimate determination over whether students get well under our tutelage. Anyone who knows addiction knows that we are powerless over it and people who have it.

If you really start believing that students are getting well simply because of your masterful command of counseling techniques rather than the benevolent conspiracy of caring atmosphere, available services, personal crisis, the "forces that be," and students' self-determination, then you also have to take commensurate "blame" when a student does not get well. Student assistance programs cannot afford either position, and to take one necessitates taking the other. We can, of course, work hard to insure that our part of the benevolent conspiracy is intact anytime a student needs to utilize it for personal change.

CONTINUING EDUCATION

The field of addictions is fast changing, and it is particularly incumbent on SAP people to keep up to date. Not only is it the ethical and professional thing to do, it will help you to feel less isolated in your position if you are involved in continuing education of some kind. Meeting fellow professionals can help you weather the rigors of SAP work. Courses are offered through local colleges and universities, and workshops are offered all the time. Plan to attend as many as you can. If you hear yourself saying that you can't get to *any,* then there's something else going on. If it has been a few years since you took a course, it is time to take another one.

Branch out, and take a course in something you know very little about. How about art therapy or dance therapy? Or, if you have no experience in these areas, try a course in special education or school administration. We are role models for the students we serve, and if they see us taking positive risks, they might follow in our footsteps someday. After all, growth is the only true evidence of life.

Continuing education is not just for people who are pursuing degree programs. On the contrary, it is probably the people with the master's degrees and the doctorates who run the greatest risk of becoming complacent and believing that they know it all. When we think we've learned everything we need to, we're in trouble! If you find yourself in this position, put down this book and sign up for a course or a workshop *today.*

Survival Tip: Most schools have tuition reimbursement plans for their faculty and staff. If you are new to the system, find out what you are eligible for right away because sometimes there are deadlines for informing the business office when you want to take a course. If you miss the deadlines, they won't pay. In other systems, you pay up front and then the school reimburses you. However, often you need to get approval first, so don't just take a course and then submit for reimbursement later. You may have an unpleasant surprise. If you are anxious about coursework or very overextended, look into auditing a course or taking it pass–fail. Check with the school first to see if they'll reimburse you if you choose these less traditional options.

USING INTERNS

Internships with your SAP serve multiple positive purposes. First, they allow young people coming up in the profession to learn about SAP operation and thereby eventually attract experienced people to the field. Interns in an SAP operation can expect a lot of direct client experience. (I tell mine that they can expect a "trial by fire.") Second, a well-chosen intern can help out a great deal in day-to-day SAP operation, making the load a little easier on the SAP person. Third, individual students may "connect" well with an intern. Sometimes a student who cannot relate well to us will find a real confidante in an SAP intern. Additionally, interns create a bridge from local colleges and universities to SAPs. As colleges and graduate programs learn more about SAPs and how they operate, eventually they will train their students to staff them.

If you decide to elicit internships for your SAP, try to work with a college or university that has an established internship program that provides faculty advisors for the student interns as well as a coordinator for the program. This way, you can be in contact with the coordinator of the internship program if there are any problems, concerns, or bugs to work out of the system. Choose interns from programs in psychology, counseling, school counseling, substance abuse counseling, etc. Master-level interns may be the most appropriate choice, though I've had great luck with undergraduates as well.

Because of the intensity of SAP work, student interns must exhibit maturity, responsibility, empathy, and the highest ethical standards. And because SAP directors are ultimately responsible for the work the interns do, SAP interns must be closely supervised. Interview prospective interns carefully, because you will be working with them closely. Luckily, most internship programs require "learning contracts" between the intern and the site supervisor. These are added paperwork but a necessary inconvenience because they insure that you both agree on the terms. You have them in writing for future reference. Always include an "escape clause" so either the intern or supervisor (you) can get out of the agreement gracefully in the event that there are irreconcilable problems. If there is no such paperwork provided by the college or university, make up your own, and have students "sign on" to your expectations of them (and theirs of you!). Interns should be included in core team trainings, meetings, etc. Include interns as cofacilitators in two or more groups on an ongoing basis, but do not include them in every group. Interns should be working in your program for a reasonable length of time so you don't spend a lot of time training them and then, just as the students are getting used to them, they leave. I would rather have an intern at school one day a week for a year than two days a week for one semester. The continuity is well worth it.

Also remember that interns are there for the learning; internships are not paid positions. As a result, an intern's day should end on time, even if yours doesn't. They have vacations from their studies, which means they have vacations from their internships as well. It is easy to forget and to treat them like employees, asking them to take more than their due share of work.

Interns can also be utilized to take on specific projects *if these are outlined from the start.* It is unfair to invite an intern into the operation saying that he or she will be involved in running groups, etc., and then have the intern concentrate solely on administrative tasks. However, some interns might want to work on a grant application, start a newsletter, or design a survey as a separate internship task. Try to include a balance of duties for interns. They should be involved in as many aspects of SAP operation as possible without compromising the quality of the services. Take care that you don't pile on mundane paperwork tasks without including interns in the more substantive workings of the program.

Survival Tip: Sometimes having an intern can be more work than not having one. Make sure that your prospective intern is a self-starter but not so independent that he or she will need to be chased after. Interns need to understand the intensity of SAP work before they get into it. After having them read the confidentiality regulations, I also require that my interns sign a statement indicating their understanding of the regulations and their willingness to follow them.

PICKING YOUR BATTLES

There are a million different places where you could put your energy in a given day, but in the SAP business, it is important to pick your battles. Make sure that the things you really mean to fight for are worth having. For instance, allowing students to attend group on a rotating class schedule is a battle well worth fighting, but when you get there, you don't want to be haunted by ghosts of other, less important battles.

For example, the first spring as an SAP director, I noticed that the senior class was selling beer mugs etched with the year and school name as prom souvenirs. This is clearly inappropriate in a school which espouses that it is trying to promote a chemical-free prom and graduation, but no one seemed to see the inherent mixed message. At the same time, we were negotiating with the administration to get a full-time group room for the following school year; I was trying to gain permission for the recovery group to meet with other recovery groups in the city, and the chemical use policy was being adopted. After some thought, I chose not to engage in the beer-mug battle that year because it wasn't worth jeopardizing the other battles at that time.

Picking your battles means understanding what is at stake and remembering the priorities of the SAP as outlined in your mission statement. In the preceding example, it was more important to secure the group room than to wage a campaign to abolish the beer mugs, and we didn't have the required energy for both. (I also do not have the authority to veto prom souvenirs.) The real trick would be to get to the members of the next senior class before they decide on souvenirs, and explain the mixed message that alcohol-related paraphernalia creates. Then, when they make the decision not to order those souvenirs, they are saying something to their class about their class, to the manufacturer of prom souvenirs, and to the school community at large. Successfully choosing which issues to go after and which to leave alone is part of avoiding burnout.

AVOIDING BURNOUT

A lot of the survival tips offered in this chapter are intended to help you avoid burnout. As you can probably gather, and may know firsthand, people who do student assistance work are highly susceptible to burnout, and programs suffer when the turnover of counselors is heavy. Following are some of the most easily recognizable symptoms of burnout:

Becoming Preoccupied with the Problems of Students: If you find that you are still thinking about students' problems long after you get home, you're too involved. This is not to suggest that SAP people can't care, but that they can't care beyond their capacity to care. Caretakers must treat themselves with the same respect they give to their clients, and this means doing your work in such a way that it doesn't rule your personal life as well.

Believing That You are Irreplaceable—That if You Left, Everything Would Fall Apart: If you begin to believe that you are the only person who could possibly do your job, then you are putting too much pressure on yourself. This is not self-congratulatory behavior, it is controlling behavior, as you begin to believe that the outcome of students' lives is dependent solely on you. This is the quickest way to burn out, because you see every student as a personal drain on your precious store of energy. Your best bet is to attend Al-Anon to learn the skill of detachment.

Frequent Physical Illness: If you find that you are experiencing more colds and flues than usual, chances are that your resistance is down. This may mean that you are beginning to burn out. (Or in certain cases it simply means that you are susceptible to physical illness.) Some people, however, regard physical illness as the body's way of getting its driver to "pull over" for a while. If you feel this is the case with you, you need to operate at a pace that won't continually overheat your engine.

Feeling Completely Overwhelmed or Depressed: If you feel that you "simply can't go on like this" or feel that you're headed "over the edge," chances are you're right. When people describe their feelings this way, they are overwhelmed, full of despair, almost unable to cope. It is easier than you might think to feel this way as the head of an SAP, as you stomp through the muck and the swamp of tragedy every day. If you feel these things, you *must* make adjustments in your workload or in the way you absorb your workload.

Ways to Prevent Burnout

If you like your work, and want to do it for a while, you need to take certain precautions to avoid burnout.

Build Bridges in Your Workplace: Isolation heads the burnout parade, and if you can avoid it, you can make great strides in avoiding burnout as well. It is difficult to develop relationships in the context of SAP work, but it is absolutely necessary. Working with a core team, cofacilitators, fellow counselors, interns, faculty members, and administrators helps you feel less overwhelmed at work. Make a point to reach out to people, even if it feels awkward at first.

Leave Work at Work: You could do this work twenty-four hours a day if you didn't check yourself. Try to leave it at school. Visualize all your students in your office, and when you close your office door, wish them all safety through the night or over the weekend, and then leave. Try to leave school on time. Obviously, there are times when everyone stays late, but never make a habit of it. Especially, don't see students after hours on a regular basis. It poses ethical concerns, your safety may be compromised, and, because you are lengthening your work day, it increases the likelihood that you'll burn out sooner.

Involve Yourself in Support: We who are so good at dispensing support need to make sure that we are partaking of it as well. If you work in SAPs, you're affected by other people's addiction. By definition, anyone involved in SAP work could also be involved in Al-Anon, which is a tremendously supportive self-help fellowship. There are also some relatively new organizations such as ProCODA, which is designed specifically for people who work in the addictions field. (Check your local telephone listings, or ask around.)

If you are in recovery yourself, continue your meetings. If you are in therapy, continue that as well. It is not okay to consider working in this field a means of addressing your own alcohol and other drug issues.

Care for Yourself: For your physical self, you need to eat right, sleep enough, and get some exercise. These things seem so simple, and yet sometimes we don't pay enough attention to them. For your mental, emotional, and spiritual self, you need to cultivate close friendships, take some quiet time for yourself, continue outside interests and hobbies, stay in touch with your spirituality, and have a good laugh at least once a day.

Survival Tip: Clinical and peer supervision are great burnout preventatives. Having a positive working relationship with school administration and guidance provides other sure ways to prevent isolation and the requisite overwhelming feeling.

ORGANIZING THE DAILY SAP OPERATION:

Because SAPs deal with large numbers of students and fairly frequent crises, you do not want to spend a lot of your time or energy looking for things or getting bogged down with administrative details. Obviously, everyone will have slightly different solutions to these organizational challenges, but there are a few tips which might make the job of organizing your office a little bit easier.

Letting Students Know Where You Are: Taking the lead from Lucy in "Peanuts," make a sign that says, "The Counselor (or your name) is:" and hang it on your door. Attach a hook to the door under the sign, and then make up a few signs on heavy cardboard that say things like, "At lunch in the teachers' room," "In the group room," or "At an outside meeting." Punch holes in the signs so you can easily hang them on the hook. If you want to get fancy, add another permanent sign that says, "I'll be back at" and, on another hook, hang signs that say "Period C" or "tomorrow." Put the interchangeable signs in a heavy envelope hung next to the door on the inside of the office. As you leave for a group or for an outside meeting, you can hang your cards to let students and faculty members know where you are going. Then, if there's an emergency, you can be contacted.

Sending Out Group Reminders: If you choose to send out group reminders, it is best to get a system going right away. Try to make out the passes several days in advance (in case you get behind) and have them ready to go. If you have access to a computer system that can produce such passes, this would be ideal. However, the system must be secure so others cannot gain access to the information about who is in groups. If you write out the passes by hand, design a pass that is easy to complete, one that has the information circled or checked off (see chapter 9). If you have to deliver passes to teachers' mailboxes, alphabetize the stacks of passes by teachers' last names.

If you are working alone, remember that many hands can make light work. Bring a stack of passes into your groups and have each student fill out ten passes for themselves with everything except the date and period when the group meets. Then, at least you have ten group sessions' worth of passes partially filled out. It seems like an unnecessary step, but it can save you some time in the long run. Also, have students who are involved in your groups fill out a class schedule just in case you have to get in touch with them. That will save you time later.

Keeping Records: Confidentiality regulations stipulate that you must have a locked place in which to keep SAP records. Ideally, you would keep any records in a locked file cabinet in a locked room. Depending on your caseload, you may come up with some creative ways of keeping track of students who use the program.

Some people use notebooks to record their daily contacts with students. Another helpful tool, hailing from education, is the traditional "rank" book. If you are unfamiliar with schools and rank books, ask a teacher to show you his or her rank book, and try to imagine how you could alter one to keep personal notes about students. These books are particularly helpful because they already have spaces for great numbers of names and dates. Some people keep their group attendance records in rank books as well. Other SAP people use them to record daily contacts with individual students.

Scheduling Your Time: Student assistance program people need a large, wall-type calendar on which to schedule groups by number or color code. However, you will also need another calendar to schedule individual appointments, because you can't list individual student names on a large wall calendar that the whole school has access to. Some people go the educational route here as well and use a teacher's plan book. Because these are set up by school periods, they may be helpful. Others use a daily calendar book, and still others create a daily log. Make sure you have a secure place to keep them. It is advisable to keep daily logs and schedules so you can check when students need to confirm their attendance with you or when an emergency arises. A sample daily log follows.

You may want to photocopy your daily log in an obnoxious, attention-getting color so you can find the corner of it sticking out from under a pile of mail or forms.

Keeping Forms Handy: In an attempt to get organized, you may stow everything away to the back corner of a locked file cabinet. You won't appreciate your impeccable organization when a student arrrives for an individual appointment and you can't find an intake form. This may seem obvious, but keep copies of very important paperwork (not filled out!) on your desk in an organizer. Keep at hand the following:

- Referral forms (for teachers who come in wanting to refer)
- Daily logs (Start a new one every morning. Create a ritual like putting your cup of coffee on top of the log first thing in the morning.)

DAILY OFFICE LOG

M T W TH F

Before school _____
_____

A _____   **To do** _____
_____   _____
                                _____
B _____   _____
_____   _____
                                _____
HR _____   _____
_____

C _____   **Phone calls** _____
_____   _____
                                _____
D _____   _____
_____   _____
                                _____
E _____   _____
_____

F _____   **Notes** _____
_____   _____
                                _____
G _____   _____
_____   _____
                                _____
H _____   _____
_____   _____

After school _____ _____
_____   _____

- Intake forms
- Release of information forms (for students)
- Group sign-up sheets
- Chemical Use policy
- A sheet explaining the federal confidentiality regulations
- Pamphlet describing SAP services
- Verification passes
- Group attendance (You need to lock this up when you are not around, but it builds credibility when you can check on a student's attendance for a teacher in a matter of seconds.)

INVESTING IN PEACE OF MIND: GETTING INSURANCE

One sure-fire way to insure your piece of mind and therefore aid your effectiveness is to make sure that you are covered by personal liability insurance. Student assistance program people especially need to find out where the school's coverage begins and ends, and, if you're a teacher, whether you can be covered while doing SAP–type functions. Some SAP people carry additional insurance through a professional association or carry an umbrella policy on their personal insurance.

Though it is extremely unlikely that you will be sued, conduct yourself as though the likelihood is great, and you'll be fine. Carry additional insurance if you find that the school (or the agency for which you work) cannot cover you to your satisfaction. (Many cannot.) If school systems cannot cover you adequately, a good argument could be made for them to foot the bill for the additional coverage, especially if it is through a professional organization. If the school cannot or will not purchase it, it can still be a good investment—mostly in your own sanity and serenity.

SETTING THE PRECEDENT

Not only are SAP personnel defining their own jobs and the parameters of their programs; they are also creating these positions for the people who will follow. Most likely, these positions will evolve over the years, but we must take great care to set precedents which indicate respect for ourselves and those that will come after us. Just as teachers who don't follow the attendance policies make it hard on those that do, SAP personnel who refuse to adhere to the confidentiality regulations make the position doubly difficult for the next person who comes along who *does* adhere to them. If you begin clinical supervision outside of the regular school day and treat it like a luxury, future SAP people will have to live with it that way. Always consider that you are setting the precedent, so take the ultimate effectiveness of these positions into account, not just for you but for the people who will follow you.

PART II
Three Group Curricula for Use in School-Based Programs

12
Friends' Group

CHAPTER 12

Friends' Group

Students who are worried about whether they are going to find their parents at home drunk after school cannot concentrate well while they are in school. The same is true of children who live with relatives who are addicted to other drugs, including prescription tranquilizers and amphetamines. These young people have much more troubling concerns than whether they get assignments in on time, and their erratic behavior has baffled educators for generations.

Recently, much has been written about this particular group of youngsters; they exhibit behavior which is sometimes disruptive, sometimes exemplary. Whichever behavior they exhibit, they do so because they are acting out some role which helps them survive the dysfunction of their families. Recent progressive teacher trainings have tried to help teachers identify the manifestations of these roles that students may act out in the classroom. Preferably, these trainings have been available to your school or district; if not, they can be arranged.

There is a great deal of information about these children of alcoholics and addicts available, including a large subcategory of literature about adult children of alcoholics, which examines the behavior and dysfunctional relationships of these children as they grow into adulthood untreated. For the sake of simplicity and inclusiveness, I refer to these young people as children of addiction, or COAs.

Student assistance programs hope to intervene so the COAs we meet in adolescence don't necessarily have to develop the characteristic tangle of emotional and relationship problems typical of adult COAs. Junior high and high school SAPs can borrow from information about both children and adults when looking for good resource, reading, and support materials. After all, our students straddle those lines of semiadulthood all the time, particularly in the older grades of senior high school.

We have chosen the name "friends' group" for this group because it is inclusive and the intentional vagueness of the name poses no threat. Calling your group a "children of alcoholics" group can exclude the student who is concerned about the drinking or drugging of a close friend or relative, but, in the typical pattern of familial denial, is loathe to label him or her alcoholic.

REASONS FOR FRIENDS' GROUP

Rarely is the educational directive for student assistance programming so close at hand as when we are talking about friends' group participation. It is not a frill to treat COAs' anxiety so they can get back to work on the academic, social, and developmental challenges which face them. If we noticed symptoms which made it clear there was a physical ailment—hands that could not grasp a pencil correctly, for instance—we would insist that the condition be treated so the student stands a chance of success in school. We must maintain the same standards for students who display characteristic symptoms of dysfunctional or abusive home lives. It is neglectful to ignore these symptoms.

Children of addiction make up a larger percentage of the population than many people are ready or willing to imagine. Current research estimates that as many as one of every four of our students hails from a family with addiction of some kind. Imagine, as you gaze at your homeroom class, a group of freshmen on the first day of school, or your graduating seventh-grade class, the worries that these students may be dealing with. Addiction is present in all types of homes, from well-manicured suburban tract houses to urban triple deckers, so don't skip over any students in your count because you just "know" there can't be anything like that going on in that family. No matter which face these students present to the world, statistically they are at extremely high risk for developing addiction themselves and for developing survival skills which can lose their original purpose and become developmentally detrimental.

The underlying assumption in all attempts to treat COAs, both in therapy and in schools, is that addiction is a family illness: that if we conceptualize the family as a single organism, each connected part suffers pain if one limb is diseased. These children are suffering from the disease of chemical dependency just as much as the addicted parent, but differently, and, in some cases, less starkly. Because we are school based, we are not hoping to have students undergo intensive psychotherapy at our hands, or to heal the family organism; on the contrary, we are striving to manage the chaos, to lessen though not eliminate the anxiety, so students can do an adequate job of getting an education while they are with us. Since we are unable to provide a cure for the illness, we provide reassurance, validation, and support amid the symptoms.

Friends' Groups and Alateen/Al-Anon

Although friends' group participation has a similar objective to Alateen or Al-Anon participation, they are not one and the same. While Al-Anon and Alateen rely heavily on a spiritual component, friends' groups rely on an educational one. This is appropriate because of the context in which friends' groups meet—namely, school. Because Alateen and Al-Anon participation is life giving and promotes healthy emotional living, you should encourage participation in these programs, always having right at hand a list of meetings, a reliable contact person, and information to create a "bridge" for students who are reluctant to try. If your SAP effort does nothing else, it must have a ready list of resources so students can leave the office of the SAP contact person with a fistful of pamphlets and telephone numbers.

If you are involved with an in-school friends' group in any capacity and have never been to an Al-Anon, Alateen, or adult COA meeting, try to get to a handful as soon as possible. It will give you a much greater understanding of the significant issues for these youngsters.

PLANNING FOR A FRIENDS' GROUP

Your SAP can wait for referrals from teachers and counselors to fill a COA group, or you can canvass your student body for self-referrals, or both (see chapter 9). Depending on your school climate, you may get enough responses through a survey sign-up to start a group right away. Clearly, all the logistics for groups must be set up before you embark on eliciting referrals, because in all likelihood, when you "advertise" the availability of these groups, you will get a response.

Decide ahead of time whether you will be requiring parental consent, and get this step out of the way at the start by sending a letter either to all parents announcing the availability of the groups generally or to parents of COAs specifically. If you are in a junior high school, parental consent is wise because some students will be twelve years old or younger. This can be done well in advance (see chapter 3).

Screening for a Friends' Group

If you conduct a canvass of every student in your school and ask students who would like to join friends' groups to sign up, a significant number will sign up right off the bat, with no other prompting than your announcement of group availability. If you're going to do this type of canvassing, do it in person, going classroom to classroom, and make sure you are ready to roll with groups starting in a couple of weeks so students who signed up don't spend a lot of time anxiously awaiting the start-up of group. They won't tell you, but they will be very nervous waiting for group to start. The students who do sign up like this have exhibited a certain amount of self-selection. They are willing to admit the existence of the addiction problem at home. To some extent, they have already begun the process of externalizing the locus of the problem; they know the problem is at least partly outside of themselves and has to do with a parent's, relative's, or friend's drinking or drugging.

It is the students that don't come forward during the start-up of groups who are perhaps in greater need of group participation, just to make it emotionally to where these other students are who have volunteered. Student assistance program people, teachers, and guidance counselors will see these less-forthcoming students in individual appointments and extra-help sessions, and they usually will not tell you what is going on *unless you ask*. This is why it is essential that SAP intake forms and interviews with guidance personnel include routine questions about parental drinking and drugging so students have the opportunity to tell someone what they've been keeping secret for so long.

Screen to see which students are appropriate for group and which might benefit from a referral to an outside therapist. Most students can do very well in a friends' group format, including some who may act out quite a bit in classes or who have distinguished themselves as being aggressive or extremely withdrawn. On the other hand, students who are suicidal, in extreme crisis, or extremely disruptive may create obstacles to other students' positive experience.

Including Others Who Identify

There are some students who do not have alcoholic parents or relatives who can benefit from friends' group participation. Children from homes where there is serious mental illness, anorexia nervosa or bulimia, violence, compulsive gambling or sexual behavior, and a variety of other serious dysfunctions may identify with many of the feelings of children of addiction. In many ways, their situations are tragically similar, but the decision to include these students should be made on an individual basis. It can be difficult to convince a student to join a group when the situations seem so different, but it can work well. I have been touched by students' willingness to embrace other kids who have concerns slightly different from their own. Having a slightly different perspective in group can underscore that what is important is the way students deal with the dysfunction, not exactly what the dysfunction is. There are also cases when students are being raised by one or more untreated adult children of addiction, who may display the mood swings, irrationality, temper, or silent treatment characteristic of alcoholics, but where there is no drinking behavior present. These students may benefit from friends' group participation as well.

Creating Working Groups

You may have great numbers of COAs sign up for SAP group participation, in which case you'll need a way to split the students into appropriate groups. This can be a difficult process, and it is best done in consultation with those who know your student body, your system, and your style. Children of addiction groups seem to operate best with between eight and twelve students, but I have heard of groups running with as few as four and as many as twenty. Whatever you do, don't elicit for referral in such a way as to gather more than you can handle. Then you have to go through the process of eliminating students for participation, a process that even students with hardy self-esteem don't take well. This can be devastating for COAs and should be avoided at all costs.

You may want to consider single-sex groups, particularly in the lower junior high school grades, if you feel it will help discussion. You may want to split up best friends, or keep them together, depending on your group composition. My experience has been that young women COAs are easier to locate than young men. This by no means suggests that there are more of them, but it could be indicative of their ability to access the "helping systems." I have located most of my young female COAs through self-referral, and most of my young male COAs through referrals from teachers and involvement with the disciplinary system. (Perhaps this is an unscientific comment on how some young men and young women manage their anxiety differently.)

Sibling COAs pose certain challenges because many of them are reluctant to join without the other, or when one joins, the other(s) may feel incredible hostility toward the one who joined, experiencing some feelings of betrayal. When siblings are in the same group, it can be difficult because each sibling in the dysfunctional family experiences the family completely differently. Expression is the goal for COA participants, not consensus. One sibling's experience of the family can deter the other from speaking or can propel the other into self-doubt. If it can be arranged, split siblings up, but if it can't be arranged, let it be. We want to help as many as we can. Try not to exclude students who are too frightened to take the leap alone.

FINDING LEADERS FOR FRIENDS' GROUP

Compassion is not all that's required of a leader for a COA group, although anyone who runs one of these groups will need plenty of it. At least one of the group leaders should have specific training in the areas of chemical dependency and surrounding family issues. Because a great deal of people come from homes where addiction is an issue, there is a chance that group leaders will have come from a home affected by addiction. (Probably a good chance; it has been suggested that many adult COAs, seek out the caretaking fields of education, medicine, and counseling.) The worst possible scenario is to have a person who is an *untreated* COA leading a friends' group. Not only is it impossible for students to garner any positive role modeling from an untreated COA, but the feelings the group provokes may be so difficult for the adult that he or she goes into emotional overdrive, experiencing anything from feelings of vulnerability to self-doubt and deep depression. It is essential that a COA group leader has his or her issues treated before trying to help others gain recovery from the family disease of chemical dependency. You cannot give away what you do not have.

Adult COAs who have been working on their own issues, who have knowledge of the literature, some coursework, and dedication make great group leaders. Self-disclosure, of course, is a highly personal decision. SAP personnel, who may be both teacher or counselor and group leader, should probably avoid self-disclosure, keeping their role as leader distinct from participant. However, some people seem to manage a fair amount of self-disclosure while keeping appropriate boundaries and making the distinction between counselor and participant.

Other people have a natural affinity for helping students who are affected by chemical dependency, just by employing their basic counseling techniques, listening ability, and tremendous empathy. If these folks can augment their existing talents and skills with workshops, coursework, and reading about the latest research on COAs and surrounding issues, they become great candidates for COA group leaders within the context of a school-based SAP.

DESIGNING A FORMAT FOR FRIENDS' GROUP

Children of addiction want and need as much appropriate adult support and attention as they can get. This makes sense since the attention they get at home is erratic, at best, and constantly negative or fear-producing at worst. This makes the job of deciding on a format for COAs a difficult one. If you have very few resources, and no SAP counselor, you may want to start out your effort by running a short-term COA educational group, giving students just the basics: that they're not alone in their situations or their feelings, that they didn't cause the addiction, and that they can't control or cure it. This will help to relieve some of the anxiety these students have felt for years, but it also may leave some students hanging. You will have then identified the problem, but you won't have allowed too much time or growth before they are back on their own dealing with the situation in the same way they always have. Still, something is better than nothing, and you can design a short-term educational group format that encourages students to join self-help groups afterward. If you do nothing else in an SAP direction, a dedicated individual, either a counselor or teacher, can get a small COA group off the ground in your school or district, finally breaking the silence that usually surrounds this issue.

Short-Term Educational Group

A short-term educational effort for COAs tries to take the responsibility and the subsequent guilt for the parental addiction away from the adolescent. In so many situations, children are told time and time again, "If you'd just get better grades (stop going out with that guy, do your chores around here, get a job to help out, get into a better college, etc.), your mother (or father, stepfather, etc.) wouldn't have to drink/drug the way she (he) does." The relief from this responsibility is the primary and most profound gift we can give to these COAs—the unequivocal message that it's not their fault. In eight to ten weeks, there's not too much chance that anything else will sink in.

Short-term educational efforts are appropriate in situations where you have large numbers of COAs who need services. Particularly where you have no SAP counselor, and teachers or counselors are leading the groups, you can run three or four groups throughout the school year. Impress on your administration how this only scratches the surface of the problem. With an average of twelve students per group at ten sessions each, one pair of leaders could serve thirty-six students in a school year if they ran the group once a week. In a school of only 400, statistically speaking, three times that number would still need services.

This is not meant as discouragement, but rather encouragement to get an SAP counselor where there isn't one, even if it is only half-time. And if that has been researched and is completely impossible, encourage more teachers and counselors to join the SAP effort. Convince your administration to give teachers and counselors release time or fewer scheduled classes to do this important work. Whatever exists, improve on it!

Day-Long Workshops

Another way to manage the educational component of COA groups is to run day-long workshops (see chapter 11) for these students, after which they would be ready to embark on longer-term support-group participation. Logistically, this can be a challenge, but an SAP counselor and interested counselors can put together a day-long set of workshops for a group of ten or twelve students at a time to teach them the basics of chemical dependency and surrounding issues. What's worse—eight class sessions taken out of eight weeks, or students missing an entire day once?

Ongoing Support Groups

Children of addiction really thrive on continuing support to remind them and validate them in their efforts to repair their self-esteem and to imbue in them a sense that no matter what has happened in the past, the future is theirs. Only students who have done the essential work of detachment can get on with this process. Students who are well on their way in COA recovery understand that though they don't have any responsibility to repair their parents, they do now possess the right and indeed the responsibility to help themselves. To do this work, young people, who rely developmentally so heavily on peer interaction, need weekly support and validation from one another. They need a place to process the unfathomable actions of mothers who bail abusive boyfriends out of jail, parents who wake them up in the night to move out of apartments, and parents who get quietly and morosely drunk in their living room night after night. They need to share common disappointments, embarrassments, resentments, and the inevitable internal conflicts of growing up in this situation.

Ongoing support groups for COAs are the way for school systems to go if they can possibly be arranged. In an ongoing support group, students can see progress in each other and serve as one anothers' mirrors. New students to the group can gather hope from the growth of students who have been in group longer. Entire support networks can be born, and group participation can become very important for these students. The only danger in planning ongoing support groups is that the numbers can get unmanageable so quickly.

There are arrangements that can minimize the time spent out of class for each student—try running the groups every other week if once a week is too much. You also may want to have each student who signs up for friends' group participation go through a ten-week structured program or day-long educational program before they "spill over" into an ongoing support group.

PROVIDING STRUCTURE IN FRIENDS' GROUPS

Children of addiction tend to respond well to structure within the group experience, but they also need time to share what is current for them, so, especially at first, your structure should include planned activities as well as "open" time for sharing. As groups evolve and members get to know one another, they may not want any more activities, preferring more time for sharing.

A typical friends' group meeting consists of the following:

1. Preamble (a welcome and reminder about group rules)
2. Activity
3. Check-in or topic
4. Closure.

Group Rules

Clear group rules are essential for the smooth running of a COA group. Make sure rules are explained, using a group rule checklist (chapter 7) or a brainstorm-refine-adopt procedure in which all participants are given the chance to question rules and the final rules are adopted and posted. Keep them simple, but try to troubleshoot obvious stumbling blocks in your particular setting. (For example, our group room is near the school store. Should students be allowed to stop at the store before group to get a candy bar, soda, etc.?)

Preamble

A brief but powerful preamble helps set a tone of respect and underscores the adopted rules for COA groups. A good first or second group session activity is to have students split up into groups of two or three and compose preambles. In composing them, ask them to think about the following questions:

- What do I want from this group experience?
- What do I expect from other group members?
- What can I offer other group members?
- What issues bring us together?

When they are completed, the group can pick one to use at the beginning of each group session, or they can rotate several. A sample preamble follows:

Hello and welcome to a friends' group at _____
(name of school)

We are all affected in different ways by the drinking or drugging of a close friend or relative. We meet here to share our experiences and learn new ways of coping with things. What many of us have learned is that while we can't change the drinking or drugging of a loved one, we can begin to change ourselves and our reactions to it. We can speak freely here without being judged, knowing that whatever we say here, stays here. If you are new today, we welcome you to our group.

Activity

The activities included in the friends' group sample sessions (later in this chapter) are intended to help students interact and to break some of the isolation many of these students have felt. Utilize and adapt these exercises to fit your style and group comfortably. While an ongoing support group might utilize an activity once every other week, and on alternate weeks choose a "chairperson" format (like Alateen), a short-term, structured educational group should include a focusing activity every week.

Check-in

The check-in time for friends' groups may have to be more structured than for any other type of group, because one of a COA's greatest coping skills is to hope against hope that if he or she just doesn't think about it, the problem will go away. Without gentle direction by the group, check-in time can become very superficial, students talking just on the surface about how their week in school is going. On the other hand, almost any topic brought up by a COA can be related to other COA'S experience. The other check-in style you want to avoid is one where students play "Can You Top This?" every week, detailing horrific accounts of parents' drinking. You want to encourage open sharing, where students can identify with each others' feelings, not necessarily with the exact details. As a group leader, at first, your job may be to extract the common *feeling* described so others can identify. For example,

> *Student:* ... and my dad was so drunk, and he was yelling at my uncle so loud that he couldn't even hear me. I kept asking him about whether I could go to the game, but he couldn't even hear me.
>
> *SAP counselor:* It sounds like you were really shut out.
>
> *Student:* Yeah, he couldn't even hear me, and I was loud.
>
> *SAP counselor:* Can anyone identify with that feeling of being shut out?

Check-in styles will vary greatly, depending on the counseling style of the group leaders. The object is to allow students who want to share the chance to do it and to encourage those who are not accustomed to sharing to try. It can be a very structured procedure, going from student to student, or it can be very free flowing. My experience has been that adolescents need more structure than we sometimes think, and a little direction makes them feel safer sharing. As the group members become more comfortable with each other, the check-in period may take up the bulk of the group experience, and that is fine if the cofacilitators are comfortable with that format.

Using Topics for Discussion (Optional): The topics included near the end of each session's agenda follow naturally from the activities. They are included in case the group is not at the point where it can simply check in without some prompting. If there is time left in the session after the activities and the leaders want direction for the discussion, these included topics cover a range of issues pertinent to COAs.

Providing Closure

Groups of COAs often talk about very serious issues when they are together. It's important to have a group closing which is predictable to settle things at the end of group and to remind students of confidentiality. Closure is best if it is the same thing every time. Students can compose a short closing for someone to read or to be said in unison at the end of the group session. This activity is another good project for a group session because it helps clarify to students and counselors what the participants feel is important about group participation. This is an example of a closing:

> Remember the trust we have built here today and the courage we have gained. Who you see here and what is said here, stays here. See you next week.

The following ten sample sessions can be used consecutively for ten weeks, to provide a brief educational training on the most basic issues surrounding the family disease of chemical dependency for identified COAs. They can also be used to augment existing COA programming or could be used to generate ideas for a daylong workshop format. Be flexible with the sessions and worksheets, bearing in mind that different groups will want to spend more time on certain subjects than others.

FRIENDS' SESSION 1

Objectives

- To help students begin to feel comfortable with the idea of group participation and sharing previously concealed thoughts and feelings
- To establish rules of group and have participants gain "ownership" in group

Agenda

1. Preamble: Read prepared preamble.

- *Option:* In a group which has some familiarity with one another, ask students to think about what they would like to use as an opening for group, and have them compose such a preamble in subgroups.

2. Rules: Present the rules to the group either as an amendable rule checklist, or as an activity in which students brainstorm their own rules for the group and adopt a set they all agree on.

3. Leaders' Check-in: Leaders should introduce themselves to the group to establish rapport and also talk a little about what the group will be about. Be sure to include specific rules of confidentiality, what can and must be reported. (After this, leaders take a less active role, providing structure and direction to the group when they need it. Facilitators are not participants.)

Activities

A: *Use an ice-breaker* that encourages students to learn each others' names. Have students identify themselves by first name and then some interesting identifying information. For example, "I'm Suzanne, and I like to lace my sneakers backwards sometimes." Everyone adds his or her name and characteristic to the list until everyone has said everyone's name.

- *Option:* In a group where students already know each other, have the identifying characteristic include a way of coping with the alcoholic or addict. For instance, "I'm Suzanne, and I can tell my mother's drunk by the way she looks at me sideways. I always tell her I have to babysit and I go to my friend Marsha's house." In this version, students do not have to repeat the characteristic, just listen. At the end of the sharing, ask one student to summarize all of the various ways of coping he or she has heard from the group.

B: *Use "Reasons for Friends' Group Participation handout* (page 259) to generate discussion, underscoring that "a lot of kids in your various situations join groups for the following reasons." Ask students to identify (on the handout) several reasons why they chose to participate in group. This preliminary impersonalization makes it easier for students to identify with the statements safely. Expect that students will say very little in this first session.

5. Check-in: When there is a new group, explain the process of check-in, but do not require that students do it on this first day.

Optional Topic(s) for Discussion

* How keeping secrets makes you feel
* Deciding to join group (was it a difficult decision?)

6. Closure: Tell students the purpose of a group closure, and assign them the task of thinking of a good closing statement. If there is time, have students work on it as a closing activity and share whatever they have at the end of group. If there isn't time, assign it as "homework."

FRIENDS' SESSION 2

Note: Some preparation may be required for this session if group leaders are not familiar with the disease of chemical dependency. If necessary, borrow some materials from session 4 of the challenge group (see chapter 13) to explain the progression of chemical dependency.

Objective

* To help students understand the symptoms of the disease of chemical dependency so they can begin to understand that the drinking/drugging is not their fault

Agenda

1. Preamble: (see previous session)

2. Activities:

A: First, ask students for closing statements they completed as homework, and choose one for group.

B: Have students quickly brainstorm a list of the characteristics of the word *disease*. Set the list aside for later discussion. Whichever leader is more well versed in the issues of chemical dependency can explain the disease concept and the progression of the disease. Use materials from the challenge group, session 4 (see chapter 13) if you need to, and make the session as interactive as you can, listing the various stages and asking participants for examples from their own experiences. Remember that students at this stage are likely to be absorbing the material and may still feel too intimidated to share much information. Relate the symptomatology of the disease of addiction back to the list of symptoms the students generated.

REASONS FOR FRIENDS' GROUP PARTICIPATION

People who are willing to help themselves join friends' groups to try to find new ways to cope with difficult situations. You may relate to all of the following statements or maybe only one or two. No matter why you're here, you're in the right place and you're welcome.

Some of Us Are Here Because it's difficult to concentrate in school when a loved one drinks or drugs too much at home. We worry about them even when we're trying to concentrate on other things.

Some of Us Are Here Because we want to learn as much as we can about alcohol and other drugs. We are concerned about someone we love.

Some of Us Are Here Because we live in difficult situations and feel as though not too many people would understand our situations or our feelings.

Some of Us Are Here Because we are sick and tired and angry!

Some of Us Are Here Because we think we have experience which might benefit other people.

Some of Us Are Here Because someone talked us into it. We're here to give it a try.

Some of Us Are Here Because we feel frustrated, alone, sad, and scared by the way things are happening in our lives.

Some of Us Are Here Because we need a place to come and talk about our feelings.

Some of Us Are Here Because we think it will be a good way to make some new friends who understand us and who understand our situations.

Some of Us Are Here Because we get blamed for everything, and we don't think it's our fault.

Some of Us Are Here Because we can't be quiet any longer!

C: Hand out the "Effects of Chemical Dependency" worksheets, and have students complete them individually. Reassure students that they will only share what they are comfortable sharing. When they are done, go through each symptom of the disease and ask students to volunteer to share their examples. For instance, you might say, "People suffering from dependency sometimes use when they say they won't." (The first example from the worksheet.) "Has that ever happened to anyone here?" Depending on the comfort level of the students, you may get verbal feedback, or simply a round of nodding heads. If someone looks willing to share, you can prompt gently; "Suzanne, you're nodding your head. Can you give me an example?" Suzanne might answer, "Like, they say they won't drink for a special occasion or something, and then they do." Again, at this stage of the game, you may have to prompt, trying to make your interventions inclusive so that all students can identify. Try something like, "That's true. Like birthdays, and maybe holidays and vacations or when you're doing something special like being in a play or a game or something. Has that ever happened to you?" Suzanne might go on to describe a specific event in her experience. For instance, "Yeah, last summer, my Mom said she wouldn't drink for my cousin's wedding, and she got really drunk and made a fool of herself. I was a bridesmaid and it was embarrassing." The more examples you can give (or prompt them to give) the more students have a chance of identifying.

- *Option:* If you are doing this without an SAP counselor but have access to an alcohol and other drug professional who can volunteer time or can be hired by the school, your efforts will be well rewarded. His or her expertise can help make the information presented more believable to students.

3. Check-in: Check-in may have to be abbreviated during these educational presentations.

Optional Topics for Discussion
- How the world views addiction
- Denial: How it affects the family

4. Closure (see previous session)

FRIENDS' SESSION 3

Objective
- To help students understand that they are not alone in their situations or feelings

Agenda

1. Preamble: Have a student read the adopted preamble. Underscore the need for trust, confidentiality, and sharing.

EFFECTS OF CHEMICAL DEPENDENCY

Because chemical dependency is an illness, the people who have it often exhibit certain symptoms. Sometimes they are unable to do things that are expected of them. Listed below are some symptoms of the disease. Write in some examples of how that symptom is apparent in your situation.

**People Suffering from
Dependency Sometimes**   **Your Example**

Use when they say they won't: _____

Break promises: _____

Are grouchy when they can't use: _____

Forget what they do when they use: _____

Say mean things: _____

Have other health problems: _____

Do irresponsible things: _____

Get mad for no reason: _____

Are nicer when they use: _____

Have trouble communicating: _____

Become violent: _____

Cry or get sentimental: _____

Have mood swings: _____

Have others care for them: _____

Deny having a problem: _____

2. Activity: Pass out large paper and markers of some kind. Instruct participants to draw a representation (picture) of their family situation. This can be a drawing, a graph, "map," any visual representation of the family. Ask them to include all important people, including grandparents, aunts, uncles, etc., and perhaps even family friends who are close enough to warrant inclusion on a "family tree" of sorts.

- *Option or addition:* If you are familiar with the procedure, ask students to complete genograms instead, asking them to shade in addiction of any kind. For an explanation of genograms, see chapter 8, "Assessment and Referral."

3. Check-in: This week's check-in will be the first in which students are asked to volunteer something about their situations. Use the family pictures or genograms to generate discussion, asking each student to present his or her representation to the rest of the group. Encourage group interaction by asking questions. Though it may seem strained at first, keep gently after each group member to share more. Consider asking the following questions:

- Which person in your picture drinks and/or uses drugs?
- Who in your picture can you talk to about the drinking or drugging?
- Who is the most secretive?
- Does anyone in your picture know that you're in this group?
- Do you have to be the "surrogate parent" for any people in the picture?

Optional Topics for Discussion
- Why it's difficult to talk about your family
- "Fantasy families" (what we think of as perfect)

4. Closure: During this first session when students are asked to share, it's advisable for leaders to prepare them for the vulnerable feelings they may have when they leave, explaining that since they have begun to break the rules of dysfunctional homes by talking about the problem, they may feel that they have betrayed the family. Assure them that these are normal feelings that they may all experience to greater or lesser degrees.

FRIENDS' SESSION 4

Note: You will need four different-colored blown-up balloons for each four or five students to do this activity.

Objective

- To underscore that all members of the family are affected by the addiction of another family member

Agenda

1. Preamble

2. Activity: Have students stand, holding hands in circles of four or so each. Tell each group that it represents a family. Give each group the first balloon, explaining that it represents school and work life. The "family" must keep this balloon up in the air to manage it successfully, without breaking its grasp. When these balloons have been up in the air for a while, ask students to stop and add another balloon, which represents family life. Keeping these both in the air will be a task! Now add a third, saying it represents community life (friends, neighbors, civic responsibilities) and explain that most families have all this to deal with and it is a lot to manage. Now ask students to stop and add the last balloon (black is a good color for this balloon), which represents one family member's addiction. This is a very important balloon, and it must stay in the air at all costs. Let the students watch as family life, work life, and community life fall to the ground in service of keeping the addiction balloon in the air. If you really want to make members work, don't blow up the addiction balloon all the way; that way, it will sink faster. Use this exercise to generate discussion.

- *Option or addition:* Cast one group member in each subgroup as the chemically dependent person. Tell him or her to keep the last balloon in the air, no matter what, even if it means breaking the grasp.

3. Check-in

Optional Topics for Discussion:
- How my experience may be different from my sibling's
- What loved ones have given up to use their substance

4. Closure

FRIENDS' SESSION 5

Objectives
- To introduce students to the typical patterns in a home where there is addiction
- To give students some new "tools" for coping

Agenda

1. Preamble

2. Activity: Hand out the worksheet "Some Typical Rules of Play in Families Where There Is Addiction." Ask students to work individually, coming up with

Some Typical "Rules of Play" in Families where There is Addiction: Following are some common characteristics that students have shared about homes affected by addiction. Can you identify with any of them? If so, write down an example of a time this rule applied to you, or write down how this rule makes you feel.

1. Keep the Secret: This rule is sometimes clear, as in "Don't tell your friends what goes on here," or sometimes subtle, as in a glare or a look that tells us not to say anything about what goes on at home. This can make us feel secretive, ashamed, and very isolated and may make it difficult for us to talk about ourselves and our problems. We may feel afraid to let people close to us in case they learn the secret.

_____

_____

_____

_____

2. Don't Share Feelings: We learn early not to share feelings because sometimes we are betrayed or told that our feelings don't count. Sometimes we are laughed at, or when we cry we're told, "I'll give you something to cry about." This can make it very difficult to share feelings with others, and we may "stuff" our feelings or even deny that we have any by saying, "Oh, it doesn't bother me anymore."

_____

_____

_____

_____

3. Mixed Messages: Sometimes we get mixed messages. Our parents tell us to grow up and act responsibly, and then they act very irresponsibly themselves. They tell us not to lie, and then they make up excuses for their drinking or drugging. When they're sober, they may tell us they love us, and when they're using, they may scream at us or call us names. This can make us angry and very confused. For a lot of us, it makes us depressed, or makes us feel like rebelling.

_____

_____

_____

_____

4. "My Intentions Were Good": Sometimes alcoholics and addicts promise things and then don't come through. Then, sometimes they want credit for just having the thought. Because they break promises, we can learn to be cynical and not to trust people.

_____

_____

_____

_____

5. There is _Not_ a Problem Here: This is denial, when people are too fearful or confused to see the real problem in proper perspective. When others deny there's a problem, we either start to do it too, or wonder if we're crazy.

_____

_____

_____

_____

_____

6. Don't Ask for Help: All the other rules are made worse by this one. In many homes that are affected by addiction, getting help seems out of the question because of the secrecy, shame, and denial.

_____

_____

_____

_____

_____

some examples from their own experience. Then, have students share some responses from the papers. The best way to conduct sharing such as this is to concentrate on one issue at a time, rather than one student at a time. For instance, start with the first rule and ask if anyone is willing to share an example. Stay on that rule until all students who are willing to share have done so. You may also want to draw out the discussion by asking some other questions about each rule. For instance, "We've heard a lot of examples of 'keeping the secret.' How does that rule make you feel? Does it prevent you from doing anything you'd like to do? What are some problems that could arise from that rule?"

- *Option or addition:* Have students compile a list of as many "feelings" as they can, to be used when these people, so unaccustomed to discussing feelings, need a hand in thinking of feeling words to describe them. Post this list conspicuously.

3. Check-in

Optional Topics for Discussion
- Other, unspoken "rules" in the participants' homes
- Different kinds of silence at home
- Mixed messages given at home, or in school

4. Closure

FRIENDS' SESSION 6

Objective
- To help students learn to identify the benefits and drawbacks of certain coping strategies

Agenda

1. Preamble

2. Activity: Present the "Different Ways We Cope" worksheet about the helping strategies played out in the context of dysfunctional homes. Individually or in small groups, have students identify any coping strategies they have tried and the resulting benefits and drawbacks. Also, have students check off the two strategies they use most often. Direct the discussion toward the fact that the strategies listed are all attempts to help, but that sometimes helping unintentionally makes the situation worse. For older students, you may want to introduce the concept of enabling (see chapter 6), making sure that you don't inadvertently "blame" students for enabling a parent. Enabling is something we do when we love someone and don't know what else to do.

DIFFERENT WAYS WE COPE

When we face difficulties, we often try different strategies to help. Most of these coping strategies have benefits and drawbacks, and most of us have tried one or more of them at some time. Try to come up with both benefits and drawbacks to the strategy. Put a checkmark next to the two that you do most.

☐ **Ignore it.**

Benefits _____

_____

Drawbacks _____

_____

☐ **Work really hard yourself to "make up" for the difficulty.**

Benefits _____

_____

Drawbacks _____

_____

☐ **Laugh it off: Make jokes about the problem**

Benefits _____

_____

Drawbacks _____

_____

☐ **Try to stay quiet and out of everyone's way.**

Benefits _____

_____

Drawbacks _____

_____

☐ **Give them a dose of their own medicine: Get in trouble yourself.**

Benefits _____

_____

Drawbacks _____

_____

DIFFERENT WAYS WE COPE, continued

☐ **Try to leave as often as possible.**

Benefits _____

_____

Drawbacks _____

_____

☐ **Try to take care of things that no one else is doing.**

Benefits _____

_____

Drawbacks _____

_____

☐ **Act as if nothing bothers you.**

Benefits _____

_____

Drawbacks _____

_____

Strategize with a small group to come up with some new strategies that might have more benefits and fewer drawbacks.

Strategy 1 _____

_____

Strategy 2 _____

_____

Strategy 3 _____

_____

Strategy 4 _____

_____

- *Option:* (for senior high school students) Ask students to split up with others who chose similar coping strategies. Have them come up with an additional list of how these same strategies help or hinder them in the rest of their lives, aside from their families.

3. Check-in

Optional Topics for Discussion
- Siblings' roles
- How these roles spill over into my life at school, with friends, etc.

4. Closure

FRIENDS' SESSION 7

Objective
- To give students some "tools" for coping with their situations

Agenda

1. Preamble

2. Activity: Hand out the "Tools for Coping" list. Use this list to generate discussion about different and new ways of coping with the old situation. There are a number of ways to use this handout.

1. Ask students to identify one aspect of their home life (relationship with the alcoholic/addict, relationship with siblings, family responsibilities, keeping up in school, etc.) which they find very problematic and ask them to present it to the group. Ask the group to provide feedback to the student, using the handout to identify the "tools" that could be used to ameliorate the existing problem.
2. Ask students to check off which strategies they already use and ones they'd like to try. For the ones they already use, ask them to share their examples with the group.

3. Check-in

Optional Topics for Discussion
- Why asking for help is so difficult
- How other family members cope

4. Closure

TOOLS FOR COPING

We all need tools to do our job. For us, our "job" is growing up into positive adults. Because we are affected by addiction, we need specialized tools to cope with our situations.

Stop Blaming Yourself: It's important to remember that you didn't *cause* the addiction, you can't *control* the addiction, and you can't *cure* the addiction. Once you take the blame off yourself, things start to get a little easier.

Set Priorities: Think through what you really want for yourself and the best way to get it. If eventually getting a good job is your number one priority, you must concentrate on staying in school today. When you face a number of choices, pick the one that is really in your best interest.

Live One Day at a Time: If you think too far ahead, you can get discouraged. If you always focus on the past, you can stay stuck in negative experiences. The way to cope is to live one day at a time—to know that if you can get through today, you can start over again tomorrow.

Easy Does It, But Do It!: Sometimes it's easy to go a million miles an hour and still not get much accomplished. In this case, you must slow down, be nice to yourself, and work at a steadier pace. On the other hand, sometimes it is easy just to say "forget it," and stop doing anything. It's important to remember to take it easy, but to keep plugging away.

Break It Down: Sometimes large problems overwhelm us. Break down every problem into manageable parts. If finding a job seems impossible, break it down into parts: dressing for the interview, going to the business, filling out the application, etc. Each part is do-able.

Ask for Help: When you feel overwhelmed, discouraged, or just sad, share your feelings with someone else. Another way some people ask for help is through a personal spiritual connection, an organized religion, or community service.

Have the Courage to Change Yourself: Sometimes you wish that you could change a parent, but you can only change yourself. Change is scary, but it is also positive. Be willing to look at ways you can change, using the other tools on this sheet.

FRIENDS' SESSION 8

Objective

- To help students recognize patterns of thinking and behaving which they can work on changing

Note: This session utilizes information from the adult children of alcoholics literature. The assertion is *not* that adolescents and adults are the same, but that adolescents can benefit from this information and can incorporate some of this vital information into their task of identity formation. I recommend using these handouts at the high school level, where students are likely to identify more closely with the characteristics presented. Adolescents certainly respond well to any intimation that their thoughts and feelings are closer to the realm of the adult, rather than the realm of the child.

Agenda

1. Preamble

2. Activity: Use worksheet called "Characteristics of Adult Children of Alcoholics." Explain that as COAs grow into adulthood, these are some of the characteristics they sometimes develop. Because adolescents are on the threshold of adulthood, some of these characteristics may now be forming and are within their power to work on and change.

- *Option:* Ask students to privately write down three things they would like to work on in themselves, *before* you proceed with the aforementioned activity. At the end of activity, ask students to compare their three characteristics to those typical of adult COAs. Do any of them correspond?

3. Check-in

Optional Topics for Discussion:
- Are our parents themselves children of alcoholics?
- What is the difference between adolescence and adulthood?
- What kind of a person do I want to be when I grow up?

4. Closure

FRIENDS' SESSION 9

Objectives

- To help students believe that change is possible
- To help students break the cycle

CHARACTERISTICS OF ADULT CHILDREN OF ALCOHOLICS

The following list characterizes what some adult children of alcoholics feel. After each characteristic, write in an example from your own experience or a comment. If it doesn't apply to you, write in "does not apply." You should share with the group *only* that which you feel comfortable sharing.

1. Adult children of alcoholics guess at what normal is. _____

_____

_____

2. Adult children of alcoholics have difficulty in following a project through from beginning to end. _____

_____

_____

3. Adult children of alcoholics lie when it would be just as easy to tell the truth. _____

_____

_____

4. Adult children of alcoholics judge themselves without mercy. _____

_____

_____

5. Adult children of alcoholics have difficulty having fun. _____

_____

_____

6. Adult children of alcoholics take themselves very seriously. _____

_____

_____

7. Adult children of alcoholics have difficulty with intimate relationships. _____

_____

_____

CHARACTERISTICS OF ADULT CHILDREN OF ALCOHOLICS, *continued*

8. Adult children of alcoholics overreact to changes over which they have no control. ____

_____

_____

9. Adult children of alcoholics constantly seek approval and affirmation. _____

_____

_____

10. Adult children of alcoholics feel that they are different from other people. _____

_____

_____

11. Adult children of alcoholics are either super responsible or super irresponsible. _____

_____

_____

12. Adult children of alcoholics are extremely loyal, even in the face of evidence that the

loyalty is undeserved. _____

_____

_____

13. Adult children of alcoholics are impulsive. _____

_____

_____

Which of these characteristics *most* describes you? _____

_____

Which of these characteristics would you like to work on in your life? _____

_____

_____

Agenda

1. Preamble

2. Activity: Have students complete the "Recovery Means: Positive Changes I Can Make" worksheet and share responses with the rest of the group. Students can also use the "Tools for Coping" list from session 7 to complete this session's worksheet.

- *Option or addition:* If you have a reliable contact person in the Al-Anon or Alateen fellowships in your area, ask that person to come to your group to talk about the concept of detachment and to share that part of his or her story which is appropriate and helpful for school-based groups.
- *Option or addition:* Borrow "Balancing the Scale" from the challenge group materials (see chapter 13). Have students give each other feedback about the changes they have seen in each other since the beginning of the group. Ask students to share a change in themselves that they haven't previously shared with the group.

3. Check-in

Optional Topics for Discussion

- How have other family members changed?
- How have my relationships outside my family changed since I started coming to group?

4. Closure

FRIENDS' SESSION 10

Objectives

- To help students apply the knowledge they have gained in group to their daily lives
- To provide closure for short-term group

Agenda

1. Preamble

2. Activity: Have students complete the worksheet "Wrapping Up Group Participation" and share their responses with the group.

- *Option or addition:* Ask students to compile a list of the things they have learned about chemical dependency and the disease of addiction since they began group participation. Ask them to reflect on the different phases of

RECOVERY MEANS:
POSITIVE CHANGES I CAN MAKE

Identifying the ways living with addiction has affected us is just the beginning. Making positive changes in our own lives is a part of feeling better about ourselves. If you identify with any behaviors on the left, share with other group members the new strategies you have developed.

I Used To

Now I Try To

Blame my parents for everything:

_____
_____
_____

Not tell anyone what was going on, act out my feelings by fighting or rebelling:

_____
_____
_____

Worry all the time:

_____
_____
_____

Feel responsible for my parent's drinking or drugging:

_____
_____
_____

Try to do everything alone:

_____
_____
_____

Cover up my feelings by acting like I didn't care:

_____
_____
_____

Not work hard in school because I felt, "Why bother?"

_____
_____
_____

Be so wrapped up in myself and my problems that I had trouble being a good friend:

_____
_____
_____

WRAPPING UP GROUP

Leaving a group can sometimes bring on mixed emotions. You may be happy that you had the experience but sad that it is over. Think carefully about what you have gotten from this experience.

The Most Important Thing I Learned in Group Was _____

_____

_____

The Most Difficult Part of Group Was _____

_____

_____

The Best Part of Group Was _____

_____

_____

An Attitude of Mine That Changed Was _____

_____

_____

Because of Group, I Have Figured Out _____

_____

_____

Before I Leave, I Want to Say to Other Group Members _____

_____

_____

_____

_____

the group, creating a chronology of what transpired and how their feelings changed in each phase.

- *Option or addition:* If you have an active Alateen group in your area, ask a representative speaker (or two) to come and explain the program to the participants. Particularly if you have no ongoing support group at school, this can provide a bridge into community self-help programs. Ask Alateen members to bring pamphlets and meeting lists with them so students can find out the necessary information to get to a meeting.

3. Check-in

Optional Topics for Discussion

- Saying goodbye
- Continuing to gain support (SAP participation or outside)

4. Closure

13
Challenge Group

CHAPTER 13

Challenge Group

The challenge group (for use in schools) is adapted from the Challenge Course[1] (for use in community projects) developed by the New Hampshire Office of Alcohol and Drug Abuse Prevention. The primary purpose of the program is to "curtail further involvement and trouble" with various chemical use, by "challenging" adolescents to remain abstinent from all chemicals for at least the duration of the group experience and to evaluate their own drinking and drugging patterns through various structured group activities. If it is discovered that students cannot meet the challenge of staying clean and sober for this short-term group, the program may ask them to seek additional help to curtail their use.

Using a modified challenge course format in the context of a comprehensive student assistance program can be very successful. The group provides the opportunity for students to take a closer look at how chemicals are affecting their day-to-day lives and motivates some to seek treatment for alcohol or other drug-related problems. It is essential to have the means available for students to take a long, hard look at their own use within the context of a comprehensive, school-based SAP. The challenge group can be used in two ways. The first is to offer it to students who want to take a good look at their own drinking and drugging patterns. Although it may seem that you won't get too many volunteers for this, surprisingly many students *do* want to take a journey into this honest and rigorous terrain.

The second way to use the challenge format, which shaped its original design, is to offer it to students who have experienced some negative consequences as a result of their drinking or drug use. In other words, it could be offered either on a voluntary basis, or students who are caught in violation of the chemical use policy of your school could choose to undergo the challenge group versus participating in another, more lengthy and uncomfortable consequence. With a little planning, you can also combine these two populations. You can be creative in designing how best to use this program.

Whichever way you choose to utilize this curriculum, it is essential to include an element of choice for the students involved, even if that choice is to participate in the challenge group for a total of twelve class sessions, or serve detentions after school every day for a couple of months. Clearly, there's a choice there, though it's not much of one. If you don't make participation the student's choice, you make a

---

[1]The Challenge Course was developed in 1989 by Tim Comings, Pat Seaward-Salvati, and Dick Utell for the New Hampshire Office of Alcohol and Drug Abuse Prevention. Development of the course was originally funded by Drug-Free Schools and Communities: New Hampshire Governor's discretionary funds. This *adapted and shortened* version is printed with permission of NH OADAP, 6 Hazen Drive, Concord, NH 03301.

lot of work for your group facilitators because they will have to win over eight or ten angry adolescents. Why not make it the students' choice from the start and dispatch with the winning over?

However it is structured, the argument for joining a challenge group can be made convincing. Fortunately, once challenge groups have been running in school, word will get out that they are "not so bad." Some students will report that they actually learned something and enjoyed themselves.

Major Goals of the Challenge Group

- To educate the participants about alcohol and other drug use and surrounding, relevant issues
- To create a supportive environment
- To provide an opportunity for at-risk students to forge relationships with the challenge facilitators
- To encourage each participant to assess his or her own relationship with alcohol and other drugs
- To provide for healthy group interaction—teaching communication and coping skills
- To make appropriate follow-up recommendations for each group member
- To leave the door open for students to make contact with the SAP at a future time

WHAT YOU NEED TO RUN A CHALLENGE GROUP

- *Two challenge group facilitators,* preferably one male and one female. It is much more difficult for the program to be successful with only one facilitator. Challenge groups can be confrontational and emotionally draining, and facilitators need to have back-up in one another. At least one must have a working knowledge of adolescent chemical dependency, familial addiction, and surrounding relevant issues. An SAP person and a guidance counselor would be a great pair.
- *A room,* available for two consecutive class sessions, that is big enough to accommodate the group comfortably
- *Authorization* from the administration to run the group six times, for two consecutive class sessions each week (a total of twelve classes in six weeks). Or, the authorization to hold the challenge group after school.
- *Photocopying privileges* to copy the materials for students
- *Supplies:* Newsprint and markers or a blackboard and chalk, a package of 5 × 8 index cards, and large magic marker, large drawing paper, envelopes, and paper for each student (In some cases you'll need stamps, too.)
- *Optional:* Film on familial addiction
- *Optional:* Folders in which students keep their accumulated challenge group materials

GROUP SIZE AND COMPOSITION

In schools, the challenge course can be run with as few as five students and as many as nine or ten. It is difficult, in larger groups, to establish trust in such a short period of time; on the other hand, groups that are smaller than five can suffer if even one student is absent. If at all possible, try to keep disciplinary referrals who have been involved in the same incident in separate groups. Preformed alliances will make group functioning more difficult. In volunteer groups, having groups of friends can be either very powerful, as they confront each other about their patterns of use, or very challenging for group facilitators.

Screening Students for Participation

The intake/screening procedures will vary widely depending on whether the students are participating voluntarily, or as part of a consequence of being caught in an alcohol or other drug situation. In all cases, the intake interview determines the eligibility and appropriateness of each participant.

During the intake interview, the challenge facilitator or team should at least get the basic information: name, family history of chemical use, alcohol and drug use history, involvement with legal troubles and/or school discipline. In the context of an SAP, if you are dealing with a tremendous number of students, the intake interviews may have to be brief and to the point. The main task of the screening process for an SAP challenge group should be to insure that students who ought to be in chemical dependency treatment don't end up in the group. While the curriculum lends itself to a rigorous self-evaluation, it does *not* constitute treatment for someone whose life is imminently threatened by the disease of chemical dependency. You can use a simple questionnaire-style diagnostic test to screen for this. Use the "Youth Diagnostic Screening Device for Problem Drinkers" (found in chapter 8) or any other assessment tool you are familiar with. (It is not absolutely necessary to conduct formal chemical dependency assessments if you are fairly comfortable with screening for it informally.)

In school, the challenge group is designed for students who may be experiencing beginning difficulties with their pattern of use. Though children of addiction may end up in the group, it is not meant to treat their issues specifically. If the major presenting difficulty is that a student lives with addiction, a friends' group would be more appropriate placement.

Even if your screening is thorough, students who are chemically dependent, and many who are well on their way, will no doubt make it into challenge groups. It is important that the challenge (to stay clean and sober throughout the group experience) is understood by all parties so parents can be contacted and treatment procured for students who distinguish themselves as being chemically dependent during the tenure of the group experience.

Be sure to explain the challenge in the screening interview so students know that they will be expected not to use alcohol and other drugs for the duration of the group experience. If you don't tell students early on, they may feel "tricked" and your relationship with them may turn adversarial.

The school-based, challenge group experience is not designed to break the denial of currently active, late-stage chemically dependent students. It is designed for students who are in the early stages of chemical dependency or for students who are in an abusive pattern of use that could be altered. It is important for facilitators to understand that a six-week group experience alone is unlikely to "get" any student sober—but it may plant a seed, or help to keep a student from becoming more seriously involved with alcohol and other drugs.

Involving Parents in the Process

In some cases, where students have been caught in violation of a school alcohol or other drug use policy and choose participation in the group as part of a disciplinary consequence, the parents may be informed of a student's participation. When parents are present for the intake/screening interview, it is advisable to have the student sign the challenge and the informed consent (the preliminary paperwork) during the initial screening, though you should ask students about their personal alcohol and other drug history when the parents are not present. This way, you maintain trust with the student while both parents and students are aware of what will be asked of them. Many parents want to believe that it will be "no problem" for their kids to stay clean and sober for six weeks. It is sometimes sobering indeed for these parents to learn that their youngsters couldn't make it past the second weekend without a drink or a drug.

It is much more likely that you will be able to motivate a student to consider further treatment at the end of the challenge group experience if his or her parents are involved in the challenge process, but you must consider whether motivation into treatment is in fact your final goal for the group. An atmosphere of pure self-evaluation rather than parental evaluation, particularly for volunteers, could motivate more students into giving the challenge group a try, which may have more sweeping effects on your school community than getting two or three students into treatment. One way to manage this dilemma is to have the parents involved in cases where the chemical use policy has been violated, but to let volunteers participate without parental consent in states that would allow that arrangement.

Voluntary Participation

The students who come to the SAP office wanting to join a challenge group are a different breed. You hope these students want to take a hard look at their use, but they also might just like to get out of a few classes and talk about alcohol and other drugs (particularly if they know a lot about them!). Challenge group facilitators will have to make it clear in the intake/screening interview that once they sign up, participation is no longer voluntary—that they need to make the commitment to the rules and the duration of the program. If challenge groups are run during the school day, students who are involved in another SAP group may have to make special arrangements with teachers for the duration of the challenge group, since it takes two class periods a week. If challenge groups fall directly under the jurisdiction of the SAP and you do not require specific parental consent for SAP group participation, challenge group participation for *volunteers* would be handled in the same manner.

Recovering students often volunteer for challenge group participation, and, depending on the composition of the group, this arrangement can work well.

Leaders must never depend on recovering students to act as confronters or to provide an example to other students, however. The recovering students are there to gather their own information. One recovering student remarked in her evaluation, "[Challenge group] helped me stay sober because I could see myself when I was using in every member of the group. My denial was so strong and so subtle."

One procedure that has worked well with volunteers is to hold a preliminary meeting for one class period before the actual group meets. During this meeting, underscore what is expected of group members: honesty, feedback, consistency, and commitment. Outline all the times and dates of group meetings, emphasizing the attendance requirements. At the end of the informational group meeting, give each student a piece of paper which again gives him or her the choice to participate:

☐ YES. I want to participate in the challenge group. I am making the necessary commitment to attend all meetings and participate actively.

☐ NO. I have decided not to participate in the challenge group at this time.

_____ , _____
(student signature)   (date)

If you collect these as students head out the door of this preliminary meeting, they have the opportunity to bow out gracefully after they have heard what is expected of them.

Participation as a Result of Grades/Disciplinary Policy

Some SAPs have used academic failure as a challenge group screening device. Students who fail a certain number of classes are given the opportunity to participate in a challenge group, on the reasonable assumption that they might be having a problem with chemicals which may be affecting their ability to perform at school. Your program could offer participation to any subset of students who seem to be experiencing difficulty—repeat dropouts, truants, students who are repeat offenders in the disciplinary system, and so on. This sort of sweeping criteria for participation can provide a good "net" for students who wouldn't otherwise receive SAP services.

Take care, though, not to design screening criteria which will produce more student referrals than your program can handle in a reasonable period of time. In a large school, you would be amazed at how many students fail three or more classes in a given semester, for instance. Even if a student meets these sweeping criteria, you still want to conduct screening interviews to give each student the choice and to assess the appropriateness of involving the student in a challenge group.

Parents can and should be contacted if you choose to use the group in this way. Legal confidentiality is not a concern at this point, because nothing yet identifies the student as an alcohol or other drug abuser, only as meeting whatever screening criteria you have set up. A phone call to parents from the challenge facilitator or, better yet, from a school administrator, is the safest way to inform parents of their child's participation, because letters informing parents of their children's school troubles have a tendency to get "lost in the mail."

Students who are referred to the challenge group because they have met some sweeping criteria (like failing three classes, or being in suspension for five or six times in a semester, or carrying a record of very bad attendance not attributable to illness) are least likely to arrive at screening interviews with smiles on their faces. The facilitators will have to deal with being seen as school policy enforcers, a role most SAPs should avoid. So there should always be some alternative to the challenge group which makes a good argument for challenge group participation, so even these students are there by choice. Pay special attention to students who choose a much more "difficult" alternative than taking a look at their own use of alcohol or other drugs. Either they don't use at all (and therefore feel they can't benefit from participation) and then the source of their difficulty needs to be examined further, or they are very reluctant to look at their own patterns of use. Both scenarios signal trouble. Make a referral to guidance and/or attempt to forge a relationship with the student by involving him or her in another group.

Participation as a Result of Chemical Use Policy Violation

Those students who are in violation of a school alcohol and other drug policy should have the opportunity to participate in a challenge group, because they have so clearly experienced a negative result directly attributable to their chemical use. Challenge group participation can be made part of the automatic consequence of violation of the chemical use policy of the school, if you choose, and if you have a sufficient volume of infractions to fill challenge groups in a timely fashion. Parents should definitely be notified of a student's mandatory involvement (by school administration) and should be kept informed of the follow-up recommendations provided by the challenge group facilitators. To follow up with parents, use a release of information signed at the beginning of the group. Challenge group used in this way is a *consequence* of violating the alcohol and other drug policy—not a punishment for it. Be aware that records of mandatory challenge group participants are protected by federal confidentiality regulations because they identify the student as an alcohol or other drug abuser.

CHALLENGE GROUP FACILITATORS

Challenge group facilitators need working knowledge of adolescent alcohol and other drug issues, adolescent development, group dynamics, and group process. At least one member of the team should have experience working with alcohol and/or other drug-related groups (recovery groups, DWI programs, inpatient treatment, etc.). At no time should a challenge group facilitator promote the participants' use of substances. Prospective leaders for SAP-based challenge groups can be found in schools, community agencies, or self-help programs, but they all must do the following:

- Provide a positive adult role model to student participants
- Be able to work as part of a leadership team
- Fill gaps in their knowledge about alcohol and other drug-related issues
- Be empathic and able to establish rapport easily with adolescents
- Have their own use of alcohol or other drugs and other personal issues resolved to avoid any negative impact on the group
- Be willing to work within school rules
- Have, or get information about, twelve-step programs and other available local self-help programs.

Creating a Positive Leadership Team

Allow half an hour or so before group participants arrive for cofacilitators to prepare for the session and to remind each other about what happened the week before. If there are difficult personalities in the group, leaders should strategize ways to minimize the distractions. Allow a similar amount of time at the end of group so leaders can process what happened in group and share their observations with each other. Work out any problems between group leaders before the group meets and decide ahead of time how particular crises will be handled (i.e., a student coming to group under the influence).

Some Final Words about the Challenge Group: The challenge group provides a fairly structured but flexible curriculum presented here in six sessions of two consecutive class periods each. It cannot be done justice in less time, and there is even a fair argument for making the experience longer. However, in the context of an SAP, there are many considerations, not the least of which is missed class time. You will find that using this curriculum is always exciting, as students begin honestly to take a look at their own patterns of use. While the curriculum can't claim to stop every student from using chemicals ever again, it may plant the seeds of self-knowledge that can motivate young people to break abusive patterns of use.

CHALLENGE SESSION 1

Objectives:
- To create an open, supportive, confidential environment
- To establish group rules
- To encourage group interaction
- To encourage sharing about personal alcohol or other drug use

Agenda
1. Introduce program (why students are here).
2. Students sign informed consent, agreement to respect confidentiality,

SAP special group rules; the challenge is reviewed and explained and the welcome is given.

3. Review group rules and post them on newsprint.
4. Challenge group pretest
5. Preview of the challenge group (what students can expect)
6. Break
7. Ice-breaker
8. Check-in
9. How I got here
10. My first time (handout)
11. Daily log homework (handout)
12. Closure

1 and 2. Introducing the Program and Setting the Tone: Although all this paperwork seems to create a tone of stuffiness or formality, in practice it creates a tone of respect and trust. So while you may be tempted just to go over the rules verbally, experience has shown that having students sign the rules indicating their understanding helps them adhere to them. Have students complete all the paperwork that wasn't completed in the intake/screening interview. (See forms provided.) Introducing the challenge and going over the rules together insures that everyone is on the same footing from the start. Explain the students' mutual responsibility to respect one another's confidentiality and the confidentiality of the group leaders.

The challenge course may be used as part of a consequence, but it is *never* intended as a punishment. In fact, the challenge course motivates the most change when it becomes an enjoyable experience—when students feel comfortable sharing their drinking and drugging experiences and getting honest feedback from group participants and caring group leaders. Students will be understandably nervous, defensive, and perhaps hostile during this first session. Setting a friendly and honest tone while reassuring students that they will not be "punished" in group is the leaders' main task in this first session.

Explaining the Challenge: There is the possibility that some students will be angered by the challenge to stay clean and sober for the duration of the group experience. For this reason, it is always best to include this as part of your screening interview. However, you may still get grumbles when you reexplain it at the beginning of group. It helps to have some ready reasons for the requirement:

- Staying clean and sober helps you monitor your level of comfort: For instance, if you are very uncomfortable with the requirement, it may signal trouble.
- Staying clean and sober helps you stay honest: Alcohol and other drugs cloud your judgment.
- Staying clean and sober yourself helps you confront others.
- Staying clean and sober gives you distance and helps you see your own use more objectively.

- Staying clean and sober may help you break abusive patterns.
- Situations in your life may change while you are clean and sober, giving you insight into the way alcohol and other drugs had affected you previously.

3. Putting the Group Rules on Newsprint: This interactive activity lets students review the rules plus add any which might seem appropriate. For instance, in a school in which meetings are not held over lunch periods, it might make sense not to allow eating or drinking in the group room. Facilitators might want to ask for a student volunteer to write down the rules, just to set the tone that it will not always be the facilitators who will be in front of the group. First, the leaders will want to outline the nonnegotiable rules for group.

The nonnegotiable group rules are as follows:

- Attendance is required at all sessions.
- Be on time for each session.
- Confidentiality must be respected.
- Each participant must be alcohol and drug free at each session.

Ask students to come up with other rules, if they'd like to add any. Leaders should add any which are specific to your setting. Examples of other rules are as follows:

- One person talks at a time.
- Use only "I" statements.
- Do not judge others.
- Be respectful.
- Do not identify any other people when describing your own behavior. (For example, say, "I was at a friend's house last time I drank," rather than "I was at John Jones's house last time I drank.")

4. Pretest: Administer the challenge group pretest, emphasizing to students that it is not a test as they know tests, but simply a measure of what they know now and what they'll know at the end of the group experience. If students have folders for their group materials, have them keep the pretest in the folder. If not, collect the tests to compare with the posttest.

5. Preview of the Challenge Group: Facilitators should let the participants know what will be covered during the challenge group by writing the following list on the newsprint and explaining a little about each section:

- Pharmacology of alcohol and other drugs
- High-risk behavior
- The disease of chemical dependency
- Family issues and chemical dependency
- Decision making
- Communication skills
- Self-evaluation

6. Break: Take a five-minute break, and be consistent about restarting on time or you'll have trouble with it later. During the challenge group, students should be encouraged to do their business (getting drinks of water, going to the bathroom, etc.) during the designated break time to minimize distractions to the group process.

7. Ice-Breaker: You can use any activity that will aid student interaction. One familiar ice-breaker is to ask students to split into pairs with a partner they don't know well and to each conduct a five-minute interview of the other. Then have students introduce one another to the group. The purpose here is simply to get students to open their mouths and let some personal information pass hands. If you know ice-breakers which have worked well, use them.

8. Check-in: Give participants the opportunity to share how they think they'll do with the challenge and anything else that is on their minds about the group. This exercise will be most difficult the first week. The leaders should explain that in subsequent weeks, the check-in will focus on the daily log. This exercise can lead quite naturally into the next one.

9. How I Got Here: Ask students one by one to share the circumstances that brought them to the challenge group or, if they are volunteers, why they chose to participate in this experience. Encourage students to "flesh out" cryptic explanations. There is likely to be hostility from students who are mandatory participants, and it is important for leaders to listen without judgment. Trust can be built simply by letting students know that you understand their situations as *they* understand them. Repeat their assessments back to them to underscore the way they see it, even if they see it through tremendous distortion and denial. "So you're angry because you think it's unfair that your other two friends didn't get caught and you did. And they drink a lot more than you do. You feel like you're kind of taking the fall for them, is that what you mean?" You can help lead students out of that denial later on in the process. Don't try now.

10. My First Time: Ask students to complete the handout entitled "My First Time." Encourage them to be detailed about this first drinking or drugging experience. Then ask students to share this information with the group. Encourage group interaction by asking each student specific questions about the experience, and encourage students to ask similar questions of each other. This exercise sets the tone for what is ahead: honest sharing about alcohol and other drug use. It may be difficult for students to share at first—consider how challenging it is to share with adults what has previously been kept from them.

11. Challenge/Homework: Explain the daily log and ask students to record when they are tempted to use chemicals, when they resist, or when they feel pressure to use. The daily log should include both instances when students used and when students refused. Specify that names of other people should not be included on these forms.

12. Closure: Remind students about the confidentiality ground rules.

WELCOME TO THE CHALLENGE GROUP
(This is the beginning of the adventure.)

The challenge group gives *you* the opportunity to assess your relationship with alcohol and other drugs.

There are some things you should know about yourself since you took the risk to sign up for the challenge group. It's important that you give yourself the credit you deserve for being here today:

☐ You respect yourself.

☐ You are courageous and willing to take a risk.

☐ You are willing to look at your own behavior.

☐ You are willing to make a commitment to yourself and to the other participants.

☐ You are willing to face the truth straight on—even if the truth contains things you really don't want to face.

☐ You are willing to work with this group of people.

☐ You have the rare opportunity to see yourself as others see you, if you choose to listen to the feedback you'll get.

☐ You have the opportunity to make positive changes in your life with the support of friends.

GIVE YOURSELF A HAND!

SPECIAL RULES FOR THE CHALLENGE GROUP

Name _____ Date _____

Participating in a challenge group comes with some responsibilities.

The group will function most efficiently if we can work as a team. Here are the rules we'll all play by. Next to each statement, please write your initials, indicating your understanding and your willingness to adhere to these rules.

_____ The challenge group meets for a total of twelve periods. You must be present for all twelve. In cases of illness, please bring a note for or talk to one of the challenge group facilitators.

_____ You can bring your lunch or snacks to the challenge group if we are meeting during your lunch period.

_____ Please arrive on time.

_____ You are responsible for the work you miss in class, and it is your responsibility to let your teachers know when you will be or have been absent due to challenge group participation.

_____ We will take a break *approximately* halfway through each session.

_____ Dishonesty wastes everybody's time. Please be honest in all your interactions in the challenge group.

_____ Everything that is said here, stays here. This is the principle of confidentiality, and this is the most important rule.

_____ , _____
(student's signature)   (date)

INFORMED CONSENT FOR INVOLVEMENT
WITH THE CHALLENGE GROUP
Through the Student Assistance Program

I, _____ agree to participate in the

challenge group at _____
                    (name of school)

I understand that I am protected under Federal Regulation 42 CRF Part 2 regarding confidentiality of alcohol and drug abuse records. Information will not be shared without my consent.

Participation in the challenge group is voluntary. The challenge group facilitators expect that during my participation in this program I will follow the explained rules.

I have been informed of the rules and procedures of the challenge group.

Signed _____ , _____
       (participant's signature)   (date)

Witness _____ , _____
        (witness's signature)   (date)

Interviewer _____

Date _____

Parent's signature (if applicable) _____

THE CHALLENGE

I, _____ , hereby challenge
myself to

1. Remain free of alcohol and other mood-altering drugs for the duration of the challenge group

2. To assess honestly my personal relationship with alcohol and other drugs

3. To discuss openly with the group my progress with the previous two challenges and any issues that arise as a result

4. To apply the knowledge and skills that I will acquire in the challenge group to make positive changes in my life

5. To seek follow-up help if I need assistance in meeting these challenges.

Student _____ Date _____

Parent _____ Date _____
    (optional)

THE CHALLENGE GROUP PRE/POST TEST
(Circle One)

Name: _____ Date: _____

1. Your driving ability is impaired if your BAC is
   a) 0.10%.
   b) 1.0%.
   c) 0.05%.
   d) all of the above.

2. BAC means
   a) Before Arrest and Conviction.
   b) Breath Analysis Continuity.
   c) Blood Alcohol Content.
   d) none of the above.

3. Rationalization is
   a) a way of avoiding personal issues.
   b) a type of denial.
   c) a psychological defense mechanism.
   d) all of the above.

4. Marijuana
   a) is a dependency-producing drug.
   b) interferes with testosterone levels.
   c) can cause memory loss.
   d) is all of the above.

5. Alcoholism
   a) is a fatal disease.
   b) can be cured.
   c) doesn't affect anyone but the alcoholic.
   d) is all of the above.

6. The family scapegoat
   a) is the person in the family to whom everyone turns for help.
   b) usually gets blamed for things.
   c) is very quiet and obedient.
   d) is none of the above.

7. Children from alcoholic families
   a) often grow up and marry alcoholics.
   b) often become alcoholics.
   c) often become drug dependent.
   d) can be all of the above.

8. A primary developmental task of adolescence is
   a) taking care of "unfinished business" from childhood.
   b) identity formation.
   c) developing realistic goals.
   d) all of the above.

9. Cocaine is a
   a) stimulant.
   b) depressant.
   c) hallucinogen.
   d) none of the above.

10. Chemical dependency begins when
    a) a person admits he or she has a problem.
    b) a person drinks alcohol or uses a drug every day.
    c) a person uses alcohol/drugs repeatedly, despite having negative consequences.
    d) all of the above events happen.

TRUE OR FALSE

	T	F
11. The process by which someone makes someone else aware of his or her own behavior is called confrontation.	☐	☐
12. An alcoholic blackout is what happens when someone passes out from drinking too much.	☐	☐
13. A person who does not get high every day is not chemically dependent.	☐	☐
14. Drinking alcohol to avoid a hangover is a symptom of alcoholism.	☐	☐
15. A person can become chemically dependent without realizing it.	☐	☐
16. Alcohol and drug use can interfere with normal adolescent sexual development.	☐	☐
17. Family members are often responsible for an alcoholic's drinking.	☐	☐
18. The younger you are when you start using alcohol or other drugs, the quicker you can become addicted.	☐	☐
19. Drug abuse is a part of normal adolescent development.	☐	☐
20. Alcohol and drugs are the number one killer of Americans under the age of twenty-five.	☐	☐

THE CHALLENGE GROUP DAILY LOG

WEEK OF: _____   NAME: _____

	Sun.	Mon.	Tues.	Wed.	Thurs.	Fri.	Sat.
Midnight to 6 A.M.							
6 P.M. to Midnight							
Noon to 6:00 P.M.							
6:00 A.M. to Noon							

Please keep track of the times, places, or circumstances in which you experienced a desire, craving, opportunity, or pressure to use alcohol and other drugs. Write down when you used or refused, and any alternative things you chose to do.

MY FIRST TIME

Name _____

The first drug (including alcohol) I ever used was _____

_____

Age at first use _____

Who I was with _____

_____

What I was doing _____

_____

Why I decided to try it _____

_____

How I felt before I used _____

_____

How I felt while I used/was under the influence _____

_____

How I felt after I used _____

_____

Did you get into any trouble as a result of your use? _____

_____

How soon did you do it again or try another drug? _____

_____

Why? _____

_____

VOLUNTARY AGREEMENT TO RESPECT
CONFIDENTIALITY OF CHALLENGE GROUP

I, _____ , agree to keep confidential names and private information that are shared during the group time. I also understand that other students are making this agreement to respect my confidentiality. We make this promise so people can feel comfortable sharing in the group.

_____ , _____

(student's signature)   (date)

CHALLENGE SESSION 2

Note: Facilitators will need to do about an hour's worth of work prior to this session to create the "pharmacology game." Once it has been made, you can use it over and over again. See 3A in this section for instructions.

Objectives

- To present alcohol and other current drugs, their various classifications and effects
- To explore alcohol and other drugs and high-risk behavior
- To encourage healthy decision making

Agenda

1. Check-in
2. Review agenda
3. Pharmacology game
4. Break
5. Blood alcohol content
6. High-risk behaviors/decision making
7. Closure

1. Check-in: Encourage students to share any progress or problems they are having with the challenge. Share daily logs. If students are cryptic in their responses, gently urge students to share more thoroughly. Encourage students to ask each other questions. Facilitators will want to keep a close eye on the time spent during check-in. At this point, ten or fifteen minutes should be sufficient. It is easy, particularly in the later weeks of the group, to let check-in go on almost indefinitely. The curriculum is designed to be flexible, but try to make sure that the time is being used productively.

I have had good results from requiring students to explicitly address whether or not they met the challenge. For instance, asking, "John, were you able to meet the challenge this week?" John answers either, "I was able to meet the challenge," (whereupon he gets a hand of applause) or, "I was unable to meet the challenge." I also ask students to record weekly whether they were not able to meet the challenge.

2. Review Agenda for Session 2

3. Pharmacology Game: The pharmacology game is intended to make relatively dull subject matter more tolerable.

    A. *Preparation:* Facilitators should copy each name and slang term for drugs (the list is found on the following page) onto separate index cards. Once that's done, you will have a stack of cards with the names of all the different drugs and their slang names on them. Now make a card for each of the five classifications listed on the "key," page 301. Make these five cards different somehow from the drug cards by putting a border around them or coloring in the letters.

B. Put the five classifications of drugs onto the floor. (See illustration.) Now shuffle the stack of drug cards thoroughly, split them up among the students, and ask them to put them under the correct classification. Do not let the students ask the facilitators any questions—they can only ask among themselves, the way it is in real life. Adolescents don't go up to teachers before they're going to buy some marijuana and ask the teacher whether he or she thinks it's a depressant or a hallucinogen.

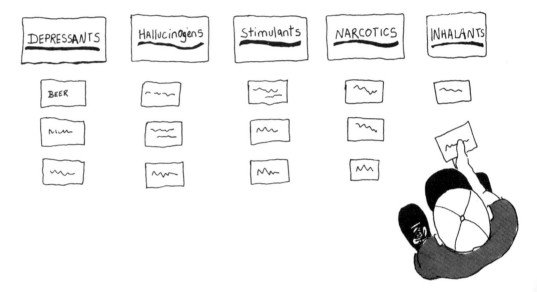

After the students have put the drugs into the classifications, have the students check the floor against the key (included, next page) to see how they did. (Or, the facilitators can do it.) Then the facilitators can lead a discussion of the various effects of the different classifications. It is essential that at least one facilitator be well acquainted with pharmacology to answer questions as they arise. Keep the conversational flow two-way; drugs change so quickly that there may be new ones that need to be added to the game that students will know. Keep a few blank index cards for adding newer drugs that students may know or additional slang terms for existing ones.

When discussing pharmacology, important points include the following:

- Potential for dependency with all chemicals
- Medical consequences
- Alcohol is a drug
- Tolerance and withdrawal
- Effects of combining drugs

Focus the discussion on those drugs which are most commonly used by the participants in the challenge group, staying away from the notion of "hard" versus "soft"

ALCOHOL AND OTHER DRUG CLASSIFICATION

Stimulants

Nicotine	Coke
"Speed"	"Snow"
Amphetamines	Meth-Amphetamine
Caffeine	Ice
Cocaine	Crack

Effects:

General speeding pu of central nervous
  system
Nervousness
Paranoia
Insomnia
Cardiac arrest

Depressants

Alcohol	Quaaludes
Barbiturates	"Downers"
Sleeping pills	Liquor
Beer	Valium
Wine coolers	V's

Effects:

General "slowing down" of central
  nervous system
Lowers inhibitions
Sometimes violence
Impaired judgment
Shuts off bodilt functions (overdose)

Narcotics

Heroin
Opium
Codeine
Morphine
Methadone

Effects:

Sleepiness
Inability to concentrate
Nausea

Hallucinogens

Acid	Marijuana
LSD	Hash
Peyote	Hashish
Mushrooms	PCP
"Shrooms"	Angel dust

Effects:

Lose touch with reality
Possible hallucinations
Erratic, bizarre behavior

Inhalants

Nitrous Oxide
Gasoline
"Whippets"
Glue

Effects:

Confusion
Nausea
Passing out

drugs. All drugs have the potential to harm. One mistake of drug education in the 1970s was to tell students that if they used marijuana, for instance, they would definitely become heroin addicts and end up living on the streets. Since students knew that this simply wasn't true for everyone, it damaged the credibility of drug education efforts. Remind students of the *potential* risks, making no specific predictions.

Answering Questions about Pharmacology: If students raise questions facilitators can't answer, and they probably will, be honest and say you don't know but that you'll find out during the week and report back. As challenge group facilitators, we're not required to have every answer, but we can act as resource people by finding out.

I make it a rule never to answer questions which seem to be asked in service of getting a better high, which defend one drug against another, or which beg reassurance for using a particular drug. Questions like "I've heard that if you snort cocaine after drinking, it will clear your head and make your drunk so much more intense" or "Marijuana is safer than alcohol, right?" or "Is it true that you can't overdose on LSD?" should be answered very carefully, with great attention paid to what I call "quotation potential." I cringe as I imagine a student taking a long haul on a joint and saying, "My challenge group leader said that marijuana is safer than drinking." Or as a student pops three hits of LSD into his mouth, he grins, "My challenge group leader said LSD isn't addictive, so I gave up everything else and now I'm tripping every day." Answers like, "All drugs are potentially addictive to some people," or "Both drinking and marijuana use have potential dangers. I can't really say which is better or worse," answer the questions without giving any implicit permission to use. Remember that as SAP people, we are considered the next best thing to experts, and our opinions about alcohol and other drugs really matter to kids. Be very aware of what you say.

An alternative to the pharmacology game is to show a film on the effects of drugs or to photocopy the "key" and run a discussion using it. The game, however, helps students interact and tends to generate more discussion.

4. Break

5. Blood Alcohol Content Level:

A. Hand out the "Blood Alcohol Content" worksheet and explain what BAC means—0.10% equals one part alcohol per one thousand parts of blood. Find out what your state's legal limit for intoxication is and what the penalties for driving under the influence are. Use the legal limit as a point of reference. While BAC is usually used in connection with impaired ability to drive, expand the discussion to include other impairments.

B. *Levels of impairment:* Discuss how behavior, thinking, judgment, driving skills, and coordination are affected at different levels of BAC. Draw on the experience of participants and emphasize levels of impairment even under the legal limit for your state. Have students use the sheet to calculate their approximate blood alcohol content during their last drinking episode.

6. High-Risk Behavior and Alcohol and other Drug Use: Use the "High-Risk Behavior" handout. Ask students to list high-risk behavior which a person might be more likely to do while at the listed BAC. Compile a group list of high-risk behaviors on newsprint. Direct the discussion toward the relationship between alcohol and other drug use, peer pressure, and high-risk behavior. This is a good place to present an informational piece on AIDS, the contraction of which can be a deadly consequence of alcohol and other drug-related behavior. (Use "AIDS: Facts or Fallacies," included.)

7. Closure: Remind students about the confidentiality ground rules. Also remind students to record use, and temptation to use, on their daily logs.

BLOOD ALCOHOL CONTENT CHART
BODY WEIGHT VS. DRINKS CONSUMED

Body Weight	Number of Drinks											
	1	2	3	4	5	6	7	8	9	10	11	12
100	.038	.075	.113	.150	.188	.225	.263	.300	.338	.375	.413	.450
110	.034	.066	.103	.137	.172	.207	.241	.275	.309	.344	.379	.412
120	.031	.063	.094	.125	.156	.188	.219	.250	.261	.313	.344	.375
130	.029	.058	.087	.116	.145	.174	.203	.232	.251	.290	.320	.348
140	.027	.054	.080	.107	.134	.161	.188	.214	.241	.268	.295	.321
150	.025	.050	.075	.100	.125	.151	.176	.201	.226	.251	.276	.301
160	.023	.047	.070	.094	.117	.141	.164	.188	.211	.234	.258	.281
170	.022	.045	.066	.088	.110	.132	.155	.178	.200	.221	.244	.265
180	.021	.042	.063	.083	.104	.125	.146	.167	.188	.208	.229	.250
190	.020	.040	.059	.079	.099	.119	.138	,158	.179	.198	.217	.237
200	.019	.038	.056	.075	.094	.113	.131	.150	.169	.188	.206	.225
210	.018	.036	.053	.071	.090	.107	.125	.143	.161	.179	.197	.215
220	.017	.034	.051	.068	.085	.102	.119	.136	.153	.170	.188	.205
230	.016	.032	.049	.065	.081	.098	.115	.130	.147	.163	.180	.196
240	.015	.031	.047	.063	.078	.094	.109	.125	.141	.156	.172	.188

This chart shows the estimated percent of alcohol in the blood after a number of drinks in relation to the body weight of the individual. This percent can be estimated as follows:

1. Count the number of drinks:

   Remember: 1 drink = 1 oz. 100 proof
   12 oz. beer
   5 oz. table wine.

2. On the chart, find the number of drinks and then read across from your body weight. This figure will give you the estimated percent of alcohol in the bloodstream.

3. From this figure, subtract the amount of alcohol metabolized during the time passed since your first drink. The figure used for this rate of metabolism is 0.015% per hour.

Example: A 150-pound person has 5 drinks in 2 hours
.125% minus (.015 times 2 hours) .030 = .095%
This person's BAC is 0.095%.

BLOOD ALCOHOL CONTENT, ILLUSTRATED

.1

.4

.02

.16

HIGH-RISK BEHAVIOR AT DIFFERENT LEVELS OF BAC

LEVEL OF IMPAIRMENT	POSSIBLE HIGH-RISK BEHAVIORS
0.02%	**0.02%**
JUDGMENT IMPAIRED	_____
INHIBITIONS REDUCED	_____
0.06%	**0.06%**
FINE MOTOR SKILLS IMPAIRED	_____
REACTION TIME INCREASED	_____
LOSS OF ABILITY TO PERFORM DIVIDED ATTENTION TASKS	_____
0.10%	**0.10%**
VISION AND HEARING REDUCED	_____
SPEECH IMPAIRED	_____
BALANCE DISTURBED	_____
GROSS MOTOR SKILLS IMPAIRED	_____
0.16%	**0.16%**
DIFFICULTY WALKING AND TALKING	_____
DISTORTED PERCEPTION/JUDGMENT	_____
IRRESPONSIBLE BEHAVIOR	_____
FEEL CONFUSED OR DAZED	_____
0.40%	**0.40%**
ABSENCE OF PERCEPTION	_____
UNCONSCIOUSNESS	_____
POSSIBLE COMA AND/OR DEATH	_____

SELF-TEST ON AIDS:
FACTS OR FALLACIES

For each statement below, circle the letter (T, F, or U) that reflects your belief about the statement. This sheet is for you. It will help you identify how much information you already have and what information you need.

ANSWER KEY: T = True; F = False; U = Undecided

T F U 1. Everyone infected with the AIDS virus is sick.

T F U 2. The AIDS virus itself usually does not kill the person.

T F U 3. A person having the AIDS virus can pass it on even though there are no AIDS symptoms present.

T F U 4. Sharing IV drug needles and syringes puts a person at very high risk for getting the AIDS virus.

T F U 5. Most people who become infected (test positive) for the AIDS virus will go on to develop AIDS.

T F U 6. A person can get the AIDS virus from giving blood.

T F U 7. Only homosexual and bisexual men get AIDS.

T F U 8. Women can transmit the AIDS virus to sex partners.

T F U 9. Heterosexual men or "straight" men can transmit the AIDS virus to sex partners.

T F U 10. The AIDS virus can be spread through casual contact such as shaking hands, touching, or being near a person with AIDS.

T F U 11. Youths who have practiced high-risk behaviors such as IV drug use, had multiple sexual partners, or whose sexual partners may have engaged in high-risk behaviors can get free, confidential, or anonymous (no name) testing and counseling.

1. FALSE: Many people who are infected with the AIDS virus have no symptoms at all.

2. TRUE: People with AIDS die of "opportunistic infections" which take over their bodies because their own immune system is unable to fight them off.

3. TRUE

4. TRUE

5. TRUE: Some people may develop AIDS quickly, within months; others may not get sick for years—some experts say up to fifteen years later.

6. FALSE: You can develop AIDS from receiving blood contaminated with AIDS virus. However, the blood supply has been tested since March 1985.

7. FALSE

8. TRUE

9. TRUE

10. FALSE

11. TRUE

CHALLENGE SESSION 3

Objectives

- To increase levels of trust in the group
- To encourage honest interaction and positive risk taking
- To introduce the various types of denial
- To present a model for positive change

Agenda

1. Check-in
2. Review session 3 agenda
3. Feelings
4. Denial
   A. Definition of denial
   B. Different faces of denial
   C. Breaking through
5. Break
6. Balancing the Scale
7. Significance of Feelings
8. Closure

1. Check-in: In these later sessions, the check in may be longer (twenty to twenty-five minutes) as students share their struggles with the challenge. Encourage appropriate student interaction.

2. Review Agenda

3. Feelings: Use this list of feelings to help students identify their feelings. On newsprint, have students generate a list of as many "feeling" words as they can think of. This will help enlarge students' "feeling vocabulary." Encourage students to come up with at least 50 feeling words. Save this list for the end of the session.

4. Denial

A. *Definition of Denial:* This series of exercises hopes to make students aware of denial, a characteristic of alcohol and other drug addiction. The least threatening way of presenting it is to explain that denial is a natural process that the body utilizes to keep unpleasant information from our consciousness. In alcohol and other drug addiction, denial becomes disproportionate and, ultimately, makes addiction fatal. Following are several ways to explain denial—putting them all on newsprint or on the board allows students to choose which makes the most sense to them.

- Denial is an unconscious process that protects us from threatening realities.

- Denial is the psychological process by which human beings block knowledge of painful realities, thereby protecting themselves from things that threaten them.

- Denial is a buffer between unacceptable reality and our feelings.

B. *The Different Faces of Denial:* Denial comes in many packages, most expertly disguised as something else. This exercise exposes all the wrappings and lets students evaluate their own means of denial. This list of different types of denial is for facilitators. Present these different types of denial on the blackboard or newsprint.

THE DIFFERENT FACES OF DENIAL

Simple Denial: Maintaining that something simply is not so. Insisting that something is not a drug-related problem despite convincing evidence that it is. *Example:* "Hey, they say I was drinking at the dance, but I wasn't. I was just sick from the pizza."

Minimizing: Admitting there's a problem, but in such a way that it appears to be much less significant or serious than it in fact is. *Example:* "Okay, so we went out drinking, but I had less than I usually do. Anyway, it's *no big deal.*"

Rationalizing: Finding reasons, excuses, or alibis for drinking or drugging or for related consequences. *Example:* "It was just that I was so tired after the track meet. That's why I got so drunk and did all those embarrassing things."

Intellectualizing: Using intellectual analysis of situations to deflect personal involvement or responsibility. *Example:* "Do you really think it's constitutional for the drinking age to be twenty-one?"

Blaming: Maintaining that the responsibility for the drinking or drugging behavior lies with someone else. *Example:* "It wasn't my fault that I got drunk that night. She's the one who broke up with me!"

Diversion: Avoiding the subject, especially by using humor. *Example:* "I had to drive. You expect me to walk in that condition?"

Hostility: Using anger to insure that people don't talk about your drinking or drugging behavior. *Example:* Becoming angry, yelling, and using the "you don't trust me!" accusation when parents bring up drinking or drugging behavior.

- *Exercise:* After explaining each type of denial, hand out "Umbrella of Denial" and have students break into groups of two or three to come up with examples of each type of denial that *they have used in their own lives.* If you feel it would be more comfortable for students, have them complete this exercise alone and then share their examples with the rest of the group.

Remind students that denial as it relates to alcohol and other drug use is a process that sometimes occurs without the user being aware of what he or she is doing. Denial is not something you can wish away. It takes some hard work, honesty, openness, and willingness to break through it.

C. *Breaking through Denial:* Breaking through denial requires two techniques:

- Leveling—being honest about ourselves
- Confronting—when others give us information about ourselves by being honest with us

Both techniques require that people take an emotional risk, but it is the only way change is possible. Facilitators should list these two techniques on the blackboard or newsprint and tell participants that the next exercise will help them level and confront. Gently challenge participants to be willing to take these risks.

5. Break

6. Balancing the Scale: Everyone has a balance of things they know about themselves and things they don't share with anyone. Similarly, we all know things about other people that we don't necessarily share with them. The more information we share about ourselves, and the more information we let others tell us about ourselves, the more balanced our scale will be.

Exercise: Hand out "Balancing the Scale." On the left-hand side of the sheet, ask students to write several things they know about themselves. Encourage them to take the risk of putting down at least one thing that they haven't previously shared with the group. This is an exercise in *leveling* (being honest about ourselves). Urge participants to write something honest about themselves that relates to the challenge group. Let the students know that they will be passing this sheet around, so other group members will see it.

Then ask students to pass the sheet to the person next to them. That person should write something about the person whose name is on the top of the paper. It should be something that the person may not be aware of. This is an exercise in *confronting.* When the papers have gone all the way around the room, have students share their feelings about leveling and confronting in this manner. Remind them that leveling and confronting are the only way to self-discovery and the best way to stay honest about alcohol and other drug use. The purpose of this exercis is to encourage students to level with and confront one another in later sessions. For example:

John Doe

"I was really afraid to come in here, even though I just acted like I was mad."

John—You really listened to me when I was talking about my experience at the railroad tracks. I think you're a good listener.

John—You never look at anyone when you say you want to quit using alcohol, but you do look at people when you say you want to quit drugs.

7. Significance of Feelings: Talking about feelings is very appropriate in the context of the challenge group, because many people begin to use chemicals as a way to manage their uncomfortable feelings. Use the feelings checklist compiled at the beginning of the session to help with the discussion.

Include these important points in the discussion, relating them back to alcohol and other drug use:

- If our behavior is opposed to our values, then we can take on one or more of the following behaviors/emotions: hostility, anger, self-pity, fear, defiance, phoniness, arrogance, etc. Direct the discussion toward the questions, "Have you behaved according to your values while under the influence of alcohol and other drugs?" and "If not, what emotions/behaviors have you taken on for cover?"
- We are threatened by disapproval from others—therefore, we develop defenses and a shield of negative feelings that others can't penetrate. Direct the discussion toward how students respond when someone (parents, friends, teachers) disapproves of their drinking or drugging behavior.
- The more we shield our feelings, the more we are out of touch with those feelings. This creates a barrier to self-discovery. Seeing and accepting reality becomes more difficult and, ultimately, the shield of denial grows. Direct the discussion toward the progression of denial.

8. Closure: Remind students of the confidentiality ground rules and remind them to record use and temptation to use on their daily logs. This week, remind students to be especially aware of their own defenses and denial.

UMBRELLA OF DENIAL

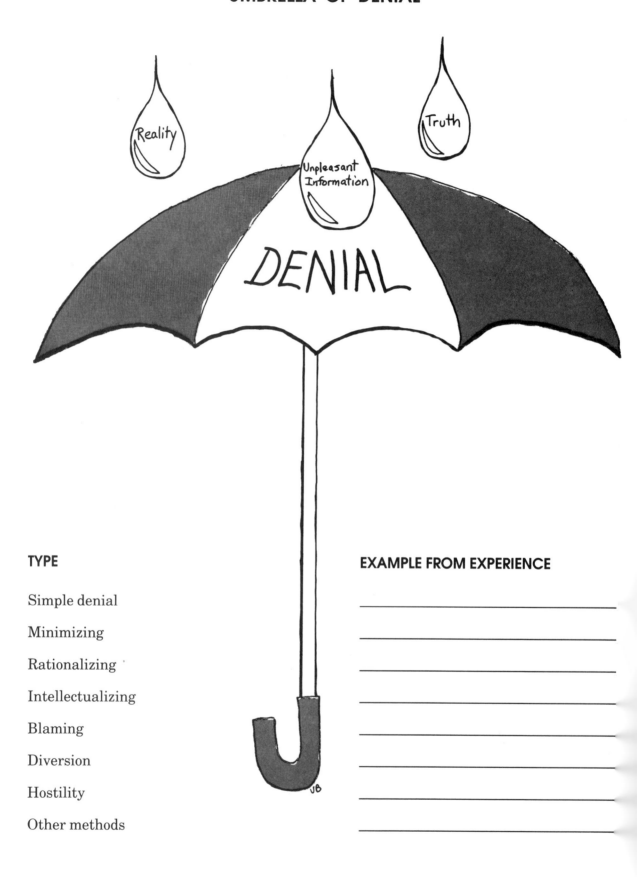

TYPE

Simple denial

Minimizing

Rationalizing

Intellectualizing

Blaming

Diversion

Hostility

Other methods

EXAMPLE FROM EXPERIENCE

_____

_____

_____

_____

_____

_____

_____

_____

Name _____

BALANCING THE SCALE

Something I know about myself that I haven't shared (leveling):

_____

_____

Things others know about me that they can share (confronting):

1. _____

_____

_____

2. _____

_____

_____

3. _____

_____

_____

4. _____

_____

_____

5. _____

_____

_____

CHALLENGE SESSION 4

Objectives

- To give participants a clear understanding of the progressive nature of chemical dependency
- To dispel some myths about chemical dependency
- To encourage honest and accurate self-evaluation

Agenda

1. Check-in
2. Review agenda
3. Good and bad aspects of drinking/drugging
4. "Picture" of chemically dependent person
5. Break
6. Explanation of chemical dependency
7. Rapid-onset addiction
8. Definite signs of trouble/self-evaluation
9. Closure

1. Check-in: Twenty to twenty-five minutes

2. Review of Agenda for Session 4

3. Good and Bad Aspects of Drinking and Drugging: Have participants complete the handout "Good/Bad Drinking/Drugging" by describing five aspects of *their own* drinking and/or drugging which are good and five aspects which are bad. Compile a master list of "good" and "bad" aspects of drinking and drug use on newsprint, directing the discussion toward the short-term versus long-term effects of each list and encouraging discussion of personal experiences.

4. "Picture" of Chemically Dependent Person: Split group into subgroups of two or three. Give each group a large piece of paper and some large magic markers. Ask each group to draw a composite picture of a person who is a *stereotypical* addict or alcoholic. (Emphasize that you do not want pictures of specific, real people known to group members.) As a team, they should draw this person in as much detail as they can, making it very clear that this person has a problem with alcohol or other drugs. Ask students to come up with a name for this person (i.e., "Dougie the Druggie"). Take about fifteen minutes for this exercise. Ask for a spokesperson for each group to introduce the picture of the stereotypical alcoholic or addict to the rest of the group. Engage the group in asking the spokesperson questions about the chemically dependent person, so this picture becomes more three dimensional. Some questions might be as follows:

- How old is this person?
- What is his or her drug of choice?
- Does this person have a job? A family? A love relationship?

- How is this person's health?
- Does this person like himself or herself?
- What dreams does this person have?

Have the spokesperson write some of the answers to these questions on the paper next to the drawing.

The purpose of this exercise is to expose stereotypes about addiction and to dispel some of the myths associated with addiction. Facilitators should pay close attention to the characteristics students use to "diagnose" addiction so they can later dispel those myths in discussion. Many students will draw pictures of IV drug users who use every day, for instance—this can lead into a discussion about how a person can be addicted to any drug, and he or she doesn't have to use every day to constitute addiction. Use this exercise to introduce the disease of chemical dependency, to explain that the people they have drawn comprise only about 3 percent of all the people in the world who are chemically dependent and that these stereotypical alcoholics and addicts are in the last, terminal phases of the disease. These stereotypical alcoholics and addicts, created by participants, probably had the disease of chemical dependency when they were in high school, but the symptoms weren't so obvious.

For the most part, students who participate in the challenge group will be exhibiting very early symptoms of trouble with chemicals, as evidenced by their mere participation in the group. Most are there because they have experienced some trouble as a result of drinking or other drug use, or, if they are there as volunteers, something about their use concerns them. This is not to suggest that every student involved in the challenge group will develop full-blown alcoholism or other drug addiction, but chances are good that without a change in pattern, some will. Facilitators should use this exercise as a springboard to lead in to the early warning signs of addiction and should concentrate the discussion on the *early* signs of addiction, always stressing that without treatment, people exhibiting early signs will begin to experience the stereotypical symptoms.

5. Break

6. Explanation of the Progression of Chemical Dependency: This is perhaps the most vital information dispensed in the challenge group. A facilitator familiar with chemical dependency should present the information, concentrating on the earlier symptoms and thought patterns associated with addiction. It's advisable to warn students that this information may be difficult for some of them to hear, because it brings them face to face with their patterns of use and perhaps the patterns of use of some of their loved ones. There are many good models available for explaining chemical dependency. Please use additional resources if you have any available.

A simple way to explain the progression of addiction follows. The examples used tend to focus on adolescent, rather than adult, issues. Use the blackboard or newsprint to present this information, and try to make it as interactive as possible. It is during this discussion that your rapport with students will pay off. Without playing the "heavy," it is the facilitator's job to present this information factually, but in a way that students can understand. This explanation holds for any drug addiction, including addiction to alcohol:

THE PROGRESSION OF ADDICTION

PHASE 1. Experimentation: This is the first time someone uses. It is literally an experiment because they've never done it before. Once the person knows what the effect will be, he or she is no longer experimenting. So it is erroneous to say, "Joe is experimenting with marijuana on the weekends." Once Joe knows what the effects of marijuana feel like, and he does it again, the experiment is over. He is then using marijuana on the weekends, rather than experimenting with it.

PHASE 2. Seeking the Buzz: This is the next phase, where the user knows what the effect of using the substance will be and goes after it, because he or she likes it. In this phase, people may experience some small[2] negative consequences as a result of their use.
　　Examples of the first negative consequences are as follows:

- Hangovers
- Decline in grades
- Loss of trust of parents
- Embarrassment from behavior while using
- Getting sick
- Doing something you wish you hadn't done.

Those who recognize the trouble as being related to the drinking or drugging will moderate or eliminate their use to insure that there are no more negative consequences. Once a person has experienced this sort of trouble, those who are going to "turn it around" will make a conscious decision to avoid the same level of chemical use to avoid a repeat of the trouble. For example, a student drinks five beers at a party, gets into a fight with his girlfriend, and gets grounded when his parents find out about his use. A healthy response to this situation would be to moderate or eliminate the use, the rationale being, "Last time I drank five beers, all sorts of terrible things happened." Next time, the adolescent drinks significantly less (or none) to avoid the negative consequences. Many participants in challenge courses are in the process of making these sorts of decisions.
　　Others, who are in trouble with chemicals (but don't necessarily think they are) and who cannot make the connection between the negative consequence and their drug use, are already experiencing denial in its earliest form. They will endeavor to manipulate the surrounding *circumstances* (rather than moderate or eliminate the use) in an effort to use the same way but not have the associated trouble. They will continue to

---

[2]The word *small* is used for lack of a better term. No consequence related to alcohol or other drug use can be considered "small." These are the negative consequences which seem less devastating at the outset but could nevertheless be indicative of trouble ahead.

use despite negative consequences. Using the preceding example, instead of moderating or eliminating the use, the adolescent will drink the same amount (or more) but make sure his girlfriend isn't at the party (or he'll get another girlfriend who doesn't mind his drinking) and he'll make sure his parents don't catch him this time. In his mind, full of denial, the problem has become the girlfriend and the parents, not his use of chemicals.

PHASE 3. Trouble: Although these people have experienced negative consequences due to their use, they continue to use. This phase is when denial becomes strong. As the tolerance for the substance increases, they have to use more, which usually increases the seriousness of the consequences.
The following are examples of more trouble:

- Problems with family and friends—arguments, fights, hurting loved ones' feelings, neglecting nonusing friends, etc.
- Emotional pain—guilt, shame, embarrassment, anger, depression, etc.
- Drug side effects—hangovers, memory loss, vomiting, loss of coordination, inability to concentrate, lack of sleep
- Psychological problems—denial, conflicts in values, low self-esteem, low tolerance for frustration
- Other problems—drinking and driving, poor school performance, missing work, accidents, unwanted pregnancy, sexually transmitted diseases, etc.

At this point, people experience negative emotions because of their use (embarrassment, shame, guilt, anger, etc.) and cover the negative feelings with yet more use and more denial. When facilitators are explaining this part of progression, it is wise to use an example of a teenager to bring it close to home. "Okay, so let's say we have our user Bob here and after the first trouble, Bob's still smoking pot between classes. Now his grades are all in trouble, and he feels pretty bad about it, so what does he do? Right! More smoking between classes, etc." Follow this progression to its logical end, emphasizing over and over again that Bob has the option of treating his addiction *at any stage.* Underscore that people who are in this phase of addiction need treatment.

PHASE 4. More Trouble: The negative consequences of the previous phase become more apparent. (Your stereotypical addicts and alcoholics are all in this deadly phase.) The user in this phase continues to use despite overwhelming negative consequences. If untreated, this progressive disease ultimately leads to death. If your challenge group screening procedures are working correctly, you shouldn't have any students who are in this stage of addiction in the group—but there is always the possibility that they will somehow get past you. Addiction is a clever opponent. The self-evaluation component, following, gives students the opportunity to assess themselves in the context of this new information. Treatment in this phase is absolutely crucial.

7. Rapid-Onset Addiction (Also known as the 5/15 Rule): Explaining dependency as a process, not an event, illustrate the startling relationship between age and the rate of onset. Use the "Rapid-Onset Dependency" handout which follows, and explain that someone who begins to use in adulthood has the potential to develop all the symptoms of addiction in five to fifteen years. A person who begins a pattern of use in adolescence can experience the same progression in five to fifteen months, and the child who uses in preadolescence (ages nine to thirteen) can experience the same symptoms in five to fifteen weeks. This section is included to dispel the myth that "It can't happen to me. I've only been using for a year and a half!"

8. Definite Signs of Trouble/Self-Evaluation: Using the "Definite Signs of Trouble" handout and the information just presented, give students a few minutes to conduct a self-evaluation. Ask students to share with the rest of the group what phase of addiction they believe they are in. Each student can ask for feedback from fellow participants. Facilitators should be prepared for the possibility that a student will identify himself or herself as being in the latter stages of addiction. If this happens, steps must be taken to insure that the student gets access to appropriate treatment. Have self-help literature available, and draw on the challenge the student accepted to encourage this student to think about getting more help.

9. Closure: Remind students about the ground rules of confidentiality, and congratulate them on their willingness to assess themselves honestly.

GOOD/BAD DRINKING AND/OR DRUGGING EXPERIENCES

Name _____

Using the space below, list five good things and five bad things about your drinking/drugging experience. Remember, these lists are about *your* experiences, no one else's.

Five good (positive) things about my drinking/drugging experiences:

1. _____
_____

2. _____
_____

3. _____
_____

4. _____
_____

5. _____
_____

Five bad (negative) things about my drinking/drugging experiences:

1. _____
_____

2. _____
_____

3. _____
_____

4. _____
_____

5. _____
_____

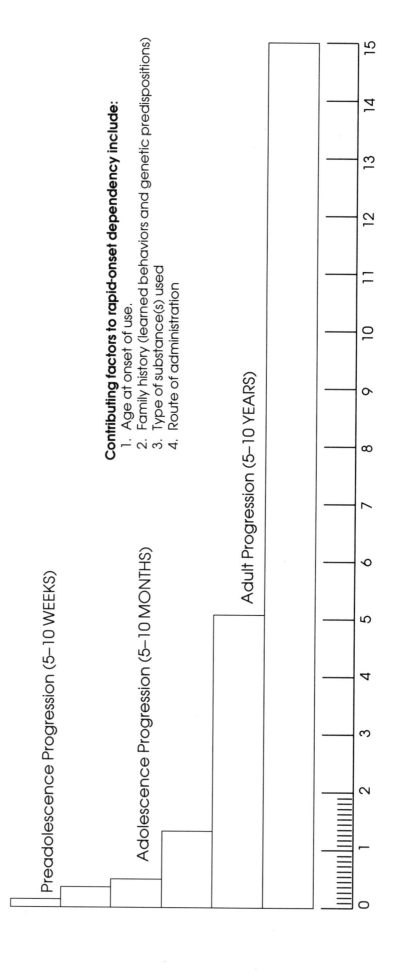

RAPID-ONSET DEPENDENCY

THE RELATIONSHIP BETWEEN AGE AND THE RATE OF ONSET

Preadolescence Progression (5–10 WEEKS)

Adolescence Progression (5–10 MONTHS)

Adult Progression (5–10 YEARS)

Contributing factors to rapid-onset dependency include:
1. Age at onset of use.
2. Family history (learned behaviors and genetic predispositions)
3. Type of substance(s) used
4. Route of administration

DEFINITE SIGNS OF TROUBLE

Any of the trouble listed below indicates serious involvement with alcohol and other drugs. If you identify with any of the behaviors listed, seek help right away.

1. **Preoccupation:** Occasionally being preoccupied with thoughts about the next time you can use. Getting excited over a future event where you can use. Planning the weekend all week. Talking about getting high/being high with your friends. Currently having mostly friends who use like you do.

2. **Protecting the Supply:** Feeling more secure if you have some extra alcohol or other drug squirreled away for your own use. Keeping extra beer in the car "just in case they run out at the party." Keeping a "private supply" of marijuana to make sure you always have enough for yourself.

3. **Increased Tolerance:** Needing more of the substance to get the desired effect. Ability to consume considerably more than a social drinker, and, though impaired, still *appear* okay both mentally and physically.

4. **"Power Hitting":** Drinking or drugging in such a manner that the drug will act more quickly or powerfully. Includes gulping drinks, shotgunning, funneling, etc.

5. **Using alone:** Includes using in a group of people where no one else is using.

6. **Using alcohol or other drugs as medicine:** Drinking or drugging to avoid life's unpleasantness. Drinking or drugging to "medicate" feelings. Drinking or drugging to medicate problems that should receive medical attention (i.e., drinking because of a toothache).

7. **Using when you hadn't planned to:** Drinking or drugging more than you had planned to or when you hadn't planned to at all.

8. **Blackouts:** Inability to remember parts of what happened during a drinking or drugging episode. This is a very serious symptom of addiction.

CHALLENGE SESSION 5

Objectives

- To expose participants to elements of healthy and unhealthy family functioning
- To encourage the recognition and acknowledgment of feelings
- To increase self-awareness
- To prepare for termination of the challenge group

Agenda

1. Check-in
2. Review session 5 agenda
3. Healthy family functioning
4. Less healthy family functioning
5. Break
6. Breaking the cycle
7. Self-awareness exercise
8. Preparation for termination of challenge group

Note: This session deals with family issues. In a challenge group, it is likely that you will have several children of addiction and others who will identify with the issues presented. Facilitators must be sensitive to the needs of these students and must be prepared to deal with a student who wants to seek further help. Make sure you have either SAP groups for identified children of addiction or access to self-help fellowships in the community to refer students.

1. Check-in

2. Review of Session 5 Agenda

3. The Healthy Family: For participants to understand what is less healthy in families, they must understand what is healthy. The purpose of these exercises is to underscore the interdependence of family members.

Exercise: Ask participants to brainstorm the elements of a healthy family and as a group (or subgroups) come up with a one- or two-sentence definition of a healthy family system. Facilitators should ask questions which provoke thought. For instance, Do family members have responsibilities to each other, or is it every person for himself or herself? Are families just parents and children?

After the definition has been generated, ask participants to come up with a fictional family that is healthy in most respects. (No family is perfect!) Briefly role-play what interaction in this healthy family would be like. Facilitators should encourage students to try to be "real" and draw from their own experience with healthy families, not from TV families. If the group is comfortable with doing so, ask students to come up with a very short skit depicting a small crisis and how it would be dealt with in a healthy family system.

If students cannot generate a list of healthy aspects of a family, you can get them started using this list:

- Family members can disagree.
- Family members are able to talk, trust other family members, and share feelings.
- Family members spend time together.
- Family members are individual people; no one "owns" anyone else.
- Family members have privacy.
- Family members can switch from role to role; no one is stuck in a role.
- Parents are parents and children are children.

4. Less-Healthy Family Functioning: Then ask students to imagine another family with similar members, except that one of the members has one of the follow conditions:

- Chemical dependency
- Compulsive gambling, overeating, or spending
- Mental illness
- A parent who was raised in an abusive home
- A violent parent.

Brainstorm a list of the characteristics of a family who is dealing with one of these conditions. It is important to underscore that not every family that must deal with one of these issues will do it in a dysfunctional manner, but there are a lot that do. Have students generate a list of these dysfunctional characteristics. Then have students briefly role-play what would happen in this family with the same crisis depicted in the earlier skit. Would it be handled differently? How would the children in the less healthy family feel about life, relationships, school, etc.? During this exercise, it is possible that students will volunteer that their families operate this way. Facilitators should gently ask about the child's coping skills— how he or she deals with it—and point out that although these have been helpful survival skills, as adults they may want to expand their repertoire of coping skills. (During this exercise, be sensitive to cultural differences in family functioning.)

In this session, it is essential for facilitators to underscore that children growing up in situations like these are affected by the dysfunction. The effects may be apparent, or may not. (They may be very apparent to the challenge leaders and not at all apparent to the student.) If the SAP person is a challenge group facilitator, it would be a good time for him or her to introduce the fact that children of addiction are at much greater risk for developing chemical dependency themselves and to introduce groups for children of addiction that are available through the SAP. Encourage anyone who identifies to take the risk to join the group once the challenge group experience is over.

- *Options:* If you have a current film available on the roles played in dysfunctional families, this would be the place to show it. You may also have handouts on children of alcoholics and the roles typically played out in dysfunctional homes. If one of the challenge leaders has facility with this subject, it would be appropriate for him or her to introduce the roles.
- If you are familiar with genograms (see chapter 8), you can have students create their own genograms, having them shade in all chemical dependency and compulsive behaviors.

5. Break

6. Breaking the Cycle: Students who grow up in difficult family situations are first of all concerned about surviving the situation until they can get out on their own. Unfortunately, the struggle doesn't end there, as many are also concerned that they will continue the dysfunction in their own lives and some feel fated to repeat the same mistakes. The greatest gift you can give these students is the knowledge that it doesn't have to be the same for them when they have families of their own; that there is hope that they can live a different way. Compile on newsprint a list of ways for students to break the cycle, reminding them that their participation in the challenge group may be the first step in breaking the cycle, as they either treat their own addiction or avoid becoming addicted in the first place. Facilitators can build this list around the following suggestions:

- Accept the disease concept of addiction.
- Take responsibility for yourself; don't enable others.
- Don't blame others for your problems; recognize your own denial.
- Recognize that you have the right to talk about these issues and you have the right to feel.
- Learn to ask for help.
- Develop a support system by making those close to you aware of your decision to seek help.
- Become involved in Al-Anon, Alateen, and/or Adult Children of Alcoholics. Seek counseling when appropriate.
- Utilize available resources such as parent support groups, parenting courses, etc., when you have children of your own.[3]

Exercise: Have students complete the handout "My Family," which asks them to outline traditions and elements of their families that they like and things they'd like to do differently in their own families. Have students share traditions in their families or things that they think their families do well. Then have them

---

[3]Reprinted with permission of the publisher, Health Communications, from *Adult Children of Alcoholics,* by Janet Woititz, © 1983.

share what they will change when they have families of their own. This exercise gives challenge facilitators great insight into what goes on for these students in their families. The student who reports that he or she would have a family where people talked to each other without yelling clearly comes from a situation where people are angry with each other a lot of the time.

7. **Self-Awareness Exercise:** Have students complete the handout "My Feelings" and share results with other participants. Ask students to reflect on whether any of their moods are caused by what happens in their families. Direct the discussion toward how some people use chemicals to mask the unpleasant feelings they experience in their families.

For example, a student might complete the worksheet "I feel happy when my friends are over. In my family, when I'm happy, I try to stay out of everyone's way because my older brother always tries to ruin it."

8. **Prepare for Termination of the Challenge Group:** At this time, begin addressing termination issues and participants' feelings and attitudes about ending the group. Encourage students to think about next week's ending and to prepare mentally for the task of termination.

MY FAMILY

List four things you like about the way your family interacts, different traditions, things you do together, ways you support one another.

1. _____

_____

2. _____

_____

3. _____

_____

4. _____

_____

List four things you'll do differently if/when you have your own family.

1. _____

_____

2. _____

_____

3. _____

_____

4. _____

_____

MY FEELINGS

Directions: Complete each statement below, and share your responses with other group members.

I feel happy when _____

_____

In my family, when I'm happy, I _____

_____

I feel sad when _____

_____

In my family, when I'm sad, I _____

_____

I feel anxious when _____

_____

In my family, when I'm anxious, I _____

_____

I feel angry when _____

_____

In my family, when I'm angry, I _____

_____

I feel hurt when _____

_____

In my family, when I'm hurt, I _____

_____

I feel insecure when _____

_____

In my family when I'm insecure, I _____

_____

CHALLENGE SESSION 6

Objectives

- To address any unanswered questions or concerns
- To give participants basic knowledge of adolescent development
- To present the concept of wellness
- To provide students with the opportunity to set some short- and long-term goals
- To terminate and bring closure to the group experience

Agenda

1. Check-in
2. Review session 6 agenda
3. Adolescent development
4. Break
5. Wellness
6. Goal Setting: Letter writing and time line
7. Closure/termination

1. Check-in: This final week, check-in may be lengthy (thirty to forty-five minutes), as students evaluate the experience they have had as a result of challenge group participation. Some will report that they have had real trouble staying clean and sober, which is a message loud and clear to facilitators that there should be some immediate follow-up, if at all possible. Consistent with group process in general, during this last session, students usually feel more free to share feedback with one another. This interaction should be encouraged while leaving time for the necessary termination and evaluation exercises.

2. Review Session 6 Agenda

3. Adolescent Development:

A. *Eight Stages of Man:* Briefly present Erikson's eight stages of development for the purpose of pointing out the crucial role of adolescence in overall human growth, emphasizing that the primary task in this stage is identity formation. Emphasize in interactive group discussion how chemicals can affect one's ability to form a positive identity.

Since an adolescent's main task is identifying a sense of self, direct the discussion toward the issues, How does alcohol and other drug use help you form a sense of self? Is it a true or a false sense?

B. *Adolescent Issues:* Engage group in discussion about adolescent experience based on Erikson's definition. Compile a list on newsprint concerning these issues:

ERIKSON'S EIGHT STAGES OF MAN

1. Trust vs. mistrust: Learning to trust one's environment (first year)
2. Autonomy vs. shame and doubt: Learning to do some basic things on your own (2–3 years)
3. Initiative vs. guilt: Beginning to be creative (4–5 years)
4. Industry vs. inferiority: Beginning to take on tasks (6–11 years)
5. *Identity vs. role confusion: Developing a sense of self, long-term goals, and taking care of "unfinished business" of childhood before moving on to full independence (12–18 years)*
6. Intimacy vs. isolation: Developing meaningful relationships and adult responsibilities (young adulthood)
7. Generativity vs. stagnation: Developing social consciousness and responsibility to others (middle age)
8. Integrity vs. despair: Reflecting and "adding up" the course of one's life and accomplishments ("golden years")

- What factors influence identity formation?
- What are the major tasks/issues in adolescence?
- What does it feel like to be an adolescent?
- What is a healthy adolescent? Draw one which can be compared to the drug-dependent drawing (See challenge session 4).

 C. *Identity:* Have students complete "My Heroes and Antiheroes" worksheet (page 331). Discuss which traits they would like to have or see in themselves, and which traits they find undesirable and why. Facilitators can take this opportunity to explain the importance of positive adult role models. Ask students to share the true-life role models in their lives.

 4. Break

 5. Wellness: Introduce the concept of wellness, emphasizing that wellness includes many different aspects of life. Have students complete the "Wellness Chart" handout (page 332) and share results with the group. Invite students to challenge each other gently to work on different aspects of the wellness chart after the experience with the challenge group is over.

 6. Goal Setting

 A. *Letter to Myself:* Have students compose a letter to themselves with their goals concerning where they want to be or what they want to be doing in six months, using the wellness chart as a resource. Have them describe the most valuable thing they have learned from the challenge course and any challenges they have for themselves. Have students self-address envelopes and seal the letters. Collect the letters, which will serve as a vehicle for the six-month follow-up appointment with the SAP. Ask students whether they'd like the letters to be sent home, or delivered to them at school through their homeroom, or whether they'd like to be called to the SAP office to retrieve them at the end of six months.

B. *Time Line:* Using the "Time Line" handout (page 333), have participants develop a time line of what they'd like to be doing in six months, one year, two years, five years, ten years, etc. Encourage both short-term and long-term goal setting in many areas (education, career, family, personal, financial, etc.).

7. Closure/Termination: Distribute the post-test (same as pretest in session 1) and collect it. Schedule individual exit interviews, but emphasize that this is the end of the group experience. Complete peer/self-evaluation and the challenge evaluation. Give participants the opportunity to process the results, share feedback, and say goodbye.

MY HEROES/ANTIHEROES

List three people that you admire greatly.

List the traits that these people have that make you admire them.

1. _____

_____

_____

2. _____

_____

_____

3. _____

_____

_____

List three people that you least admire.

List the traits that these people have that make you dislike them.

1. _____

_____

_____

2. _____

_____

_____

3. _____

_____

_____

THE WELLNESS CHART

Evaluate yourself for each aspect of wellness. When you are done, connect the circled numbers to see if the "landscape" is smooth or filled with hills and valleys. Share your results with the rest of your group and challenge yourself to make an improvement.

SOCIAL	PHYSICAL	INTELLECTUAL	CAREER	EMOTIONAL	SPIRITUAL
10	10	10	10	10	10
9	9	9	9	9	9
8	8	8	8	8	8
7	7	7	7	7	7
6	6	6	6	6	6
5	5	5	5	5	5
4	4	4	4	4	4
3	3	3	3	3	3
2	2	2	2	2	2
1	1	1	1	1	1

Social: Ability to have close relationships, family functioning, community
Physical: Ability to do the things you want to do, recreation
Intellectual: Working to academic potential, curiosity, creativity
Career: Working on goals, satisfied with progress and prospects
Emotional: Self-esteem, self-concept, feeling good about yourself
Spiritual: Values, morals, meditation, worship, ethics

TIME LINE

What do you hope to be doing in six months, a year, and so on? Include different aspects of your life: education, social life, family, employment, alcohol and other drug use, etc.

6 months

1 year

2 years

5 years

10 years

THE CHALLENGE GROUP
Peer/Self-Evaluation

Name _____ Date _____

Write a brief statement that describes a behavior or an attitude that has changed while you have been in this group:

_____

_____

_____

_____

_____

NOW PASS THIS PAPER TO THE PERSON ON YOUR RIGHT.

Write a brief statement that describes how you think the person above has changed while in this program. Then pass the paper to your right.

1. _____

_____

2. _____

_____

3. _____

_____

4. _____

_____

5. _____

_____

6. _____

_____

If there are more people than numbers listed, please use the back of this sheet.

EXIT INTERVIEWS AND FOLLOW-UP APPOINTMENTS

Each student should be scheduled for an exit interview within a few days of the last group meeting. Some students will have evidenced signs of serious dependency throughout the group experience, and when you have signed releases of information, parents should be contacted and recommendations for placement or treatment made. When you have no release of information, use all your powers of persuasion to convince the student to sign one so appropriate follow-up treatment can be procured.

Exit interviews are the appropriate time to bring up whether a student wishes to join another SAP group or seek outside help through a private therapist, agency, hospital, or program. A number of your challenge group participants may wish to join your recovery group. Some challenge group participants may have identified themselves as children of addiction, in which case they may want to join one of the SAP's groups or get information about local Alateen meetings. From these exit interviews, also try to glean a sense of what students liked and didn't like and use it in designing the next challenge group experience.

Using the Six-Month Follow-Up Letter

The letters the students write to themselves in the last group session can be a valuable tool in terms of following up. One way to utilize them is to send a notice to each student in six months asking them to come to the office to pick up their letters. Most will come, simply because it is a novel idea. When they come to pick up the letter, you can conduct brief, informational interviews or use the challenge group "Follow-Up Questionnaire" to determine whether the challenge group has had any (relatively) long-lasting effects. Students who may not have been very vocal during the initial exit interview may have needed more time to process the experience, and this six-month checkpoint may be a good time for you to contact them. Another benefit to this contact is that some students who did not feel able to come to the SAP office without invitation will be encouraged to regain contact.

If students do not seem to be making noticeable changes in their lives as a result of challenge group participation, be patient. Many students need to "sit" with the information a while and may need to test the alcohol and other drug waters more before they are really convinced. If the group experience hurries up the process of an adolescent recognizing his or her dangerous patterns of use, then it is a worthwhile pursuit. In my experience, many students who have gone through the challenge group have sought additional treatment for alcohol and other drug issues, some as much as a year or two later. With this in mind, try to keep a positive relationship with students who go through the challenge group. Some of them may utilize the SAP to access treatment somewhere down the road.

CHALLENGE GROUP EVALUATION

Was participating in this group generally a positive or negative experience for you?_____

_____

_____

Please list three things you learned here:

1. _____

_____

2. _____

_____

3. _____

_____

What was the most valuable thing you learned about yourself during this group? _____

_____

_____

If you were running this program, what changes would you make ?_____

_____

_____

Do you think your drinking or drugging behavior will change in any way because of your

participation in this group? (please explain) _____

_____

_____

Please evaluate the group leaders: _____

_____

_____

Additional comments: _____

_____

_____

FOLLOW-UP QUESTIONNAIRE

Note to all former participants in the challenge group: This questionnaire is confidential. It is not necessary for you to sign your name any where on this sheet. You may identify yourself if you wish, but no identifying information (such as name, address, etc.) will be utilized by anyone from this or any other agency. The purpose of this questionnaire is to gather information about the effectiveness of the program and how we might better serve the community. If you are having problems of any kind, or would just like to say hello, please do not hesitate to contact us. We would love to hear from you.

Sincerely,

_____

The Challenge Group Coordinator/Facilitator

When did you complete the challenge group? _____

Since then, have you used alcohol or any other drug?   Yes   No

If so, what drugs and how often? _____

_____

Have you attended a self-help group (such as AA, NA, Al-Anon, Alateen, or others)?

Yes   No

If so, which one(s) and how often? _____

_____

Are you currently in counseling?   Yes   No

If so, what type? (family, school counselor, substance abuse counselor, or other)

[specify: _____])

Are you currently in school?   Yes   No

If yes, what grade? _____

If no, why did you leave school? (suspension, quit, expelled, illness, other)

[specify: _____])

Are you employed?   Yes   No

If yes, part time or full time? _____

Since you were in the program, have you joined any new group club, team, or other activity?   Yes   No

FOLLOW-UP QUESTIONNAIRE, continued

Are you currently dating or "going steady"?   Yes   No

If in school, have your grades improved?   Yes   No

Do you have a family member who is currently abusing alcohol or other drugs?

    Yes   No

Do you feel responsible for things that other people do?   Yes   No

Do you take on too much responsibility?   Yes   No

Do you isolate yourself?   Yes   No

How do you rate yourself on the following:

BAD	POOR	FAIR	GOOD	EXCELLENT	
1	2	3	4	5	My ability to concentrate
1	2	3	4	5	My ability to socialize
1	2	3	4	5	My self-esteem
1	2	3	4	5	My ability to accept criticism
1	2	3	4	5	My ability to communicate
1	2	3	4	5	My ability to handle stress
1	2	3	4	5	My ability to resist peer pressure
1	2	3	4	5	My grades (if in school)

What problems are you experiencing now? _____

_____

If you need help, *please* call us at _____ .

Please enclose the completed form in the enclosed envelope and get it back to us as soon as possible.

Thank you.

14
Recovery Group

CHAPTER 14

Recovery Group

The purpose of an SAP recovery group is to support students who have made the decision to live completely alcohol and other drug free. Many students who are in recovery, though not all, will be active in self-help programs like AA and NA in their communities and will use SAP participation to supplement their recovery programs and as a vehicle to meet socially with other clean and sober youth at school. The social element of SAP participation for recovering students is very important, because recovering students need to locate and cultivate a positive, nonusing peer group. Recovery groups are not designed for students who are still abusing chemicals, nor are they designed to motivate students into treatment. On the contrary, recovery groups are designed to support and validate the efforts of those students who have already made the decision to abstain both from alcohol and other drugs.

REASONS FOR RECOVERY GROUP

Having a school-based recovery group is essential and is part of bare-bones SAP programming. The first benefit of having such a group available is measurable in climatic change—the mere existence of the group legitimizes the decision to live alcohol and drug free at your school. Second, it underscores to school and community alike the struggle that exists for adolescents to stay clean and sober while negotiating the rigors of high school life. Third, and most important, the recovery group provides a "landing pad" for those students returning from chemical dependency treatment. It is imperative for students returning from treatment to hook up with the recovery group immediately upon their return to school. If they don't meet this new peer group of sober individuals, they may fall back in with their old using friends and the lessons of treatment may be lost.

For a small but significant percentage of students, the recovery group will be a mainstay of support, for SAPs occasionally encounter students who get sober, and stay sober, using school-based programming only. The hope is to hook up these students with self-help groups in the community to insure their commitment to sobriety during the summer months and after graduation. While it is natural to be nervous about the seriousness of such students' commitment to staying sober, we shouldn't waste too much breath complaining about students who seem to gather their own momentum from minimal services.

The recovery group is vastly different from other groups because the SAP's role is to sustain a process that is presumably already happening. There is some responsibility to educate students about chemical dependency and surrounding issues, but, more importantly, the SAP simply provides the time and space for students to recover together. Recovering students need a place to "check in" a school, with someone who understands the struggles unique to recovery from addiction. Recovery groups could benefit from meeting more than once a week, if a schedule could be designed that was not too disruptive to academic schedules (perhaps a regular rotating group time with supplemental meetings either before or after school, or during a mid-week lunch period). Group participation can also be viewed as a relapse prevention strategy; if recovering students are consistent in coming to group and receiving feedback, they can glean some self-knowledge and work on preventing relapse. Student assistance program participation gives recovering students the chance to celebrate recovery and share its inevitable trials with others who can relate, firsthand, to the particular peaks and valleys of adolescent recovery.

Whole recovery from addiction includes a myriad of physical, mental, spiritual, and emotional tasks, but a great deal of what SAPs do is provide the forum for students to catch up on developmental tasks they may have missed due to their use of alcohol or other drugs. Some may not yet have conquered very basic developmental tasks of adolescence: managing schoolwork, making friends while sober, talking in a direct and honest way, effectively managing time, identity formation, taking responsibility for one's actions—things they didn't give much thought to when they were using chemicals. So, in a very real way, recovering kids are a little behind and need a "leg up" developmentally. The very process of being in a recovery group is life affirming and opposed to the illness of addiction. Being open about behavior and thought processes is directly in opposition to the denial and secrecy chemical dependency fosters.

Recovery Groups and AA/NA

The twelve-step programs have without question saved millions of lives, and without them the current movement toward recovery might well have stalled. It is important for SAPs to have close ties with the twelve-step communities and to be aware of reliable contact people in each of the pertinent fellowships for students and their families who are going to take this step. While taking care to maintain our separateness, we must encourage our students and their families to take advantage of these life-saving programs. In public schooling, however, we must recognize as well that the spiritual nature of twelve-step recovery may not settle comfortably with every student, and personal differences must be respected. Not every student who gets sober will do so using a twelve-step program, and an SAP must offer additional strategies to young people who can't or won't join twelve-step fellowships.

An afterschool AA or NA young people's meeting can be held in your school building, underscoring the school's commitment to self-help programs. However, members of the fellowships themselves would have to set up the meeting. If you have a student who is active in a twelve-step group, try to encourage the start-up of a meeting designed for young people held in the school building or near it. It is probably best if the SAP director is in no way officially connected to outside groups, but he or she can facilitate the start-up and serve as the school contact.

Student assistance program personnel must keep one thing clear: An in-school SAP recovery group is not an AA meeting or an NA meeting. As an SAP person, you are taking this time with these recovering students to make their *educational* journey through school easier and more productive. Let the students who participate know that school provides the opportunity for recovery group to help them get through their education successfully. Staying alive is the bottom-line benefit of staying sober for those affected by chemical dependency, but good school attendance, improving grades, and better school functioning are also major objectives of a school-based recovery group.

PLANNING A RECOVERY GROUP

To run a recovery group, you need some students who are in recovery. This is not as easy as finding COAs, because there are certain preconditions about students in recovery—they usually have experienced some negative consequences as a result of their use and through some significant event, or series of them, they now have a commitment to staying clean and sober. Some will have been to treatment, and others will have quit through self-help or on their own. You will encounter some students who have been sober for six months or a year and who seem very nonchalant about the whole thing, and you will also encounter students who have been sober for a week but have become very vocal about it. Some will be very motivated to stay sober, and some will be very unaccepting of their condition and angry that they cannot use their drugs of choice.

It can be quite a challenge to find these students for an SAP just starting out. During my first year directing an SAP, one motivated recovering student and I had "group" for three weeks before we could locate another recovering student. Then, for almost two months, we ran the "group" with only two, and this was in a school of 1,800 students! Plan for a small but intense group, and keep your expectations in terms of numbers low at first. Recovery groups take years to build, as more students and their families understand that there is life, and a better one, after they give up the alcohol and other drugs.

If there isn't an established recovery group in your school and you are trying to start one, canvass the guidance department to find out whether they are aware of any students that have gone through chemical dependency treatment and who are still in school. Advertise the existence of the group, even if you don't have any students in it yet, just in case you stumble across a student who is ready to join. If you can get hold of even one student who is willing to give it a try, you can make a slow beginning. Chances are, that student may know of one or two others who are in recovery as well and who might like to join a group. When you have three or four, you can make a start.

LEADERS FOR A RECOVERY GROUP

At least one of the leaders of an SAP recovery group must have facility with the language of twelve-step recovery and must have experience working with adolescent chemical dependency and surrounding issues. Though it is impossible to prescribe the exact qualifications of the person who will run this group, no matter how well qualified through education and experience, it is essential that the leader(s) have their own alcohol or other drug-related issues properly treated. It could be disastrous for the leader and students alike if one of the leaders, for instance, had not worked out his or her issues with an alcoholic spouse, parent, or child.

People who are themselves recovering are a seemingly obvious choice for recovery group leaders, but recovery alone does not qualify a person to do this work. Some combination of education, life experience, and work experience provides the proper balance. If you feel inexplicably anxious about the issues of alcoholism, drug addiction, and recovery, you should let someone else run this group. Some leaders who are unfamiliar with the issues of recovery have invited recovering people into the group to colead. This can be mutually useful: While one gains knowledge about group counseling and group skills, the other learns about those issues surrounding recovery.

Leaders' Recovery and Twelve-Step Fellowships

Some leaders will be in recovery themselves and may be active in twelve-step fellowships. Should your students know that you are in recovery? This is a delicate subject because people have such strong and conflicting views on how the leader's own recovery should be handled in an SAP. The other issue is that if you are a member of a twelve-step fellowship and go to meetings in your city or town, you are likely to run into students who are also in recovery. You can't simply forsake your own recovery and stop going to meetings. Without making major changes in your program of recovery, however, you can frequent meetings that students don't go to often, and if you by chance meet a student there, without snubbing him or her, you can make it a point to mingle with those people your own age. An SAP leader who is also in one of the Anonymous programs probably should not become a twelve-step sponsor to one of the students in the SAP, and certainly should never "hang out" socially with students. The roles are far too muddled and the professional risks significant. Alcoholics Anonymous publishes informational pamphlets which are applicable to all the twelve-step fellowships for those counselors/educators and psychologists who "wear two hats."

If you are a member of a twelve-step fellowship, remember that as an SAP group leader, you are not on a twelve-step call but, rather, are employed by some educational body to help students help themselves in the context of the school. Your professional purpose cannot be to get these students to go to meetings; however, the information that twelve-step programs are statistically successful can be part of your message.

Considerations about Self-Disclosure

For recovery group leaders, self-disclosure of any kind is *always a risk.* Self-disclosure to make the leader more comfortable is *never appropriate.* When a leader should take that risk is a highly personal decision, but to err on the side of extreme caution seems appropriate. Particularly if you come from a treatment orientation where recovery is viewed as a gift and an accomplishment, you may be surprised at how suspiciously it is viewed on the "outside." School systems do not have the same understanding of recovery as the treatment industry or twelve-step programs. For instance, people on the "outside" of recovery often mistakenly think that someone with ten years of sobriety who still attends AA is right on the verge of taking a drink, and that's why they still "have" to attend. Although this is hardly ever the case, you must be prepared to deal with others' perceptions and their subsequent treatment of you. Others feel that they must be a power of example of recovery, no matter what the personal risk.

SCREENING STUDENTS FOR RECOVERY GROUP

This seems like it would be easy, but it isn't. In fact, screening students for the recovery group is a difficult task because it means nailing down exact eligibility requirements for group participation. Students coming back from chemical dependency treatment facilities are clearly eligible for participation, but what happens if they relapse? And keep relapsing? Some recovery groups require that a student have a certain length of sobriety (two or three weeks, let's say) before joining, but this can be construed as exclusive and prohibitive to the student who wants to get sober but may not have the resources for any other treatment except school-based services and self-help programs. And what do you do with the student who really wants to stay clean and sober but isn't making it very well, and every week monopolizes the group with tales of recent binges? Suggested solutions include the following:

- Within recovery group, have specific rules around the telling of "war stories." Certain groups prohibit any recounting of drinking or drugging episodes which serve to glorify past use.
- Limit each student's time to share to insure that students don't monopolize the group time.
- If the student cannot stay sober for any length of time, more drastic measures may need to be taken. Suggest challenge group participation as a starting point.

These are issues you'll have to wrestle with to come up with a comfortable solution. If you turn over the decision to the students, they will usually come up with a fair but complicated solution. One of the recovery groups I have had the pleasure of knowing came up with the solution of having "open" and "closed" meetings (something like the twelve-step tradition, but not exactly) on alternate weeks. Open meetings are for anyone who wants to *try* to stay clean and sober. Closed meetings are for students who are already doing so successfully and want to talk about the new challenges that they face as sober people.

A student who poses a significant threat to the continuing sobriety of other group members should be removed from group participation until he or she establishes a stronger commitment to recovery. Recovery groups are not coercive in nature, so trying to get a student sober in the context of a recovery group is a losing battle for everyone involved, particularly for the other students who are already sober and want some support and validation. Most adolescents need more invasive treatment to break through the strong denial that characterizes adolescent chemical dependency. If you encounter this situation, remove the student from recovery group and try to motivate him or her into a more coercive experience, ranging from the challenge group to inpatient chemical dependency treatment.

FORMAT FOR RECOVERY GROUP

Most school-based recovery groups are open-ended, providing ongoing support for students throughout the school year and perhaps into the summer. It's possible that you'll stay in contact with some recovering students for as long as four years, if they stay (or try to stay) sober freshman through senior year. This will inform your format because your recovery group will become a very cohesive group of students who may know each other for a long time. The group is meant to provide long-term support. You probably won't need an activity for each group session, though if you are just starting out, you may feel more comfortable utilizing activities.

Because many students may be active in AA and NA, they may be accustomed to a "discussion group" format, wherein one student shares his or her experience using alcohol and other drugs and subsequent journey into recovery, and then other students relate their experience to that student's, and topics are formed as they go along. If the leaders are comfortable with this and feel they can either direct the discussion or feel they don't need to, then this may be the approach to take. Students who are not familiar with AA or NA may need some prompting to tell their "stories" in the proper time frame. If this is the case with your group; use the activities provided here in the recovery group sample sessions to supplement or provide variety to your existing framework. Recovery groups are not structured with a formal beginning and a "graduation," because recovery is a day-by-day effort from which one can't graduate. You and your recovery group can decide which format is the best for your particular SAP.

The following ten session samples can be intertwined into an existing recovery group; bits and pieces can be used for ice-breaking activities, or, if you are just starting out, use them to start off the year until you are comfortable with the forming group. The format for the sample sessions is as follows:

1. Preamble
2. Check-in
3. Activity
4. Closure

Group Rules

The rules for all groups need to be simple and to the point. Chapter 9 includes a "Group Rule List" which is helpful in underscoring the importance of adherence for proper group functioning. Make the rules simple, and don't include rules you can't enforce. It's always good practice for leaders to present the rules as amendable and to tell the students that they're willing to consider any reasonable suggestions. The final rules, as agreed on by the leaders and the membership, should be posted, adopted, signed into "action," or whatever ceremony makes them "official." For a recovery group especially, there must be specific rules about the consequences of students coming to group under the influence of alcohol and other drugs. Because such an event would indicate a relapse of a life-threatening illness, SAP personnel should think seriously about this issue and agree on how such a situation will be handled before it happens, because it will happen eventually.

Preamble

Because recovering students are accustomed to upheaval in their using days, they respond very well to structure within the group. Then they know exactly what to expect every time they come to group. Having and using a preamble at the beginning of every group meeting is also a good way to insure that every newcomer to the group hears the rules and the same welcome. The predictable reading of the preamble can calm students and set the tone for the meeting. Following is a sample preamble:

Hello and welcome to the _____ recovery group.
(name of school or SAP)

This group's single purpose is to support students who want to stay clean and sober. We are all recovering students who meet here on a weekly basis to share our past and present experiences and our new ways of dealing with things. While we are here, we can speak freely without being judged, knowing that what we say here stays here. If you are new today, welcome.

Check-in

As your recovery group evolves, check-in should become the bulk of the group experience as students share what is going on in their lives, and especially how they are dealing with the many facets of life as a clean and sober individual. There are many different ways to conduct check-in:

- Group leaders can go around the circle, asking each student to check in briefly about what is going on in his or her life, and especially how it relates to sobriety.
- Like "dealer's choice" in poker, whoever is designated as the student chair person gets to decide on the format for that day's meeting.
- You can appoint a chairperson or have that person volunteer, and that person begins the check-in and asks fellow participants to follow suit.
- As in twelve-step meetings, one student can share his or her "story," and then others can relate their experiences to that student's and comment on topics brought up through the story.
- The leaders can ask, "Who needs time today to check in?" and those students who are having particular difficulties or need to share specific situations can do so. If this is done consistently, it gives students the opportunity to participate actively when they feel like it, and to take a less active role on other days, which is probably more true to human nature. Students who either monopolize check-ins or never speak may need some feedback from leaders or participants to regulate their behavior.

Bear in mind that though the leaders come prepared with activities and topics galore, there is always the possibility that participants will bring up issues during check-in which will take the rest of the group time to process effectively. It's helpful to be flexible in recovery groups.

Sample Session Activities

The activities included in the sample sessions are intended to help students focus their thoughts about recovery and to aid group interaction. Many of the activities in the challenge group (chapter 13) could also be worked into a recovery group format—as long as the leaders remember that recovering students need support to continue the process they are already in, not consternation from leaders for past use.

Optional Topics for Discussion

The topics included near the end of each session's agenda can follow naturally from the activities. If there is time after the activities and leaders feel they need to direct the discussion, these topics cover a wide range of recovery issues. Anytime you are looking for a topic in recovery group, you can use those suggested in the sample sessions. However, chances are that students will bring up their own topics.

Another way to utilize the optional topics for discussion is to copy each topic onto an index card and keep the stack of cards with the materials for recovery group. Keep a few extra blank index cards so students and leaders can add new ones to the pile. During a "Chairperson's Choice" meeting, students can use these in a number of ways, either choosing a topic for the meeting by "cutting the deck" or having each participant choose one and addressing that issue as part of check-in.

Though some of the topics are fairly sophisticated and require some knowledge about recovery issues, you will doubtless be surprised at how well recovering students can address these issues. At least some of your recovering students will have gone through treatment, and others will be involved in twelve-step programs; both require rigorous self-honesty and examination of actions, motives, etc.

Closure

Particularly in the context of the SAP, it is important for group to come to some sort of closure before the bell rings and students gather their belongings and dash to the next class. Following are four simple ways to close group:

- Repeat the preamble. If your preamble is simple, and it reminds students about confidentiality, repeating it can be an adequate closing.
- Summary: Have one student summarize what has gone on in group.
- Closing statement: Have students compose a very brief closing statement. It can be read, or students can memorize it and say it in unison at the end of group.
- Goal and commitment: This is a way for each student to verbalize his or her short-term goal(s) for the week. In goal and commitment, students ex-

press their goal for the week and their commitment to the group (whether they will come back to recovery group next week). This closing is used in the sample sessions provided.

Additional Activities

Because recovery groups are usually long-term support groups, additional worksheet activities are included at the end of this chapter. Use these handouts to identify signs of relapse or to provide self-evaluation opportunities for recovering students. These are simply additional resource materials that you can use as you see fit.

RECOVERY SESSION 1

Objectives

- To have students gain "ownership" in the recovery group
- To set rules

Agenda

1. Preamble: Read the preamble and ask students if they like it or if they would like to see anything changed. Or, leaders can ask students what they would like to hear in a preamble.

2. Activity:

A. It is important for students to feel invested in the rules of the group. I you are using a rules checklist (chapter 9), introduce it, asking fo: amendments and additions. If you aren't using a rules checklist, have students brainstorm a list of rules of their own. When they are complete post them.

B. Utilize one of the following ice-breakers to get students more familia with one another:

- Have students split into pairs and interview each other for a few minute each. Then they can introduce the other person to the group.
- Starting with one student, have him or her say his or her first name an something that rhymes with it or starts with the same letter. For instanc "Hi, my name is Ray, where there's a will there's a way" or "Hi, I'm Radic: Ray." Then the next person repeats "This is Radical Ray here and I'm Aw some Annie." The last person, of course, will have to repeat the who room's worth of names.

Students may moan and groan about these get-to-know-you activities, but the are effective in getting students to learn each other's names, which is an impo tant part of showing one another respect.

- *Option or addition:* Ask students to share "how they got here" with the re of the group. (This can be part of check-in.)

3. Check-in: This first week, the leaders may have to prompt the check-in, telling the students that this will be part of group every week, when students can share how their week is going with this group of people who support them. Ask students to share a little of what is going on and how their struggles and triumphs with sobriety are going.

Optional Topics for Discussion:

- What does support really mean? How can we support one another in group?
- Why is confidentiality important? What happens when confidentiality is broken?
- What do students expect out of recovery group participation?

4. Goal and Commitment: Explain goal and commitment as the closing, asking students to think carefully about their goal. While staying clean and sober is a good goal, it is also somewhat of a given, and we should hope that that is part of each participant's goal. A more thought-out goal might include staying clean and sober and an effort to work on some issue that might have been brought up in group. For instance, "My goal is to stay clean and sober this week, and since I really admired John's honesty today in group, I'm going to work on staying honest with myself and others. My commitment is that I'll be here next week."

RECOVERY SESSION 2

Objective

- To help group build trust by sharing experiences

Agenda

1. Preamble

2. Activity: Have students complete the "First Time/Worst Time/Last Time" worksheet and share their responses with the rest of the group. Encourage interaction by drawing parallels between students' experiences. Ask additional questions of each student so they become accustomed to speaking to the whole group. Ask students why they used again after the worst time. What made them decide to quit using after the last time? Can you identify with anyone else's experience?

During these first few weeks, you may have to remind students to

- Speak to the whole group, not just the leaders
- Offer feedback to other group members
- Speak one at a time.
- *Option or addition:* Have students complete only the first part of the exercise, collect the worksheets, and have students complete subsequent sections on subsequent weeks.
- *Option or addition:* Have students complete the worksheet, and then ask

for a volunteer to "tell his or her story" start to finish. Collect and keep other worksheets for students to tell their stories on subsequent weeks.

Optional Topics for Discussion:

- Progression of the disease from first use to last use. Did you have to use more to get the same high?
- "Hitting bottom": What convinced you that you can't use safely?
- What was lost while you were using? Were all your losses material things, or did you lose values, relationships, friends?

4. Goal and Commitment

THE FIRST TIME/ THE WORST TIME/ THE LAST TIME

Try to remember the first time, the worst time, and the last time you used. Write what you are comfortable sharing with the rest of the group.

The first time I used alcohol or other drugs I was (age) _____

I was with _____

What we were doing _____

Why I decided to try it _____

What happened? _____

How I felt before _____

How I felt during _____

How I felt afterward: Physically _____

   Emotionally/mentally _____

The worst time I had with alcohol or other drugs I was (age) _____

I was with _____

What we were doing _____

Why I decided to do it _____

What happened? _____

How I felt before _____

How I felt during _____

How I felt afterward: Physically _____

   Emotionally/mentally _____

Did you use again after this experience? _____

Why? _____

The last time I used alcohol or other drugs I was (age) _____

I was with _____

What we were doing _____

Why I decided to try it _____

What happened? _____

How I felt before _____

How I felt during _____

How I felt afterward: Physically _____

   Emotionally/mentally _____

What made you decide to quit? _____

RECOVERY SESSION 3

Objective

- To help students explore the physical aspects of the disease of addiction

Note: Physical health is important to eight- to twelve-year-old children, and then it rapidly ceases to hold the interest of high school students, as they begin to believe themselves immortal. This imagined invincibility is developmentally appropriate for this age group, but dangerous nonetheless. Particular attention should be paid to physical health for recovering students, as they are by nature self-destructive and have probably mistreated themselves physically.

Agenda

1. Preamble

2. Activity: Have students complete "My Physical Health" and share their responses with the group. Offer suggestions to benefit physical health, and ask students to share whether they feel better physically since they quit using. If you can arrange it, have an outside health professional speak to the group about the physical benefits of getting and staying sober. (Ask the group members first whether they want a guest speaker from the outside coming into the group.)

- *Option and/or addition:* Compile a master list of bad health factors associated with alcohol and other drug use (on the board or on newsprint using the completed worksheets as a guide.
- *Option and/or addition:* Use the "Wellness Chart" from session 6 of the challenge group (see chapter 13) to generate discussion about whole-person wellness.

3. Check-in

Optional Topics for Discussion:
- How I stay well physically, mentally, and spiritually (whole-person wellness)
- Physical health and ability to succeed in school
- What physical withdrawal from chemicals was/is like
- What the psychological withdrawal was/is like

4. Goal and Commitment

MY PHYSICAL HEALTH

Complete the worksheet, recording your physical health when you were using and then changes since you have entered recovery. Also include changes you would like to make in the future.

WHEN I WAS USING	NOW	FUTURE

Drug effects:

Diet:

Sleep patterns:

Exercise:

Accidents:

Violence:

Colds/flu/illnesses:

Self-destructive patterns:

RECOVERY SESSION 4

Objective

- To help students understand the mental aspects of the disease of addiction, especially denial

Agenda

1. Preamble

2. Activity: Have students complete the worksheet "All My Excuses" in subgroups of two or three, and then share their responses with the group as a whole. Then have students compile a master list of the "Ten Most Typical Excuses" (leaders—stay out of this one; it should be completely a student effort!). Post this list conspicuously somewhere in the group room so group members can confront one another if they hear these typical rationalizations and justifications from one another. If you need additional resources to talk about the concept of denial, use the explanation found in the challenge group, session 3 (see chapter 13).

- *Option or addition:* Borrow "Umbrella of Denial" from the challenge group materials (chapter 13).

3. Check-in

Optional Topics for Discussion:

- How denial can lead to relapse
- Why addiction is called the "disease of denial"
- How I still use denial in other areas of my life
- Under all my denial, how I really felt when I was using

4. Goal and Commitment

ALL MY EXCUSES

Being really honest with yourself, check off all the excuses *you* used when you were using alcohol and other drugs. Then, think of ten more that were your all-time favorites.

☐ My mom/dad uses, so it can't be so bad, right?

☐ I was just celebrating.

☐ I was just drowning my sorrows (trying to forget).

☐ Using makes me less shy around the opposite sex.

☐ Only dull people don't use.

☐ People will think I'm a jerk if I don't use.

☐ What's the *big deal? Leave me alone!!!*

☐ It's school vacation.

☐ It's the weekend!

☐ I was hanging out with the wrong crowd.

☐ I don't have to use, I choose to use.

☐ I could quit anytime I want to; I just don't want to.

☐ If I'm an alcoholic/addict, so are all my friends.

☐ My family treats me badly. You'd use if you were me, too.

☐ You guys are jerks. Get off my back. (outright hostility)

☐ I'm a heavy-hitter, that's the way I am. Take it or leave it.

☐ I don't have a problem. If I had a problem, I'd quit, but I don't, so I won't.

☐ Drinking/drugging makes me feel older, more accepted.

☐ My relationships with people drive me to drink or use other drugs.

☐ Everyone I live with uses, so I had to also.

My Ten Favorite Excuses/Justifications/Rationalizations

1. _____
2. _____
3. _____
4. _____
5. _____
6. _____
7. _____
8. _____
9. _____
0. _____

RECOVERY SESSION 5

Objective

- To help students understand the spiritual aspects of the disease of addiction.

Note: Spirituality can be a delicate subject. People who have worked in chemical dependency treatment will have a deep understanding of the relationship twelve-step group members have to a "Higher Power." Public school personnel, in particular, may feel a bit uncomfortable around student AA members who are vocally grateful to God for their recovery while in an SAP group. While encouraging those students to keep doing what they're doing if it's working for them, there has to be room for students who are recovering in different ways. In the context of an SAP, we have to be careful that students do not feel excluded if their recoveries are not connected to reliance on a "Higher Power," and each student's recovery must be valued equally, regardless of our own beliefs. You should also be sensitive to cultural differences that will become evident as you discuss values.

Agenda

1. Preamble

2. Activity: Have students complete the "My Values" worksheet individually and share those responses that they feel comfortable sharing with the group. Discussion can spring from any of the values listed (e.g., why honesty is important to staying sober, how patience is important in getting through school). When possible, direct the discussion toward school performance, both academic and social.

3. Check-in

Optional Topics for Discussion:

- How I went against my own values when I was using and how it made me feel
- How relying on chemicals made me feel
- How I have learned to accept my addiction and/or alcoholism

4. Goal and Commitment

VALUES

Your values are very personal things. Under the influence of alcohol and other drugs, sometimes people do things that are against their own values and end up experiencing emotional pain as a result. Being clean and sober gives people the opportunity to live within their own values and to work on themselves, which is difficult or almost impossible when you're using.

Rank in importance from 1 to 16 (1 being most important, 16 the least) the values listed here. Then rank yourself on each quality on a scale from 1 to 10. Use this sheet to share with the group that which you are comfortable sharing.

Rank in importance to you	Rank yourself for this quality

____ Intelligent	1	2	3	4	5	6	7	8	9	10
____ Honest	1	2	3	4	5	6	7	8	9	10
____ Hard-working	1	2	3	4	5	6	7	8	9	10
____ Considerate of others	1	2	3	4	5	6	7	8	9	10
____ Faithful, loyal	1	2	3	4	5	6	7	8	9	10
____ Friendly	1	2	3	4	5	6	7	8	9	10
____ Good student	1	2	3	4	5	6	7	8	9	10
____ Religious	1	2	3	4	5	6	7	8	9	10
____ Good sport	1	2	3	4	5	6	7	8	9	10
____ Accepting of others	1	2	3	4	5	6	7	8	9	10
____ Patient	1	2	3	4	5	6	7	8	9	10
____ Ambitious	1	2	3	4	5	6	7	8	9	10
____ Leader	1	2	3	4	5	6	7	8	9	10
____ Respectful of self and others	1	2	3	4	5	6	7	8	9	10
____ Tolerant	1	2	3	4	5	6	7	8	9	10
____ Committed to principles	1	2	3	4	5	6	7	8	9	10

Since you got clean and sober, what quality have you worked on the most?

_____

_____

Do you need to work on any areas that you ranked as important to you?

_____

_____

RECOVERY SESSION 6

Objective

- To build a larger repertoire of nondrinking activities for recovering students

Agenda

1. Preamble

2. Activity:
Have students pair off and complete the "Clean and Sober Activities" worksheet. At least half of these responses should cost nothing. Students may protest that they can't think of fifty activities, but you should encourage creative responses, underscoring that students are going to need a lot more than fifty alternatives up their sleeves if they want to stay sober for any length of time. The students can then share their responses.

- *Option or addition:* Engage the group in the task of designing a drug-free field trip for the recovery group that will cost nothing.

3. Check-in

Optional Topics for Discussion:

- Accomplishments I am proud of in sobriety (both actual things I have accomplished and personal growth)
- How do I measure my progress in sobriety?
- How I handle boredom in sobriety

4. Goal and Commitment

CLEAN AND SOBER ACTIVITIES

Together with a partner, list fifty activities that you could do without alcohol or other drugs. At least twenty-five of them should cost nothing.

1. _____
2. _____
3. _____
4. _____
5. _____
6. _____
7. _____
8. _____
9. _____
10. _____
11. _____
12. _____
13. _____
14. _____
15. _____
16. _____
17. _____
18. _____
19. _____
20. _____
21. _____
22. _____
23. _____
24. _____
25. _____

26. _____
27. _____
28. _____
29. _____
30. _____
31. _____
32. _____
33. _____
34. _____
35. _____
36. _____
37. _____
38. _____
39. _____
40. _____
41. _____
42. _____
43. _____
44. _____
45. _____
46. _____
47. _____
48. _____
49. _____
50. _____

RECOVERY SESSION 7

Objective

- To help students recognize that change in recovery is possible

Agenda

1. Preamble

2. Activity: Have students sit in a circle and, starting with one student, begin a story, every student adding a sentence or two to the progression and plot. Leaders should tell the group this story is about two teenagers who are actively using alcohol and other drugs and who are running into trouble with it. Leaders can start the story if they want to. For instance, "Bartholomew and Angela were a boyfriend and girlfriend who would rather smoke pot (or whatever you think the students can relate to most closely) than do almost anything else. One day . . ." and let it go! Expect some laughs! Let the story go for a few minutes until it has run out of steam.

Then, leaders introduce a new story about recovery to the group: "Angela and Bartholomew both ended up in treatment, and Bartholomew came home today. When he got home, the first thing he did was . . ." Use these stories as a way to talk about how life changes when teenagers get clean and sober.

3. Check-in

Optional Topics for Discussion:
- What coming home from treatment was like
- The progression of recovery: how it changes after six months, a year, or more
- How I let go of old friends, attitudes, and places

4. Goal and Commitment

RECOVERY SESSION 8

Objective

- To help students give positive feedback and receive constructive criticism

Agenda

1. Preamble

2. Activity: This activity helps students give each other feedback about changes they have seen in each other since the group started. Write each student's name on a small paper bag (lunch-sized) and place the open bag in front of each student. Give each student small slips of paper on which to write. (Give each student as many slips of paper as there are participants in the group.) Instruct students to write on each slip feedback about changes they have noticed in each group member or positive strides they have made in recovery (one comment per slip). Put the slips in each student's bag. Have students open the bags, share those pieces of feedback they feel comfortable sharing, and discuss the feelings the activity produces.

- *Option or addition:* Use this activity around the holidays, asking for positive feedback only, so each student leaves with the "gift" of self-knowledge. Instead of using slips of notebook paper, use holiday gift wrap and have students write on the wrong side. When folded, these slips of paper become holiday "gifts."

3. Check-in

Optional Topics for Discussion:
- How to identify and avoid perfectionism while still holding ourselves to high standards
- Giving and getting honest feedback: different ways of doing it
- Why self-awareness is important in sobriety
- How am I "working on" myself today to avoid relapse?

4. Goal and Commitment

ECOVERY SESSION 9

Objective
- To help students share and practice overcoming common obstacles to sobriety

Agenda

1. Preamble

2. Activity: Have students set up an "obstacle course" in your group room with different props representing different obstacles. Students have to devise ways "past" obstacles, and then each group member runs through the obstacle course once. For instance, a chair could represent the obstacle of loneliness. For students to get past the chair, they need to step onto the chair and reach out to another recovering person. The obstacle course should include at least three or four obstacles to sobriety. These obstacle courses sometimes make good skits when they are complete.

3. Check-in

Optional Topics for Discussion:

• Handling peer pressure

• How I used to deal with anger, and how I deal with it in sobriety

4. Goal and Commitment

RECOVERY SESSION 10

Objective

• To have students recognize positive changes in themselves as a result of recovery

Agenda

1. Preamble

2. Activity: Have students complete the "Recovery Can Change Attitudes" worksheet and share their responses with the rest of the group. If your group is comfortable interacting, have students tell each other how they have seen attitude changes in one another. Additional worksheets that can be used as needed in future group sessions are also provided.

3. Check-in

Optional Topics for Discussion:

• Choose any of the areas on the worksheet "Recovery Can Change Attitudes" to discuss changing attitudes about school, friendships, honesty, or family.

• How I handle fear in sobriety

• What are/were some of my unrealistic expectations about sobriety?

• Why living one day at a time is so important to staying sober

4. Goal and Commitment

RECOVERY CAN CHANGE ATTITUDES

ABOUT SCHOOL

Old attitudes

I used to think that school was . . .

_____

_____

New attitudes

Now, I think school is . . .

_____

_____

ABOUT FRIENDSHIPS

Old attitudes

I used to think that friends were . . .

_____

_____

New attitudes

Now, I think that friends are . . .

_____

_____

ABOUT HONESTY

Old attitudes

I used to think that honesty was . . .

_____

_____

New attitudes

Now, I think that honesty is . . .

_____

_____

ABOUT FAMILY

Old attitudes

I used to think that family was . . .

_____

_____

New attitudes

Now, I think that families are . . .

_____

_____

ANOTHER ATTITUDE OF MINE THAT HAS CHANGED IN RECOVERY IS:

_____

_____

_____

RECOVERY REPORT CARD

You are going to "grade" yourself on certain aspects of recovery. Try to be honest with yourself. Where you are not reaching your potential, you should seek some "extra help."

A = Excellent
B = Very good
C = Average
D = Passing, but in trouble
F = In serious trouble

Did not use alcohol and other drugs: _____

Attended meetings through self-help groups, aftercare, or through school: _____

Stayed honest with myself: _____

Was positive in my relationships with friends: _____

Was positive in my relationships with family: _____

Completed my schoolwork: _____

Got enough rest: _____

Healthy diet: _____

Participated in something fun, playful, or recreational: _____

Checked myself for signs of relapse: _____

Additional comments: _____

_____

_____

_____

_____

_____

_____

_____

SIGNS OF RELAPSE

Before recovering people relapse, there are often signs that warn of the dangers ahead. If you are aware of some of these signs, you can check yourself and others. If you notice these symptoms in yourself, take action to keep yourself on the right track.

Increasing Dishonesty and Denial: Finding yourself lying to other people and even to yourself. Being unwilling to accept reality.

Hopelessness: Thinking that it will never get any better; that there's no point in trying to stay clean and sober because nothing gets better anyway.

Reliance on Relationships for Sobriety: Saying, "Oh I have a new friend, and she'll keep me sober, no matter what." No one can guarantee your sobriety but you.

Unreasonable Resentments: Getting mad unreasonably can make you pick up your drug of choice. Also, you can forget that *you* get hurt if you use alcohol or other drugs and you can mistakenly think, "Boy, will *he* be sorry when I get drunk. It will be his fault."

Impatience: Not being able to give yourself the time you need for you to get well and for things in your life to change as a result. Wanting everything *yesterday*.

Isolation: Not wanting to see anyone or to discuss your sobriety. This may mean that you are setting yourself up for a fall and don't want anyone close enough to confront you on it.

Overconfidence: Thinking that you are "cured" and that you don't need to be careful. Putting yourself into dangerous situations where other people will be using.

Depression: Feeling overwhelmed or unable to cope with day-to-day happenings. If you feel this way, tell someone right away, before you use.

FEELINGS

Draw in a face that shows how you are feeling today. At the bottom of the sheet, write a few words describing your feelings.

_____

_____

_____

APPENDIX:

Additional Resources

SELF-HELP GROUPS:

Alcoholics Anonymous

Box 459
Grand Central Station
New York, NY 10168
(212) 686-1100

Self-help fellowship. Members share their experience, strength, and hope with each other to solve their common problem and to help others recover from alcoholism.
    Also check your local phone book under Alcoholism to find local chapters of AA.

Al-Anon

World Service Office
P.O. Box 862
Midtown Station
New York, NY 10018-0862
(800) 344-2666

Help for family members and friends of problem drinkers. Also check local telephone listings to find local meetings for both Al-Anon and Alateen.

Alateen

World Service Office
P.O. Box 862
Midtown Station
New York, NY 10018-0862
(800) 344-2666

Help for teenaged family members who live in an alcoholic family situation to learn new ways of coping.

National Association for Children of Alcoholics

NACOA
P.O. Box 421691
San Francisco, CA 94142

Narcotics Anonymous

> P.O. Box 9999
> Van Nuys, CA 91409
> (818) 780-3951

NA is a self-help fellowship of recovering addicts. Also check local telephone listings to find local meetings.

ALCOHOL AND OTHER DRUG INFORMATION:

National Clearinghouse for Alcohol and Drug Information (NCADI)

> P.O. Box 2345
> Rockville, MD 20852
> (301) 468-2600
> (800) SAY-NO-TO

Extensive offering of alcohol and other drug information at little or no cost. Publishes a catalog of available titles. Funded by the Office of Substance Abuse Prevention.

AIDS INFORMATION

National Aids Information Clearinghouse (NAIC)

> 24-hour hotlines:
> (English (800) 342-AIDS
> (Spanish) (800) 344-SIDA

STATE GOVERNMENT AGENCIES FOR DRUG AND ALCOHOL INFORMATION

Alabama

Alabama Department of Mental Health
and Mental Retardation
Division of Substance Abuse
200 State Park Drive
Montgomery, AL 36109
(205) 270-4648

Alaska

Division of Alcoholism and Drug Abuse
P.O. Box 110607
Juneau, AK 99811-0607
(907) 586-6201
(907) 465-2185

Arkansas

Governor's Partnership in Substance
Abuse Prevention
DADAP, P.O. Box 1437
Little Rock, AR 72203-1437
(501) 682-6656

Arizona

Arizona Department of Health Services
Division of Behavioral Health Services
411 North 24th Street
Phoenix, AZ 85008
(602) 220-6478

California

California Department of Alcohol and
  Drug Programs
1700 K St
Sacramento, CA 95814-4037
(916) 445-0834
Resource Center (800) 879-2772

Colorado

Alcohol and Drug Abuse Division
Colorado Department of Health
400 South Colorado Blvd.
4th Floor Suite 410
Denver CO 80222
(303) 331-6530

Connecticut

Connecticut Alcohol and
  Drug Abuse Commission
Prevention Division
999 Asylum Avenue
Hartford, CT 06105
(203) 566-7458

Delaware

Division of Alcoholism, Drug Abuse
  and Mental Health
901 North Dupont Highway
New Castle, DE 19720
(302) 577-4460

District of Columbia

Office of Health Planning and
  Development
1660 L Street
Suite 715-16
Washington, DC 20036
(202) 724-5637

Florida

Department of Health and
  Rehabilitation Services
1317 Winewood Blvd.
Tallahassee, Fl 32399-0700
(904) 488-0900

Georgia

Division of Mental Health, Retardation
  and Substance Abuse Prevention
  Resource Center
Suite 319
878 Peachtree Street, NE
Atlanta, GA 30309
(404) 894-4785

Hawaii

Alcohol and Drug Abuse Division
Department of Health
Queen Emma Building
1270 Queen Emma Street
Room 706
Honolulu, HI 96813
(808) 586-3986

Idaho

Substance Abuse Program
Division of Family and Children's Services
Idaho Department of Health and Welfare
450 West State
Boise, ID 83720
(208) 334-5934

Illinois

DASA
Division of Prevention
100 West Randolph
Suite 5-600
Chicago, IL 60601
(312) 814-3840

Indiana

Indiana Department of Family
  and Social Services
Division of Mental Health
Bureau of Addiction Services
402 West Washington Street
Room 353
Indianapolis, IN 46204
(317) 232-7800
Information line (317) 232-7816

Iowa

Bureau of Prevention and Training
Division of Substance Abuse and
  Health Promotion
Department of Public Health
Lucas State Office Building
3rd and 4th Floors
Des Moines, IA 50319
(515) 281-3641

Kansas

Alcohol and Drug Abuse Services
300 S.W. Oakley
Biddle Building
Topeka, KS 66606
(913) 296-3925

Kentucky

Division of Substance Abuse
Department for Mental Health and
  Mental Retardation Services
275 East Main Street
Frankfort, KY 40621
(502) 564-2880

Louisiana

Division of Alcohol and Drug Abuse
1201 Captol Access Road
P.O. Box 3868
Baton Rouge, LA 70821
(504) 342-9351

Maine

Office of Alcoholism and Drug Abuse
  Prevention
Department of Human Services
State House Station #11
Augusta, ME 04333
(207) 289-2781 (207) 289-1110
(207) 626-5404

Maryland

Alcohol and Drug Abuse Administration's
  Prevention Services
201 West Preston Street
4th Floor
Baltimore, MD 21201
(301) 225-6543

Massachusetts

Division of Substance Abuse Services
Massachusetts Department of Public
  Health
150 Tremont Street
Sixth Floor
Boston, MA 02111
(617) 727-1960

Michigan

Michigan Department of Health
Center for Substance Abuse
3423 North Logan Martin Luther King
  Blvd.
P.O. Box 30195
Lansing, MI 48909
(515) 335-8831

Minnesota

Chemical Dependency Program Division
Department of Human Services
444 Lafayette Road
St. Paul, MN 55155-3823
(612) 296-4711

Mississippi

Department of Mental Health
Division of Alcohol and Drug Abuse
1101 Robert E. Lee Building
239 North Lamar Street
Jackson, MS 39201
(601) 359-1288

Missouri

Department of Mental Health
Division of Alcohol and Drug Abuse
P.O. Box 687
Jefferson City, MO 65102
(314) 751-4942 FAX 751-7814

Montana

Department of Corrections and
    Human Services
1539 11th Avenue
Helena, MT 59620
(406) 444-2878

Nebraska

Division on Alcoholism and Drug Abuse
Department of Public Institutions
P.O. Box 94728
Lincoln, NE 68509-4728
(402) 471-2851

Nevada

Department of Human Resources
Rehabilitation Division
505 East King Street
Carson City, NV 89710
(702) 687-4790

New Hampshire

New Hampshire Office of Alcohol and
    Drug Abuse Prevention
    Hazen Drive
Concord, NH 03301
(603) 271-6100
(800) 852-3345 ext 6100

New Jersey

New Jersey Department of Health
Division of Alcoholism, Drug Abuse and
    Addiction Services
N 362
Trenton, NJ 08625-0362
(609) 292-4414

New Mexico

HED/BHSD Substance Abuse Bureau
1190 St. Francis Drive
Santa Fe, NM 87503
(505) 827-2601

New York

New York State Division of Alcohol and
    Substance Abuse
(518) 474-3377

Two mailing addresses:
(Alcohol abuse)
194 Washington Ave
Albany, NY 12210

(Substance Abuse)
Box 8200
Albany, NY 12203

North Carolina

North Carolina Department of Human
    Resources
Division of Mental Health,
    Developmental Disabilities and
    Substance Abuse Services
325 North Salsbury Street
Raleigh, NC 27603
(919) 733-4670

North Dakota

Division of Alcoholism and Drug Abuse
Department of Human Services
1839 E. Capitol Ave
Bismark, ND 58501-2152
(701) 224-2769
(800) 642-6744 (ND only)

Ohio

Department of Alcohol and Drug
    Addiction
2 Nationwide Plaza
280 North High Street
12th Floor
Columbus, OH 43215-2537

Oklahoma

Department of Mental Health and
  Substance Abuse Services
P.O. Box 53277
Oklahoma City, OK 73152-3277
(405) 271-8755

Oregon

Office of Alcohol and Drug Abuse
  Programs
1178 Chemeketa Street, NE
Salem, OR 97310
(503) 378-2163

Pennsylvania

Division of Prevention and
  Intervention Services
P.O. Box 90
Room 929
Health and Welfare Building
Harrisburg, PA 17108
(717) 783-8200

Rhode Island

Department of Mental Health,
  Retardation and Hospitals
600 New London Ave
Cranston, RI 02920
(401) 464-2336 (TDD); (401) 464-2191

South Carolina

SCCADA
Director of Programs and Services
700 Forest Drive
Suite 300
Columbia, SC 25204
(803) 734-9520

South Dakota

South Dakota Department of Human
  Services
Division of Alcohol and Drug Abuse
East Highway 34
500 East Capitol
Pierre, SD 57501-5770
(605) 773-3123

Tennessee

Department of Health
Bureau of Alcohol and Drug Abuse
  Services
Room 255
Cordell Hull Building
Nashville, TN 37247-4401
(615) 741-1921

Texas

Texas Commission on Alcohol and
  Drug Abuse
720 Brazos Street
Suite 708
Austin, TX 78701-1214
(512) 867-8700

Utah

Alcohol and Drug Abuse Clinic
50 North Medical Drive
P.O. Box 2500
Salt Lake City, UT 84132
(801) 581-6228

Vermont

Office of Alcohol and Drug Abuse
  Programs
103 South Main Street
3 North Building
Waterbury, VT 05671-1701

Virginia

Department of Mental Health, Mental
  Retardation and Substance Abuse
  Services
P.O. Box 1797
Richmond, VA 23214
(804) 786-1530
Information Line (804) 786-3921

Washington

Division of Alcohol and Substance Abuse
P.O. Box 45330
Olympia, WA 98504-5330
(206) 438-8200

West Virginia

Division on Alcoholism and Drug Abuse
West Virginia Department of Health and
  Human Resources
State Capitol Complex
Building 6, Room B 738
(304) 558-2276

Wisconsin

Office of Alcohol and Other Drug Abuse
1 West Wilson Street
Room 434
Madison, WI 53707
(608) 266-9485

Wyoming

Department of Health
Division of Substance Abuse
Room 451 Hathaway Building
Cheyenne, WY 82002
(307) 777-7115